THE SERPENT COILED IN NAPLES

THE SERPENT
COILED IN NAPLES

Marius Kociejowski

First published in the UK in 2022 by
Armchair Traveller
An imprint of Haus Publishing Ltd
4 Cinnamon Row
London SW11 3TW

This paperback edition published in 2023

A CIP catalogue for this book is available from the British Library

The moral right of the author has been asserted

ISBN 978-1-914982-02-6
eISBN 978-1-909961-80-7

Typeset in Sabon by MacGuru Ltd
Printed in the United Kingdom by Clays Ltd (Elcograf S.p.A.)

www.hauspublishing.com
@HausPublishing

for Chiara Ambrosio

I lived for a long while in a truly exceptional city … It had everything: good and evil, health and suffering, the most joyous happiness and the most agonising pain … all of these things were so tightly fused and confused, so mixed together among themselves, that a foreigner arriving in this city had, at first glance, a strange impression, as if quite normal human beings with regular instruments in the orchestra were not under the intelligent baton of the Maestro, but had wandered off to play on their own, producing an effect of marvellous confusion.

—Anna Maria Ortese, *L'infanta sepolta* ('The Buried Infanta', 1950)

Contents

The Serpent Coiled in Naples

Spare a thought for Jacopo Martorelli, *il professore*. Born in 1699, this most erudite figure was a philologist and Royal Professor of Greek antiquities at the University of Naples. We remember him, if at all, for his ability to believe absolutely in his own theories and to be unruffled by anything as trivial as solid evidence to their contrary. In 1756, he published a 738-page treatise, *De regia theca calamaria* ('On a Royal Inkpot'), complete with prolegomena and detailed notes, which drew on the recent discovery in Puglia of a bronze octagonal jar that was subsequently housed in the museum at Portici where it first tickled his imagination. I would have known nothing of the book were it not that a few years ago a copy of it strayed into the antiquarian bookshop where I work and where it is still available for inspection and improbable purchase. I shall blow the dust from it for the first comer. Its previous owner told me its chief value for him lay in the reproduction of an ancient inscription, one of several in the book, the original of which disappeared not long after publication. The book therefore provides the only proof of its former existence. Sadly I neglected to make a note of which one it was, and as this was secret knowledge that apparently only the seller was privy to, the link is now forever broken and an ancient artefact has been twice lost. Since then, the book has been the object of nobody's curiosity except, very briefly, mine. What I was able to glean of its contents came of my having had to catalogue it, and resorting to the instant information the internet provides. The book is bound in plain vellum, unlettered on the spine although there would appear to be traces of interference, possible erasure, or even, judging from the razor-like scoring in the material, excision, and it weighs roughly the same as two bags of oranges. The Latin text is liberally sprinkled with Greek and Hebrew, which makes the typography attractive to the eye. It is, I repeat, for sale. When finally somebody falls for it, which could be any time between now and forever, it'll be a small miracle.

Quite incredible was the effort that went into Martorelli's researches, the findings of which might nowadays fill up to ten pages of a quarterly magazine devoted to antiquities. After all, just how much can be said about an object so simple? It resembles all inkpots in that whatever it might look like on the outside, and this is a handsome enough example, on the inside it is designed to do what inkpots are meant to do, which is to hold ink. So what was so special about this one? A great deal, apparently. This is where things begin to unravel. The 'prophet and founding hero of modern archaeology', Johann Joachim Winckelmann, writes of his Italian contemporary that he had 'grasped this public opportunity of revealing everything he knows' and that 'the gods opened for him a wide field, in which he could indulge himself in mythology and ancient astronomy. At the same time he pours out whatever can be said about inks, pens, the art of writing, and the works of the ancients.' This is a polite enough verdict on a case of severe logorrhoea. The only cure that works in such instances is total abstinence because one does not whittle away such verbiage – one expands, as does this sloppy old universe, with ever bigger areas of darkness between the tinselly bits and pieces.

Martorelli set out to prove, on the basis of a single object, that the earliest use of a pen and inkwell could be dated to the Jews of ancient Egypt and Greece. As theories go, it was not such a bad one – a fledgling science has to begin somewhere. The Romans had their inkwells ranging from the simple *terra sigillata* to highly ornate ones with mythological scenes depicted on their surfaces. My hunch is that the less literary minded of them went for the more decorative style in much the same way our possessors of fountain pens inlaid with jewels tend to use them only in order to sign fat cheques or wobbly peace treaties. The Egyptians began to use inkpots when their writing shifted from stone to papyrus, which is a natural enough progression. The Jews of ancient Palestine had them too. There was one discovered in the scriptorium in Qumran. The Greeks, I don't know what the Greeks did, but presumably they, too, used them. Clearly there was a work to be written on the subject and in all probability there would be inkpot enthusiasts such as one finds nowadays for military memorabilia, tram tickets, postage stamps, cigarette cards, salt and pepper shakers, sugar cube wrappers, and barb wire. It may be reasonably assumed that in his research Martorelli did not poach the work of other scholars nor, for reasons that will become clear, would they later poach his. Were he playing forward for S.S.C. Napoli he would have had the field to himself.

So why the glum face? Sadly for him the Neapolitan government forbade circulation of his book on the grounds that it leaked confidential information on the archaeological discoveries then taking place in nearby Herculaneum, which were the province of the newly established and highly distinguished Accademia Ercolanese, the fifteen elected members among whose names Martorelli's is most pointedly *not* to be found. Booksellers also refused to stock the title because much of it was devoted to denigrating the work of a fellow philologist and archaeologist by the name of Alessio Simmaco Mazzocchi who, incidentally, was one of the esteemed Ercolanese circle and much revered by his contemporaries. Academe, even then, was prone to mudslinging exercises. This might serve to explain the illegibility of the book's title on the spine. Although it was not a work one would care to have seen on one's shelves it might have afforded private amusement all the same. We know that Herr Winckelmann owned a copy although it is not the vellum-bound book he is holding in Raphael Mengs's portrait of him. *De regia theca calamaria* is too cumbersome to pose with in one hand. It can't even be read in bed with ease.

Those were the very least of Martorelli's troubles, however, because his theory might have held water, or even ink, had the inkpot been an inkpot and not, as was clearly the case, a jewellery box. A whole reputation was skewered on a single mistake. One can easily imagine the mortification he must have felt at seeing so much effort go to waste. One can just about hear the distant laughter emanating from the gang Ercolanese. According to the potted biography in the *Dizionario biografico degli Italiani*, Martorelli entered a period of 'profound existential crisis' during which time – and here, one might say, is a sure pointer to his character – he blamed his publishers for having given the go-ahead to the book's publication. Thenceforth, as a result of the self-inflicted harm done to his reputation, he would publish all further academic studies under a different name.

It is hard to say what goes on in a man's mind at the best of times, but it was soon after that Martorelli began to lose his proverbials and diverted his vast mental energies towards proving that Homer – yes, the very same – lived in Naples and founded the university there. We will have to suppose it was not, as previously reported, Frederick II, Holy Roman Emperor, *stupor mundi* – 'astonishment of the world' – who opened it in AD 1224, it was Homer, author of some agreeable verses. Maybe, though, Martorelli had blundered onto something. There has been a theory doing the rounds of late to the effect that much of what we take to be Greek culture was in fact exported from ancient Italy to Greece and not, as most historians would have it, the other way round. There is a major work, published by a major university, devoted to that very premise, Giovanna Cese-rani's *Italy's Lost Greece* (and before we say of her what has been said of Martorelli, here's something to tease the brain a little: why are the best instances of Greek temples found not in Greece but in southern Italy? And what about their chronological sequence? Paestum looks *forward* to the Parthenon). Still, the idea of there having been a University of Naples some centuries before Christ is a bit of a stretch and, worse still, according to our heroic scholar the heroic poet created the Chair of Greek Studies which, centuries later, he himself would fill, and which would leave no one in doubt with respect to his academic pedigree.

This is not to suggest all his other academic efforts were without value. On Via Tribunali one can step into the Pontano Chapel built in 1492 by the humanist Giovanni Pontano in memory of his wife Adriana Sassone, where, in 1759, at the order of the king, Carlo di Borbone (otherwise known as Carlo III, King Charles III of Spain, Charles V and VII, the intricacies of which are better left to the historian to disentangle), Martorelli oversaw its restoration and had the Greek and Latin memorial inscriptions on the floor moved onto the walls. It was done with exquisite taste. Among them is Pontano's epitaph, the last words of which contain the astonishing message, 'You know who I am, or rather who I was: But I, good Stranger, cannot know thee in this Darkness: Pray Heaven, thou may'st know thyself. Farewell.'

Would that Martorelli knew enough to know himself he might have been spared our mirth. Author of some learned treatises on Greek tragedy and comedy, and a master of Greek syntax for which, to give him his due, he developed a most effective teaching method, Jacopo Martorelli died on 21 November 1777 in the pleasant surroundings of the Villa Vargas Macciucca di Ercolano, not so very far from the scene of his professional suicide.

Why should I settle on a fool, albeit a learned one, when Naples was, and had been for a long time, the seat of philosophical enquiry? After all, St Thomas Aquinas, the greatest mind of the Middle Ages, wrote the third part of his *Summa theologiae* there. Why not begin with Martorelli's contemporary, Raimondo di Sangro, a genius in so many spheres? The composer Giovanni Battista Pergolesi? The great thinker Giambattista Vico? The answer is this: I find in Martorelli a strange brotherhood. We who pursue, and seek to finesse, a single line of thought, who do so regardless of the consequences, and who take our bearings not from the stars above but from their reflection on choppy waters, do we not dip our pen into the same inkpot sometimes? Are there not a thousand intellectual premises that amount to little more than a thousand hot air balloons, only for them to be shot down one by one? Are there not scores of Martorellis beneath our very own noses? If, as I believe, enthusiasm is the engine that drives the universe, ought we not to stifle our laughter a little? Jacopo, hear me. I, too, may have fallen victim to an *idée fixe*.

Which is this: all over Naples I showed people a sentence that, for quick access, I wrote on the inside cover of my notebook, and which, if my source is correct, is a Sicilian proverb: 'Mai temere Roma, il serpente se ne sta attorcigliato a Napoli' ('Never fear Rome, the serpent lies coiled in Naples'). It's the sort of line one likes to trot out at dinner parties although there's got to be sufficient menace in one's voice for it to chill the blood a little. It was used in an American TV film, *Gotti: The Rise and Fall of a Real Life Mafia Don*, which one critic dismissed as being 'too detailed for casual viewers and too inaccurate for enthusiasts' and whose total aesthetic value may not have been equal to its single most quotable line. Admittedly I seized upon the proverb before I ever got to Naples. It provided me with a title before I knew what the book's contents would be. It was like being handed a physical law for which I had yet to find a theory, one that I'd make fit no matter what, there being something of the Jacopo in me. Would it be too much to say that by tenor alone the line carries its own inner truth? Sadly I've been unable to chase the serpent to its source, but then what makes a proverb a proverb is its anonymous nature and the way it has been polished by time. And then there's the problem of how best to interpret it. Matthew 10:36 has been cited: 'And a man's foes shall be they of his own household.' It's what most gangsters learn by rote, but never fully absorb because sooner or later they make a mistake. The serpent for them tends to strike from within the family circle. There is, I think, even more juice to be squeezed from the pomegranate. The proverb seems to be loaded with metaphysical significance. What applies to Naples applies to the universe. Soon I began to see that serpent everywhere. I place the emphasis on *attorcigliato*, which means 'twisted' or 'coiled', a thing so tightly wound it might snap at any second, at which point it's best not to be anywhere within striking range. Admittedly the serpent occupies but a tiny place in the city's mythology and so while I do not want to push an image at the expense of veracity it serves as my personal take on the lives of the people I met there. So tightly wound are the hairsprings in their watches that a single turn more and all their best efforts come to naught. The Naples I have come to love breaks hearts.

What the sentence brought out in the Neapolitans I showed it to was, in the main, puzzlement or a shrug of the shoulders until finally one man roared with laughter, saying, 'Yes, perfect! Very *nice*!' Domenico Garofalo is a mover, a man who makes things happen. Certainly he has done his bit for culture, and, among other things, he is involved in organising festivals and contemporary dances, which was how I met him. I had lost my way in the Spanish Quarter when I stopped to ask for directions, and after giving them to me this friendly man in his early forties suggested I come back later for a performance he had organised at the theatre opposite the café where he was lording it over his coffee, as did Garrick in front of his theatre. I made my excuses. I walked on. I dined. I mulled it over. I went back. A couple of days later, I met him again in the quietest spot in Naples, the newly restored, staggeringly white, courtyard of the Convento di San Domenico Maggiore. Domenico's enthusiasms took me in a hundred directions, from jazz and dance to a Neapolitan rap band called La Famiglia (in particular a song of theirs called 'Odissea', which compresses into five minutes the whole history of Naples beginning with ancient Parthenope), the films of Pier Paolo Pasolini, the writings of Hegel (about which I know little, although I was made to understand Naples is a Hegelian place) and Blaise Pascal, and onwards to Giacomo Leopardi and Curzio Malaparte. There was no saying where next he'd take me. Willing to go high and low, eclectic by nature, Domenico was a most reliable guide.

A few minutes later, in the Piazza del Gesù Nuovo, he pointed to the statue of the Virgin Mary on top of the baroque Obelisco dell'Immacolata. 'Look,' he cried, 'there's your creature!' And indeed, beneath the foot of the Virgin, was a coiled serpent. Nothing so unusual in that, it being a common enough feature in Christian iconography, but I had been vindicated by the very best of authorities. *She* wouldn't stand for any nonsense. Domenico invited me to look again at the statue and tell him what else I could see because it would bear on another matter we'd been discussing only minutes before, which had to do with the inextricable relationship in Naples between the living and the dead and how one might simultaneously inhabit both worlds. We'd agreed that any description of the city's duality was best located there. We had spoken of skulls and of the people who adopt them, the cult of *anime pezzentelle*. What was I meant to be looking at? I squinted my eyes a little. All became clear when Domenico pointed it out to me. When viewed from the sunny side, so to speak, the front of the statue of the Virgin represents life, but when seen from the dark side, and with perhaps somewhat deliberate eyes, it becomes, especially at night, the Grim Reaper. It is an optical illusion and probably accidental, although there has been the suggestion it was so rigged by members of the Sanseverino family, whose noses were put out of joint when their palace was perforce turned into the church of Gèsu Nouvo as punishment for their having taken the wrong side in a political row. Whatever the case, the statue's dualistic nature has entered the city's folklore.

The folkloric: this, apparently, is where I've been required to take extra care. I had been warned by certain people solicitous of its reputation that I was to avoid any depiction of Naples as a *folkloric* city. A bit of me thinks this is a species of political correctness because while its inhabitants are quite right to avoid stereotypes of themselves, it does seem to me that there is nothing as purely illustrative of a people as its folklore. Or could it be that *talk* of the folkloric gets in the way of the *actively* folkloric, such that it becomes a species of embarrassment or, even worse, a call to arms? My solemn warners have a point. As soon as one summons the folkloric it dies. We have seen what happens when it is recruited for nationalistic causes. Those pretty little folk costumes all of a sudden become sinister. The Polish writer on theatre, Jan Kott, who visited Naples in 1962, writes: 'Never before did I realise that folklore means a view from outside, from an alien circle. One cannot consider *oneself* as a part of folk-lore; or rather one cannot do so with impunity ... Folklore made conscious immediately becomes a stall with readymade souvenirs, a circus, or a masquerade.' So yes, one wants to come up with something better than an oleograph in which there is only a tenuous connection between the subject and the prefabricated brushstrokes. And besides, one doesn't go looking for truth in Naples because one is liable to plunge headfirst down an intellectual sinkhole. This is no idle simile. The sinkhole has become a feature of Neapolitan existence, whole buildings disappearing into the cavernous spaces below. There are times when from the bottom of one of them one can hear Jacopo's ghostly voice.

So when did the folkloric acquire such a negative connotation in a city where one might still purchase for oneself a red horn pendant to ward off ill fortune? There's the first mistake. The red horn, which really is a repackaging of the apotropaic phallus the ancients wore, has no power unless it is presented to someone else as a gift. I do not wish to put the red horn sellers, those purveyors of 'readymade souvenirs', nice people many of them, out of business, and tourists ought not to be discouraged from the belief that good fortune can be purchased for as little as a couple of euros, but maybe they ought to be educated as to how the red horn operates and instead of buying one for themselves buy a dozen or so for friends and relatives. One does see those pepper-like shapes from time to time at the entrances to houses, maybe not quite as plentiful as in bygone days but still to be found where modernity has not taken all the gusto out of life. I saw one at the entrance of a car repair on the road going up to the cemetery at Fontanelle. If ever there was a need for a red horn it was there.

The truly folkloric begins to disappear when the conditions of life improve. There is poverty in Naples, plenty of it, some of it very raw indeed, but not as physically wretched as when the great social commentator and novelist Matilde Serao wrote of it in the 1890s. She pleads after the end of a cholera outbreak:

Do not abandon Naples again, when you are caught up in politics or business; do not leave this place – which we all must love – once more to its death throes. Of all the beautiful and good cities of Italy, Naples is the most graciously beautiful and the most profoundly good. Do not leave Naples in poverty, filth, and ignorance, without work and without help: do not destroy, in her, the poetry of Italy.

Serao's book *Il ventre di Napoli* ('The Belly of Naples', 1884) is at once a damning indictment and a cry of love. Would she still make claims for the city's goodness, I wonder, or would her heart have snapped at the pyramidal crime zone that is Scampia? She may have caught a whiff of the biblical Gomorrah (not the film and, later, the TV adaptation of Roberto Saviano's *Gomorrah* which Neapolitans say is wildly inaccurate, although it keeps them glued to the screen). Old fools say things get worse. I reckon Serao would love it still but with a more desperate love. Contemporary poverty resides in a pile of empty syringes and may be all the worse for it, a species of spiritual as well as physical malaise. The composer, ethnographer, and writer, Roberto De Simone, informs me there are now ex votos, made of gold, of syringes given by people who have recovered from drug addiction. It is human nature that when people are defined as one thing or another, they tend to squeeze willingly into the mould made for them, a trap difficult to escape. A school teacher and friend of mine, Mariagrazia Barsanti, when speaking to me of the Neapolitans and of the terrible generalisations visited upon them, both from inside and outside Italy, could not have been clearer: 'They want, and deserve, deliverance.' We were sitting at the outside café just off Via Toledo. There was a bit of a cool breeze. As the sun moved we had to shift our chairs in order to stay in the warm light. *They want, and deserve, deliverance*. Profound words, I shall seek to keep them before me at all times.

Can we really speak of deliverance without its sister, survival?
Giuseppe Marotta in his book of short stories *L'oro di Napoli*
(1947) writes:

> An ability to get up again after every fall; a remote, heredi-
> tary, obstinate and intelligent endurance. Rolling the centu-
> ries away we may perhaps find its origin in the convulsions
> of the earth, the sudden gusts of deadly vapour, the waves
> of lava engulfing the hills, and all the dangers that have from
> time immemorial beset human existence in this corner of the
> world. This endurance, then, is Neapolitan gold.

A few lines later, he is more specific.

> Only a few steps away is the sea, distant and solemn before
> the city's martyrdom as if it were a basin of holy water. As
> soon as there is no more danger from the skies, I told myself
> in May of 1943, the Neapolitans will dip their fingers in this
> kindly water, make the sign of the cross and go back to their
> work and play.

Marotta walks to one side of me on this journey, a melancholy figure, gentle to the point of hate, and on the other side of
me is Malaparte who is merciless, cynical, and cruel to the point
of love. They stare in separate directions, not a word passing
between them.

There is a Neapolitan saying that compares the city to another
north of it: 'If Naples were to open all its doors, Rome would
disappear.' A hidden city, it most certainly is. I was to have
physical evidence of this. I was in the Museo Diocesano when a
terrible heaviness pulled at my eyes, something akin to weariness
of its baroque excesses. I had been excited only by a stone slab
with the letter 'Y' carved into its surface. I will speak further of
its significance. I was about to leave when I noticed a small door

at the back. I passed through it and found myself in what was an older church, the Santa Maria Donnaregina Vecchia, when I felt a sudden rise in my spirits, and, as I went deeper into it, the only visitor there, I found myself entranced by the frescos, the greater number of which had turned a reddish hue after a fire in 1390. And then there was another door and behind it yet more extraordinary treasures. This idea of a door leading to another door and yet another serves perfectly as a way to understand Naples.

Domenico had one more thing to show me. I could have stood all day staring at the wall of the Gesù Nuova and missed out on yet another aspect of the city's secret lore. The building, constructed in 1470, renovated between 1584 and 1601, was originally the palazzo of the Sanseverino family. The original façade, done in the so-called ashlar or *bugnato* style, with small jutting pyramidal stones, was preserved when inner structural changes were made. The overall effect is rather grim, a bit like a prison wall, and gives little hint of the opulence to be found inside, which, again, is rather too baroque for my taste. I strained to see what Domenico said was there to be seen. Again I failed. Barely visible to the naked eye are seven different marks spread, in various combinations, over the entire surface of the building. It used to be said of them that they constituted some kind of secret code, carved into the volcanic stone by stonemasons, and that they were positive symbols meant to drive out the negative. If so, then I hope the stonemasons got out of town quickly because there would be fires, earthquakes, and two collapses of the church's massive dome. It was also suggested that the marks refer to the caves from where the volcanic stone, called *piperno*, originally came. Now there is an even more extraordinary theory. According to the art historian Vincenzo De Pasquale the incisions are Aramaic letters, each, as was briefly the practice at the time of the building's construction, representing a different musical note, so that in effect the entire façade of the church is a vast musical score, most probably for plectrum instruments, lasting some forty-five minutes. It is impossible at ground level to read them from right to left and from bottom to top, as the scholar invites us to, and so only the Grim Reaper, if his eyes are equal to the task and if he could turn his head at a sharp angle, would be able to grasp the whole. The music, which has been given the title 'Enigma', is there to be listened to, on the internet, arranged for organ rather than strings. I begin to wonder whether Professor De Pasquale might not have taken the Jacopo route. Quite simply, it's boring, there being insufficient variation in the music, if that's what it's meant to be, to hold the listener's attention for more than a couple of minutes. The best that can be said for it is that it is a shade sinister, the soundtrack to a low-budget horror film. The mystery is not so much solved as deepened. If, to begin with, the building was a palace and not a church then the presence of these symbols would surely have had an esoteric rather than religious purpose. All in all, it was a strange thing to do. Small wonder it has entered the city's folklore. *Basta!* We mustn't go there. The city's got a hard nose. The coffee, though, is exquisite. What do they do to it that a single shot of it takes one into the realms of the divine? The playwright Eduardo Di Filippo, in his play *Questi fantasmi* ('These Ghosts', 1946), says it must be toasted to 'the colour of a monk's mantle'.

One might suppose that the erection of the Obelisco dell'Immacolata, which doubled up as a plague column (or votive spire), would have passed without argument, but when plans for its construction were announced the owner of a nearby palazzo, Duke Nicola Pignatelli, objected, saying he feared the obelisk might tumble into the entrance of his home. This was not such a peevish complaint given that the city sits in an earthquake zone. On the other hand, the entrance at the far corner of the Piazza del Gesù Nuova, at 53 Calata Trinità Maggiore, is just a little too far away for any real damage to be done to it. He was well out of shot of a flying halo. So what was Pignatelli's complaint exactly? Surely it was the Virgin's close proximity that set his

teeth on edge. What would She say to what was going on behind
the handsome façade of his home? In 1761, at the time of the
obelisk's construction, one of Pignatelli's guests was Giacomo
Casanova. There is not room enough here to go into the latter's
complex relationship with women, and besides he was consider-
ate enough to leave behind ten volumes of his life and times and
amatory adventures. The scholar Judith Summers remarks of
Casanova's ability to move among women: 'He has the knack
of addressing them as if they were his equals, and undressing
them as if they were his superiors.' It was at the Palazzo Pignatelli di Monteleone, within sight of the Virgin, that he took an
amorous interest in the 'mistress' of the impotent duke. Leonilda
was, in modern vulgar parlance, Pignatelli's 'eye candy'. Casanova saw in her an opportunity for more than merely greets the
eye and then writes that 'the seductive features of this charming
girl were not altogether unknown to me'. When one evening he
was introduced to her mother, Donna Lucrezia, all became hor-
rifyingly clear. Eighteen years earlier, when Donna Lucrezia was
married to a man called Castelli, another semi-willing cuckold,
Casanova had a fling with her and, unknown to him, nine
months later, she gave birth to a daughter, Leonilda. Casanova
describes his immediate reaction: 'My hair stood on end, and I
relapsed into a gloomy silence.' A rekindling then took place,
such as sometimes happens with old flames, and it was with
their daughter in attendance, as voyeur, that Casanova demonstrated he was nothing if not inventive in his sexual escapades:

> I must draw a veil over the most voluptuous night I have ever
> spent. If I told all I should wound chaste ears, and, besides,
> all the colours of the painter and all the phrases of the poet
> could not do justice to the delirium of pleasure, the ecstasy,
> and the license which passed during that night, while two wax
> lights burnt dimly on the table like candles before the shrine
> of a saint.

If Leonilda was not physically involved with Casanova that night, she would be several years later, on the occasion of her marriage to yet another cuckold. It's amazing what the incestuous Casanova shouts at full volume in his prose. The wonder of it all is that the Virgin did not of her own accord climb down from the top of her obelisk and, despite the two threatening anthropomorphic faces at the tops of the columns glaring down at her, pound her fists on the entrance to the Palazzo Pignatelli di Monteleone.

Very few are the historical centre's buildings and monuments that do not have a story to tell. Blood, tears, and semen have seeped into, and ooze from, every crack of the old town centre. Quite often, *very* often, it's blood. Walk the five minutes it takes to get from the Piazza del Gesú Nuova to the Piazza San Domenico Maggiore, and inside the entrance to the palazzo diagonally opposite you'll find the spot where the composer Carlo Gesualdo dumped the repeatedly stabbed corpses of his unfaithful wife, Donna Maria d'Avalos, and her lover, Duke Fabrizio Carafa. When, late on the evening of 16 October 1590, Gesualdo told his manservant Pietro that he was going out hunting the latter remarked on the improbable hour for such activities. 'You shall see what hunting I am going to do,' his master answered. Already I can hear the low thunder of timpani, an explosive crescendo, and then the music ebbing in diminuendo along with the lives of the leading lady and her very handsome lover. One can imagine Verdi setting the line to music. Actually there are several operas based on Gesualdo's life, one by the Russian Alfred Schnittke, another by the Italian Salvatore Sciarrino and, most intriguingly, yet another by the Neapolitan Francesco d'Avalos who was a descendant of Donna Maria's uncle. At one point it was rumoured that the composer owned the bed in which Donna Maria was murdered and that one night he'd left a tape recorder running on it, just to see whether there were any noisy spirits on the loose. When morning came he discovered on the recording a strange singing voice, which he immediately transcribed for one of the arias in his opera. '*Non é vero*,' he confessed shortly before he died in 2014, 'it's not true', but there are times, especially in Naples, when denials are taken for avowals, and there are stories that Donna Maria's scantily clad ghost is still to be met with in the small hours.

Where there's space on a wall there'll be a scrawl of some kind for sure, and where there's mess to be made it'll be made. A man walking past my café table throws his empty cigarette pack on the ground where there are plenty of other bits of rubbish. There is no getting around the fact that Naples is a bit of a shambles. I have become a subscriber to James Q. Wilson and George L. Kelling's 'Broken Window Theory', which can be summed up best by quoting the article they wrote for the *Atlantic Monthly*: 'Consider a building with a few broken windows. If the windows are not repaired, the tendency is for vandals to break a few more windows. Eventually, they may even break into the building, and if it's unoccupied, perhaps become squatters or light fires inside. Or consider a pavement. Some litter accumulates. Soon, more litter accumulates.' As theories go, it is remarkably, indeed pleasingly, simple. It allows for that nebulous thing known as human nature. What they describe can be just as easily extended to the graffiti covering so much of Naples, even the churches. If there are three instances of it, why not add a fourth or a fifth? It has reached the point where there is so much graffiti one doesn't notice it any more. I can almost swear those natives who extol their city's beauty haven't noticed the mess, which, in a way, is not such a terrible thing because it means they have been able to penetrate mere surfaces.

There are times when the graffiti congeals into something perversely aesthetic, something which photography captures

better than the human eye. The street art is another matter altogether. Some of it, in particular the paintings by cyop&kaf in
the Spanish Quarter, are on a level of excellence rarely encountered anywhere, but only Banksy's *Madonna con la pistola*
in the Piazza dei Gerolomini is treated with reverence. It was
covered with plexiglass after a petition of over 16,500 signatures
was raised in order to protect it from damage. An earlier work
of Banksy's was vandalised, although what is one to say when
the vandals vandalise the vandals? What is one to make of the
handgun above the Madonna's head where a halo is meant to be?
Sacrilege? Or are we to understand that religion and crime are
the polarities of Neapolitan existence? The *Madonna* is under
the auspices of the Pizzeria Dal Presidente whose owner Agostino 'o Pazzo ('Augustine the Crazy'), born Antonio Mellino,
was famous for his daring exploits on a motorcycle in the streets
of Naples during the 1970s. Youths have been following his
example ever since. Meanwhile, the latest word on the street is
that Banksy may be of Neapolitan lineage. It is not such a distance from Bristol to Naples.

A lady from South Carolina, a lemony squeeze of Tennessee Williams in her voice, told me that Naples would be a great place if only someone took a hoover to it. She said this with an accompanying hand gesture worthy of a native of the city she professes to love. She sees possibilities for the place, which begs the question: were Naples to be given the 'once-over' might it not cease to be Naples? It has been described by its own inhabitants as a paradise occupied by devils ('Napoli è un paradiso abitato da diavoli'), a saying so old it has become something of a proverb if not an actual cliché. It has been credited to countless people. Certainly there is enough to appal the visitor, but it never ceases to amaze me how many tourists are oblivious to the city's many treasures. It is also a city in whose historical centre people still actually live. Irene Vecchia, Pulcinella *maestra*,* in order to demonstrate the truth of this, took me to the covered arches of Via dei Tribunali where she pointed to a curious groove, probably centuries old, in the stone pavement. She invited me to follow it to its source. A fishmonger sloshed water over his fish, which then ran from the basin into the groove and from there into the street. 'You see,' she told me, 'there has always been a fishmonger in this spot.' What she was demonstrating is that life, *real* life, continues here as it always has done, which makes the historical centre of Spaccanapoli almost unique among Italy's old city centres. The fact that much of it and the Spanish Quarter have been gentrified of late is no cause for celebration, although at the same time it is be wondered why the inhabitants do not respect their surroundings more.

There is another view of Naples, which is that rather than being populated by devils it is a place where the poor find it close to impossible to climb out of the rut of their lives, and so, guided by a sense of fatalism, they become irresponsible. Why

---

* Pulcinella is a stock character in the Neapolitan puppetry tradition. We will be gradually making his acquaintance throughout this book.

not throw your cigarette butt on the street if the street's a mess anyway? *Broken Window Theory.* And yet they love their home. What Harold Acton says of eighteenth-century Naples holds true: 'The large population of the people, including the sturdy *lazzaroni* who lived from hand to mouth, were united by certain quasi-religious sentiments, of which the most intense was the love of home. Naples was their home, associated with all that makes life beautiful and sacred.' I spoke to a young woman of eighteen who comes from the district of Secondigliano, a rough zone, and she spoke of it with something that sounds a lot like love. Acton continues: 'Those who had no private property and who could neither read nor write were bound to Naples by a deep and poetic tie. They belonged to this land, this sea; here they multiplied and luxuriated in the benign climate, accepting their lot without questioning the inequalities of fortune any more than the caprices of Vesuvius.' Neapolitans may complain about their city, and certainly it is in many respects deplorable, but then they hate to see it derided by others. Some of the saddest songs, 'Santa Chiara', for example, are about being separated from the city they love, and at the same time being reluctant to return to it for fear of what they might find gone.

Domenico Garafalo speaks of his city in terms of Eros and Thanatos, love and death, death and love. Domenico is a 'believer', which is to say he believes Naples is the cultural capital of the south of Europe. If only more people would believe it as well, so he finds it all a bit of a struggle. Barcelona, he says, doesn't compare. It's pretty, but fake. Naples as the manifestation of Eros and Thanatos was our big theme.

'It is a city of love,' he told me, 'a city of music and art, and on the other side we have darkness – the Camorra, murders, robberies. Those people care only about what they can touch. Their end is simply to survive. This is the dark side of Naples. Many of my friends from high school and university have left here, all of them looking for happiness, but what is saddest of all is that they leave thinking nothing can be changed. So why bother any more? Who is going to change things, however, if everyone leaves?'

I think I saw something in Domenico's eyes, which maybe his mind had not yet had time enough to register, that one day soon he'd be leaving Naples. And indeed he did, and the fact of it makes him ache.

'An old man I met a couple of months ago,' he continued, 'is a wine entrepreneur and before that he was an engineer and now he is working on this new venture. He asked me, "In your opinion what is the most important quality required to do something risky in this place?" I answered that you have to be brave. "No," he scoffed, "you have to be stupid! You have to have the courage to be stupid because if you think too much about starting up something you won't do anything at all. Just do it!" Over these past ten years I have done and maybe changed things a little and now I'm quite happy to be here. I want to see the world, of course, maybe even live elsewhere, but for now I want to believe in the dream that this, my city, can be my home. It is not so easy. A lot of people here feel it's not really their home. Pasolini said, "The last part of a human being is Naples." He found in the people here a humanity that he never found elsewhere. It was the same with Leopardi. It's incredible that a man like him could at the end of his short life have felt so alive here. Naples is a city of life but at the same time it is a city of death. One mirrors the other. They have to be together in order for either of them to exist. St Augustine said something nice on the subject of good and evil. When people asked him why, if God is so good, did He invent the Devil, he replied that in order to understand the light one needs shadow. Only then will the light be important, like a star or a lighthouse. This, for me, is the real war between good and evil, this continual battle between shadow and light. First, however, they have to co-exist. If there is no shadow, the light is too strong. Without the light, it is too dark. This is our human condition, somewhere in the middle. We are made of both light and dark. In this respect Naples is a real mirror to humanity. Where I disagree with many Neapolitans is that they don't accept a part of our city which is true. We are angels and devils at the same time.'

We discussed Curzio Malaparte's *The Skin*, the most searing book ever written about Naples, a depiction of the city in 1944 when, after getting shot of the Germans, the Neapolitans fell before the Allies, the women turning to prostitution in order to feed their families. Domenico sprang a surprise on me.

'We are the bitch of the Mediterranean for sure. We dominate the dominators. This is a matter of history, it's what happened here over the centuries. We are almost addicted to this idea. It's not cultural prostitution, it is physical, and as such it becomes a way to understand the world. It's deep inside our language. There is a story about our word for orange, *purtuallo*. Whether or not it's true I don't know, but legend says that every so often the French gave out oranges for free and they'd say to the people *Pour toi* ("for you") and gradually the word became *purtuallo*.* There are many such situations where domination has changed the language. This improved the culture of Naples. Someone said if you can understand Naples you will understand the world. We live so close to each other, one on one. The actor Marcello Mastroianni when he was asked his thoughts on Naples replied, "If I am in Milan and bump into an old friend, he'll say, 'Oh my God, you've aged!' but if the same thing happens in Naples the response will be, 'Oh God, *we* are getting older. Let me get you a coffee.'" We have this Neapolitan phrase "Tien'm ca te téng", which means "Hold onto me and I'll hold onto you." We know we need each other because it is too tough to handle things here alone. This sense of a collective is deeply felt here. If someone in

---

* The stronger possibility is that the word derives from the Greek for orange, *portokalia*.

the street gets sick four or five people will stop. People care, but at the same time you might lose your watch.'

I was reminded of a joke, most probably concocted by someone from the north of the country. A man is sitting on a train when the conductor passes. 'Excuse me,' he says, 'can you tell me when we arrive in Naples?' The conductor answers, 'Hold your wrist level with your eyes and study the minute hand on your watch. Keep it there. When your watch disappears, you'll know we've arrived.'

'When I was in Brazil three years ago,' Domenico continued, 'I worked in the *favela*, the slums, with a Canadian NGO who was taking pictures with his cell phone. I said to him, "Put that thing down, we could have problems." He replied, "Yeh, but I'm free to take pictures." "Yes," I replied, "and they are free to rob you of your cell phone and your wallet." It is not a question of rights, it is a matter of respect. If I go into the Spanish Quarter dressed *au couture* or wear an expensive watch they might rob me. You have to be smart enough to understand what it is you are going into. It is not a question of freedom because *they* live there. *You* are not living there. You go into their territory and so you have to respect what might happen there. It is not right, of course, it may not be fair, but it's the truth. As it turned out I was the only person in the group in Brazil who was not robbed. They joked, saying it was because I'm Neapolitan. And I said, "No, it's because I take care of myself. C'mon, you see children here sniffing glue. There is something more important than the picture you can take of them." This is common sense, of course, but I got this from living here in Naples. Often I read in the newspapers about tourists who are robbed here. I feel badly for them and I feel badly for my city, for the negative publicity this creates. I repeat, it is not right, but it is a matter of taking care. What I hate is when I see the kind of tourism in Naples that resembles a kind of safari in which people go into the poorest, most raw, quarters to see the human beasts living there. They see people from afar. They see something that scares them and excites them at the same time. This is not the right way to behave.'

It was time for Domenico to go. Just before we parted company he told me something else. Was it mischief I detected in his voice or had he himself been taken for a ride?

'And don't forget Dracula's grave is here.'

A local Italian newspaper, *Il Gazzettino*, on 11 June 2014, ran a short article to the effect that the tomb of Vlad the Impaler, the horrid original for Bram Stoker's rather more elegant Dracula, had been discovered in the church of Santa Maria La Nova in central Naples. The tomb had everything going for it – the image of a dragon, a couple of sphinxes, an inscription in some indecipherable language, and a mysterious heat radiating from the stone. I won't go into the painstaking details that 'prove' the symbols spell out the name of Vlad III Drăculea or indeed Vlad Țepeș, but word of the discovery quickly spread throughout the world and it is not without a little national pride that it can be announced the first newspaper in England to pick up the story was the august *Daily Mail*, whose better headlines include 'Angry Queen Punches PM In Drunk Rage'. According to the scholars (whose names I will not repeat here because I would rather not embarrass them back into the limelight they created for themselves, and, besides, they may have been suffering from the enthusiasm of innocence), Vlad the Impaler, previously believed to have been killed in battle, was instead taken prisoner by the Turks who then ransomed him to his hitherto unheard-of daughter in Naples, Maria Balsa, which, in the circumstances, was most generous of the Turks given that Vlad won his moniker after impaling so many of them. Our scholars, meanwhile, staked their reputations on proving this was indeed his tomb, which would have been news to its occupant Matteo Ferrillo, Count of Muro. The best we can say is that the closest Dracula ever got to Naples was through the budding genius of Bram Stoker who was not unfamiliar with the place, having visited his parents there in 1875, some twenty-three years before the publication of the book that later spawned a thousand movies. As for the discoverers of 'Dracula's tomb', the spirit of Jacopo Martorelli watches over them, whispering *molto bene*. So, too, say the tour guides, extra coinage spinning in their eyes.

What Neapolitans cannot be accused of is mediocrity. Their normal life exists at the poles of high and low, and hardly ever in-between. What one observes on any day in the street is pure theatre. This is not to present a folkloric picture, but simply to say that the boundaries between public and private have been long dissolved. There is no place for the theatrical to spill but onto the street. When summer comes, people move their cramped dining area outside. Jean-Paul Sartre, who was not deeply enamoured of the place, had to concede that Neapolitans are 'the only people you can actually watch living their lives, from top to bottom, head to toe'. The modern Neapolitan writer, Luciano de Crescenzo, puts it slightly differently, 'I have a concept of Naples that is not so much of a city, per se, but rather an ingredient of the human spirit that I detect in everyone, Neapolitan or not.' Love the place or hate it, very rarely is it met with indifference.

There is, I think, another element peculiar to Naples, and that is the degree to which people inhabit, and are inhabited by, time. Admittedly this may come across as a rather ludicrous statement, a bit like saying the sky is blue, and so I'd better rally my forces. Peter Gunn, author of a notable book on Naples, also wrote an essay called 'Some Thoughts on Time in Naples', which contains maybe the most profound of many brilliant observations he has made:

It is a strange fact that a sojourn in Naples has the quite extraordinary effect of evoking and stimulating in one a lively awareness of the existence, the actual presence, of Time. And *presence* is perhaps the operative word: presence, rather than passage … It does appear curious that in Naples, to a degree perhaps not experienced in other cities, one has a peculiarly heightened awareness of the present moment, a sense of sensuous immediacy, the enveloping, luminous present, the here and now … It is the vividness, the vivacity of the momentary impressions, that impinge on us with such compulsion. The impact of these heterogeneous sensations on our mind is such as to arouse in us an acute awareness of our surroundings – and of ourself. This self-consciousness is instantaneous – the momentary now of self-knowledge. In this heightened consciousness of self one may be equally well aware of the soul's health or the soul's malaise.

I have never been anywhere that, in the moment of one's being, so perfectly mirrors my inner spiritual anarchy as Naples does.

A knotted rope of associations lies at the beginning of what promises to be a circumbendibus as opposed to a straightforward journey, a series of markers that serve no purpose other than to demonstrate that any place one chooses to map is ultimately unmappable. Ennio Flaiano, author and scriptwriter for Fellini, writes: 'In Italy, in fact, the shortest line between two points is an arabesque. We live in a network of arabesques.' Maybe, though, one can describe to some degree the conditions that ensure the unmappable stays unmappable. It would be quite awful to know a place so well that one couldn't see anything of it any more. The familiar swallows our eyes. This said, the lacunae in this book will be immense. I know that by sticking for much of the time to the city centre, I am, in a sense, playing it safe, although where I'm staying is a crime zone. Still the very worst of what I see there is no match for the outlying districts, the rise of which are so memorably depicted in Francesco Rosi's 1963 film *Le mani sulla città* ('Hands Over the City'). Any depiction of them is beyond my ken, but there is no getting out of my mind the aerial shots at the beginning of that movie. If ever mankind created hell on earth it is to be found there. It is what wraps old Naples in a deadly embrace. And yet I know there is a teeming humanity to be explored in those places. This is not to say the one is less real than the other, but the creeping gentrification in the city centre may one day force me to re-evaluate things a little.

There is the small matter of a volcano, a coiled serpent if ever there was one, slowly biding its time. Where's the formula by which one might calculate the degree to which its brooding presence shapes the minds of those who live in its shadow, whether it serves to explain the fatalism of Neapolitans or if it's merely to be shrugged at because if nobody knows what tomorrow brings why bother the Fates with personal anxieties? There is a belief that Vesuvius contains magnetic forces that bring out either the best or the worst in those who are in contact with them. It is therefore advisable to be on good speaking terms with Vesuvius because the consequences of being disrespectful might result not only in it covering what has never been covered before but also all that which so much painstaking work went into uncovering in the first place. When I asked someone what it's like for people who live there, knowing that it can explode any time, she responded, 'Yes, but we have a solution. We call it a mountain. We speak to it, ask it to remain calm. We even have a popular song that goes, "I live with you. Does that mean nothing to you?"' The actress Valeria Vaiano is so physically sensitive she should hire herself out to the Vesuvius Observatory. She told me that every night when she goes to bed she feels the earth tremble. Otherwise it pays not to dwell too much upon the unavoidable, certainly for the 600,000 people who live on its slopes. In *Die fröhliche Wissenschaft* ('The Gay Science', 1882) Friedrich Nietzsche writes, 'The secret for harvesting from existence the greatest fruitfulness and the greatest enjoyment is: to live dangerously! Build your cities on the slopes of Vesuvius!' And then who would forsake a glass of Lacryma Christi, literally 'tears of Christ', although, and here it becomes easy to conflate pagan and Christian, the tears are not His but those the god Bacchus shed when he saw the loveliness of the surrounding landscape. And wherever his tears fell there grew vines. The wine is the closest to what the ancient Romans drank and its excellence is due to the volcanic ash in which the vines grow. Christopher Marlowe makes mention of it in the second part of his play *Tamburlaine the Great*. Jesus, weeping over Lucifer's fall from heaven, was perhaps a bit late on the scene to be considered the producer of Lacryma Christi but there can be no denying the beauty of the name.

There has been some unpleasantness with respect to Vesuvius issuing from the football fans from Verona who taunt the Neapolitan fans with '*Oh Vesuvio lavali col fuoco!*' ('O Vesuvius, wash them with fire!'). Their chant carries unpleasant connotations of the cholera epidemics that have hit Naples from time to time, which well-scrubbed northerners put down to the uncleanliness of southerners. The Neapolitan response is '*Giulietta è 'na zoccola!*' ('Juliet is a slut!'). One overheated journalist, appalled by the behaviour of the Veronese, claimed that this banner of abuse was much more than a typical stadium slogan, that it was an intellectual masterpiece of irony, a nod to the genius of Shakespeare, and if that were not sufficient, a conception of true life as opposed to the idiotic vulgarity of the opposing force. Another sign in the Naples stands read '*Romeo é un cornuto!*' ('Romeo is a cuckold!'). The Veronese got their own back with '*Napoletani figli di Giulietta.*' If Neapolitans really are Juliet's bastard children then the Veronese ought to reconsider the reputation of their heroine. This last strikes me rather as an own goal.

Also worth recalling, especially when one is feeling sure-footed, is that the greater part of the city is built over empty space. So it is threatened from below by structural collapse, sink-holes and the like, and from above by Vesuvius feigning sleep. Meanwhile, at ground level, almost everything is in a permanent state of chaos. Actually, the biggest threat to the city comes from 20 km to the west of Naples, the Campi Flegrei (also known as the Phlegraean Fields), a volcanic complex of eight square miles that has all the ingredients of a supervolcano, the eruption of which would dwarf the events of 24 August AD 79. It could take down the whole of Europe. The people living there seem to be even more sanguine about it than the Neapolitans are in relation to Vesuvius. One of the forty calderas, Solfatara, which bubbles and heaves, was until recently a popular camping site. It is darkly appropriate that the Phlegraean Fields might seal our fate given that so much of the world's mythology concerning Hades comes from there. It's no good trying to ask the Sibyl at Cumae when that'll be. She was last seen washing cups in a Naples café.

An Octopus in Forcella

Where I have my room, on Vico Scassacocchi, which is one of the oldest streets in Naples, my window on the fourth floor looks out into what the architectural glossaries describe as a 'lightwell', too small to be a courtyard, too big to be a mere shaft, not enough space in which to take one's repose in style, but wide enough to be able to hang one's laundry, although three bedsheets would be one too many. It is too confined a space to be able to hold onto its daily ration of direct sunlight for more than a few minutes. The sun moves, the well's in shade, my room darkens: this proves once and for all that Copernicus and, before him, Aristarchus of Samos, got it wrong about it being the earth that moves. This planet, with all its woes, is going nowhere. At night, when I'm sleepless or else kept awake by the noise, the well becomes for me a kind of *temenos* filling up with disembodied voices. It is impossible to determine from which direction those voices come, whether they be from ground level, the top floor or somewhere in the middle. The way the sound travels probably has something to do with the precise dimensions of that space.

At midnight a man screams, clearly in a rage, although it is hard to determine who his audience is, if in fact there is one, because there is never any response. Several times he's done this and I detect trauma of some kind in his voice. A screaming woman one might hold close because it is just possible that she'll recover her equilibrium, if only for a while, but for the screaming man there is little hope because he hurtles through space forever ... unreachable, *unsavable*. At 1:15 a.m. a child moans, then retches. I hear the flushing of a toilet, a mother's consoling voice. Approaching 2 a.m., I listen to a couple, she in tears, he trying to comfort her although at times, judging by the exasperation in his voice, I think he'd rather throttle her. You could be fooled into thinking the way to love is through hate. What is so striking is that almost every other sentence of his ends on a musical phrase and I wonder whether this ability to shift from spoken to sung language is his alone. This goes on for maybe half an hour or more, there is silence for about twenty minutes, and then they make love. I detect in her weepy voice some resistance and then, finally, surrender.

What I hear is what everybody on every level of the building hears, and tomorrow, when they pass each other on the stairs, A will ask B how her child is and both A and B will have a pretty good idea of the state of C and D's marriage. As for the shouting man there'll be a shrug of the shoulders because they already know Signor E. has seen and experienced too much for a single lifetime. There are no secrets in Naples although for me it is all a secret because the inhabitants here speak 'o napulitano, a language – *not* a dialect – impenetrable even to Italians from elsewhere. It is said to be a great language in which to deliver curses. This is a fairly mild example: 'Soreta nu' me da maie 'o rieste' ('Your sister never gives me my change'). *Mild* but strong enough to warrant her older brother's clenched response. One can lay siege all night long to the language, but it will release not a single hostage. There are times when, in my sleeplessness, I begin to think that if only I could crack the code, if suddenly all these disembodied, nocturnal voices were to become comprehensible, then a complete history of Naples could be located in them. If I describe the space through which they move as a *temenos* I do so without apology because what I would most dearly like to decipher is the sacredness of ordinary existence.

The morning following these nocturnal ruminations, Irene Vecchia, puppeteer, sent me a video link of an octopus escaping the fishmonger at the far end of my *vico,* where it meets up with Via Tribunali, and headed in my direction. It slobbered over ancient volcanic stone. There was laughter and, I suspect, taunting words from the fishmonger and his buddies. Cruelty I can take, if only in tiny doses; humiliation, never. A cephalopod, the octopus has three hearts, and, so say the biologists, plenty of brain, making it the smartest of a smart bunch, although I wonder how one goes about measuring its intelligence. It's not as if one can ask it to recite the alphabet or a poem by Salvatore Di Giacomo. Obviously it knows enough to be able to read signs of danger and thereby effect an escape, as the star of my video has. So why doesn't it avoid capture more? Why doesn't it stay further away from shore? The heart-breaking answer is that it's a curious creature. It will stretch a leg in the direction of whatever it wishes to understand better. We all know where curiosity gets one, either heaven or hell, sometimes both together, but then probably the octopus can't fully appreciate what goes on above water, just as we have trouble fathoming what lies outside our universe or, for that matter, our neighbourhood – and besides, what is humankind seen from below but a broken shadow upon the water's choppy surface? Who'd ever expect it to plunge from one dimension into another? Can we ever anticipate what we can't imagine? Suddenly I'm put in mind of the Tomb of the Diver, found close to the ancient city of Paestum in Magna Graecia: a fresco of a young naked male figure in mid-air, behind him a primitive tower of sorts, ahead of him the unbroken surface of water, this suspension believed to represent the transition from life to death. Whoever painted this must have taken his cue from one of the dead youth's pleasures. This octopus's escape is another kind of plunge into the unknown. I wish I could wish it well, that is, with some expectation of its emancipation, but such wishes are in vain when it's destined for somebody's dinner plate. I watched the video in a state of semi-amused horror. The octopus has 10,000 more genes than man does. One day, perhaps, it will make a better fist of things than we have. Maybe it's already higher up the evolutionary scale than we are. Should I take as much pleasure as I do in the grilled version of this most intelligent of God's invertebrates? Come evening, I think I'll feed on a dimmer species.

Vico Scassacocchi is in the heart of the Forcella neighbourhood reputed by some to be the toughest in central Naples, although the Quartieri Spagnoli has been more often accorded that dubious honour. Secondigliano and, on the city outskirts, Scampia are by some distance the more dangerous areas with the highest murder rate in Europe, but Forcella is bad enough. An old man, when we spoke about the area, told me of how things used to be, the dark along with the bright in his memories, but when I encouraged him to speak of the present he replied, 'If I told you what I know, and if you wrote about it, when you come back to Naples I won't be here any more.' Sometimes at midnight, he tells me, there's a knock at the door, somebody asking a favour of him. Most likely, given his age, it will be to stash drugs at his place.

My landlady, Melania Russo, who I quite adore, who is more than a couple of decades younger than me and has a serpent tattooed on her foot and takes me on her motorbike and does U-turns in the middle of the Corso Umberto and knows what I'm about, is a proud citizen of Forcella. She would like me to give it a shot at redemption, but although she redeems it with her every gesture, with every slice of her mother's cakes, I'm afraid she may not be pleased with such words as I write. I'd happily change the world for her, but Forcella may prove too much of a stretch. Still, without wishing to tempt the Fates, I like it here. Also, maybe foolishly, I feel quite secure. While Neapolitans only a five-minute walk away tell me there are safer places to be, Melania informs me that hereabouts I'm a known figure and only a drunken idiot from another part of Naples will mug me. I'm not sure how true this is, but she may be my guardian angel who nobody would dare tackle.

Pole dancing is her chosen form of exercise. She speaks like she dances, with much nimbleness and no indication of which direction she's about to take. She is also a master psychologist. The woman in the flat below kept telling her there was a leak from the upstairs bathroom. Melania investigated her neighbour's ceiling and found no tell-tale signs. And still the *signora* complained. This went on for several months, brought on, so I was made to understand, by a case of jangled nerves. A year ago, the woman's refrigerator had caught fire and so, given that misfortune loves nothing more than to be one in a series of misfortunes, it was natural enough for her to suppose that after fire, water would be the next catastrophe. Finally, weary of the woman's complaints, Melania called in a plumber. When he pulled up the floorboards and exposed the pipes she invited the woman downstairs to come up and take a look, which she did along with a female contingent of neighbours, a bit of theatre which I suspect Melania orchestrated but in such a way that she allowed the woman to think it was her own idea. I was chewing on a croissant when they all trooped through with their loud voices and then trooped out, each of them in turn apologising for the interruption to my breakfast. Melania wore a poker face. No sooner was the neighbour satisfied that something was being done than Melania told the plumber to cover everything up again. The plumber, realising he had been made a dupe, flew into a rage. The trick worked though. There were no more complaints from downstairs. I had just been given a lesson on the illusory nature of Naples.

Scoundrels and thieves, liars all of them, Neapolitans have had quite a bit of bad press, not least from their own countrymen, that is if Naples can be considered a part of Italy. I think it is fair to say that visitors either love or hate the place with there being little in between. I have looked for, and cannot find, a lukewarm response. John Ruskin, of whom one might expect better, describes Naples as 'the most loathsome nest of human caterpillars I was ever forced to stay in', but then he loved more the things of this world than those who made them. The American novelist John Horne Burns, whose novel *The Gallery* is a fascinating though sometimes rather hatched picture of wartime Naples, written when its populace was at an absolute moral and physical nadir, was a swine both before and after the war, but at least here he was brought to love. And whoever is brought to love is led to truth:

> I remember that in Naples I learned that everything in life is a delusion, that all happiness is simply a desire for, and unhappiness a repining of, love. Nothing else matters. All of life is a preparation for, or a retrospection on, those brief hours when two people are together and perfect in each other. Then we're the slaves of a power outside ourselves, that brings us together for its own ends and tricks us into a joy and an equality.

All the more pity, then, that for him love had such a short battery life. There is nowadays a tendency to believe what he wrote was true, which is where his admirers swallow any number of assertions. If there really was a gay bar in the Galleria Umberto I during the war, no other record of it exists. Still it's a book one should read even if sometimes the prose turns purple.

It has been my remarkable good fortune that the people I've met have not been scoundrels and thieves, and, unless I am especially gullible, not even liars, which leads me to conclude that all the others must surely be. Generalities ought not to be the province of any writer, but there are reported generic trends which are difficult to ignore. It is not so much that the Neapolitan lies as that he operates within *a kind of truth* with just enough room for him to be able to wiggle his toes. Some of the happiest moments of my life have been those spent in the company of Neapolitans but then maybe I'm a rogue, fibber, and cutpurse.

The irony is that Melania, who would have me paint a rosy picture of life in Forcella, took me a few doors down the *vico* to visit an elderly woman and her middle-aged daughter. She said they would show me another side of life. When Melania gets an idea there is no power in the universe that can stop her. All one can do is tag along. She had even obtained a small bouquet of flowers for me to present to them. I went not really knowing what to expect although what she calls *another side* is, for me, almost always *this side*. If it's the zone through which I prefer to move, it is not because I think there is exoticism in poverty, although rough humanity, even with its attendant cruelties, often shines for me more than where people fade into abundance. Nor is it an intellectual choice. It is something that comes from deep within the wellsprings of my own life. Shall I say it might have been the best thing my parents inculcated in me? I'd be a fool to say what it is, but I know it's there.

I'd seen the two women many times before, and I'm sure they saw me, a stranger in these parts, but we willingly entered a charade of first introductions. We might have just arrived from opposite ends of the universe. They were, as Neapolitans tend to be, welcoming and generous with what little they had. On the right-hand wall of their *basso** were three photographs – two

---

* A *basso* ('low') is a dwelling of one or two rooms on the ground floor opening directly into the street. It is where the poorest people, quite often whole families, live. They are romantic only from the

men and a boy. What was it about those images that told me they were no longer alive? Could it have been their size, just a bit bigger than regular family photographs, which made them tokens of remembrance? Was it that their faces were so full of life they suggested the opposite? Such things make sense only where nothing makes sense. There's no measure for it, for what soul alone sees.

The older woman spoke of her childhood experiences during the war, recalling how mothers and wives hid husbands and sons from the Nazis in the underground water supply. She laughed bitterly when she described how the German soldiers were the first to flee the bombs dropped by their own side. She was spared what another woman I spoke to saw with her own eyes, a group of children executed by a firing squad or maybe, as is commonly the case with people who've been through hellish times, she did see such things but was unable to give them voice. She spoke of the food shortages, the water queues, and of how people were brought to such a level of desperation they began to steal from each other. It was not, in other words, the official version of mutual kindness although a rough kindness was there. She spoke of the women who, after the Germans left, prostituted themselves to the soldiers of the Allies – the brothels in the Quartieri Spagnoli, the quick transactions on the Corso Umberto close to the port – and was oddly ambivalent with respect to their plight because, after all, she told me in a matter-of-fact voice, they would have starved otherwise. There is no question of right or wrong when those very words have been stripped of all meaning. Curzio Malaparte and Norman Lewis wrote unsparing accounts of what those women did in order to feed their families. I'd spoken earlier to an elderly man

---

outside, their inhabitants subject, especially in earlier times, to pestilence. Privacy is a virtual unknown for the families who eat, sleep, and die in those places.

who, aged ten, pimped for the American soldiers. This he told me in front of his granddaughter. I was surprised. She wasn't. He, too, shrugged it off because the will to survive sweeps aside moral imperatives. And then there are the 'black Neapolitans' born of the union between black American soldiers and prostitutes. Who can honestly pronounce judgement on those men who for the first time in their lives found themselves without fear in the arms of white women and who on the following day might take an enemy bullet? A woman's body sweetens death, makes it easier to die. It is all too easy to judge at a distance. Any verdict is as harsh as the realities people had to endure. Although terrible, prostitution is not the same as rape, which is what many women and girls had to endure, particularly at the hands of the Moroccan conscripts, the most unruly of all who fought in that theatre. And now an elderly woman on Vico Scassacocchi was telling me of the lucky ones who followed their lovers back to America. She had no bitter words for the Allies who, after all, she said, had got them out of this mess. Once a year she leaves flowers for them, the fallen soldiers and the women who sold them their bodies.

The situation after the war continued to be desperate.

'We had to move to the outskirts of the city, to Via Marina, where we built shacks in the woods. I remember the mice. We had to walk almost a mile for water. Also there were no toilets. When we got back to the centre of town my husband started selling fruit and vegetables. The only way to survive was to sell them for just a little profit, also fireworks, which are part of our Christmas tradition. We grew up in the street. I got married and had children, five or six of them.'

I wondered for a moment whether in this abbreviated history of hers she had lost count or whether there were complexities she'd rather not go into.

'My husband's sisters worked in restaurants where instead of a salary they were given food. Close to my husband's shop there was a flower shop where I worked, bringing water and delivering flowers. We suffered a lot. I and my other two sisters went to work in people's houses, washing floors. Some years later, I took a job in a school, as a superintendent, looking after the cleaning. I spent twenty years there. My husband, in order to earn more money, sold contraband cigarettes. We kept big bundles of cigarettes in here. One night he moved one of the boxes which had got a little bit wet in the rain and it touched the overhead light by mistake. An electrical shock went through his brain, almost killing him. After this he was sick all the time, shook a lot, and then he started to drink. He always hid money in his socks and because everyone knew this they stole it from him when he was drunk. This happened many times. During this difficult period our son Antonio, aged fourteen, got cancer in the leg. Two years later, it was amputated, and he died.'

She began to weep silently, her daughter holding her hand. The smiling boy's photo was the middle one.

'And then, a couple of years later, my husband died from exactly the same thing.'

His was the photo on the left.

'We are not happy here. I have a monthly pension of 580 euros, but the rent alone is 300 euros. I iron shirts and wash sweaters to make a little extra money. A couple of black people live next door. We are happy with them … there is no problem with respect to colour or religion … they are quiet and they are our friends … but with respect to the Nigerians living down the street I am racist. They are crazy people. They drink and then fight. A couple of years ago, one decapitated another with a broken bottle. *Bella Napoli!* It is an unlucky city. It has changed and we suffer. I don't recognise it any more. When other people still lived here they'd keep their doors open, but now it is no longer possible.'

The daughter chipped in.

'One Sunday we were eating and a Nigerian burst inside, bleeding from the head. He locked the door behind him and there was another Nigerian outside, looking for him, shouting and screaming. The first Nigerian said the second was out to kill him. We ran into the bathroom and locked ourselves inside. We knew that if he had a gun he might have killed all of us.'

What neither mother nor daughter said is that the Nigerian immigrants have fallen into the hands of the Camorra who use them as hit men because, after all, they are expendable. A dead Nigerian doesn't raise too many queries. One darkly ironic consequence of this is that the Neapolitans – or rather, the more deeply compromised of them, who were the hit men once – have complained bitterly, saying their jobs have been taken away from them.

The daughter continued.

'I used to sweep the street outside and I'd always sing while doing so. We have this proverb "If we do not sing, we die", but now I don't sing any more. I've suffered too much.'

The third photograph on the wall was the final piece in Death's not-so-intricate puzzle.

'Like my father, my husband also sold cigarettes. The newspapers said he was in the Camorra, but it's not true. One day he saw something he shouldn't have and so they came and shot him in the face.'

I left mother and daughter in each other's arms. Melania was right, of course, they had a story to tell me, but there came a point when I felt I'd become a voyeur of lives I was not privy to. What I'd heard was more than any stranger had a right to hear. They would no more escape their situation than would the octopus in Forcella his. And now comes word that a few months after our meeting the older of the two women died.

On Via Vicaria Vecchia, in what was a cinema once, there is a free library and youth centre set up in memory of Annalisa Durante who, aged fourteen, was caught in the middle of

Camorra crossfire. The serpent will strike any time, from any direction it chooses. Roberto Saviano in his book *Gomorrah* gives a vivid description of the girl's funeral. One small detail he provides doesn't quite make sense at first – a cell phone is placed at the foot of her coffin – but as we turn the page a seemingly naff gesture becomes tragic in its resonance. 'As her body is being carried away in its white coffin,' Saviano writes, 'a classmate calls her cell phone. The ringing on the coffin is the new requiem. Musical tones, a sweet melody. No one answers.' The slogan for the free library and youth centre, which, with help from the City of Naples, was set up by Annalisa's father, Gianni, is 'La cultura salva le anime' ('Culture saves souls'). Would that it were so. Would that I could believe it.

Saviano doesn't quite finish the story, however. As with so much else in this city a thread dangles. Annalisa's father, who for hours on end sits in front of the youth centre, which very few youths ever go to, has been made the unlikely hero of a sorry tale. Many times he has been interviewed and every time he speaks passionately of the need for change, although he is reluctant to name those who necessitate that change – but the question nobody wishes to pose is what he did for a living before tragedy overtook him. It was nothing so terrible really, and in no way can it be said to have led directly to catastrophe. After all, a man's got to bring the bacon home, but the deeper story reveals a social fabric the threads of which, when seen from afar, compose a bigger, darker pattern than one might first suppose. Gianni Durante used to sell CD-ROMs for the PlayStation Console, which, given the circumstances, could not be more ironically named. Whereas the original Sony product cost anywhere from thirty to sixty euros, tech-minded people in 'the System'* found

---

* When speaking among themselves, almost invariably Neopolitans speak of *'O Sistema*, which is what they call the complex economic and political web of the Camorra.

a way of reproducing them that would cost no more than a euro each to make. The market was soon flooded with cheap copies. Somebody had to distribute them, of course, and, willy-nilly, Gianni found himself in 'sales'. It can't have been all that hard to put a mental divide between himself and the illegality of this activity because, after all, he was dealing in mere fripperies. I'm sure Sony would not be pleased to hear their product described thus, but surely the selling of illegal CD-ROMs must count among the lesser crimes. So what does this say? It says that a man can, unwittingly almost, find himself working for the very power that will one day rob him of a beloved daughter. The heart aches. The only positive thing to have come of this was that he was now able to reinvent himself and do something in memory of her and for the community. So far so good, but then there are heroes and there are heroes.

'Can you understand it?' my informant told me. 'This is an *illogical ambiguity*. We are all deeply sad for Gianni's loss, of course. Maybe I'm too honest but, listen, if one day a man in however small a way works for the System, selling pirated CD-ROMs, and the next day he becomes a paladin of justice, it's not fair. The judges Falcone and Borsellino, the journalist Giancarlo Siani, all three of whom paid for their courage with their lives, *they* were paladins of justice. Death does not make you an honest man. The life you lead does.'

The judgement seems a bit harsh and yet not wholly unreasonable.

Gianni Durante sits there, day after day, in front of a place where nothing much happens any more. The interviews have stopped and so, too, the publicity machine. Quite simply, he is old news. Sometimes he shoots the breeze, other times he stares into space. You might think he actually owns the building but no, it's only on extended loan. It might be said that everything in our lives is on loan and we are but temporary owners or rentees, but the empty space he guards is a curious form of compensation such as only a government with its own 'illogical ambiguities' can make. As such, there is a kind of dumb perfection in an order where *nothing comes of nothing*. Saviano notes that the people directly responsible for an innocent girl's death showed up at the funeral in their shiny automobiles. This was the ultimate absurdity in that they should have wished to appear to be on the side of justice. The bitter irony is that the Camorra are at pains to profess their Catholic faith. So it must have come as a terrible blow when in 2014 Pope Francis excommunicated them en masse. The Camorra at prayer, such piety as they have amounts to no more than a good luck charm on the bracelet of a whore. Underlying their presence at the funeral was the message that we must let bygones be bygones. Shut up, in other words. At the church service nobody dared utter the dreaded 'C' word and, sure enough, the man who fired the bullet is shortly due for release. I wonder what goes through Signor Durante's mind, whether his youth centre is a fantasy he lives or whether at times he realises he is living a lie. Surely, though, it beats petty crime. Or does it? Which is worse for the soul, selling pirated CD-ROMs or doing something that ought to be worthy but which in reality is futile? At least with the first one may come out of confession with an *ego te absolvo*. Was he aware that I was looking at him, trying to work out the riddle of his existence? What he is, others are. They feed upon the same silence. Small wonder he is disliked by those whose lot he shares.

As one emerges from the shadows of Vico Scassacocchi and, squinting a little, enters the sunlit market on Via Forcella what one sees on the other side of the street is the entrance to the mediaeval church of Sant'Agrippino and there, chiselled into the marble portal, is the Latin inscription.

AD BENE AGENDVM NATI SVMVS

The old motto of Forcella, it translates as 'We were born to do good.'

＊

There are times when I suspect Forcella is being made to pay the price for the rest of Naples, just as in any group of children there is the bad boy who is the lightning rod for his fellows and willingly takes the rap for their misdeeds as well as his own. As for staying in Forcella there are the strategies one may adopt, although this is perhaps too cold a word for the social inter-course one happily has with the people who live and work here. The shopkeeper from whom I buy mozzarella jokes with me. I buy my bread from elsewhere. So, too, the cheap wine that I quite enjoy although when I remove its plastic cork there is a small purple cloud of gas that bespeaks additives. Spreading oneself about, it's a way of establishing a presence. I exchange simple courtesies with the neighbours in the belief that their neighbours will have neighbours who will protect me. I speak to the man who sells me fruit, Alberigo, who, when I ask him in Italian how he is, repeats the question in Neapolitan as if in Italian he could

never be more than fair to middling. Alberigo's got a good face. I'm sure he could weigh an orange with his eyes alone.

I look people in the eye. This is to let them know I'm not about to fall victim to the old skulduggery of *scartiloffio*. *Scartiloffio?* I'll explain. You see a nice cake at a stall you've never seen before, you buy it as a gift for a beloved someone back home, and the seller offers to wrap it up handsomely, which you agree to, and so, out of view, he does just that and the parcel he gives you really does look handsome although you might have paid more for the wrapping than for the cake. You get it back to London safely and the beloved presentee removes the ribbons and the wrapping and what she finds in lieu of that cake so happily spotted in Naples is a piece of stone wrapped in many layers of newspaper. You've been had. This is *scartiloffio*. It is one of the gentler forms of theft, to be admired almost, the stuff of comedy routines. There's a short film in which the master comedian Totò, his face shaped like a jellybean, goes to Rome and, pretending to be its owner, sells the Trevi Fountain to the first mug he sees. *Scartiloffio!*

Often, when I give people my address, if their response is not a raising of the eyes or a look of alarm it is a nod of approval because I'm staying in the *real* Naples. Other times, I am greeted with laughter. It has taken me a while to get the joke. Scassacocchi is closely related to the slang word *scassacazzi* or 'ball-breaker' although often it is translated as 'a pain in the arse'. I have been advised to take care of my pronunciation because to begin with I'd got the second double consonant wrong, taking the sound of the word a pitch closer to its impolite relative. There are various theories for the name, one of which being that in times past the paving stones were so uneven that carriages trying to go down the *vico* would suffer damage to the wheels (so the impolite version is not perhaps so far off the mark). There used to be a courtyard where they would go to be fixed although it is a funny old state of affairs when one goes down the very street that will necessitate repair. Such a poor neighbourhood, it is hard to imagine that at number 49 once stood the Palazzo Piscicelli, the royal chambers of Joanna I, Queen of Naples, who is one of history's more colourful figures. Boccaccio thought she was a good thing, which probably was why he was made to feel welcome at her court. Sexually voracious, a killer to boot, she met her end smothered between two mattresses. Admittedly we are less inclined to allow a woman the behaviour that in a man would pass unremarked. It doesn't help either, judging from the surviving images of her, that she was a great beauty. 'Beauty is but a painted hell,' the poet Thomas Campion writes, 'Aye me, aye me.'

Vico Scassacocchi shows up in Renato Carosone's song 'Giuvanne cu a' chitarra', and again in Eduardo De Filippo's script for the film of *Napoli milionaria!* in which Pasquale Miele, played by Totò, lives on the fifth floor of 17 Vico Scassacocchi, and finally it is given another airing in his play *Quei figuri di trent'anni fa* ('Those Figures of Thirty Years Ago') when Donna Assunta says, 'So you and I will pack up and return to live on the sixth floor of Vico Scassacocchi.' The audience laughs knowingly at this point and, besides, it is such a funny name. And then there is a popular comedy skit *La Smorfia* ('The Grimace') with Massimo Troisi, Lello Arena, and Enzo Decaro, where it is described as 'un vicolo notoriamente tranquillo e pacifico' ('a notoriously quiet and peaceful alley'), which, yet again, invites knowing laughter.

Where I stay is a funny place to be.

Forcella's symbol, although few people living there seem to remember this, is the letter 'Y', and it is here that we enter a wonderful tangle of meanings, so dense one could get stuck inside there forever, getting loopier by the minute. Although the esoteric can be a fatal trap, especially for any writer who favours historical accuracy, it is hard to resist the idea there is rather more to this 'Y' than meets the eye. If one prefers to stick to plain thinking on the matter, it can refer simply to the bifurcation in the main road running through Forcella – *forcella* in Italian means 'fork' – not the fork with which we raise a piece of octopus to our mouths, which is *forchetta*, but a forked implement, stick or tree or even the fork on a bicycle. Dig deeper and what comes up is the symbol of the Pythagorean School that was located somewhere in the area, when Naples was as much Greek as it was Latin, and in fact a bridge between those two cultures. (Pythagoras himself lived in the Greek colony of Kroton, what is now Crotone in Calabria.) 'Y' was known as the *Furca Pythagorica* ('Pythagorean fork'), which lends further weight to it being the origin of Forcella's name. The Latin 'Y' is the Greek *upsilon* which in turn is derived from the Phoenician *wāw* which is further echoed in the Hebrew, Arabic, and Syriac alphabets, and thereabouts often invested with mystical properties. There is even a legend that Pythagoras himself added the letter to the Greek alphabet. According to the seventh-century scholar, Isidore of Seville, whose mighty twenty-volume work *Etymologiae* was the first attempt by a Christian writer to create a summa of universal knowledge:

Pythagoras of Samos was the first to fashion the letter 'Y' into a pattern of human life. The straight portion at the bottom signifies the first, uncertain age, which at that point has been given over to neither vices nor virtues. The bifurcation at the top, however, begins at adolescence. The path to the right is difficult, but it tends toward a blessed life. The path to the left is easier, but it leads to ruin and destruction.

Any youth growing up in Forcella ought to have 'Y' emblazoned on his T-shirt because sooner or later he'll be faced with a similar choice of which direction to take in life, the one of virtue (*arete*) or the one of vice (*kakia*). Amplified in verse, there are lines wrongly ascribed to Virgil, which are possibly by Maximinus but, if not, then of similar vintage. Sir Thomas Stanley translates them:

> The Pythagoric Letter two ways spread,
> Shows the two paths in which Man's life is led.
> The right-hand track to sacred Virtue tends,
> Though steep and rough at first, in rest it ends;
> The other broad and smooth, but from its Crown
> On rocks the Traveller is tumbled down.
> He who to Virtue by harsh toils aspires,
> Subduing pains, worth and renown acquires;
> But who seeks slothful luxury, and flies
> The labour of great acts, dishonour'd dies.

'Y' was a late addition to the Roman alphabet, put there in order to ferry words over from the Greek, although the sound in Latin was more like an *oo* than a *yeh*. (The French *ygrec* points to Hellenic origins as well.) Over time it would signify the forked cross depicted in many mediaeval paintings of the Crucifixion, and which, depending on where you are in Europe, is variously known as the *crucifixus dolorosus*, the *ypsilon* cross, Y-cross, thief's cross or the *crux furca*. The shape makes its way, via the Holy Trinity, onto the priest's chasuble. Such crosses tend to come from the mystical notion that in shape they resemble a tree, or, more specifically, the Tree of Knowledge whence sin comes. While it is believed there were no such crosses in reality, one of the most curious features of the Turin Shroud is that the blood runs down the length of the arm rather than across the wrist, which would suggest that Christ was crucified on a Y-cross and not the regular T-shaped cross which in some mediaeval paintings is reserved for the thieves on either side of him. If the Turin

Shroud is a fake, then it is a most extraordinary fake. I wonder why nobody seems to have considered the alternative: that it is neither real nor fake, but rather a work of devotion. There are only two surviving instances of the Forcella 'Y', which used to be a common feature, carved on the doors of houses as a ward against evil. One of them is on the outside of the church of San Lorenzo Maggiore on Via Tribunali, the other inside the Diocesan Museum on the Largo Donnaregina, a sixteenth-century marble escutcheon that bears the letter 'Y' resembling a heavily pruned tree.

When read on a more primitive level 'Y' becomes a visual pun on the private area of the female and, when placed upside down, the male, and from there it is no great distance towards it being perceived as the Tree of Life. One could go further still and investigate its signification in other cultures. And although one shouldn't push the image too hard, it could also recall the shape of the stick employed by the ancients to catch serpents.

If any of this sounds like poppycock, just look to the philosopher, cartographer, and geographer Dicaearchus of Messana, one of Aristotle's followers who, when speaking of the foundation of the ancient city, said it was constructed upon both scientific and sacred principles. Urban planning has its beginnings in the soul and when this is forgotten or ignored it becomes the nightmare Francesco Rosi depicts in his movie, *Le mani sulla città* ('Hands Over the City') in which the Devil provides the blueprints and greedy men follow suit. Somewhere close to where a Pythagorean school was, where the street divides at the Piazza Vincenzo Calenda, is a group of stones which is erroneously referred to as 'il cippo' or milestone. It is a happy enough mistake for it gave rise to the Neapolitan expression 's'arricorda 'o Cipp' a Furcella' ('This reminds you of the Cippo of Forcella') which refers to something really, really old. It can even refer to the teenager's common lament about a thing that is no longer fashionable. Old it most certainly is, probably the most ancient survival of Hellenic Naples, dating back to the third century BC, the remains of the ancient Greek wall of Neapolis or even the ancient gate, the Porta Herculanensis, later called the Porta Furcillensis. A sign hangs on the protective railing surrounding the stones, calling upon passers-by to remember Maikol Giuseppe Russo, a young father of two, who became yet another innocent bystander fallen victim to random gunfire.

A few feet away from those stones, I sat drinking coffee with Ciro, breathing in the Neapolitan bouquet of traffic fumes; there are no flowers, no trees, to dissipate it; the pollution is pure. Ciro is a bright spark hereabouts. A young academic, not yet done with his studies, he could just as easily be the drummer in a band. Maybe it's the jazzy T-shirt or the diamond in one of his ears or the closely shaved head favoured by so many young Italian men. If the jacket he wears seems a couple of sizes too small, it's meant to be. Style rules. There is something lithe and rather beautiful about him. As a photogenic child he showed up on the cover of Elisabetta Valentini and Simona Filippini's photo-essay on Forcella and Sanità, 'Alza gli occhi e guarda' ('Raise Your Eyes and Behold'). There is a quality which sets him apart from the crowd and its clichés, a depth of perception. I had just been telling him that when walking through the neighbour-hood I always look people in the eye. What was I doing telling a man less than half my age that I'm streetwise?

'Don't be afraid.' He laughed.

'I'm not, not really, but then people do get caught in the middle.'

'It happens. A year ago, on New Year's Eve, a group of six guys on their bikes drove through here and fired into the crowd. That night I walked with a friend of mine in the same place only ten minutes earlier. One person died. And it was done just for demonstration, nothing else. These were just kids, seventeen, maybe twenty years of age.'

Suddenly I twigged that the dead man was the same one whose name is on the sign in front of the old stones. Sooner or later, and this is what makes a city of a million people feel like a village, everything links up. I asked Ciro whether he thought it's true that Forcella takes the rap for the rest of Naples, and he began with what perhaps is the best measure of change, the market, the market being the most intensely human of theatres.

'I am proud of Forcella and I'm ashamed of it too, which is how I feel when I am away from here. I love Forcella and I love some, though not all, of its people. I hate Forcella and some of its people. Wherever I go, I take Forcella with me. If I have to compare the old with the new, I'd say the present is much more competitive. Maybe it is because I have grown up and I am not a child any more, but I really think this is the case. Definitely, in the street market, there has been a change. One of my ways of measuring this is through my father who is a kind of milestone. He is intelligent not only in a working way but also in an aes-thetic one, and it's because he has always lived and worked in the street. When he was a child he worked with his father, same place, same work, and I could have been the third generation.'

'Had you not gone down the dubious route of academe,' I quipped.

I suspect Ciro reads Dante's terza rima with a trader's eyes.

'Nowadays Forcella is poor not only in an economic way but also in a human one. When I was young it was very crowded but, again, in a rather different way. Maybe it is the nostalgia speaking in me, but I don't think so. There were many shops and their owners knew each other. There was a friendly way to make business. My father made business with the shop opposite and the man in that shop dealt with his neighbour and so forth. This creates a recognisably human economic circle. It's the thing I miss most here, this element of human nature. I don't see it any more or else it has become diminished in scale. Forcella started like a normal market, but in the 1980s there were the beginnings of a parallel market of goods that were either stolen or fake. Maybe a tourist seeing Forcella for the first time will say to himself "This is the *real* Naples, the one I have seen in the movies or read about in books", but for whoever was born and raised here it is not the same. I am not alone in thinking this. My father will tell you that old Forcella is gone.'

What I didn't say to Ciro is that for me this *is* the real Naples, the one I've seen in movies, and which, God willing, others will read about in these pages. It is a vexing issue, this question of how things used to be, because too often it becomes an excuse for disappointment or even bitterness. Maybe it is best kept in check by restricting one's memory to what was once the cost of an ice cream cone. There's nothing we see that will not be one day gone. What survives are memory traces. One thing Ciro told me, which surprised me, is that one of the old nicknames for Forcella was 'Casbah' which reinforces the sense of déjà vu I've had from time to time, when the streets of Damascus, a city I was once close to, seem to superimpose themselves onto those of Naples. Ciro thinks the nickname derives from the chaotic nature of the neighbourhood, but then it might be a survival just in the way the Nilo area of Spaccanapoli contains within its name some aural memory of the Egyptian traders who used to live there.

'Would you say these changes manifest themselves in other, darker ways?'

'This is not to defend the Camorra, but once upon a time they had a certain honour. Honourable men do not exist any more. Saviano has published a book called *La paranza dei bambini* ["The Gangs of Children", recently translated as "The Piranhas"] which talks about Forcella and the phenomenon of the baby Camorra. This is something completely new. When I was a child there was another System, which is the word we use rather than "Camorra", and those who were in it were more respectful of the people who lived and worked here. Those people are gone, either dead or in hiding or in prison, and the power void that was created has resulted in a new system made up of youngsters who with just a little money can purchase weapons and make business with drugs. The old respect is gone.'

'How young are they?'

'They range from fourteen to nineteen. Statistically by the time they are twenty, or maybe a bit more, they are dead. The other night, a boy of sixteen was shot here and nobody knows who did it. What is here one day is gone the next. It is a general phenomenon not only in Forcella but also in Sanità and on the periphery of Naples.'

'These are things everybody knows but will not discuss?'

'I don't know the real reason. Maybe it is fear of revenge. I talk about these things all the time when I'm elsewhere in the country in order to explain my background to other Italians. Once upon a time in Forcella there was a very compact group whereas nowadays there are small groups that fight each other. We do not know who is in charge any more. Maybe this is why we don't talk because we don't know who is in charge.'

'It is such a strange attitude,' I ventured, 'because normally if one wants power one dreams of having it forever, but here, as you say, people die young.'

'*These* people, not everyone. The young boys who choose to lead this path know very well the lives they'll have to live. When they say, "I didn't know what I was doing" or "I was unconscious at the time" they lie. They are aware of *everything*. Even a sixteen-year-old boy is conscious of what he does, and that is very scary to me, the fact that he can already think like this. That's the reason I think that over time Forcella will get even worse than it is now. Maybe I am cynical or pessimistic, but the things I have seen or heard force me to think this way, not only me, but my friends and relatives too.'

'What about their parents, do they know what their children are doing?'

'Of course, and they are happy because these families, just like the planets going round the sun, revolve around the System. They are happy if their kids can introduce themselves into the System. It is a symbol of power. Maybe their boy will live five years, one year, one month, one week, one day. They don't care! Once a kid of this mentality becomes an adult it is not the problem of the family any more. This kid does as he likes. The important thing is that he brings money home. It is not important how, whether it is in a legal or illegal way.'

'Is there glory in death when someone is killed?'

'They say "É uno buono", it's a good one. This kid is one who *made it*. It is a different conception of the self-made man. The parents cry and are desperate, of course, when one of their children dies, but the death is of one who made good although not, of course, in any moralistic way.'

Saviano in a recent interview remarked upon this change in the Camorra, saying that it is no longer a matter of living differently but of dying differently and if someone lives to the ripe old age of thirty he is considered a failure, someone who has not 'made it' in life.

'Eros and Thanatos,' Ciro continued, echoing my earlier conversation with Domenico Garafalo, 'love and death, this is our situation in Naples. My people are capable of the biggest acts of love and the biggest acts of evil. This is why Italians from elsewhere, especially in the north, hate us.'

I tried to remember who it was who said or wrote that Naples is a metaphor for the world. I'd probably dismissed it at the time as being the easy product of a single brushstroke, but now, listening to Ciro, the words began to feel true.

'My father struggled through at least five or six System wars. Those wars were big and important, such as nowadays we don't have any more. It was very scary. I can't imagine how my father went to work every day, every week, every month, in that climate where the danger is a stray bullet. Some of these people he knew because they were his customers. One day they'd come with a shopping bag, the next day with a gun. And he would have to thank them for spending money with him.'

'So without doing anything you can find yourself compromised?'

'It is a difficult job maintaining your balance because there are so many temptations. Of course it is much easier to live like these people. It is much more difficult to live, as does my father, as an honest person. My father does not pay protection because his is one of the old shops. I'll give you an illustration. When I was a child I did not speak Neapolitan, only Italian. I was meant to be this nice Italian boy. A man buying fruit and vegetables at my father's shop heard me and was surprised. Next to him was his lawyer who also heard me and he said to my father, "When your child grows up he must work with us because we need good surface men [that is, the people of good appearance and respectable positions]." This was only because I spoke good Italian, and as speaking Italian was a step up from Neapolitan it could be very useful for them. My father said to him, "Yes, yes, we'll see later." My mother was terrified. "Leave it," my father told her. "This man is crazy. What he's saying is nonsense. Ciro will grow up and decide for himself what he does." Still, when you hear something like that, "when your child grows up" et cetera, if you are an honest person you tremble. A father of another kind might have been very happy with this proposal. The story went in another direction. The lawyer was either shot or dropped into the sea with his feet in cement. Maybe he'd lost a case. Make a mistake and you have to pay. The lawyer and his "Boss" are long gone, and me, I'm still alive. Some years later, when I was at secondary school, my father came to me and said, "As of now you can't go outside the house because there are some people from different gangs in search of someone physically very similar to you." So for two weeks I could not go outside at night just because of someone who looked like me.'

'What this would suggest is that your father and everybody else knew who this other man was.'

'Yes. This guy who looked like me was about twenty and had committed something like three or four murders. Now he is in prison. The police arrested him before one of the other groups got to him. This was his good fortune! It was better in this case to be taken by the police.'

Later, we went to Ciro's family home. Sitting in the living room one could almost reach through the window and touch the pink wall of the house opposite. The *vico,* like all *vicos,* was narrow and if one could not quite reach the other side, one could without too much trouble jump the space between.

'I was thinking of the danger of your growing up here. Is there a time when the young go this way or that?' I may have been thinking of the letter 'Y' again, the two branches between which a young person may choose. 'Is it just hopelessness or wanting to live and die on the edge?'

'There is only one fortune in my life and it is my parents. They have not only protected me, but they also provided me with a special education, that of the street. This last came from my father. When I was a child my mother wouldn't allow me to go in the street to play with other children because she was scared, but my father argued with her, said, "No, Ciro has to learn and understand how to live in the street. He has to talk with the good guys and the bad guys." This was an important lesson my father gave me. Nowadays, when I walk in the streets, I am not scared because when I was a child I learned how to approach people. You have to have many eyes, otherwise it is difficult to survive. If we didn't have those eyes we would be tourists here rather than citizens. One day I was walking hand in hand with my mother and suddenly people started to flee. A guy who probably just committed a robbery was running with a gun in his hand, holding it high so everyone could see it. This way he could escape more easily. He was like Noah parting the waters. I used to be friendly with a boy three years older than me. We played football. There was one important thing, however. He was the son of the Boss. In the end he was a kid just like me. I didn't have problems with him. The Boss had an apartment, the one just outside this window. He was close friends with Diego Maradona. It was a normal thing at that time. So why was Maradona with this man? It was because he got cocaine from him. See how things get tangled up? It is just like a jigsaw puzzle in which every person is a separate piece contributing to the whole picture – Maradona, the Boss, the kid with whom I played. If you choose these pieces well it comes out looking like this, a puzzle of life and death. The razor is represented by this kid who was the son of the Boss, the Boss means the Camorra and the Camorra means death. Life is represented by the children playing together. Football means joy and joy means life. All this fits together like a big puzzle. The Boss is no longer boss because he collaborated with the law many years ago and now there are immigrants living there.'

'So it was true about Maradona being a drug addict.'

'The hand *and* nose of God. I remember when the Justice Department took over the Boss's apartment and sequestered the family treasures. This is common procedure. The money obtained from the sale goes to the government. There was a gigantic, very kitsch bathtub in a form of a shell, straight out of Botticelli's *The Birth of Venus*, exactly the same shape, all gold-plated. You can see on the internet a photo of Maradona, the Boss, and his brother in this bath. I remember watching as the policemen lowered it upside down into the street with ropes. They put it on sale. It was just like Macy's.'

'Maybe the bath was sold as a piece of Maradona memorabilia.'

'Your next book will be about a voyage in search of this bath.'

Actually, if I were so inclined, it might have been *this* book. Later, I went on a wild goose chase because, quite by chance, and from a wholly different source, I heard about a shell-shaped bathtub in the possession of a politician whose reputation was not, shall we say, the cleanest in town. Surely, I reasoned, there couldn't be two such bathtubs in such close proximity, and I could find no trace of the whereabouts of the bathtub sequestered and then sold by the police. Maybe it wasn't sold but presented to the worthy one. It seemed the most symbiotic of all relations that it should pass from gangster to politico. I went so far as to write to his office, with what for me was a rare lie, saying I was writing a book about Maradona and I was curious to know whether this was the same bathtub in which he was photographed with friends. I was careful to avoid Maradona's friends' names. I have been waiting for a response. I may wait forever.

'Ciro, this is surreal!'

'Not at all! It was normality in the 1970s and 80s, the kitsch and the extravaganza. They had too much money and then with all this wealth they had to somehow change their face and put on a business front, reinvest, and be respectable, become "clean" in other words, although underneath the shiny surface it would be as dirty as ever. The number of people killed in the 1980s was the highest in the criminal history of Naples. They shot, they stabbed, and they drowned. The Camorra in Scampia and Secondogliano and the periphery, which Saviano describes, were crueller than in the historical centre. They had bigger economic interests, not only selling drugs but also money laundering, and, of course, politics. The Camorra in Forcella didn't do as much in those lines because those were different times and they were, I repeat, the old Camorra. There were five or six wars. The main clan lost their power. Now there is a lack of leadership. There were other groups affiliated with the old clan for various reasons, marriage, for example, just like in the Middle Ages when two reigns became one. I wasn't yet born when the Boss offered to buy this apartment from my parents. Why? Because it was so close to his own apartment. If the police came he could jump from one balcony to another and escape through here. Quite a few buildings around here belonged to the clan. The whole area was like a stronghold with many escape routes. In the 1980s, the main mechanism for maintaining power was to have a strong physical presence in the territory, which meant apartments and in them people who belonged to the clan. They *had* to live in the neighbourhood. The new Camorra prefer to show their presence by riding their bikes and shooting in the air or through shop windows or doing what happened here last New Year's Eve.

This is the new way of displaying power and, unlike before, we are not sure who they are.'

'So tell me about the happy side of Forcella.'

'My closest friends are from this neighbourhood. It may be strange for you to hear this after all the bad things I've said about Forcella but it's true. We have known each other for maybe fifteen years. When I'm away from here the fact of my friends and my family makes it a joyful place to come back to. Friendship in these parts is strong. We were three guys. One was the chief of security at the train station, the second had two university degrees, and the third was depressed because he couldn't find work. He was in bed with the sheet pulled over his head. His mother phoned us to find a solution for her depressed son. From that alone you can understand our friendship. I don't know whether this is a southern Italian thing, the fact we are always together, but if I have to pick a symbol for the depth of our friendship it is the fact that the mother of any one of us can call upon the other two friends for help. This is a reflection of the bigger way of life here. With our very different situations we are an illustration that there can be another way to life here. As Neapolitans we have one important quality: we can appreciate everything. When we need to complain we complain, but when we appreciate something we appreciate it deeply, and from this comes a philosophical approach to life with both its bad and good elements because ultimately one has to appreciate life.'

'And yet there would also seem to be, in addition to a philosophical attitude, a strong sense of victimhood.'

'It's quite true that many people in Naples look upon the north of Italy as the great evil because they have robbed us. I don't think so. I am not a Bourbon supporter, thank you very much. Maybe I am *modern*. I think that if you have a fault you have a fault. If you fail you've failed, no excuse, and the same holds true for this city and its history. If the city has failed then it has failed. There can be no excuses. This is one aspect of the

Neapolitan people I do not like, their victim mentality, so that when we point to the bad it is never our fault but the fault of someone else. I want them to be honest. The bad and the good are always with us, but honesty is the first thing for me.'

We spoke of the great Neapolitan writers and Ciro told me the city's great masterpiece is Raffaele La Capria's *Ferito a morte* (translated as 'The Mortal Wound') which I'm going to have to read again because several people have told me it's a masterpiece. Certain works make me feel stupid before they make me wise. It has got a fair wallop of James Joyce in it, such as might have confounded even James Joyce. (Oddly enough, I had recently found myself at a party in the Villa D'Anna where the author spent his youth, in Posillipo, the posh bit of Naples. He would dive from the balcony into the bay.) And we spoke also of Malaparte's *The Skin*, which really is a masterpiece, albeit a screwy one, and in which barely a story does not end with some kind of Grand Guignol. Doubtless it was the way by which Malaparte could arrive at the truth, via exaggeration, which Ciro told me was also the mannerism of the times in which he wrote. Some people accuse Malaparte of lying, while others take every word he writes as the gospel truth. I visited the Pendino Santa Barbara where, according to him, one went to find dwarf prostitutes. There was no evidence of them or of the bakery famous for its *taralli*, the hard toroidal biscuits that are so moreish one empties a bag of them in no time at all. I asked people whether the prostitutes on the *pendino* really were dwarves and they said yes, of course. One of them went so far as to say there was an epidemic of achondroplasia at the time. My own take on this is that Malaparte made them dwarves in order to describe the depths to which women had fallen or, worse still, that they were children forced into prostitution. There was plenty of it, none of it happy, women who indulged in sexual practices on the street, in front of the stacked tins of meat, one or two of which would be their wages. So wrote Norman Lewis who might not have had Malaparte's imaginative flair but was more reliable. Naples has never really recovered from the humiliation it endured during the war, first at the hands of the Germans and then the Allies, but then Ciro told me self-humiliation has been a feature of Neapolitan existence from at least the end of the Bourbon period, perhaps even longer.

'Naples from that moment on has been insulted ... morally, materially ... by governments and strangers ... and by the Neapolitans themselves. Dickens, in his *Pictures from Italy*, touches on this tendency we have for self-humiliation when he describes these women, all crazy and dirty, working in the streets, yet behaving naturally. In the eyes of a man like him this was madness, but this was how people here lived. This is the question we have to ask ourselves. Why do we have to live in a manner such that a man coming from another country sees it as an animal way? As yet I haven't arrived at an answer to this. I don't know if you have noticed it, but I can see it still. There is another important factor. Not knowing the history of this city is to me a form of self-humiliation. Knowing nothing about the place in which you were born and raised is a sort of crime. You don't have to know everything but at least *something* about the place where you live. Something *important*. I have studied Neapolitan history. Nobody forced me to. I think one has to know one's roots in order to be able to continue. This is important not only for Neapolitans but for people the world over. I say this not because I am Neapolitan, but because I've never seen another city like this, not only archaeologically or aesthetically but also morally, mentally, and ethically. Some places in Sicily might be comparable, but then not deeply so because there is always something different about them, something that I can recognise, which I can't see, but I know is there.'

'Yes, it seems to me Neapolitans live much of their lives in an invisible world.'

'Naples is a city where any level can suddenly intrude upon another level. There is a constant shifting. The underworld enters the centre, the sky the earth, so that the city lives in a sort of limbo. It is not such a bad thing really, this limbo. It is a suspended region. Also Naples is a razor's edge. At least I see it like this. If you use a razor correctly you can shave your face and give yourself a fresh look, but if you don't use it properly you'll hurt yourself. Naples is like that for me.'

I went to bed full of what the day gave me. Although I didn't actually dream of that escaped octopus it sat somewhere on the borderline between wakefulness and sleep, its arms drooping over either side. It's a mistake to call them tentacles. They're *arms*. Another common mistake is to describe all eight as legs. Only two of them are. The octopus in the video employed its two legs to give itself a boost while with its six arms it pulled itself forward. Again I heard those mocking voices. I became that octopus, feeling my way, sucker by sucker, over the obdurate Neapolitan language, no wiser to it now than I was the night before. I calibrated the unevenness of the ancient stones beneath me. They're old enough to have known the swish of togas, the slap of sandals, the clatter of spent cartridges. Outside, so close I thought at first it was gunfire, I heard the sound of fireworks. A birthday, a saint day, a victory for S.S.C. Napoli? Those fireworks can also be the signal for the arrival of a new shipment of drugs or the release of someone from prison. Take your pick. Whatever it was, it was in order to celebrate, and I was reminded of what Ciro told me earlier, that with all the good and bad one finds here, life is a thing to appreciate. *Ombra e luce*, shadow and light, there's no having the one without the other, the darker the shadow the brighter the light, which probably is what so attracts me to this place, the wedding of opposites. 'The shadow dresses you,' writes the novelist Giuseppe Marotta, 'the sun undresses you.' And now, with that octopus stretching for a metaphor, anything that might give it hope, I repeat a certain lady's words: 'They want, and deserve, deliverance.'

The Street of the Solitary Woman

Melody was born in Naples.

So they claim, and who am I to dispute what people say of themselves? They may overdo the sauce a little, but I'd much rather it be them for a change and not me. Some people flee an unsupported assertion as if suddenly sprayed with insecticide. Others reach for their intellectual weapons of choice. We are, on the whole, expected to be reasonable. The poet Giacomo Leopardi, whose ghost I will later pursue, says we place too much value on reason for it is the enemy of nature and he was no subscriber to the *Whole Earth Catalogue*. Melody was born in Naples. The claim, wild though it is, is not wholly without substance.

Pasquale Scialò, composer and musicologist, has written extensively on music – on the young Mozart in Naples, Raffaele Viviani, and, most recently, *canzone napoletana*.* Quite inseparable from his colourful crocheted skullcap and patterned scarf,

---

* *Canzone napoletana* is the traditional form of Neapolitan song, notable for its melody line and, often, its nostalgia for the city as it once was. Although sung in the Neapolitan language, the genre has had a worldwide impact on popular music, from Frank Sinatra to Elvis Presley.

he cuts a *bella figura*, there being also something of the oriental about him, which is augmented by his white moustache. You could easily imagine him selling watermelons in Istanbul if he weren't already a pasha in Naples. Where he and his wife Valeria live, in the *centro storico*, when you step out onto the balcony, one of the highest in the area, you get a panorama of the city that truly astonishes. It feels like the centre of the universe. It may well be. The sounds from the street below have a bit of a struggle getting up there. And so, a man in his castle, with words alone, Scialò took me down to ground level on what was to be a sonic tour of Naples. Actually this is what he does from time to time, going about the streets with a recorder, scooping up sonorities in the same way someone on an English beach might gather pebbles.

'The first important thing is to learn how to listen to Naples,' Scialò began. 'It is like going through a composition that builds up in real time. The wonderful thing is that sounds come from all these different settings and so you have this juxtaposition, these different layers, which, as you walk through the city, fade in and out like in a movie score. If you go out of my home and head towards Piazza Dante you will hear the sound of young people playing in the streets. As soon as you get closer to Piazza Dante, which is an open space, you will hear the tolling of bells. And when from there you go beneath Port'Alba, which is an enclosed space, the sound changes. There is a different reverb, a different acoustic, and then you come close to the conservatory where there is another kind of interference, snatches of Pergolesi and Scarlatti, and further on there is the *posteggiatore** in front

---

* The *posteggiatore* or parking valet is a feature of Neapolitan life, bordering on the folkloric. A rascal he may be, but with a coin, or preferably a note, he will assure your car is spared the dents and scratches of outrageous fortune. You don't have to pay him if you don't wish to, but then neither will he feel obliged to know the

of a restaurant singing popular songs. And then three steps later you find a *cantante neomelodico** who sings a song of the *malavita* or criminal underworld, maybe some *latitante*.† You have these continuous layers of sound and interferences. You are completely enfolded into this soundscape and it takes you to where you may feel through your feet the underground train or the telluric motions of the earth, the rumbling of an earthquake, which equally could be the sound of your belly reacting to something that upsets you or is something so nice it is almost erotic. And then there is the music of the hands ... many Neapolitan singers move their hands as if they are melodies ... there is the music of the heart which involves another part of the body ... and the music of the head, which is an intellectual music, a stylised sound, although really it might be only the sound of a plane flying overhead. Walking around town is like having an immersive experience that involves the whole body. Naples is like an informal orchestra where there is lots of noise, and noise is important because it has the power and strength of transgression. The way to make revolution is through noise. There is no action without noise. You listen to the noise and sometimes it becomes melody. And then there is the voice, the voices of the people. In Naples people talk like they are singing and with an intensity of sound that is greater than in Helsinki or Greenland, and because in Naples the climate is nicer they live in the street much more ... the voice is an instrument that adapts to the environment and you use it to communicate with people and so it necessarily has to be higher and so you throw your voice. *Lellucciooooooo!* This is the mother who calls her son. It is a

---

whereabouts of the car, which by the time you return may have found a new home.

* An astonishing number of these singers drift into crime. One finds its equivalent, complete with bullet holes, in gangsta rap.

† A fugitive from justice although often everyone knows where he is.

combination of sound and architecture because it is architecture that makes sound and determines the echoes.'

Valeria is an architect, and, most vitally, an architect with a lovely voice.

'Badly made music is bad for you,' she interjected, 'just like spaces badly organised are bad for you. Young people worry me because they live in a two-dimensional tablet world and they don't really care about spaces any more and they don't listen to silence. A friend of mine, an urban planner, promotes two products, silence and space. He designs places where one might have one or the other.'

'Sound touches you from afar,' Pasquale continued, 'and it is the X-ray of everything that happens. There is this continual exchange, an opposition of sound and silence. In the Piazza del Gesù Nuovo the young people are shouting and making noise, and then only a few yards away, in Santa Chiara, it is complete silence, a different world, and so, going from one area to the next, you go from loudness to silence. And with a multicultural environment it is even more interesting. In the old markets you have a real sense of what multi-ethnicity is. A street seller throws his voice in order to sell his produce and a young Romanian plays the accordion. Naples is a kaleidoscopic soundscape. Within Neapolitan music you have two poles, one the talking voice and the other the singing voice, and between them there are many different phases. A scream can become laughter, pain melody.'

I'd just been made witness to the birth of melody, Scialò its midwife.

'What do you say to those people who claim *canzone napoletana* is dead?'

'So tell me, *which* songs have died? The difference is between a song and its rendition. What in 1800 had been defined as Neapolitan song is not here any more. It can't be. Those forms are obsolete. They had three strophes, three choruses, three verses. If they are alive it's only because people still perform them, but nobody actually writes that way any more. By 1880 people were saying it was already finished. By 1944 the cycle closes. The form of the song may be said to have finished, but the way of singing it has moved on and adopted different forms. The locality may be gone, but the musicality survives. Caruso sings very differently from Pino Daniele. The *canzone napoletana* has always been polluted with different materials blending in, different matrixes. Take "'O sole mio", what is the musical accompaniment to it? It is a *habanera*.* So it's already polluted. There is a transformation over time, the emergence of different faces. If someone in the countryside tries to slip the blues into the *tammurriata*† there is complete horror. Not only is it not authentic, it is a profanation. It is the breaking of something. On the contrary, though, because it has to mirror reality, our music is blending with other sources. Tradition is betrayal. It is the same word as "betray" in Italian. The words "betrayal" (*tradimento*), "to translate" (*tradurre*) and "tradition" (*tradizione*) have the same root, from the Latin *tradere*, "to surrender" and which can also mean "to hand down". If there is no betrayal, there can be no tradition. Anthropologically speaking, the process is the same. The *canzone napoletana* is humanly organised within Neapolitan sound and connected to the language.'

'So you are more optimistic about its survival than some people.'

'I am not only more optimistic, I am more realistic because they don't know what is happening now. They are looking at the past. The fundamental thing is to listen and to have clean

---

* A style of Cuban musical dance that came into being in the nineteenth century, and which found its way into the aria 'L'amour est un oiseau rebelle' in Bizet's *Carmen*.
† The *tammurriata*, 'the dance of the drum', is a folk dance of Campania belonging to the southern *tarantella* dance, of which more later.

ears and to not have prejudice. It is prejudice that is very much linked to power because people who say this think their music is the only one.'

'I remember going in the company of a singer to hear another singer perform, who to my ear was good, but this person told me it was not authentic.'

'You should never go with one singer to listen to another! You said a word that is important. *Authentic*. When they tell you it is authentic, it is fake. An anthropologist friend of mine told me this. There is no original. You can't even say what authentic *tammurriata* is, but every singer of it will say his is performed in the authentic style.'

'My impression is that Naples has a taste for a certain kind of music that it does not wish to let go.'

'This is correct. It also has to do with language. The melody is already within the Neapolitan language. The song is a close encounter between melody and lyric. Sometimes it is a marriage of convenience and sometimes it's for love.'

'I have always heard that melody is born in Naples.'

'Some siren from the past has been singing to you!'

'The other phrase I hear is "If we do not sing we die."'

'There is a song that actually says this. You don't sing to perform – you do so to let your feelings out. In my family our seismograph was song. It measured the tension in the house. If my father was upset with us he would go to the window and sing a melody, looping obsessively, the same bit over and over. It was like he was winding up for something. We knew he was going to snap, so this was an emotional signal. This was given by the fact he was singing in a certain way. Melody goes beyond words and tells much more. This is a way to communicate. Among my circle of musician friends and singers sometimes we do not speak, but instead communicate through fragments of songs each of which has a meaning.'

'So, in conclusion, for the tradition to survive it must be constantly renewed.'

Pasquale Scialò, whose face is destined to be always young, replied, 'It's like this: I give you something, I disappear, and what you do with it is your business. When my father gives something to me he becomes my son.'

Together, over their plates of *spaghetti aglio, olio e baccalà*, he and Valeria broke into a lovely song. It's what happens here. Suddenly people sing. I wish I'd noted the song's title along with the recipe.

Any day you choose, there'll be a concert somewhere. It may be in a church or it may be, as it was that lovely April evening, in someone's house. There is the bigger picture too. Naples was one of the great centres of classical music in Europe with, at one point, four music conservatories – Santa Maria di Loreto, Pietà dei Turchini, Sant'Onofrio a Capuana, and Poveri di Gesù Cristo – which were in fact orphanages where children were trained to become singers. Pity the young boys with the best voices who, in order that their tender tones be preserved, fell to the castrator's blade. Among the city's many composers one finds Gesualdo, Pergolesi, and Cimarosa, and also those who chose to go there because it was most definitely the place to be, Alessandro and Domenico Scarlatti, for example. One may speak of musical academies, great composers, and musicians, but high culture is at its most potent when it is inseparable from low culture – think of Shakespeare's London – and what is Naples but a marriage of opposites, high and low, shadow and light? *Ombra e luce*, small wonder Caravaggio's paintings made such an impact. And somewhere between the musical extremes there is the *canzone napoletana*, those songs composed in the local dialect and which no opera singer from Caruso to Pavarotti would dare ignore.

I grew up listening to Giuseppe Di Stefano belting them out on a farm in Ontario, a smiling image of him on the cover of the record album, waving to me from a speedboat in the Bay of Naples. Was the Italian in me fathered then, challenging the

Pole? Not quite. Aged six, on Monday, 16 May 1955, I was taken by my parents to see the great Beniamino Gigli in Ottawa of all places, such events at that time being scarce, and I can remember still an aged man taking his bows in front of a plush red velvet curtain. I shouted 'Bravo, bravo!' as I had been instructed to although in truth his voice was already on its way out. It was his farewell tour, and the stress of it greatly impaired his health such that within two years he was dead. I can't remember whether he did a *canzone* for an encore. Gigli did his bit for Naples, though, with a rendition of Pergolesi's 'Tre giorni son che Nina'. (On the programme, which I've framed and hung on the wall at home, Pergolesi is spelled *Pergolese* and, dear me, Brahms *Brams*.) It was a fateful evening because as of that night I would change my name to Mario, and would be called that, even in the school records, for the next twelve years. '*Mario, Mario*'. Sometimes, though, I crave a rougher voice because, magnificent though they were, Gigli's and Di Stefano's were too polished for the genre. What I'd give to be able to go back a century and be serenaded by Gilda Mignonette. She left Naples for New York in the 1920s, it's true, but she chose to die in the place of her birth. Only she didn't quite make it in time. A boat off the Algerian coast ferried her body home. There's *appocundria* for you.

Appocundria? It is a native disease, highly contagious, and for which there is no known cure. A species of melancholy bordering on the desirable, the peoples of many countries have their own special word for it, claim it as unique unto themselves and therefore untranslatable. The Turk suffering from *hüzün* has about as much sympathy as the Russian suffering from *toska* does for the Portuguese suffering from *saudade* and all three look askance at the Neapolitan who separates himself from the rest of his country and is therefore even more isolated in his sorrow than they are. Whatever it is, wherever it is, one perishes happily from it. There is plenty of it still to be found in Naples. And melody, melody is everywhere.

✳

A tourist shop may be a somewhat unlikely venue in which to find a singer emblematic of Neapolitan culture and in particular *canzone napoletana* but it was there, in a cavern-like space at the back of the Museum Shop on Piazzetta Nilo, that I met the woman who, when I told her I was after the soul of Naples, answered, 'I *am* the soul of Naples.' Now there's an assertion with which one does not dare trifle. Pina Cipriani wears a ring with a huge stone, which she jokingly remarks doubles up as a means of quickly solving disputes. A woman in her early seventies, with a voice of one in her late twenties, she ought to be elsewhere, in a theatre of her own, with her own musicians rather than having to sing to pre-recorded music, but it is precisely the fact that she *did* have a theatre once, and that she *did* have live musicians, one of whom was her composer husband, Franco Nico, and that she *did* have a stage, that makes her emblematic of a city subject to the vicissitudes of good and ill fortune. There is something rather melancholy about it all, the sense of a fall having taken place, between what she had then and what she has now, a distance measurable only in the soul. And yet endure she does. She endures because the culture is one of endurance.

The Museum Shop occupies the ground floor of the Palazzo Panormita, and before I take the reader to my chair in front of the stage, I am once again caught up in the fantastic historical tangle that is the *centro storico*. You've already been warned this would be a circumbendibus. The singer must hold fire. The palazzo takes its name from the poet Antonio Beccadelli (1394–1471), more popularly known as 'Il Panormita' ('the man from Palermo'), whose best-known work *Hermaphroditus* is a series of erotic epigrams written, in Latin, in the manner of the poet Martial, and which, happily or unhappily, remains as obscene today as when it was first published in 1425 to the applause of humanists and the disgust of Christian apologists. The book

which has been described as 'a precious jewel in a dunghill' celebrates all forms of sexual vice, in particular sodomy, and was
dedicated to Cosimo de' Medici who, after perusing its pages,
immediately had it burned. The poet declares his intention in
the dedicatory lines: 'Cosimo, my book in two do I divide / As
many parts has the hermaphrodite.' Soon enough, he sets aside
gentility for genitalia and lets rip with some pretty raw verse.
The work has been translated into English, but the problem with
the obscene in poetry is that generally speaking it works only
when couched in technically flawless verse that is delivered with
elegance, and there is no better medium than Latin in which to
deliver a wagonload of ordure. Antiquarian filth sits better on
one's shelves than modern. By the time Il Panormita settled in
Naples he had cleaned up his act and become panegyrist to King
Alfonso V of Aragon and Naples. As for his earlier verses, he
claimed that while his poetry might be obscene he himself led a
virtuous life. It's what some call a classical stance.

Il Panormita would not have been familiar with the statue
in front of the shop because it was not there when he was alive.
Surely he would have delighted in its hermaphroditic properties:
the *Statua del dio Nilo* ('The Statue of the Nile God') was, for a
while, and for some it remains so, a woman. The area in ancient
times was known as the Alexandrian Quarter in recognition
of the fact that it was home to Egyptian traders. Even after all
traces of Egypt had disappeared the area continued to be referred
to as 'Nilo', a memory of which is preserved in the name of the
small church close to the Palazzo Panormita, Sant'Angelo a Nilo.
And the Bar Nilo opposite where there is a shrine to Maradona.
The statue was erected by Egyptian merchants during the time
of Nero as a backward nod to their own origins and religion. It
disappeared soon after the advent of Christianity but was redis-
covered minus its head in the 1100s, and then it was lost sight
of until its rediscovery in the fifteenth century, which was when
matters got into a bit of a gender muddle. The presence of putti

led people to believe that the headless figure was a female suckling its children and so it was that the statue acquired its new interpretation as 'the body of Naples', hence the Neapolitan phrase o *cuòrp' 'e Napule*, and it was venerated as such, though not always in the way the Church would approve. When in the 1600s the statue, still headless, was restored to its rightful place, the sculptor Bartolomeo Mori was commissioned to sculpt a new head, which was of a heavily bearded male. It continued to be treated as a female object, however, one of popular worship and invested with magical properties. The eighteenth-century magician Alessandro Cagliostro, everybody's favourite charlatan, visited it. And to add a further dimension, at some point during the 1950s art thieves made away with the head of the sphinx that was part of the sculptural group. It was found in an antique shop in Austria and has been returned and restored to its rightful place.

I have now paid my historical dues. I took my seat at the back of the Museum Shop, where maybe Il Panormita stored his wine. Pina Cipriani walked onstage in a velvet dress and a feather boa and stared into the small patch of darkness somewhere inside of which is the audience. She told me later she can't make out the faces, but that when people are attentive she can *see* the silence. Only then does she feel able to release her emotions to the full, which, if the conditions are right, will then play upon the audience's. 'O *sole mio*, there's a sob at the bottom of all canzone.

A potted history of Neapolitan song, the show began with the haunting 'Canto delle lavandaie del Vomero' ('Song of the Washerwomen of Vomero'), which is believed to date to the thirteenth century. It probably began life as a love song – Boccaccio notes its beauty in a letter – and then, although it sounds too tender to be thus employed, it evolved into a protest song against the domination of Naples by the Aragonese. Vomero, which now is one of the posher areas of Naples, was until the 1950s quite rural. 'Tu m'aje prommiso quatto moccatora / oje moccatora, oje moccatora!' ('You promised me four handkerchiefs...').

Moccatora means handkerchief, normally a token of love, but it evolved into what here refers to the parcels of land that Alfonso of Aragon had promised to redistribute among the people. Promises, promises, a word whose repetition amounts to little more than a politician's ruse. One reason the song endures is that the injustice it relates to, although maybe different in substance, is still visited upon ordinary people. Pier Paolo Pasolini used the song in the 'Andreuccio da Perugia' chapter of his somewhat overheated film version of *The Decameron*. It is also in Turturro's *Passione* although it's hard to believe the gorgeous singing washerwomen in his film ever came close to the smell of detergent. And then Pina moves to *Fenesta vascia,* a nineteenth-century treatment of a poem written in 1500, in which a girl watching from a window, which itself becomes a symbol of her cruel indifference, asks, 'Who is the handsome lad who sells water?' and he replies, 'They are tears of love, not water.' The water-seller may no longer be a feature of Neapolitan life, but the agonies of unrequited love are.

A military musical phrase opens "O surdato ńnammurato' in which a soldier fighting at the Front pines for his beloved. Anyone who has seen Alfredo Giannetti's film *La sciantosa* will not forget the scene where Anna Magnani, wearing a ridiculous crown and robed in the colours of the Italian flag, is brought onstage to sing a patriotic number for the troops. When she sees the wounded soldiers in the audience, one of whom is an amputee, she angrily removes crown and garb – no one did anger better than Anna Magnani – and switches to the song that speaks most directly to her audience. At first she intones the words as if to give them wing would be too painful a struggle, but once she gets going her performance brings even her musicians to tears. Yes, it's meant to grab one. It grabbed Italians in the middle of World War I the way Vera Lynn's 'We'll Meet Again' would later grab the British in the middle of World War II, laying bare the uncertainties that accompanied every goodbye.

'Luna rossa', on its 1951 release, upset the purists. What were these stains of the beguine? What place did Guadeloupe (or for that matter Martinique) have in *our* canzone? Frank Sinatra was quick to notice it. His version of 'Blushing Moon' came out in 1952. If an American, albeit one of Italian descent, could make the song his own then surely an Italian would seize it back. In 1954 Claudio Villa 'the little king' had a hit with it, and all of Naples danced. Soon it was firmly in the repertoire. The lyrics written by Vincenzo De Crescenzo, with music by Antonio Vian, speak of a man walking the streets alone at three in the morning, hoping his love might see him from her balcony. It's a red moon he addresses, asking it if it has seen his love waiting for him, and the moon, a straight shooter, replies, 'If you really want to know, there's nobody here.' It's a fool for love who thinks his object of desire lies awake, pining for him. Women are more practical, they want their sleep. Ernesto Tagliaferri's 'Passione', which dates from 1934, says all that can be said of passion: 'You have put into my veins a poison so sweet.' What does a song do but give depth to the trite?

It was midway through the performance, with Pina's rendition of 'Munasterio 'e Santa Chiara' that my eyes began to well up. The song, written by Alberto Barberis, with lyrics by Michele Galdieri, was first published in 1945 and tells of a Neapolitan exile who at the end of World War II wishes to return to Naples but at the same time is afraid to see the damage done to his city. 'Munasterio 'e Santa Chiara / Tengo 'o core scuro scuro' ('In my heart there is darkness'). And so he never goes. What is ironic, because almost certainly he had gone to the United States, is that the magnificent Gothic building referenced in the song's title was hit by American bombing on 4 August 1943 – 'six centuries destroyed in ten seconds', as people remark in Naples. All that survived of the original was the wonderful majolica-covered cloister of the order of the Poor Clares, added in 1742 by Domenico Antonio Vaccaro. Santa Chiara was restored and reopened precisely ten years after its destruction, on 4 August 1953. This was seen as a symbol of rejuvenation and the song is now listened to in that spirit.

By the time Pina sang 'Carmela', for which Sergio Bruni set music to words by the poet Salvatore Palomba, I was now completely hers. The woman in the song is, in a sense, Naples, with all its darkness and allure: 'Stu vico nera nun fernesce maje / e pure 'o sole passa e se ne fuje.' ('The black alley never ends and even the sun passes and flees'.) It could have been written with the Vico Scassacocchi in mind. Its theme is that one must love one another now as there may be no tomorrow and because love is the opposite of death. It's what one gets for living in the shadow of a volcano. And Pina ended with Pino Daniele's 1988 'Canzone nova', which hits Neapolitans dead centre, although maybe not quite as much as 'Napule è', which has become a kind of anthem. 'Napule è 'na carta sporca'. The city might be, as the song says, 'a bit of dirty waste paper' but it is also the city of 'a thousand colours'. Domenico Garofalo told me it is the most important song of contemporary Naples. 'It's a Pulcinella way of life we have here. We care only about what we can touch. Our end is simply to survive.'

Pina Cipriani lives in Santa Lucia, an area made famous by the song of that name, 'the realm of pure harmony' as one of its lines has it, although it is no longer home to the fishermen who used to sing their songs there but rather to the expensive restaurants supplied by their catches. The rather more specific area of Pallonetto remains a quintessential working-class quarter, the setting of Giuseppe Marotta's delightful stories in *The Slaves of Time* in which the nightwatchman Don Vito Cacace takes us through its seasons: 'June disembowels Pallonetto,' he writes. 'It is like an X-ray of these ancient walls and this equally ancient people. Take advantage of it. Examine and diagnose.' I shall try my best to examine and diagnose. The area is now rather less gentle than it was in Marotta's 1950s prose. The kids in Pallonetto are at loggerheads with the kids in the neighbouring Quartieri Spagnoli and invariably drugs enter the picture. The eighteenth-century building where Pina lives is on Via della Solitaria, which translates as 'The Street of the Solitary Woman'. It was so named in reference to the widows of the fishermen who died at sea.

Pina was born in 1944, in Casal di Principe, some sixty miles north of Naples, a town whose name is synonymous with dark forces. A major town now, when she was small it was one of three villages, the other two being San Cipriano d'Aversa and Villa Literno. Some years before, at the behest of Mussolini, the three villages were united into a single town called Albanova ('New Dawn'), a name that survives only with the local train station and a football team. It is to be wondered whether the name was chosen so as to put a bright face where there had been only a sinister one. The villages were connected by country roads along which it was dangerous to go at night because of the ambushes. The spirit was still one of brigandage. There was one spot in particular, a railway bridge near Frignano, where, just before one got to it, there was a sharp turn in the road, bad news to anyone who found it blocked by a parked vehicle because backing out of there in a hurry was close to impossible. The driver would then be escorted to a spot beneath the bridge. When a train passed overhead the noise it made would disguise the sound of a gunshot. Mostly this was Camorra killing Camorra, but what began as local banditry would evolve into something far worse. It isn't so provincial any more. Quaint were the times when people simply fired guns at each other. A large area of the *campania felix*, 'the fertile countryside' so beloved of the ancient Romans, has become the *triangolo della morte*. A land once rich in apples, apricots, plums and peaches is now filled with toxic waste.

'They can't grow anything there,' said Pina in a blistering voice. 'It is the truth and I am not afraid to say it. The Camorra destroyed this land. There was one particular area of it that was poor. The families living there had children who left their country to work abroad and so the parents were left alone, ageing, and with no one to work for them. They were given small amounts of money for their land, and from all over Italy the poison arrived in huge barrels and during the night they dug holes in the land and buried them. The poor farmers didn't know it was dangerous. They were told, "If you see machines digging your land, just close your eyes and mouths and don't think about it." Nobody ever said to them they would die. They started to fall ill. And not only can you not live there, you can't even breathe. The air itself is poisoned. Children are dying of cancer.'

Pina's cousin, Don Giuseppe Diana, whose parish was in Casal di Principe, in Christmas 1991 wrote and distributed a letter 'For the love of my people I will not stay silent', which called upon his parishioners to resist the Camorra. Three years later, as he was preparing for Sunday Mass, he was shot dead in his own church. Pina remembers him as a child and in particular a little song in dialect which he composed: 'Piglia 'o cane, acchiappa 'o cane, 'a capa d'o' cane, 'o cane, 'o cane' ('Get the dog, catch the dog, the head of the dog, the dog, the dog'). His religious calling came at a young age and his mother, Pina's Aunt Iolanda, cried, 'I can't believe my first son wants to become a priest.' Giuseppe's reply was, 'Don't worry, Mummy, I will go with Dad to work the land even when I am a priest.' Pina's husband would one day set the words of Diana's protest letter, altering the title a little, 'For the love of my people I have given my life'.

'They think only of money,' Pina continued. 'The Camorra are harming their own children as well. In Naples we say, "'O pesce fete d' 'a capa" ("The fish smells first from the head.") When you put fresh fish in the sun it deteriorates first at the head. All bad things begin with the government, *the head*. If the government had helped the poor farmers they would not have sold their land for money. And then there's another example. Who is traditionally considered the most important figure in the family? The father. If the children go wrong, it is him who's to blame. Who is guilty? If he makes mistakes, the children notice. The fish smells from the head. Will this crime ever end? It has been here for two centuries.'

'*Do I dare to eat a peach?*' A line illustrative of Mr Prufrock's anxiety, sexual maybe, there is no amount of commentary that will get us close to anything so simple. Suddenly, though, it begins to feel like one of the most prophetic lines T. S. Eliot ever wrote. There is a pivotal scene in *Gomorrah*, the film based on Saviano's book, where an elderly woman presents the Camorra boss, Franco, played charmingly by Toni Servillo, with a box of peaches from her orchard. 'What beautiful peaches!' he tells her. After he and his apprentice in crime, Roberto, have driven away some distance, he stops the car and tells Roberto to dump the peaches. Roberto is puzzled. 'Can't you tell how they stink?' Franco says. It is a terrible moment of realisation. Roberto gets out of the car, throws away the peaches, and then announces he is no longer willing to work in 'waste management'. Franco scolds him, saying, 'Does this job disgust you, Robbe? Do you know that we are the ones who made it possible for this shit country to enter the European Union?' Roberto refuses to get back inside the car and walks alone through the countryside which he helped to defile. 'Go make pizza,' his boss mutters. Making pizza would be, of course, the more honourable course.

Pina describes her family as one whose size was dictated by a *grande amore*. The production rate being on an annual basis, her mother gave birth to nine children, five sisters and four brothers. At that point her father was a successful owner of a bakery and grocery and also traded in grain. A man who has bread to sell in difficult times may be said to be on a better footing than his confederates, but he did what he could to help people suffering from hunger. It was the war. The Nazis were busy gathering the young men of the towns and villages in order to shoot them.

'The children in the street, when they saw them coming, would cry "The Germans! The Germans!" This was the signal for the males to hide. Mother would tell them she was pregnant, which was true. She was *always* pregnant with the next child. "My husband has run away, *the bastard*," she'd tell them.'

War or no war, there was a continual atmosphere of fear, and because fear is so often the author of unspoken laws Pina and her four sisters were mostly confined to the house. The Camorra continued to eviscerate any idea of a normal life, but there was another side, *il predominio maschile*, the male culture of the society. And then, on a positive note, there were the peasants working in the fields, *la vita naturale*. She particularly enjoyed the visits to her maternal grandparents. There all the men worked as farmers.

'I had these uncles, one of whom we called "il comandante", who wanted to direct everything but didn't actually do anything. And then there was my Uncle Luigi, a soldier who, when the war finished, didn't return from Russia. We were informed he would never come back. One morning someone banged [on] the door and everyone thought he was a beggar. "No," he cried, "I'm Luigi, I'm back!" The family didn't recognise him. His mother, unable to believe her eyes, fainted. The first thing they did was to prepare a bath for him, as if by cleaning him they'd make him the man he used to be. Luigi would say hardly anything. He'd go to work with the other brothers, but then he would just drift away between the trees, looking at the skies, standing there for the longest time. His father would cry out, "Luigi is having another ecstatic moment!" Obviously he understood his son's situation but wanted to lighten things up a little. "C'mon, why do you always wander off?" he'd add affectionately. "We have work to do." And then there was another uncle, a baritone, a singer with a natural operatic voice, who would sing "Nessun dorma" early in the morning while shaving. "None shall sleep," he sang, wakening everybody. My mother would wake me up, singing, "Piscatore 'e Pusilleco" ("Fisherman of Posillipo") and I'd sing back to her from under the covers, so there was a kind of musical lineage. It was like a theatre in the house. When my mother was tired in the evening and my brothers, who worked for the family bakery, went to bed after working collecting grain all day, she'd invite the girls and would invent stories and fairy tales for us.

'After the war there was a moment of relative wealth due to the bakery, the bread sold well, everyone wanted to spend money on food. My father was reckless though. As well as being a gambler he poured all his money in some construction scheme that was started during the First World War and which continued to be funded by the fascist state. The Opera Nazionale Combattenti was designed for war veterans whereby all these people would be given pieces of land on which they would build houses. It went badly for him. He lent money to a contractor friend, and, as was usual in the south of Italy, the buildings were not well made. The inspectors went to look at them and refused to pass them. That was the end of it for our family. After that there was no milk in the morning. We went from relative wealth to relative poverty. We would ask our mother, "Why did you make us?" we'd ask. "Because we had the money then," was her reply. Those were very hard years, a complete revolution of our previous life. When my mother got tired she'd say to the girls, "Give me peace, I'm tired. I wish I'd gone into the convent like my sister."'

Strange the way a chance remark an adult makes can have unintended consequences for the boy or girl who hears it, but then childhood is a peculiar prism through which whatever passes is not only redirected but also strangely magnified. It's why so many childish fears are inexplicable. A writer of genius will recreate it, otherwise it is close to impossible to delineate through the layers of interpretation we add over later years.

Sometimes religious fervour gets into a girl's bones. Aged twelve, Pina got into her head that she, too, must go to a convent. Her mother was horrified and with some cause. Her sister, Pina's aunt, Pasqualina entered the sisterhood. In 1943 an allied bomb hit the Benedictine convent in Piedimonte d'Alife and Suor Donna Maria Flavia, as she had then become, fled and stepped on a nail. She got tetanus and because she refused to have her leg amputated she died, aged thirty-three.

'She said when taking her vows, and my mother remembered this, "The way these roses will one day lose their scent and fall, so too will my life." I had an image of this very mystical woman with a bouquet of white roses in her arms, also this idea of the convent as a mystical place where one could have a life for oneself. There was no peace and tranquillity in the village. My mother, still traumatised by her sister's death, cried, "Do you want to die like your aunt?", but it was too late, there was nothing to be done for it. All these things I suffered in my childhood, I can still feel them inside. You absorb them, but you don't want to dramatise the pain. You want to feel it and imagine it like a flower and not as a bad thing in your life. I don't want to keep this pain, I want to cancel it.'

A seemingly insignificant thing happened three years before she entered the convent. One day she was in her brothers' room, doing the household chores, making up the beds for her brothers, and there on the floor was a clipping from a magazine called *Sorrisi e canzoni* ('Smiles and Songs'), which featured a handsome young musician and songwriter called Franco Nico, born Francesco Mastrominico, who at that point was working as a singer and musician in Ischia. She took the article and showed it to her friends, telling them about this famous singer from the nearby village of San Cipriano d'Aversa. She then put it in a drawer. She was nine years old at the time.

Aged twelve, Pina entered the Benedictine convent of San Biagio in Aversa as a novice. Saint Biagio, as it so happens, is the *santo protettore* of sore throats. A singer could not want for better insurance. She remained there for four years, during which time she learned the Gregorian chants, snatches of which she sang to me as we spoke. The *madre badessa* ('Mother Superior') was called Donna Maria Geltrude, whom Pina recalls as being very big with a wonderful face. She could be severe though. Pina related to me some of the punishments meted out for minor infringements, such as the time she broke the iron which she then had to wear on her back as a form of penance. When I asked her whether her memories of the place were bitter she was quick to respond, saying a bit of convent life would be good for everybody.

'Nothing is yours. The first time my mother brought a big basket for me it was taken from me. When I remember this, I become that child again. "Where are the things my mother gave me?" I asked. They replied, "Yours? *Ours*!" So everyone enjoyed what was brought me. This was important for creating a sense of sharing with others.'

When Pina was sixteen she became ill with a high fever, and her mother was desperate to bring her home.

'She cried, "Please leave the convent and come back home with me." The Mother Superior wanted me to stay and there was something like a tug of war between her and my mother. "If you don't leave," my mother cried, "you'll die here." The Mother Superior said, "What will we do without Pina's voice?" She finally agreed to let me go. When I was in the convent I got very fat. It was as if destiny did not want me to be a nun. As soon as I left the place I became thin, deflated like a balloon. My mother said, "Look, everything is okay, now you're better!" but no, I wanted to go back to the convent. The Mother Superior declared I should stay at home and decide what I wanted to do. I was seventeen.' Pina sang a few lines from 'Ave Maria' and laughed. 'There was the main church in the village where, after leaving the convent, I would sing at weddings. The priest said to my mother, "Why not let her study singing?" My mother said, "No, please! *Silenzio*! What would we be doing if we let her leave the convent only to become a singer?" This was *too* much. I told her, "But surely if the priest says I ought to study singing then I should do so." This set me on my life's course.'

The question of who should teach Pina arose and it was then that she remembered the article she had secreted away when she was nine.

'"You're crazy," my mother cried. "Who is this Mastrominico? Where did you get this piece of paper? How did we ever get to this point? Where can we find him?" My sister had a boyfriend who was a car mechanic with his own garage, and naturally he had clients from all over the village. Surely one of them, he said, would recognise the man in the picture. I waited and waited. One day a customer remarked, "My son is an artist, if it's my son we're talking about." He promised he would arrange a meeting with him, and a promise in rural Campania was something to be honoured. Franco was furious with his father. "You want me to meet a girl who was to become a nun and now I am to decide whether she can sing or not!" "Look," his father said, "I made a promise. All you have to do is meet her, say she can't sing, and that'll be the end of it." The day of the appointment, when I came to the house with lemon trees, I had the feeling this man would be mine. *E' successo!* It happened! When Franco saw me, he fell in love with me. I said, "I have acne all over my face", and he replied, "I don't look at this." I sang for him Milva's recent hit "Quattro vestiti" ("Four Dresses"). Four dresses, four colours, four seasons, one love. The white dress signifies the first meeting, the red dress the flame of love, the yellow dress jealousy, and the black dress the dark shadow of memories. At the end of the song, winter covers the green hills with snow as white as the nights are. Franco said I should go and study with the seventy-year-old maestro, Nino Campanino, who was pianist for Enrico Caruso and Beniamino Gigli. I did not see Franco for another month. I met him by chance, on the bus, when he asked the classic question, "Where are you going?" After two years, Campanino said I was ready to go on the stage. And it was not long after that Franco and I got married.'

What is it about this photograph that so deeply moves me? There is a marvellous sense of animation, of course, which only stillness of a kind captures. You can actually feel the speed at which they move. A marriage certificate in one hand, a bouquet of flowers in another, they've got to wherever it is they wanted to be, but, this said, the sentimental has no place in this picture. They know what they're about. Serious business is behind those joyous faces. There's rather more to it, however, and this is where I begin to fumble for a line. Quite simply, the photograph, which hardly feels like a photograph at all because it is hard to imagine anyone holding a camera in front of them, represents everything that Italy has ever been for me. It's a country some Italians are at pains to tell me no longer exists, and yet I keep finding it, again and again, such that I begin to wonder whether they can still see what I see or if I'm simply voicing what's not there. I think not. Whatever it is, it exists. It can be caught in a simple gesture. It can be heard in the snatch of a song of a woman on the street, oblivious to the fact I'm listening to her, or in a sublimely out-of-tune funeral band wherein lies musical perfection of a kind. It can be smelled in just about any marketplace. Wild fennel, *finocchio*, will be my guide. And yes, I know what those detractors are saying to me. It is not that they suffer from want of love for their country, but from too much of it. Theirs is an expression of loss, perfectly understandable, but then loss itself is a form of permanence. Always there is something being lost somewhere. Words are inadequate, and yet without them what will we preserve of anything at all much less ourselves? A few hours ago, a teacher of Italian spoke profound words to me: 'Secondo me quando muore una parola muore anche ciò che quella parola definisce'. What Adriana Vasques meant, with respect to how language has been allowed to deteriorate, is that when a word dies the very thing that word defines also dies. The sense of responsibility she places upon language is immense. What, then, can be said of this image? What am I asking it to do for me? What can it say about the fragility of existence? Adriana's words come at just the right time. There needs to be, in this season of extremes, a balance. One can speak of pain and joy, of course, but suffering is of itself no resolution and neither is a whoop in paradise. This photograph could not have been taken anywhere else in the world and it reminds me also of the Italian films of the post-war *verismo* period, which I love, so beautifully rendered on cheap stock in black-and-white. Looking at them, one can almost feel the texture of the woman's dress as her husband, worried for their future, embraces her. It was the cinema of the poor, and poverty will never again be so rich or so tactile. One does not feel emptier for seeing those films or depressed because what they say is that happiness is not anything one can hold onto, that for it to have any value it must be fleeting in nature. As long as suffering is resolved, which is what the ancient Greek tragedians understood so well, then we will be free to breathe. It is curious to note how, with the advent of technicolour, the lily began to fester a little. There can be no reconstructing that bittersweet vision. What the photograph says to me, almost in a whisper, is that *all will be gone, all we ever were will cease to be.*

The reality, as I would discover later, was slightly different. The newlyweds had just come from the church and were almost too late for the ferry that would take them to Capri. The photographer was already waiting on the dock, screaming at them to hurry, which was precisely when he took the image. The Italy I see was still a place where love might hold up a boat.

Pina sang the opening lines from Franco's 'Resta ancora a Capri' which was written before the wedding and dedicated to the island, although it is tempting to think it was just as much for her.

E' Capri la terra dei sogni che porta fortuna
E' Capri una stella caduta dal cielo nel mare
A Capri ti sento felice, non devi partire
Rimani stasera, domani, domani
E poi partirai.

Capri is the lucky land of dreams
Capri is a star fallen from the sky into the sea
In Capri I feel you're happy, don't leave
Stay tonight, tomorrow, tomorrow
And then you'll go.

'It was *un grande amore*,' Pina reminisced. 'If ever we had an argument or a moment of tension he would bring me a rose afterwards. I link all my best moments with Capri. My son Egidio was born there and my daughter Bianca was born in

Sorrento. I told Franco I wouldn't go to Ischia for fear of having another child there!'

They moved to Naples in the 1970s. At her mention of this, I asked her if she really is a bona fide Neapolitan. 'I have become so. With my voice an ambassador, I made up for all the years I wasn't there.' Franco went to school at the Liceo Vittorio Emanuele, on Via San Sebastiano, dubbed 'the street of musicians', and Pina, wife and mother, took in the city's atmosphere, her mother-in-law insistent that they be more Neapolitan than the Neapolitans themselves. And then came the momentous decision that would change their lives. There was no cabaret in Naples, and because many people hungering for it went to Rome, they decided on a new course. In 1972, together with their friend the writer Angelo Fusco, Franco and Pina started the Teatro Sancarluccio – 'the small San Carlo' – in the Chiaia district of Naples. The place would soon become the training ground for many famous actors, Massimo Troisi, Roberto Benigni, Leopoldo Mastelloni to name but three. It was a period of great dynamism, Angelo Fusco producing texts, many of them satirical in nature. While Franco Nico was writing the music for one, Fusco would already be onto the next one. 'I, Gennaro Esposito,' went one of their songs, which here I flatten into prose. 'We are four brothers. When we go out we do bad things because our mother was a prostitute and our grandmother was another, but with our fathers things were different because they changed all the time.' Six years were spent in creating a repertoire. Pina was still a young mother but determined to sing. She asked Franco, 'When will you let me sing?' and he replied, 'You'll sing, you'll sing'. Franco, responding to the creative drives of his young wife, created the theatre for Pina and so the Sancarluccio became for them home, a place where they would eat and sleep, a total experience.

'My first time on the stage was in 1978, with our group Bentornato Mandolino. Some years later, we devised a performance,

Rosa, Preta e Stella with a string quartet. When we needed other instruments we brought them in from elsewhere. We took the performance to Paris and other places. There was also a show called *Tiempe sciupate* ('Wasted Time'), written and directed by the playwright Enzo Moscato. We combined music and poetry, emphasising the relationship between them. I both sang and spoke.'

I put it to Pina that Naples seems to be one place in Italy that tries to hold onto something lyrical and, shall we say, *real* from its history. This is not to say the lyrical is confined to Naples but that it has a higher profile there than in many other cities. At the same time it is a place of corruption and violence. One might think it's because of the darkness that this lyrical voice survives. I wanted to know whether that hardship helped to preserve the lyricism, or was this perhaps too romantic a notion?

'It is not possible to separate the light from the dark in Naples. And besides the city has not two but a hundred different faces. It is about the soul that sings out of this particular city, and what you bring to it is from who you are. It is all about how you interpret the song. You can sing a song, but if you don't understand it you won't be able to give it your own interpretation. There is this simplistic view that if a song is joyous you should put joy into the way you sing it or if it is sentimental you should put passion into it. You have to look at the intention of the poets who wrote the songs, the stories behind them.'

Pina has spoken of an authentically Neapolitan way of singing and is critical of people who do not get the right tone. There must be a high and low way of singing those canzoni. Di Stefano sang them as would an opera singer, but surely it was not how ordinary Neapolitans treated those songs.

'If you do it in an operatic way then it is not really Neapolitan although, granted, Di Stefano was really good. He sang from the heart and with him it was much more than lyricism whereas with a lot of opera singers they sing merely to show off their powerful voices. The Neapolitan song does not necessarily require power.

It is quite possible to get around a song without displaying a big voice, the distinction being that it is the voice that comes from within and not the one you put out which matters most. You bring to the written song your musical instinct and education and, of course, your *feeling*. This has been given different names, *duende* and so forth, but most recently it has been expressed, strangely enough, with the English phrase 'O *feeling*, with a Neapolitan accent and article. How a song is expressed depends on the singer's background. Take "Munasterio 'e Santa Chiara", for example. Somebody from Forcella, the backbone of the *centro storico*, will interpret it in quite a different way from someone living elsewhere in Naples. It is more about the tradition of those particular songs. The song is the collective memory that travels through generations. The voices might change, but the song remains.'

Was *real* Neapolitan song, then, closer to the street?

'The way of singing has changed over the years. With the early twentieth-century singer, Gilda Mignonette, you will hear the voice you describe, but it is the voice of a city that doesn't exist any more. You can't have that voice any more. I remember my grandmother when she sang melodies. She wasn't a singer but she had that same kind of authentic voice. This was when singing still came from local people. There was no way singers from the north of Italy could have taken these songs and made them their own. You had to be Neapolitan and be able to *feel* the dialect, the mother language. There is a tendency now to emote whereas in earlier times it was the song and not the way one sang that was the first thing. Sometimes one can't even make out the words any more. It becomes a kind of display which can be interesting sometimes, but the Neapolitan songs were seen as literature first of all, a form of poetry, after which the melody followed suit. God gave me this voice. I have an orchestra in my throat. When I'm on the stage I feel I have to go up, up, and up with this voice. Music gives you passion. It is not me, however, but someone else singing. I am a simple person but when I'm on stage it is a mystery. Something *happens.* I enter every word of the poetry and the poetry gives me the emotion with which to express myself.'

The serpent, when it has a mind to do so, coils up inside a pothole. On 18 November 2008, after phoning to say he was hungry and would be at the theatre soon, Franco drove his motorbike into the tunnel at the Galleria della Vittoria and did not emerge alive. Soon after, there was a local scandal, then known as 'the Global Service bid', which, among other things, related to the condition of the streets in Naples and their 400-million-euro reconstruction. The scandal rested on the accusation that works were delayed in order to secure the bid for one particular and very influential contractor, Alfredo Romeo. A large number of politicians and administrators in the council came under investigation, and the maintenance commissioner, Giorgio Nugnes, who was put under considerable pressure and was probably fearful of being made a scapegoat, committed suicide.

The funeral for Franco at the Basilica of San Francesco di Paola, on the Piazza del Plebiscito, was grander than any that would be held under normal circumstances, with the Mayor of Naples and other politicians in attendance, and yet it was conducted within the ancient folk traditions of which the deceased was so important a champion. The accounts I have of it are vivid enough for me to be able to reconstruct the scene. Marcello Colasurdo, widely acknowledged as maestro of the tammorra,* sang a low tune or lullaby and then, to the accompaniment of his instrument, slowly danced around the coffin. As one newspaper reported, 'the rhythm reminds one of the lamentations of the *prefiche*', the professional female mourners who were most

---

* The frame drum, so much a feature of southern Italian folk music, which usually has a membrane of goat or sheep skin.

hauntingly captured in a short film by Cecilia Mangini, *Stendalì – suonano ancora* ('Still They Toll', 1960). Then Pina got up from where she sat with her family and danced as if in a trance. It was more like a shamanic act, a healing procedure for the dead and the living, a ritual designed to facilitate the passage from life into death. Whether by accident or design, what Colasurdo and Pina did was to reach into something buried deep in the region's history, the ancient Samnite funeral dances, so beautifully depicted in the painted tombs at Albanella and near Capua. Although influenced by the Greeks and Etruscans, the Samnite's dance was more solemn in execution, or so we have been made to understand from the pictorial evidence. So little do we know about the Samnites, who were exterminated by Rome, that the funeral dance they depicted now stands as a memorial to their shadowy existence. And if one reaches back a little further, the Etruscans believed the dead were ushered into the afterlife with music and dance. This is not to transmute personal grief into an historical essay but to bring alive ancient sorrow in such a way that their tears and ours are of the same lineage. Stunned by her loss, Pina could barely stand on her feet, but as an artist she knew the ritual of the ancient death ceremonies and understood that dance pushes the pain away, injects light into an atmosphere that would be only dark and desperate otherwise. Dance, in this context, is not a pagan exercise any more. It is for all time, a bond of trust, a ward against the impotence one feels at the loss of a husband and friend. The priest who was a gifted musician and director of the Conservatorio di San Pietro a Majella, and who as a child knew Franco in Capri, gave the ritual his blessing. At the end of it there was a big round of applause. The audience, timidly at first, then increasingly absorbed by the majesty of the event, clapped their hands in rhythm to accompany Pina's dance. Afterwards they surrounded her and comforted her. I am reminded of those wise words about people in Naples wanting, and deserving, deliverance.

A most theatrical event, it served to remind people that Naples had been a *matrigna* ('evil stepmother') with respect to the fate of the Sancarluccio. At the end of the funeral Pina railed against the indifference of the general public who abandoned the little theatre. 'The Sancarluccio is empty. Where are you? Why are you leaving us alone to fight the battle for survival with no weapons?' The bitter irony is that on the day of the accident Franco Nico was returning from the Council where he had gone to renew the licence for the theatre. The simple fact is that he was already in the throes of a losing battle. The funding for the theatre from the government office, Regione Campania, though promised, was several years late. Meanwhile, the rent was increased. The question always is how to keep things alive not just in Naples but anywhere. What might have been supported by one government will be irrevocably lost with the next one. Naples is a place of great energy, but there comes a point there is nowhere left for this energy to go. The Sancarluccio, at least in its first manifestation, died with Franco Nico although nominally it would continue in other hands.

Pina, who lives on the street that might have been named for her, tells me that when she and Franco married they went to live on the slopes of Monte Solaro on the island of Capri. A chairlift goes up that mountain, a scary ride for those who'd rather not dangle their feet in space, and from it the tourists would wave to a young mother and her child on the balcony of that house. One day, Pina says, she'll take me there. She already has.

There is a Fellini film I greatly admire, *Ginger and Fred*, which is about two ageing performers, played by the best actors of the day, Marcello Mastroianni ('Pippo') and Giulietta Masina ('Amelia'). Mastroianni was required to thin his legendary hair for the role. Masina had merely to show her age. They both protested, he more than she. Pippo and Amelia, who were lovers once, are Fred Astaire and Ginger Rogers impersonators who have been pulled out of retirement and thrust into a ghastly

television variety show where, as one movie critic put it, 'the shadows are more real than the figures that cast them'. Amelia does it to amuse her grandchildren, Pippo for the moolah. Vincent Canby of *The New York Times* goes on to speak of the other performers milling about backstage, some of them truly freakish, as 'souls awaiting judgement in this electronic age's only purgatory'. I think Canby got it right. Fellini certainly did. Somewhere, I can't remember where, he predicted that

Berlusconi would be the face of Italy's future. This was when the latter still had some distance to go. Sometimes prophecy is the ability to see more clearly than others what is already there in the fine print of our lives. The rest is divination: say enough things enough times, you're bound to score sooner or later. The smart ones charge for their services. Pippo and Amelia enter what will one day dissolve their species – the world of junk television, Berlusconi's in particular, an acid bath for popular culture. The commercial breaks, Fellini claimed, were 'more dangerous than the atomic bomb itself' – a bit over the top maybe, but then he was given to hyperbole. Or else he didn't rate reason quite as highly as others do. Amelia and Pippo will, against all the odds, produce a final hurrah. They may be, at times, just a little creaky, and while one is tempted to smile at them what is absolutely vital to any understanding of the film is that even in this most degrading of situations, even though Pippo reaches for the bottle, even though Amelia struggles to put on a good face and be professionally distant from old love, they never sacrifice their dignity. Miss this, and you've missed the movie. We already know Pippo and Amelia to be the stars of a world of shadows. It may not have been such a big world in the first place, but it was theirs, they made it, and what they did there was done, although maybe not to everyone's taste, with supreme elegance. Showmen both, the world owes them much. 'We are shadows,' says Pippo. 'We arise from darkness and disappear again.'

It was something I remembered as I watched Pina. She, too, battles a tacky universe. The performer, always on the cusp of disappearance, the stage an illusion of permanence, were it not for him, were it not for *her*, there'd be nothing of what we so tentatively call culture. A continuum, most perilous of zones, matters more sometimes than the bright lights dotted along it, for it is comprised of every person who with some degree of craftsmanship has sung a note, danced a step, or jotted down a phrase. They are the enablers of culture. I do not mean to strike too democratic a note here. This is not an invitation to the world to get up on stage nor is it to pull down the mighty from theirs. The woman on the stage at the back of the Museum Shop blinked into the darkness, so difficult for her to make out the faces. She would give it her all, however, whatever size the audience. She got at least one heart in her basket. She deserved a thousand. She has had many more, of course, but a thousand at this moment in time, when she had so much left to give, would have been nice.

Physicists say that time passes more quickly or more slowly depending on whether we are on slightly higher or slightly lower ground and although not many of us can afford an atomic clock like the one they have in Boulder, Colorado, if it's true what they say – and there are times when I wonder if time really does exist, whether it is not simply a measure we have devised for our puny selves – then the lady onstage was ageing something like a hundred-billionth of a second faster than me. She was up there and I was down where Il Panormita stacked his wine bottles. *Appocundria*? I've just been hit with a lethal dose of it. She ages. We both do, at slightly varying rates. I wouldn't have been able to say any of this once, but now I can do so with the sure knowledge our bones ache in the same places.

Coda

Pina Cipriani died on 29 June 2019. The last time I saw her, the year before, was at her favourite café in Piazza San Domenico Maggiore. I could not have guessed then that she would have a major heart attack a couple of days later. She was never to perform again. She spent a year in a condition of suspense. On the day preceding her death she could see from her hospital bed the Bay of Naples, Vesuvius in the distance. It is no bad image for the dying to take with them. The chapter I wrote on Pina describes a woman close to the end of her singing career, with a beautiful voice still, and, in the face of all that a cruel decade threw at her, vivacious in the extreme. The Teutonic shadow in which I placed her was mine alone. She dwelled in ultramontane light. Should anyone be so careless as to suppose what I wrote is a complete picture then he or she should listen to her rendition of 'Maronna mia', words by the poet Salvatore Palomba, music by Eduardo Alfieri. It is a magical performance. It should also be noted that her life and career were inextricable from that of her husband, Franco Nico. I wrote of her alone.

The woman died, the artist lives. A few days after she died, the mayor of Casal di Principe, Renato Franco Natale, announced that a theatre which had been built on land confiscated from the Camorra, and temporarily dubbed the 'teatro della legalità' would be officially named Teatro Pina Cipriani.

The Man Who Watches the Waters

'And the third angel poured out his vial upon the rivers and fountains of waters; and they became blood.' – Revelation 16:4. That morning Lake Avernus had a definite reddish tinge. The day before it wasn't there. I was advised that on the following morning it would be gone. It is the sort of thing one notices only when one's eyes are acutely sensitive to spectral change, otherwise, boys and girls, it'll be just another day on the lake. It was not the red that sits boldly on the artist's palette but a red that insinuates, a red one sees in the dark of one's soul, a red that says not all is as it should be. Sometimes the lake becomes ox-blood red. Other times its surface goes milky-white and what happens then is that the fish die. They stink up the place. 'And I heard the angels of the waters say, Thou art righteous, O Lord, which art, and wast, and shalt be, because thou hast judged thus.' The ancients, summoning the gods to their side, put such mysterious events down to the evil that men do, and when those gods were put to bed one by one, the one who survived them all became, by virtue of being the only one left standing, God Almighty, the angels His enforcers, the third of whom rubified the lake.

That's one explanation, more or less. Algal bloom is another. The microscopic water plankton, when it reaches the end of its life cycle, flowers and dies in a single day. There is nothing gradual about the process, no stages, no speeding up here or slowing down there – it happens all at once. The conditions, the temperature of water and air, have to be just right, which is why it is quite a rare occurrence. One might even say it's a small miracle of nature, although, in truth, algal bloom is an ecological curse. More specifically, and because there is some confusion between algal and cyanobacterial bloom, the event described here is due to anaerobic bacteria. And when the lake goes white, and we have what the environmentalists call 'fish kill', it is because the sulphur released from the volcanic depths combines with the water to produce sulphuric acid. When Giovanni Boccaccio was at the Neapolitan court in the 1330s, where he was deeply enamoured of the king's married daughter, the 'Fiammetta' of his prose romances, he describes in a letter how one day the surface of Avernus was covered with dead fish, 'black and singed, as if killed by a subaqueous eruption of fire'.

A lovely day, the air thick with mortality, I walked around the lake.

Lake Avernus, about 25 km west from Naples, is a relative youngster on the earth's surface, only 3,500 years old give or take, which in geological time is a mere trifle. The waters filled a volcanic crater, which, given the fact that nothing in the Phlegraean Fields is ever quite dead, slumbering maybe, farting sulphurous gases all the while, lends credence to Boccaccio's report. It happens still. Fish die. Legend has it that at some point in prehistory the Cimmerians dwelled here, in caves. If so, those dwellers in darkness were a long way from home. There is a charming domestic picture of them made by the fourth-century BC Greek historian, Ephorus of Cyme, which Strabo quotes in his *Geographica*:

They live in underground houses, which they call *argillae*, and it is through tunnels that they visit one another, back and forth, and also admit strangers to the oracle, which is situated far beneath the earth; and they live on what they get from mining, and from those who consult the oracle, and from the king of the country, who has appointed them fixed allowances; and those who live about the oracle have an ancestral custom, that no one should see the sun, but should go outside the caverns only during the night; and it is for this reason that the poet [Homer] speaks of them as follows: 'And never does the shining sun look upon them'; but later on [less charmingly] the Cimmerians were destroyed by a certain king, because the response of the oracle did not turn out in his favour; the seat of the oracle, however, still endures, although it has been removed to another place.

Would those Cimmerians, so wanting of Vitamin D supplements, have recognised themselves? What was their idea of fun? And where are the caves in which they supposedly lived? There are not enough of them to accommodate a sizable population. Ephorus spoke of things he saw not, and it would seem that his purpose was to substantiate, as vividly as possible, the Homeric tale. Avernus 'the realm and region of the Men of Winter, hidden in mist and cloud' is as good a literary setting as any for Odysseus's descent into the Underworld. Geographically, though, the most logical candidate for those subterranean folk, if they were ever here in the first place, is near Baiae where there is a rather more intricate network of caves. There is even a decent candidate for the River Styx, a matter that has been pursued with some imaginative vigour by Robert Paget and Keith Jones, and, most recently, Robert Temple.

The ancient Romans believed Avernus was the entrance to Hades. There's nothing I can do to make that sentence sound revelatory: it's the first thing one learns after dominoes. Very few volcanoes have not been referred to, at some point or other, as the entrances to, or the eyes of, hell. The Romans would have inherited the Avernus legend from the Greeks just as in all probability the Greeks inherited it from elsewhere. All signs point to an archaic time. There may have been witnesses to the formation of the lake, although there's no saying for sure. Whoever they were, they had no written language, but this not does preclude the possibility they kept the event alive in their oral tradition, some of which seeped into the writings of later times. There are several entrances to hell in the area, worthy candidates all of them, but then surely, says a mischievous voice in me, there are as many entrances as there are people. Strabo, in his encyclopaedic *Geographica*, wrote: 'The people prior to my time were wont to make Avernus the setting of the fabulous story of the Homeric *Nekyia* [the title the ancients gave to the eleventh book of the *Odyssey*]; and, what is more, writers tell us that there actually was an oracle of the dead here and that Odysseus visited it.' Virgil certainly knew the ancient legends, read widely, and he would have pounced with enthusiasm on such traces as survived in the folk traditions of the time. What he would make of them remains one of the most vital passages in all literature. *Facilis descensus Averno*. The descent to Avernus is easy, but the journey back, well, that's the hard bit. We have been making that poetical journey ever since.

Hannibal went to Lake Avernus in 214 BC, ostensibly to make a sacrifice to Hecate. It is said that his real aim was to attack Puteoli, the modern Pozzuoli, which may be true, but this does not necessarily preclude religious observance. After all, he was a pious man. He also knew his Homer, in Greek, and he would have known that this was where Odysseus descended into Hades and met the soldiers slain in battle. As one of Hannibal's biographers, Clifford W. Mills, puts it, 'The realm of the dead came nearest to the living here.' A memory of this survives into the present day: I've been told, although I can't substantiate the story, that until recently many of the older farmers in the area would not work in the fields at night because of warrior spirits on the loose. What of the Sibyl who is supposed to have dwelled here? There were ten of them in all scattered throughout the ancient world, according to the Roman antiquarian Marcus Terentius Varro, although sadly the book in which he describes them is lost. We know it existed, it was cited by other scholars of the time, and we know its dedicatee was Julius Caesar. The Cumaean and Cimmerian Sibyls are the ones who concern us here. One looks in vain for either of them in Silius Italicus's *Punica*, the epic poem devoted to Hannibal's exploits. There is a sibylline chronology of sorts in that Virgil's Sibyl was appointed to her position in the Avernian groves by Hecate. First, though, we must set the scene for her. What is so vividly pictured in Book VI of the *Aeneid* is not taken from anything Virgil himself saw because if, as we suppose, he went to Lake Avernus in 37 BC or thereabouts the dark forest surrounding it was already gone. Strabo describes the place:

> Avernus is enclosed round about by steep hill-brows that rise above it on all sides except where you sail into it (at the present time they have been brought by the toil of man into cultivation, though in former times they were thickly covered with a wild and untrodden forest of large trees); and these hill-brows, because of the superstition of man, used to make the gulf a shadowy place.

The Roman general Marcus Vipsanius Agrippa established a busy naval base there in 37 BC. Might he not be said to have spoiled the atmosphere? He also had a canal made, along which one may still walk, joining it to Lake Lucrinus and then he had his chief architect build a tunnel, the first major construction of its kind, joining Avernus and Cumae. The Grotta di Cocceio, now closed to the public, was in use until World War Two when it was heavily damaged. The Germans used it to store munitions with predictable results. The harbour complex, cunningly hidden from the sea, was named Portus Julius in honour of Octavian's (later Caesar Augustus) great-uncle and adoptive father. As the English travel writer Henry Swinburne notes in 1777:

> After a long reign of undisturbed gloom and celebrity, a sudden glare of light was let in upon Avernus; the horrors were dispelled, and with them vanished the sanctity of the lake; the axe of Agrippa brought its forest to the ground; disturbed its sleepy waters with ships, and gave room for all its malignant effluvia to escape. The virulence of these exhalations is described by ancient authors as very extraordinary; modern writers, who know the place in a cleared state only, charge these accounts with exaggeration; but I think them entitled to more respect, for even now the air is feverish and dangerous, as the jaundiced faces of the vinedressers, who have succeeded the Sibyls and the Cimmerians in the possession of the temple, most ruefully testify.

Swinburne accepts a Cimmerian presence.

So why does Virgil fix his attentions here? There is reason enough in the very etymology of the name – the Greek for Avernus, ἄορνος (*aornos*) translates as 'without birds'. Sophocles, in a tantalising fragment ('Frag. 748, Pearson', for those who care about such details), speaks of a 'birdless lake'. The legend was that any bird flying over the lake would plunge to its death because of the mephitic fumes rising from below. Strabo thought it a mere fable. It is by no means an implausible fable, however. The volcano still breathes from time to time, as does the whole landscape. It is perfectly reasonable to suppose the fumes were at one time so toxic the birds dropped dead in mid-flight and that whoever those people were who witnessed this backed away from the shore. Again, it's not implausible. There is an account of the volcano that convulsed the island of Lanzarote, in the Canary Islands, in 1730–4, in which the writer describes how seven or eight birds flying above the vapours dropped suddenly as if asphyxiated. This feels closer to Lucretius who with an eye to things as they are, and not as the gods would have them, writes in his *De Rerum Natura* that the birds over Avernus rather than being killed outright by toxic fumes were instead disabled by them. 'They forget to flap their wings and so fall down / With limp necks [*molli cervice profusae*] on to the ground below / If they are over land, or into the water', which is how the poet C. H. Sisson renders the lines. (That word 'limp', which in most instances is translated as 'languid' strikes me most persuasive as if one might clutch in one's own hands one of those feathered necks.)

When Swinburne went there the scene he describes had to a large degree reverted back to nature: 'Black aged groves stretched their boughs over the watery abyss, and with impenetrable foliage excluded almost every ray of wholesome light,' and he goes on to describe 'mephitic vapours ascending from the hot bowels of the earth, being denied free passage to the upper atmosphere, floated along the surface in poisonous mists'. What this tells us is that even as late as the eighteenth century the air was troubled with toxic effusions. He continues:

> Superstition, always delighting in dark ideas, early and eagerly seized upon this spot, and hither she led her trembling votaries to celebrate her dismal orgies; here she evoked the manes of departed heroes – here she offered sacrifices to the gods of hell, and attempted to dive into the secrets of futurity. Poets enlarged upon the popular theme, and painted its awful scenery with the strongest colours of their art. Homer brings Ulysses to Avernus, as to the mouth of the infernal abodes, and in imitation of the Grecian bard, Virgil conducts his hero to the same ground. The holiness of these shades remained unimpeached for many ages.

If this is pure fantasy it is not one he allows elsewhere in his narrative.

The ancient Greeks placed greater store by caves than they did by volcanoes. A cave was where one could reach into the darkness of one's own soul or where a shaman might indulge in shamanic activities. Our Sibyl beckons. On the southern bank of the lake, hidden behind brush, is the Grotta della Sibilla where one could go and consult the oracle. These days one must hold one's nose. On the path leading to the grotto there is an inexplicable amount of soiled toilet paper, as if whole busloads of people have together relieved themselves. The gate is now locked and rubbish is piled up against it. There was an amiable figure who used to take people on torch-lit tours, who called himself 'Caronte' ('Charon') – his real name is Carlo Santillo – but severe arthritis has left him largely immobile. Although the grotto is privately owned still, and a penny could be made from it, nobody has thought to continue his good work. Within the cave, although I haven't seen it, there is a stairwell which supposedly leads down to the River Styx. And if one keeps going straight, one comes to the spot where the Sibyl told her oracles. It is difficult to know what the grotto was like in Virgil's time because bradyseism has either shifted or buried whole sections of it. The word 'bradyseism', which refers to the slow vertical movements of the earth's crust, caused by volcanic action, derives from the ancient Greek *bradus* (slow) and *seismos* (movement) and as such was coined by the Genoese geologist Arturo Issel in 1883. All in all, it is a sorrowful business to observe how a place of mystery, whatever its contrivances, should have been allowed to go into such decline. *O Italia!* Stone, however, is more durable than tissue.

There is the question of whether it was this cave that belonged to the Sibyl or the Antro della Sibilla at Cumae, or even whether there were two Sibyls, the Cumaean and an earlier Cimmerian. Varro's Cimmerian Sibyl comes from his reading of Gnaeus Naevius who claimed that long before the Cumaeans the

Cimmerians inhabited the area around Lake Avernus. Maybe they really were here. If the poets of the Renaissance and after were perfectly content to accept the Grotto della Sibilla at Avernus as the place in which Virgil has Aeneas consult the oracle it is largely because it wasn't until 1932 that the Italian archaeologist Amedeo Maiuri discovered the astonishing *dromos* at Cumae, a trapezoidal passage carved out of volcanic stone, over a hundred metres in length. It had been blocked at the entrance by somebody who had a bread oven there and the first quarter of the passageway was heaped high with rubble. I am rather inclined towards this latter, more hygienic, option. It echoes Virgil's description of a place with 'a hundred openings'. It is not anywhere near a hundred, but then poets are prone to exaggerate. (A friend in Naples, consulting the Oracle at Delphi, says she was advised that Cumae was the place. The great scholar H. W. Parke, in his *Sibyls and Sibylline Prophecy in Classical Antiquity*, certainly argues for it. The dedicatee of this book favours the grotto at Avernus and she is a Sibyl of some kind.) The earliest allusion to the Sibyl at Cumae, although Cumae is nowhere mentioned, is in the Greek tragedian Lycophron's *Alexandra*, a poem known for its impenetrability and which perhaps is not even by him. There the author speaks of Italy 'and Phoebus's mountain, where the priestess maid, the Sibyl, has her awful dwelling-place, a yawning cavern roofed with arching rocks'. Wherever Phoebus's mountain is, there we will find a temple of Apollo. Certainly there was one at Cumae, the earliest Greek colony in mainland Italy – the first was on the island of Pithecusa (now Ischia) – and we know the ruins at the edge of Avernus are not, as was previously believed, a temple dedicated to Apollo but Roman thermal baths. The Sibyl for whom we have the least historical evidence is the one who looms largest in our imagination. Poets revere her, painters likewise. Andrea del Castagno captures her in youth, Michelangelo in noble decrepitude.

When I visited the Antro della Sibilla at Cumae, it was closed
for structural repairs. I badly wanted to go inside. A fierce woman
in a uniform was on duty, watching to see that nobody sneaked
past the temporary barrier. Several times I tried to outwit her
and every time I thought I might make a break for it she would
show her face. A battle conducted in silence, a game of cat and
mouse, she was the biggest cat and I the smallest mouse. It was
only when a group of yellow-helmeted archaeologists gained
admittance that, stooping low, I joined their number. The cheap-
est victories are also the most enjoyable, but there is nothing
that quite robs one of the possibility of an epiphany as being
in a group of people in yellow helmets led by a person on a
loudspeaker. It was on the journey out, which we made alone,
that one could feel the epic grandeur of the place. One cannot
walk through it without feeling one is being drawn into, or, in
this instance, departing, a place of mysteries. The Sibyl in her
uniform when she saw me emerge, realising she had been outwit-
ted, produced something like an exasperated smile.

Outside the grotto one may find there in abundance the oak leaves upon which the Sibyl is said by some, but not all, to have written her prophecies, three of which I have tucked into my copy of the *Aeneid*, the version so audaciously translated into English hexameters by Frederick Ahl. It is quite possible that Virgil seized upon the astounding structure at Cumae and for his own literary purposes relocated it to Avernus. What poet does not move about his pieces? Surely Cumae's the place. Ahl takes me there with his rendering of the trance scene, which, in his notes, he describes as 'controlling the Sibyl's mind and body in a kind of spiritual rape':

> Rather, as if Bacchus ruled her, she rages around in the
>   cavern,
> Hoping to buck the huge god from her breast. But he
>   wearies her froth-flecked
> Mouth even more, as he takes her heart's wildness, and
>   shapes her with pressure.

The Greek traveller and geographer Pausanias cites the historian Hyperochus of Cumae who wrote that the priests at the temple of Apollo showed him an urn that according to them contained the Sibyl's ashes. The Sibyl, whom they called Demo, was already something of a tourist draw. There is yet another account in the *Patrologia Graeca* of a visit that took place in AD 250 by two Christians:

> we were shown three tanks excavated from the same rock. They maintained that these were regularly filled with water and that the Sibyl bathed in them. Then, after she had put on her long robe again, she would retire into the innermost room of the basilica which was also hewn from the same rock. Then, they stated, she would take her seat on a raised platform in the centre of this chamber and would pronounce her oracles.

Also, it seems, those same priests acting as guides were quite happy to give visitors the impression that she was speaking to them from inside the urn. The early Christian apologist Justin Martyr when he visited Cumae was shown the Sibyl's cave, which he describes as 'a great basilica carved from a single stone'. It would seem the odds are in Cumae's favour, but this is not to say my affections do not also lie with the lesser Grotto della Sibilla which, after all, kept Virgilians satisfied for centuries.

One of those happy antiquaries was Mary Shelley who with her poet husband visited it in December 1818. Percy Bysshe Shelley writes to Thomas Love Peacock: 'We passed thro the cavern of the Sybil (not Virgils Sybil) which pierces one of the hills which circumscribe the lake & came to a calm & lovely basin of water surrounded by dark woody hills, & profoundly solitary.' This is all a bit puzzling. What did Shelley mean when he wrote this was not 'Virgils Sybil' and might he and Mary not have come to Lake Avernus by way of the Grotta di Cocceio, which is yet another candidate for the path Aeneas took to Hades? Maybe the most curious sibylline revival is in Mary Shelley's introduction to her novel *The Last Man*:

> At length my friend, who had taken up some of the leaves strewed about, exclaimed, 'This *is* the Sibyl's cave; these are Sibylline leaves.' On examination, we found that all the leaves, bark, and other substances, were traced with written characters. What appeared to us more astonishing, was that these writings were expressed in various languages: some unknown to my companion, ancient Chaldee, and Egyptian hieroglyphics, old as the Pyramids. Stranger still, some were in modern dialects, English and Italian. We could make out little by the dim light, but they seemed to contain prophecies, detailed relations of events but lately passed; names, now well known, but of modern date; and often exclamations of exultation or woe, of victory or defeat, were traced on their thin scant pages.

First published in 1826, and, although mocked at the time, described by one critic as the product of a 'diseased' imagination, *The Last Man* has become a key work in the development of post-apocalyptic fiction. It is also a key to the characters of two men who of themselves exceeded the boundaries of science fiction, Percy Bysshe Shelley and Lord Byron. Would that she kept those leaves, but at least she wove their contents – nothing like having the Sibyl on one's side – into the first-person narrative of Lionel Verney who is largely a stand-in for Mary Shelley herself. Adrian, Earl of Windsor and Lord Raymond are, respectively, based on Shelley and Byron.

Herman Melville, when he went to Avernus on 23 February 1857, a guide carrying him on his shoulders to 'the bath & bed of Sybil', decided it was not 'a plausible hell'. Struck by the perversity of man's thinking, he wrote in his journal: 'Surely man is a strange animal. Diving into the bowels of earth rather than building up towards the sky. How clear an indication that he sought darkness rather than light.' Naples, on the other hand, he considered the 'gayest city in the world'. 'No equipages flash like these; no beauties so haughty,' he writes. 'No cavaliers so proud, no palaces so sumptuous.' The moral for Melville lay in the 'apt representation of that heedlessness, benignly ordained, of man which prevents one generation from learning from a past. – "Let us eat, drink & be merry, for tomorrow we die." Such seems the lesson learned by the Neapolitans from their scenery. – The beauty of place, in connection with its perilousness.'

Jacopo Martorelli is on my case. I'm in danger of turning a jewellery box into an inkwell. Why am I looking for historical correspondences when the only ones that truly matter are those made in the poetic imagination? This I already know and yet something in me wants tangible proof. It is not to say a poet does not draw from reality but that several realities can be made to serve one. Virgil made of all he saw a single coherent poetic vision. And besides, the ancients were not such sticklers when it came to positioning their mythical figures. They could be in several places at once. Such traces as there are, are at best vague, and yet what better place to heap one's certainties than upon something vague? One in a sense removes oneself from criticism. While there is no solid evidence for a sibylline tradition at Avernus, only hearsay, there can be no escaping the fact that much of our later western mythology comes from just a few square miles of the earth's surface. At the same time, I salute this most memorable of the Sibyls. The truths we look for lie not so much in historical fact as in the literary depictions accorded them.

After Virgil's lines nothing hits the reader quite as powerfully as those in Petronius's *Satyricon*, which, on the face of it, seem to come out of the blue. Much of what Petronius writes he takes from Ovid's *Metamorphoses*. We find the Sibyl in a suspended jar, much demoted, a figure of mockery. She's been through bad times. All the worse for her now that it is given to that slob Trimalchio to discuss her fate. In 1922 a young American poet in the process of anglicising himself used Tremalchio's words in his epigraph to *The Waste Land*. So powerful are they, they bear repetition: *Nam Sibyllam quidem Cumis ego ipse oculis meis vidi in ampulla pendere, et cum illi pueri dicerent: Σίβυλλα τί θέλεις; respondebat illa: ἀποθανεῖν θέλω* ('For I myself saw the Sibyl indeed at Cumae with my own eyes hanging in a jar; and when the boys used to say to her, "Sibyl, what do you want?" she replied, "I want to die."') Most strikingly, the question put to her and her answer are in Greek rather than Latin. The Sibyls spoke Greek, delivered their prophecies in hexameters, lived a thousand years, and were notoriously vague. The Cumaean Sibyl's tragedy is this: she had asked Apollo for eternal life, asking to live for as many years as the grains of sand she held in her hand, and Apollo was prepared to strike a deal with her if it included her virginity, which she refused him. Apollo, petulant as gods tend to be, took revenge. As she had neglected to add that she would also like eternal youth he allowed her to age and to dwindle in size until she was nothing more than a bundle of shrunken decrepitude and, finally, no more than a voice. It is a terrible image for not only is she saddled with her diminished state but she carries more heavily than ever the disappointments of the present as well as the burden of the future. Her fate echoes throughout the whole of Eliot's poem, although of course it is his own tormented spiritual condition he describes: 'I was neither / Living nor dead, and I knew nothing, / Looking into the heart of the light, the silence.' This might be the place to remind the reader that Petronius met his end at Cumae, in AD 66 when, at the order of the emperor Nero, he was arrested. Doomed, he took his own life. Tacitus speaks of his eloquent exit:

> Yet he did not fling away life with precipitate haste, but having made an incision in his veins and then, according to his humour, bound them up, he again opened them, while he conversed with his friends, not in a serious strain or on topics that might win for him the glory of courage. And he listened to them as they repeated, not thoughts on the immortality of the soul or on the theories of philosophers, but light poetry and playful verses.

We have a rather better idea of what Lake Avernus was like in ancient times than in almost all the centuries since. There is a massive blank in our knowledge between the end of the Roman Empire, when the region was largely abandoned, and the early mediaeval period. Doubtless people kept on living here, but we know little about them. Presumably they continued to harvest their grapes, the white in particular, the wine of which sits well on the palate. There is an account by the English canon lawyer and writer, Gervase of Tilbury, who, in his early thirteenth-century *Otia Imperialia*, describes a supernatural meeting related to him by John II, bishop of Pozzuoli:

Once he was singing the office of the dead while walking along at random, unremitting as he was in prayer, when he heard the wailing of souls which, from the sound of it, were suffering in the hollow centre of the sulphurous mountain. After a while the bishop conjured one unhappy soul in the name of our Lord Jesus Christ to make known whose soul it was, and for what crime it had brought condemnation on itself. Then the soul he had addressed replied with a human voice, in familiar and sorrowful accents, saying it was the spirit of someone known to him from the neighbourhood, and that it had been sentenced to the several penal fires of Avernus there.

When the bishop enquired what might be done for him, the spirit asked for his prayers so that his soul might be released, step by step, from that purgatorial place. This story, which could be a prose transcription from Dante, neatly falls in with what a man in Naples told me, which I have not heard elsewhere. Salvatore Mazzi, craftsman, was telling me about the small wall shrines or aedicule devoted to the *anime del purgatorio*, with their small naked terracotta human figures waist-deep in flames, like strange potted plants, which are peculiar to Naples, saying they owe their origin to the mediaeval belief that swimming in Lake Avernus could kill one and that it was a purgatorial place. Signor Mazzi makes those terracotta figures. A most lovable man, may his kiln explode if what he tells me is not true.

I think I've just heard the *whumph* an avalanche of tall stories told by a short man makes. I sought support for his idea and found none. Roberto De Simone, when I put it to him, replied with a painful 'Eh?' It was more like a squeak of disgust. There is another school of thought that the idea for those shrines was introduced by the sixteenth-century priest Gaetano dei Conte di Thiene.

Gervase comes up with a puzzling description of Avernus, which he describes as 'the dried up remains of a lake, where the ground is very muddy. If any living creature is driven into this

place it dies at once. Even birds flying overhead are immediately infected by the atmosphere of the place, and died from its effects'. It is an awfully deep lake for it to have gone dry. Still the legend of flying birds falling to their deaths was very much alive in his time. A great traveller and observer Gervase may have been, but one thing will forever blacken him in my eyes. Some years before, in France, he encountered a pretty girl who, when he showed an interest in her, protested that she would suffer eternal damnation if she lost her virginity. Gervase took her for a member of the heretical *publicani* sect who were against procreation, and, as a result of this chance meeting, she was burned at the stake.

Petrarch went to Naples twice, in 1341 and 1343, and it was on the second occasion, when the city was in decline – he describes this fall in the most despairing terms – that he fled into the countryside to see the places Virgil describes. Writing to Cardinal Colonna, albeit from a deeply Christian perspective, he provides an arresting description of Avernus, which once more supports the notion it was a malodorous place:

I have seen the Lucrine lake, famous for its oysters; the lake Avernus, with water as black as pitch, and fishes of the same colour swimming in it; marshes formed by the standing waters of Acheron, and the mountain [Mount Gauro or Barbaro] whose roots go down to hell. The terrible aspect of this place, the thick shades with which it is covered by a surrounding wood, and the pestilent odour which this water exhales, characterise it very justly as the Tartarus of the poets ... I have seen the ruins of the grotto of the famous Cumaean Sibyl; it is a hideous rock, suspended in the Avernian lake. Its situation strikes the mind with horror. There still remain the hundred mouths by which the gods conveyed their oracles; these are now dumb, and there is only one God who speaks in heaven and on earth. These uninhabited ruins serve as the resort of birds of unlucky omen. Not far off is that dreadful cavern which leads, *they say*, to the infernal regions.

What ruins exactly was Petrarch looking at? Could it have been the supposed Temple of Apollo? What is important to note here is that Gervase, Boccaccio, and Petrarch agree on the toxic effect of the place.

In the 1300s, the Angevin rulers of Naples gave Avernus to the Monastery of Santa Chiara and then, in 1750, the Bourbon ruler of Naples, Ferdinand IV, as reward for medical services provided by *dottore* Giuliano Pollios, a name with classical pedigree, gave it to him and his descendants. It stayed with them until 1991 when it was sold to the entrepreneur Raffaele Cardillo who was prevented in the nick of time from transforming the lake into a gigantic tourist complex. Not since Agrippa had there been such a threat to the spiritual integrity of the place. Fortunately the Minister for Cultural Heritage, Ferdinando Facchiano, put out a decree preventing any further development. The trouble did not stop there because one of the Cardillo family, Gennaro, had close connections with the Casalesi, one of the most feared Camorra families in Naples. On 10 July 2010 police impounded the lake, which was used as a hideout by Giuseppe Setola, a hit man for the clan, who would stay at the lake's B&B after his killings. The police action was labelled, predictably enough, 'Operazione Sibilla'. 'Caronte', the guide to the Grotto della Sibilla, was interviewed. Asked whether he had noticed anything suspicious, he replied, 'I have seen nothing and anyway I have no interest in putting my nose in other people's business.' Who can blame him? The matter of who owns what has yet to be settled and, with a decision pending, which is likely to continue deep into the future, what we have here is another shining instance of Italian legal rigmarole.

Ernesto Colluta has worked on the edge of Lake Avernus for a decade although he gives the impression of having been here for centuries, maybe even millennia. It requires no great feat of the imagination to picture him in a toga although first he'd have to remove his thickset glasses. What does he do exactly? He is not really a farmer. Maybe 'agronomist' comes closer, but this would suggest he has made a science of what he does. This seems to be not quite the case, but neither does he spurn knowledge. A good deal of thought goes into what he does. The property is not big enough for him to be able to focus on any one product because there wouldn't be enough of it to make a meaningful profit and so, in addition to growing the fruit and vegetables that he delivers to nearby restaurants, he works with schoolchildren, teaching them the basics of agriculture, and to boost things a bit more, he has picnic grounds and even an outdoor theatre. The first tree one sees upon entering the site grows both oranges and lemons, which suggests that some kind of Luciferian pact with nature has been made.

The family owns thermal baths at nearby Lake Lucrino, a highly successful operation that is believed to be on the very spot where the emperor Nero sweated away his cares. There are traces of an ancient Roman structure that was later expanded in the Middle Ages. It was then abandoned for many centuries until Ernesto's father and uncle took it over in the 1960s. When the family purchased land on Avernus, Ernesto immediately volunteered to manage it. One can see the work suits him although when I suggest it might have been an escape from the semi-naked anthropoidal shapes in open bathrobes that wallow about the spa he demurs a little. 'No, *why*?' What he does he does because of the pleasure it affords him, a feeling of peace. When the day's work is done he returns to his family in Lucrino. A man who watches the waters, it was he who apprised me of the colour change. A thoughtful figure, clearly happy to be where he is, Ernesto admits that it is never with his feet on the ground because here the ground is never a constant, but maybe, just to take things full circle, the earth's mutability makes a natural philosopher of him. When he speaks it is with the voice of a man who closely observes.

'One can say everything begins here.'

We sat on a wooden bench with a full view of the lake, birds chirping in the branches, no memory in their small brains of just how dangerous it was for their ancestors once upon a time. They dart over the lake with no ill effects, maybe just a bit too sure of themselves. What Ernesto told me about beginnings makes chronological sense. The Sibyl, when Virgil sang her into verse, was 700 years old at the time and so exactly as old as the Greek presence in southern Italy. Another 300 years would see Rome decked out in Christmas lights although, admittedly, I may be guilty here of toying with time.

'I am very lucky to be able to work in this way,' Ernesto began. 'Certainly it beats the sulphur mines. Also I like the way we must adapt our way of thinking, so as to give ourselves reason to live in this territory. One must be awake because no one plans anything and every day brings something different. I must be in good order so as to be able to take my skin home. We are relaxed because we are under blue skies, we are in a good place, but without planning there can be no insurance for the future. You have to be awake. When my feet are on the ground, I don't move, but then the ground moves. So where is our anchor? We don't have one. The soil and the geological part of this territory are alive and could suddenly change our reality. We all need anchors, of course. If we don't have them then we must build them, but rather than do it with stones we create idols and miracles. It is not quite so interesting, building with stones. We require other kinds of anchors, idols we can recognise. This idol, whoever he is, may live fifty years. He dies. No problem. We'll produce another. A new one is born every other day. Totò is one such, Maradona another. These are the small fixed points that hold together the pieces of our culture, but even so we can easily lose them. We can sanctify anyone, anything. I don't know whether there is anywhere else in the world where twice a year, on the first weekend in May and on 19 September, there is a miracle. San

Gennaro. We begin to understand something important when we realise that we, too, are nature, but with our cultural evolution we have built a wall of separation between humanity and nature. Always it is man *and* nature, the injunction being to love and respect nature but only as something alien to ourselves. We gradually take over the space between ourselves and nature. The rock here is tuff. It is everywhere, but with wind and rain it soon turns to dust. I see rocks that no longer look the same as they did twenty years ago. The bigger structures require attention. The place is for me something that is alive, with everything becoming older and more fragile, and then rebuilt out of its own materials. There is a beautiful paradox because all this richness you see has come out of destruction. The grapes are as they are because of a volcano that probably caused the extinction of Neanderthal man in Europe, and yet for us it is not terrifying. It is a normal way to live. We have a volcanic phenomenon called bradyseism, which means there is a continuous movement of the ground. It is rising here like a cake in an oven. We know everything could change in a very short time. About ten or twelve years ago, after talking with other people, I began to think that there must be a connection between geological movement and our local anthropology.'

Ernesto pointed to one of the hills on the other side of the lake.

'What you see there, Monte Nuovo, was born in a single night.'

A cinder cone volcano, Monte Nuovo came into being on 29 September 1538 although it was not until 6 October that it took its present shape. It was the first volcano in modern times for which there survive written testimonies, among them Francesco del Nero's. Watching the show in nearby Pozzuoli, he wrote: 'About this time fire issued forth with such force, noise and shining light that I, who was standing in my garden, was seized with great terror.' And then we hear Antonio Russo's strangely intimate story of how, at the gates of Pozzuoli, he saw one Zizula, wife of Geronimo Barbiero, who escaped from the village of Tripergole on a horse, riding it like a man, hooded, wearing only a blouse. There's some ambiguity in his account. Was Russo saying something about the state of her marriage? Where was Barbiero? Tripergole was completely covered along with Cicero's villa. Another consequence of the eruption was that Lake Lucrino was greatly diminished in size, virtually squeezed into a pond, which did it for the oysters that in earlier days could be found there in abundance.

'Monte Nuovo is a reminder of just how quickly things here can change,' Ernesto continued. 'The effects are dual in nature. The positive is to be able to take the good of today, which is not such a bad way to live. The negative is that it is very difficult to plan for the future. You can see it everywhere, in our public administration, for example. Whatever they do is done as an emergency and so nothing is ever really planned. They do not look into the future.'

'The mythological aspect of this place must be something you feel every day.'

'Yes, I feel it. I don't know if it is a physical question or a matter of transcendence, but I feel it physically. I am not religious yet I feel something powerful coming from this soil, this nature. The real power of this place is that you feel it, but you don't get to keep it. It is strange that while we never plan anything we keep on living so strongly, so healthily. You see that nature is still mighty, stronger than our human will, and stronger than all anthropological and anthropic pressure. There is something ... I don't know if it is about the mythology. I think that this power is the reason for the mythology and not the other way round. The place itself creates myth.'

The splendidly named Salomon Kroonenberg would agree. In his 2013 book *Why Hell Stinks of Sulfur: Mythology and Geology of the Underworld* (I love the sound of the Dutch original, *Waarom de hel naar zwavel stinkt*) he wonders why Avernus and not Solfatara, with its sulphuric reek, was Virgil's choice as the entrance to Hades. Kroonenberg produces a tactful response. The latter was a Roman spa and as such it would have been bad faith to brand as hell a place advertised for its curative properties. Also, it seems likely that at the time Lake Avernus was smellier and no bird flew across it unless intending suicide. Why else would Virgil refer to 'the foul jaws of stinking Avernus'? Somewhat chillingly, Kroonenberg, a geologist by trade, notes that Solfatara is merely a part of the greater complex that is the Campi Flegrei caldera otherwise known as the Phlegraean Fields or 'the fields of fire':

> It makes no difference where Aeneas entered the underground – at Lago Averno, Solfatara, the Dog Cave, Astroni crater or Il Pericolo – because under the ground they all come together in the same magma chamber. They are all small, bubbling outlets of the same immense volcano. Hell is a little larger than Virgil imagined.

Campi Flegrei is not the sum total of its parts, it is a synthesis – and all the scarier for it. Meanwhile, in 2016, the blood of San Gennaro failed to liquefy, a sign of ill fortune, which has led the more credulous of Neapolitans to look askance at the immediate future.

Ernesto had a rather prosaic take on the efforts made by archaeologists and literary people alike to identify the places most closely associated with mythology and folklore.

'The problem began with the first archaeologists because rather than look for historical traces they sought mythical ones. They were searching for Apollo, the Sibyl, anything that might relate directly to the ancient stories. The *Aeneid*, the works of Homer, these are not historical works but poems. Still, the early archaeologists wanted verification. "So this is Lake Avernus," they said. "Okay, Aeneas came here. All we've got to do is prove it." They had to find the temple of Apollo and the Sibyl's cave. So they called the structure over there the Temple of Apollo whereas really it was a Roman spa. At Cumae you had the same problem. They were moved by enthusiasm, their love of myth and not by the historical traces. The Sibyl may have shrivelled to a mote of dust but it doesn't mean she's dead, does it?'

'It is understandable surely,' I argued. 'As a writer the temptation is to give a pattern to what one sees and make ends meet because you want everything to make sense and cohere. This said, it is still a place of mythology.'

'I'll relate a story in which you may find an interesting connection between mythology and fact, and which shocked me albeit in a good way. We know the mythological history of this lake and that it was considered the physical passage between life and death. So it stands to reason there must be a door where on one side we have life and on the other, death. I had been making the sets for a play we performed here, a rather complex retelling of the story of Nero and Seneca. The plot required a raft, so I built one. I had an old anchor, but as I didn't have a rope I bought a new one of forty metres. The depth of Lake Avernus is thirty-six to forty metres. It was a pure white cotton rope. Afterwards, I left the raft anchored on the lake. A year later, I had to move it. I pulled up the rope. As one might expect there was greenish algae stuck to it, but suddenly, after ten metres, the rope was pure white. It was like new, the remaining thirty metres absolutely white. I found this strange and I began to reflect on the mythological question with respect to this place. I related my discovery to a friend, a chemical engineer who some years before had made an analysis of the water. He explained to me why the rope was white. There is an upper level of "sweet" water measuring ten metres, he told me, which is lighter in density than the water beneath. This first level is clear, sweet water, but the rest is like a liquid fossil and heavier in density because of the minerals, gases and other chemical structures that give out no oxygen. The only thing that survives in those depths is *bacteria anorobisci*, an organism that lives without oxygen, otherwise the lower part of the lake is completely dead. One can imagine between those two layers the meeting point between life and death. Also it is where scientific fact meets up with mythological belief. It was a very good moment for me. Mythology and reality, it is a wonderful symbol for everything here, for Naples, and for our notion about life and death being inseparable.'

The realm of the dead came nearest to the living here.

All my dead rise before me.

Might not the ancients have had a more nuanced take on the afterlife than the Christians? All too often their Underworld, presided over by the deity Hades, has been taken for some old version of our Christian hell. In Hades, however, one may, depending on how virtuous one has been in life, enter the Fortunate Isles, the better precincts of Elysium, which are populated by demigods and heroes, among their number Cadmus, Peleus, and Achilles. And then we have the Asphodel Meadows where those who have neither sinned nor particularly distinguished themselves go, which is a kind of dumping ground for mediocrities. Asphodel Meadows, a good name for an old age home. And then there are the Mourning Fields where those who, like Dido, died for love go. The thing is to be sure, when the time comes, to set off with a coin under your tongue to pay that stinker Charon to ferry you across the River Styx. Clearly Tartarus is not a good place to be, so much so that it is consigned to a place deeper than Hades, as far below it as the earth is beneath the skies. There darkness rules. It is full of people with strange haircuts and tattoos.

'Welcome to Forcella,' they say.

Ciro said something to me, echoes of which I found in Ernesto's words and in what other people have told me, some of them unbelievers. I had asked him why the terracotta figures one sees in the wall shrines are engulfed with flames, as this would seem to be more suggestive of Hell than Purgatory, and he replied that in times past Purgatory didn't have an image, and so it was represented by flames. When I suggested to Ernesto that it seemed as though many Neapolitans preferred to situate themselves in Purgatory rather than in Heaven, he answered, 'We hope for the first because the second is too much to ask for. We have humility. Heaven is for saints. We know we are poor things on earth. We have this phrase, "Stare con i piedi per terra" ("Stay with our feet on the ground"). There's no guarantee we will go to Heaven so it is more pragmatic to hope directly for Purgatory because we know that even if we are in flames there will be people here who'll pray for our souls. This is at the heart of our Misericordia or, rather, our concept of mercy. For every prayer accorded them they will spend less time in Purgatory.'

The historian Jacques Le Goff wrote a book on the subject, *The Birth of Purgatory* (1981), in which he states that the idea of Purgatory, although 'it is made up of many very ancient elements, whose origins often seem to be lost in the depths of time', reached its most concrete form by the end of the twelfth century when finally it could be considered an actual place. 'It is not hard to understand,' he writes, 'why one bit of natural geography attracted particular attention when it came to locating the site of Purgatory, or at least the mouths of Purgatory, on earth: volcanoes.' When Avernus was said to have come into the possession of the Monastery of Santa Chiara it was at the very moment when Purgatory was defined and would very soon find its greatest expression in Dante's *Commedia*. Something else Le Goff writes strikes me: he suggests that the belief in Purgatory took hold 'for reasons that go beyond theology, and it is these other reasons that particularly interest me, because they tell us more than theology does about the relation between belief and society, about mental structures, and about the historical role of the imagination'. The theologians, he reminds us, look upon Purgatory not as a place but a *state*. Purgatory, in the folkloric sense, would seem tailor-made for the agnostic, one of the brightest ideas to have entered our imaginative sphere. And what an incredible bit of religious appropriation, a wondrous instance of career change, that the Sibyl of old with her wild hair, heaving breast and foaming mouth should have become a Christian figure. Her wild trance was explained away by the Augustinian monk and humanist Giles of Viterbo when he visited Cumae in 1499 as having been brought on by sulphurous fumes.

Divinae Institutiones (AD 250) was the first introduction in Latin to the Christian faith and in order to prove the supremacy of the new religion its author, Lactantius, drew heavily on classical Greek and Roman writers. He was the first to say in print that Virgil's *Fourth Eclogue* was a prophecy of the coming of Christ. It made perfect sense to Dante that Virgil should be his guide. And who actually voices that prophecy? Why, it's the Sibyl. While it is just conceivable that the saviour to whom she refers is the hoped-for child of Augustus and Scribonia, there is no escaping the fact the ancient world was in a state of expectation. 'Ultima Cumaei venit iam carminis aetas' ('The final age of the Cumaean song has now arrived'). Even the most hardened atheist would have to agree there was something in the air.

The history of religion is to a huge degree a history of appropriation and it is hard to resist the temptation that Avernus came to be seen as a purgatorial place. Once again, Gervase of Tilbury's account, although it does not mention Purgatory by name, describes such a place. Le Goff writes, 'The century in which this occurred was also the century in which the influence of folklore on the culture of the learned was at its height and the Church was most receptive to traditions that in earlier years it had rooted out, covered up, or ignored.' When presented with the choice, he continues, 'Christianity might well have followed Judaism in choosing a monistic other world – *sheol* – rather than a dualistic one like the Roman Hades and Elysian Fields, the former a place of terror, the latter of happiness. But it adopted the dualistic model and even accentuated some of its features.' So maybe signor Mazzi is not so far off the mark, after all. May his oven thrive.

Some of this is mere speculation but, if so, it comes from what other people have told me. One might say it depends on who one speaks to, but if, as I believe to be the case, the border between life and death in Naples is porous, and what Ernesto has provided me with his story of the rope is an image upon which the mind settles, then I would say Purgatory is the key to the Neapolitan soul, possibly even an escape clause from the dogma of organised religion. And then there is what he also told me: 'Hereabouts, paradise is not such a good place nor is hell such a bad one. You will not find anything all black or all white, all clear or all dark, it is always mixed so when something appears to be white we reckon it must have a black side. When a Neapolitan talks about religion he never talks about God. He talks about Jesus Christ, the Madonna, all the saints, but there is not even a word in Neapolitan that specifically refers to God. They use the Italian word "Dio". Nobody talks with God, they talk with the saints, Christ, and Mary but not with God. He exists, but is untouchable.'

The disbeliever in me concludes the lake is round, the sky blue. All else is stories. The agnostic in me thinks anything is possible, the only certainty being there must have been Sibyls once, just as there have been shamans, sorcerers, and temple priestesses, although I very much doubt they reached a thousand years of age. And now those words attributed to G. K. Chesterton, which apparently are not his at all but Emile Cammaerts on the subject of Chesterton, come back to me, a tidy sentence, proverbial in essence, highly quotable: 'When men choose not to believe in God, they do not thereafter believe in nothing, they then become capable of believing in anything.' Philosophically, though, it is just a bit sticky; mathematically there are too many snags in the filigree. I'll settle for Montaigne's 'Que sais-je?' The believer in me remembers that when I was a small child an itinerant vicar placed his hand, which oddly smelled of tar, on my head, and said to me, 'Sonny, do you believe in God?' and, no cheek intended, I replied, 'Sure, I believe in all of them.' Gods and Sibyls, Hades and Purgatory, we must treat these things as real if we are to grasp what survives of them in modern sensibilities.

'One must be awake,' Ernesto told me. As if to prove his case, he took a phone call, an urgent message saying there was a swarm of bees back at the spa and what was to be done about it. The man normally in charge of the beehives was away and so it fell to Ernesto to make the best of what for him would be his first apiological experience. The spell broken, we grabbed an empty hive, jumped into the car, and drove to Lucrino. The swarm was clamped onto a small tree, deep inside the branches, difficult to get at from any angle. It would require removing the outer branches. The Queen, as it turned out, was most elusive. You don't get her, you don't get the bees. 'Apes enim ego divinas bestias puto,' says Petronius in his *Satyricon*, 'Truly, I think bees are divine creatures.' The link between bees and human souls had already been established before Virgil's time, when, exactly, there's no saying, but when Virgil in the same Book VI of the *Aeneid* has his hero go into Hades where he meets his father

Anchises, Anchises compares the souls of the dead gathered along the Lethe to bees. Some years ago, when I kneeled over the corpse of my friend Arcangelo Riffis, I saw in the space between the raised window and the embrasure a bee hovering, almost a month too early for bees, and then, when we buried him a couple of weeks later, another bee – surely not the same one, but then maybe it was, because there can be no accounting the behaviour of psychopomps – hovered above the coffin as it was lowered into the ground.

Splendid that the swarm chose this of all places, the very spot, so I like to think, where Nero composed his verses. The ancient Romans had a special massage which involved the application of honey to one's muscles. It has been reintroduced at the spa with some success. A samurai in white cotton smock and veil, Ernesto tried to capture the Queen several times, and after each failure had to wait for the bees to re-swarm, which, of course, they did because the message to do so is deeply channelled inside them. There is talk of late, scientifically driven, that bees have consciousness. Who could ever have thought otherwise? Only latterly do the moderns discover what the ancients knew all along. The swarm gathered on one branch, which was lopped off and then they settled on another that, too, had to be removed, so that by the time Ernesto Colluta succeeded there was rather less than before of the original tree.

Street Music

With a Cursory Aside on the Sorrowful Demise of the Quarter Tone

Any day you choose, walk along the street that leads from Piazza del Gesù Nuovo towards Via Duomo; slow down a little as you enter Piazza San Domenico Maggiore, and you will hear street musicians performing anything from tarantella to jazz to opera. A Botticelli-like woman in a diaphanous sky-blue dress plays the harp at the entrance to Santa Chiara; a bearded man who looks as though he has just stepped down from the mountains, unlaced boots, holes in his trousers, plays tarantella on the accordion and sings with a rustic voice, no touristy confection there; a clean-cut man in a dark suit stands stiffly against a wall singing operatic arias with appropriate hand gestures, a deeply melancholy aspect to him. What's his trouble? *Appocundria*,* I suspect.

Street music in Naples is a joy not to be passed by with a tight purse.

So it was in the autumn of 1770 when the music historian Charles Burney visited the place:

---

* An important word the attentive reader will remember from Chapter 3.

This evening hearing in the street some genuine Neapolitan singing, accompanied by a calascioncino, a mandoline, and a violin; I sent for the whole band upstairs, but like other street music, it was best at a distance; in the room it was coarse, out of tune, and out of harmony; whereas, in the street, it seemed the contrary of all this: however, let it be heard where it will, the modulation and accompaniment are very extraordinary.

Burney, though peevish at times, hit on something: the open air is the street musician's true medium. What happens there will not necessarily fly on stage. There we sacrifice our critical faculties for what moves the heart more. So it was when the Sirens with their bonny voices tried to lure Ulysses to their fatal shore. Ulysses commands the crew to plug their ears while he has himself tied to the mast, ears unplugged, the point being he *wants* to be seduced by their song but prevented – some cod psychology here – from being able to act on his desires. One of the Sirens, Parthenope, in despair over their failure to entice Ulysses, drowns herself, thereby giving her name to the ancient city that would one day arise in her wake, which in turn became Neapolis, then Naples. A song might be said to have given birth to a city. Parthenope would later strike a deal with Christendom. At the church of Santa Caterina della Spina Corona, on Via Guacci Nobile, there is a statue of her with water issuing from her breasts, which, so the Latin inscription – *Dum Vesevi Syrena Incendia Mulcet* – informs us, douses the flames of Vesuvius. The popular, more vulgar, name for *la fontana della Spinacorona* is *la fontana della Zizze*. Neapolitans are never less than familiar with their saints and mythic figures.

So it is when one goes down to the seaside where one can listen to the fishermen, repairing their nets, singing with their grizzled voices. 'E si nun canto, io moro.' Words close to proverbial, I've heard them uttered several times: 'If I don't sing, I will die.' So it is that in Naples, another assertion we will let fly – the first assertion, remember, is that melody was born in Naples – even the deaf sing and are not wanting of tune. What's alive here is a melodic strain that has absented itself from much of Berlusconi's trash culture. It's as if for all their misfortunes, and maybe even *because* of them, Neapolitans were given a taste of something they are in no hurry to lose. There are spots on the planet where one finds a species of floating excellence – Istanbul is another such place – and maybe it's because in order to survive at street level one must always be at the top of one's game. The mediocre hasn't got a chance. It was somehow appropriate that the first street singer I should see in Naples was a stout old woman missing a couple of front teeth, clutching a microphone, and singing a popular canzone in a coarse voice against crackly music coming from a heavily bandaged tape recorder. I would see her again, a couple of months later, a slightly younger version in a yellow track suit, at the beginning of John Turturro's irresistible film, *Passione*, his personal exploration of Neapolitan music. It was like I'd been greeted by an old friend although we never spoke.

If one is looking for an image of continuity then go to the National Archaeological Museum where one may stand before a mosaic from Pompeii in which the artist Dioskourides of Samos depicts a wandering group of musicians (*musici ambulanti*), one on double flute, a second on small cymbals, and a third on tympanum which, if one squints one's eyes a little, becomes the tammorra so beloved of southern Italian folk musicians. It is not so hard to guess at the sounds those ancient figures produce. It is heartening to consider that although the clothes may be different, the hairstyles too, there are still many such scenes on the streets of Naples.

When I first saw Zena Rotundi playing her concert harp at the entrance to Santa Chiara she struck me as unapproachable, just like those very cool folk in my days of yore, in the 1960s, when the holes in one's rags had to be in the right places and

style ruled over the heart's occurrences and in order to get close to them one had to be equally cool or a bona fide figure on the pop landscape. I suspected something of that in Zena, what with her beauty and theatrical dress sense, which was why I was hesitant to approach her. When finally I spoke to her and mentioned she'd already slipped into the pages of my book, Zena, a kind of Eliza Doolittle, leapt from her place and made a whoop accompanied by a pirouette, calling out to her friend at one of the street stalls that she was to appear in the pages of *un libro*, the words italicised in her voice. She is, in short, a joyful presence. It is one of the happier, albeit confusing, aspects of Naples that one can't judge by appearances.

We met up later at the Bar 7bello on Via Benedetto Croce, whose owner, Pino De Stasio, had played a pivotal role in her life. Pino's knowledge of music, opera in particular, is profound and often he can be found behind the counter expounding on the merits of different singers, comparing recordings, plucking the high Cs out of the air as one might between thumb and index finger catch falling leaves. A man both robust and delicate, he also provides a piano upon which musicians are welcome to perform. One evening I requested he play the 1939 recording of Beniamino Gigli singing Giulio Caccini's 'Amarilli', which not only silenced the clientele but moved two of them to stand at their table in tribute. There was an audible gasp when I told them that, aged six, I'd seen the elderly Gigli on stage.

Zena Rotundi came to Naples eighteen years ago, from Foggia, which is where Raimondo di Sangro was born in 1710, of whom we shall hear more in due course. Zena strikes me as yet a further instance that the city's deep creative vigour can be so often traced to people who have come there from elsewhere. A spray of salt-water, a few choice phrases in the Neapolitan language, a philosophical shrug of the shoulders in the face of overwhelming odds, a snoot cocked at Vesuvius, and, presto, one has become a native. She went to university in Naples, the very one where, according to Jacopo Martorelli, Homer founded the chair of Greek studies. She graduated in philosophy and then she did as any sensible woman would do and found her vocation as a street musician. The street, precarious though it is, is where she finds her true mode of life. She teaches Greek and Latin on the side, as well as harp to children who can barely reach the strings but who make her feel even more at home. Although warm in nature, she has the toughness requisite to working at street level, which is why she has been dubbed *fiore d'acciaio* ('steel flower'). This is not to confuse her with the Italian title of the American movie *Steel Magnolias*, which stars Dolly Parton, and is about a sisterhood every bit as durable. You can see the metal in her eyes when tourists try to take selfies with her. She does not like to be suffocated, which is problematic because hers is a most magnetic presence.

She did not immediately take to Naples but now, like Virgil, a magus who wrote poems on the side, is quite happy for it to be her final resting place. It was only after she learned 'Pulcinella's Secret' – in 2013 she performed with the Pulcinella maestro, Bruno Leone – that she came to understand that the city would reveal itself to her in direct proportion to the readiness of the mind to open itself up to it. It opened her eyes, becoming, paradoxically, more and more a city of the esoteric. She fears, as do many people, that the light is beginning to be expunged from the historical centre, that too much of its soul is being given over to tourism. She performs there, but lives in the Quartieri Spagnoli where she feels the old Naples is still very much alive.

'I am usually found here, although this area is becoming more and more like a postcard. There is a strong contrast between light and dark in other areas of the city but not so much here any more, which is the part most tourists see. This street used to be full of music stores, but they are beginning to close and are being replaced by touristy restaurants and cafés. The old centre is losing its character. Another thing I feel intensely is the humility of the people. You know nothing about them and then you discover he or she is a musician or somebody else studies or works in some important field. The thing I love most about this place is that people are always a surprise. You have to know them and discover what they have to say. This city makes you free. I am a free spirit. Also people on the street create jobs in order to survive. There is a professor of mathematics on the street here.* There is a strong connection between what he does and the old *smorfia*†. People keep an element of magic about themselves. A friend of mine speaks regularly to a statue of Eduardo De Filippo on a balcony here in Spaccanapoli, and in return Eduardo offers suggestions to him to do this and not to do that.'

A year ago, in June, Zena made the news. She wishes it were not so, but then it was to be a blessing in disguise. The news was bad enough to become positive. She used to keep her instrument in a lock-up in a friend's theatre. One morning she went there,

---

* At his Università stradale at the corner of Piazza San Domenico Giuseppe Polone, the master of magic squares, can be found rain or shine, wearing his mortarboard, pointer in hand, mathematical charts pasted onto the wall. I did try to get his story once, but he was most elusive, the only answer he gave being when I asked him how he came to be a mathematician. Polone told me he got lost for five days in the Amazon jungle and in order to keep track of time he resorted to devising mathematical formulae. '*Dopo Pitagora e Einstein vengo io*,' he says. 'After Pythagoras and Einstein comes me.'

† *La smorfia* (literally 'the grimace') is the tradition of interpreting dreams so as to obtain the numbers to play in the national lottery. Not only objects but also the events, emotions, and people that appear in dreams are assigned numbers. A naked woman, for example ('*a femmena annura* in Neapolitan), is '21' whereas if the focus is on her naked leg ('*e ccos'd 'e ffemmn*) the number is '77'. Curiously enough, '77' is also the number for the Devil. Most likely, *la smorfia* has its origins in 'Morpheus', the Greek god of dreams. The Neapolitan system is a descendant of the ancient Greek practice of oneirocriticism, the interpretation of dreams.

the door was locked as usual, but when she opened it the harp was gone.

'There was a security camera and so I went to the police to ask them to watch the video, but unfortunately that day we were having an election for a new mayor and they were too busy to see me. Another street musician told me to come here to the Bar 7bello and talk to Pino De Stasio. I made a video with him, telling my story and asking whoever took my harp to give it back. As soon as I uploaded the video onto Facebook people came to the Bar 7bello to give money, and this was before the actual fundraising began. Then I was contacted by the police who told me in confidence they knew who stole the instrument. I think they'd made some kind of agreement with the thief. This is typical of Naples. Where I kept my instrument something else happened. They stole 10,000 euros' worth of chocolate from a woman who had stored it there to sell at Christmas. Clearly someone who had a key to the place knew our movements. A month ago, in a place near here, some people gave a performance which made 1500 euros and the person in charge of the money, who I thought was a good guy, stole it. We know he had the keys to this door. He ran away to Milan after they discovered what he'd done. Probably he was the one who took the harp, but almost certainly he did not act alone. It had been well organised, and probably he was the one who opened the door and told the others the time and the place.'

'It must be difficult to sell a stolen harp,' I said.

'I don't think they intended to sell it. It was, in a sense, a kidnapping. "You give me money, I'll give you back your harp." I started fundraising in other places and then the newspapers ran articles about me. I lost the instrument on 18 June and on 21 June it was Music Day in Europe and people organised events, with even the mayor of Naples dedicating a concert to me. My harp teacher came with three other classical harpists, professional musicians, and played in Piazza San Domenico. While they played the concert was put online. It was such a beautiful thing, all these people playing for me. This could not have happened anywhere else. I bought a new instrument in Bergamo and the guy who sold me the instrument also helped me with the price. In a single week I raised 2500 euros without working! I opened the package containing the instrument here in the 7bello. This was a great manifestation of love. A month before my instrument was stolen I refused two jobs because I wasn't ready, because I was too scared. So this raised my sense of self-worth. I had more self-confidence after this. Thinking back on what I'd been through, the thief did something good for me.'

At this point tears filled Zena's eyes.

'I named my new harp "Parthenope",' she wept, 'in honour of Naples.'

She had one more story to tell me, which at first she said ought not to go into print for fear it might create a diplomatic incident, but when I persuaded her of how people back home would appreciate its humour she relented. On 19 September 2016, San Gennaro's day, Prince Charles who is of Bourbon (or, in Italian, Borbone) descent and the Duchess of Cornwall visited Naples. Charles went north to Vicenza and Camilla, wearing a pearl choker necklace with a round diamond clasp, which is inadvisable because thieves think nothing of snatching jewellery from one's person, stayed behind and visited various local sites.

'She came to Santa Chiara because one of Charles's ancestors is buried there and when she and her retinue came out they found me. They asked about me. When the camera was off I spoke with Camilla. I told her I liked the history of the Borbone. She took a badge and put it on me and nominated me royal harpist to the Borbone. She then sent over a little girl to give me some money. It was just a few pennies. I thought to myself, "Borbone?" "No, *barboni* [tramps]!"'.

✳

A single drop of it is enough to induce oblivion. There is no gradual escalation. Suddenly you're there, and in order to survive the wrench from ordinary existence you and whoever you choose to squire might better make a space for yourselves amid the sweating bodies. One might go so far as to say those gyrating figures have been emancipated from time. A frenzy of arms, swaying hips, nimble feet, the tarantella, so very erotic and at the same time chaste, promises deliverance to young and old alike. It's the dance which legend says owes its name to the spider bite that sends one clean over the edge and the only cure for which is to dance, dance, and dance until one drops, at which point, with luck, the venom will have been sweated out, the tremors will stop, and one may rejoin the human race. Maybe one should speak of this in the past tense because spiders these days seem to act with increasing decorum in direct proportion to the worsening behaviour of the human species. One hears so little about spider bite nowadays. The state it was said to have induced, tarantism, most commonly affected women of the lower classes. Some scholars say that all this malarkey about spiders was a mere cover for the release of unseemly orgiastic desires. Small wonder ladies of distinction did not fall victim to it, although Boccaccio would say they skipped ceremony and didn't need as much to get them onto their mattresses. Others have likened the dance to religious mania and indeed there are sects whose physical response to various stimuli – some of it staged, some of it inexplicable – might be said to resemble a corybantic dance, the rapture it causes bringing one into the presence of the gods themselves. It could be a form of mass psychogenic illness, of course, a common diagnosis made by people seeking to condemn other people for simply enjoying themselves. There were similar outcries when in 1959 Chubby Checker introduced the twist, which, as I remember, rather than leading to erotic excess produced a rather nasty stitch in one's side. Still there must be something not quite right about the way these people move because in 186 BC the Roman Senate, in a fit of righteousness such as occurs from time to time, outlawed the Dionysian rites. Ancient killjoys in togas drove the Bacchanalian dance underground only for it to re-emerge, centuries later, as a cure for spider bite. The old gods were laid to rest, although I think some of them were merely napping while others disguised themselves in sackcloth and ashes, and people began to seek sanction from the Catholic Church for their euphoric activities. After a performance musicians would often place their instruments on the altar to be cleansed of whatever impurities might have seeped in from a profane mind. Between the fifteenth and the seventeenth centuries an epidemic of tarantism spread through the town of Taranto which gave its name to the local spider, not the newsworthy tarantula that from time to time shows up in crates of bananas, but the wolf spider whose Latin name is *Lycosa tarantula*. (It is all a bit confusing to one who doesn't know his Theraphosidae from his Lycosidae, and now there's another school of thought and it's that the wolf spider has been unfairly blamed and that it was a different spider altogether, *la malmignatta* or the European black widow.) The physician Giorgio Baglivi (1668–1707) wrote a treatise based on his studies, *De anatome, morsu et effectibus Tarantulae*, which describes what happens when one is subjected to the bite: 'At the moment of the bite the tarantula injects an almost imperceptible fluid, the poison, which immediately kills the patient with its contagion *when music and dance are not ready*.' The repetitive and accelerated 6/8 rhythm of the dance, he goes on to explain, induces convulsions in the dancer that release him from the spider's poison. It is also remarked that musicians would walk through the fields in the event (dare one say *hope?*) of someone getting bitten. Maybe, though, it is best not to confuse any further the solitary dance that is done to alleviate the effects of spider bite with what over time has become a dance for couples.

All this is a preamble to what I am about to relate, which is that one sunny afternoon in April 2017, in a walled garden in the neighbourhood of Rione Sanità, a woman with honey-coloured hair and freckles invited me to dance the tarantella with her. An old weakness for freckles was not enough to lure me into the mêlée. It was much too complicated this system whereby each man and each woman knows or anticipates what the other is going to do, which draws upon knowledge that has been in the blood for centuries. I would have loved to have joined her and to have shown her steps unique in the history of dance, but doing one's own thing simply won't wash in this part of the world where people will not tolerate innovation for innovation's sake. It is not because they are stubbornly conservative but because they have taken too much trouble in bringing the aesthetic into their lives for it to be squandered on egotistical exercises. They know what best to preserve, which, in the face of junk culture, has never been more difficult to achieve. I did not wish to profane an ancient ritual and so I watched from a safe distance. A man with a hosepipe sprinkled the earth to stop the dust from peppering people's eyes. The dancing couples seemed to be blind to everything around them and yet, in an order known only to themselves, were so secure that they never collided. I watched a small girl of about five, on her own, swaying her hips, absorbing what one day will be her tribute to ancient vice.

The performers were members of one of the most popular street bands in Naples, Ars Nova, with Marcello Squillante on accordion and guitar, Gianluca Fusco guitar, accordion, and *gaita* (bagpipe), Michelangelo Nusco violin, mandolin, baglamas, trumpet, and trombone, Vincenzo Racioppi mandolin and charango, the latter a South American import, Bruno Belardi double bass and Antonino Anastasia percussion, consummate musicians all of them. Apropos of Charles Burney, they fly as well onstage as they do outside. If ever there is a successor to the superb Nuova Compagnia di Canto Popolare then I think Ars Nova is a strong candidate.

I met Ars Nova at an abandoned palazzo which the local government had the good sense to allow to be used for cultural activities. Their most recent recording, *Chi fatica se more 'e famme* ('Whoever Works Will Die of Hunger'), is a musical record of a journey made through the folk traditions of southern Italy. After they did the recording Marcello discovered it was made in the very building where his father was born. The title of the CD comes from the satirical song 'Trapanarella' by Eugenio Pragliola, also known as 'Cucciariello' and 'Eugenio cu 'e lente', this second moniker probably a reference to the horn-rimmed glasses he wore. Eugenio Pragliola (1907–89), whom I briefly memorialise here, took his accordion onto trams and buses and although no master of the instrument it didn't matter because the accordion which he squeezed rather than fingered served as the rhythmic bedrock of his improvised, often satirical, verses. As he went down the aisles, he could adjust the lyrics according to the faces of people he encountered. The only music of his that survives is a private recording of eight minutes, which can be heard on the internet. I should think his ghost would be quite bewildered by this posthumous existence. 'Chi fatica se more 'e famme': what is being said in that line is that one doesn't make money by working because one would starve – you make money only if you already have money, a message that would not have been lost on the commuters from the working-class district where he lived. Ars Nova chose well for they have taken their bearings from a stock figure that is all but gone, but without whom there would have been an irreparable break in the evolutionary music chain. We must honour the likes of Signor Pragliola and every musician that has come before and after him. It was no accident that the American ethnomusicologist Alan Lomax described his year in Italy making field recordings as the happiest of his life:

> The rugged and lovely Italian peninsula turned out, in fact, to be a museum of musical antiquities, where day after day I turned up ancient folk song genres totally unknown to my colleagues in Rome. By chance I happened to be the first person to record in the field over the whole Italian countryside, and I began to understand how the men of the Renaissance must have felt upon discovering the buried and hidden treasure of classical Greek and Roman antiquity. In a sense, I was a kind of musical Columbus in reverse.

I, too, would experience that happiness many times – in Pagani at a festa in honour of the Virgin of the Hens, at Somma Vesuviana, on the steps of the municipal hall where a group of about thirty people came especially from out of town in order to sing their hearts out in Naples, and when late one night, while Ars Nova played, I watched Zena Rotundi dance over the cobblestones as if upon ice.

Speaking of their music, the members of Ars Nova describe themselves as simply the latest chapter in an enormous book, an ancient story that constantly changes over time, and whose evolution depends on the characters and features of the different performers from this and other periods. The performance of an old song sung now or even ten years ago might sound radically different from a rendition of twenty years earlier and yet the greater number of those songs have their origins in simple arrangements for tammorra and voice, which over time became more complex with the addition of other instruments. It is still, at base, music made by the people. I asked them about the *tammurriata* or the 'dance of the drum' – the folk dance of Campania belonging to the *tarantella* tradition. Marcello replied, 'There is a message behind it which is difficult to explain. It can take a whole book to describe it or just a couple of words.'

'Shall we go with the latter then?'

'It's *a moment*. It is not so much the traditional song we know as it is a moment with dance and voice, an occasion to be together and to communicate in a different way. The idea of *tammurriata* is to break the limits of people, to push them to the point of explosion. One may ask whether this is life or theatre. We say it's life. There are parties where rather than play for ten or twenty minutes, which is what we do on the street, we'll play for a couple of hours at a time. We enter another zone. Often, when we finish, we ask ourselves, "Why did we play for two hours? *How*?" We don't understand it. We just *do* it. Many people use drugs and alcohol as a way of exploring themselves, but for us it is music that takes us into another part of the mind, another part of the world or even as far as paradise. It is a way to go outside ourselves. When the people dance they are not tired whereas if someone sings for a very long time he can lose his voice or if he plays the tammorra for that period it is not easy to maintain the rhythm. It is in order to push themselves to the absolute limit.'

'Yesterday,' I told them, 'a girl with freckles asked me to dance with her. Sadly I had to decline.'

'We are glad you did not try to dance! We appreciate this because you understood it is a moment, something special.

Sometimes people come and do whatever they like, but for all their efforts they find no place for themselves. When we go to the more traditional villages where there is music and dance we always stand a bit on the outside because it would be wrong of us to interrupt *their* moment. It belongs to them alone. We don't want to push ourselves inside their picture.'

'So one does not decide but rather is *moved* to dance, is that the difference?'

'Yes, and it is a big difference. The idea of what we do is not so much the song but the dance.'

'Which is like the ancient Greeks? The dance of life and death?'

'Roberto de Simone studied this music in depth and wrote a trilogy of books in which he puts the songs he collected from the different regions into three boxes – life, death, and sex – which represent our biggest fears. A woman can be inside all three, a mother sometimes, a lover, or the face of death. Many years ago, travellers coming to Campania described the tarantella as the sexual act. Sexual and sacred, they are linked. Before we prayed to the Virgin Mary we prayed to Aphrodite or Diana. If you go to the church of San Paolo Maggiore at the end of San Gregorio Armeno you will find it is built on an ancient temple. It is a perfect image of the stratification of all that we have here, where the Virgin Mary is built over the figures of ancient Greek divinities.'

'Yes, I know in my heart Naples is half pagan!'

'We are losing our paganism a little.'

'Did you ever meet Roberto De Simone?'

'A decade ago,' Marcello replied, 'Antonino and I gave a performance for him. It was incredible. He described us as good musicians, but said of us that rather than being in the traditional mould we were an urban phenomenon, a verdict with which I agree. We were born here and so we must study the tradition of our place. Our families listened to Neapolitan music, much of it rooted in the eighteenth and nineteenth centuries. We do the same thing only with different instruments, different volume, different communities. And there are people from the poor areas like For-cella and Secondigliano who now perform Neomelodic music. Originally, though, here it was the story of guitar and mandolin whereas in the country it was the tammorra. If you listen to the old recordings you will find the singers had the quarter tone, which is incredible. You do not find this any more. They would find their notes somewhere in the middle. You will not find this in piano music. Only with the violin and the voice can you reach for those notes. Oriental music has instruments with the quarter tone. We lost this because we followed western ways. I disagree with De Simone when he says the tradition is finished because some of that story survives in the art of the old people, but then he was the first to collect and preserve this music. Without him it would have been completely lost.* The truth is somewhere in the middle. I understand him when he speaks of the young people as having destroyed this music. It's why we lost the quarter tone. All those people who go to tammorra and dance workshops destroy the very thing they are trying to save. It is an academic approach and not the right way to go. On the other hand, I do not come from farming people, I come from Naples. This is my dress code. Why, if I go to Somma Vesuviana, should I change my musical clothes?'

'Is there a quantifiable difference between performing for a special occasion and on the street?'

'Sometimes there is none. Yesterday it was like on the street, which is where we feel most comfortable. We can decide when to start and when to finish whereas if we perform in a theatre it is difficult for people there to dance.'

---

* Roberto De Simone issued much of this music, as well as folk rituals, from Campania in a monumental series of recordings entitled *Son sei sorella* ('They Are Six Sisters') which are accompanied by a 372-page book.

'Is there a kind of code of the street?'

'There are no written rules, but we know them more or less. We know each other well enough. The street is a beautiful thing in Naples because we are free and we do not hate each other. It is permitted to sing here whereas in Rome the relationship between street musicians is often very strained. We travel in a camper and there are places we would like to stop but can't. The rules are that you need documents and have to fit into a precise schedule. Sometimes people find their ideal place in the street and try to treat it as if it is their own property. This happened to us in Rome. We got into arguments with people because we found ourselves in their places. You have to be flexible.'

'The street is also a place where you can thrive or be destroyed.'

'It is difficult to survive on the street, but in terms of spirit it is a good place.

'There is one danger in Naples,' I said, thinking of a couple of musicians I'd seen. 'I am beginning to notice Neapolitan kitsch being played to tourists.'

'This is dangerous not only for us but for our society as a whole. This kind of tourism is dangerous for our relationship. It is like a form of colonisation. In the past two years we have seen our old city centre destroyed. It used to be like a village. People are now speaking of gentrification but their fears come very late in the day. There are B&Bs everywhere. For those of us who actually live here it is very difficult to pay the rent. It is incredible that our supposed intelligentsia should write so positively in the newspapers about the tourist boom in this city whereas people who actually live here understand it's not at all a good thing. The danger this poses to our music is that one day we may find ourselves playing only to tourists. It is not the fault of the tourists who work all year and then come for ten days of holidays. They pay to see what they want to see. In the eighteenth century popular music changed because of the Grand Tour, with people coming from France, Spain, and England. The musicians moved from the street into bars and small theatres and, as if in a circus, started wearing typical folk costumes and played tammorra just for tourists. This was a big change. It was like what you get now in Spain with flamenco music. You don't see any actual gypsies. After two years this place is beginning to resemble Luna Park.'

'So you are fighting for the cultural survival of Naples.'

'We are not fighting for Naples. We are playing for it. We are simple guys trying to send this message.'

Maria Cerbone, *zingara*. When I first heard her she was playing on accordion and singing 'Nascette mmiez'o mare' ('Born in the Middle of the Sea'), a song penned by Roberto De Simone although it draws on the anonymous 'Michelemmà' collected in the seventeenth century by the poet and painter Salvator Rosa. The song tells of the fate of a young woman who falls into the hands of Turkish pirates. A potted history of Naples, a story of oppression, it has been made famous through the rendition by Concetta Barra who to my ears is one of the world's most haunting voices, a voice beaten into truth in the way Edith Piaf's or Billie Holiday's were, a voice akin to those voices that in the memorable phrase of a late friend of mine 'scrape heaven, scrape hell'. The song with its thick knots of historical reference is virtually untranslatable, but at its core is the idea of Naples as a beautiful prostitute who must sell herself in order to survive.

Zingara is Italian for 'female gypsy', which is how Maria Cerbone first introduced herself to me. She even presented me with a card: 'Maria Cerbone Zingara'. She owns a smartphone too. Modernity's a bit of a damper sometimes. Still all my adolescent fantasies rose to the surface, old memories of Rowena Farre's *A Time from the World* (1962), which tells the story of the author's travels with British tinkers and gypsies before they were hard put upon by a world for which freedom of movement is anathema, when it was caravans and bangles, and when Xavier Petulengro ruled the roads and wrote the 'Your Fates in the Stars' astrology column in the *Sunday Chronicle*, and so I was a bit crestfallen when Maria confessed she was not a gypsy, not as such, a gypsy in the soul perhaps, but not in the blood, which rather took the zing out of things for me although if the O.E.D. defines *zing* as 'energy, vigour, liveliness' then she is what she claims to be. When she performs she beats time with her foot upon which there is an anklet of small bells. An Indian gold filigree nose ring could not but add to the general allure.

Aged eighteen she worked in the fields, gathering vegetables, and, a few years later, there was some unhappy business that forced her to re-evaluate things a little. This, in part, is a story of how people get to be where they are, whether it is by circumstance or by choice.

'Nothing happens without a reason,' Maria said. 'There is always an explanation behind everything. My friend gave me an accordion because he saw something in me. It was like medicine for the soul. Music filled the gaps in me and I played from Rome to Naples. It is not simple. You have to face what people think of you, the way they stare. You can see in their eyes how well you are doing. I have had to question myself, but at least people here do not have set rules. You can ask for money in the street. The thing about Naples is that it takes a lot of energy. Sometimes I need to take a breath. There is this eternal struggle. It's like a link the city offers you. Whoever lives here has to die here. There's always something that drags one back here. I may change my ideas about things but I'm convinced I'll die here.'

What's become of Roberto? Dov'è Roberto Talarico? What news of him since he set his accordion on fire? Accordions don't exactly grow on trees. Any more than harps do. Somebody told me that first he hurled the instrument with such force it came close to doing serious injury to a small girl who ducked just in time. She might have been killed, my informant cried. Not so. The 'small girl' was in fact the diminutive figure of Bruno Belardi, double bassist with Ars Nova, and even then he wasn't in the line of fire. Still it is not what one does, not according to any book of etiquette. Surely there is a clause on the indelicacy of throwing accordions at people. Who would think to bring his own butane? Was what he did some kind of symbolic gesture? A misguided sacrifice on the altar of love? Whatever made the serpent in his head strike, I don't think we'll hear from him any time soon. *Come back, Roberto, wherever you are. We'd like an explanation or, if not, then at the very least some kind of alibi otherwise how can we plead your case?*

'Are you absolutely sure?' I kept asking the people who knew him. 'Why would he destroy the very thing that keeps him alive?' Various theories were put forth, perhaps the most optimistic of them being that by wrecking his livelihood Roberto Talarico had set the stage for some kind of rebirth. *Speranza* is Italian for hope. There's a hole in the bag where I put it. Mostly drugs were held to blame for his erratic behaviour although one person swore he never touches them, at least not the harder stuff. Already I'd been put in a moral quandary, such as writers go through from time to time, when I heard that the theft of his instrument the year before was not quite as he had related it to me. Verisimilitude counts for much when one's in danger of being made to look gullible. Yet I didn't want to expose him either. I'm nobody's judge. Consider a man who is where he is. Such a one tells lies either in order to gain or so as not to lose. Whichever way he goes, what he gains or loses will be very little. Somehow, though, the business with the smashed accordion has given me licence to lift the seal I'd placed upon my tongue. A man who destroys his instrument destroys a sacred bond and, with it, the possibility of human discourse. There is a story here that goes straight to the heart of the city's myriad ambiguities.

When I last saw Roberto a beautiful young woman with the sensuality of a panther stalked back and forth in front of where he played in his customary spot opposite the entrance of the Monastero di Santa Chiara. I don't have to dig all too deeply into my encyclopaedia of clichés to come up with that description of her, but then nothing else in the animal kingdom comes close. She was more panther, say, than Welsh corgi. She was carrying a tammorra which might have been for decorative purposes. Although not yet eighteen she had the operatic haughtiness of a woman twice her age. They had holed themselves up in an abandoned house close to the sea, at Posillipo, no electricity, no water, she several steps down from a comfortable home life, he a step up from the homelessness of the year before. Apparently their neighbours gave them food and water, which was awfully nice of them although I wouldn't bet on their good nature lasting beyond threshing time. Country life produces in the minds of certain people a strange belief in the ability of nature to provide sustenance without so much as having to pick up a hoe. A turnip is not necessarily one of God's miracles whereas the man who grows one may well be. Might one not say the same for instruments and those who play them?

A year ago, there was warmth in his eyes. This year I wasn't so sure. I thought it would be a grand reunion. It was a fizzle. Maybe he was distracted by a new romance. 'Sono stanco,' he said as he packed away his instrument. 'I'm tired.' That was the last I saw of him. It did occur to me he might have felt he'd revealed too much of himself the year before. Was there something he would like to have clawed back, blanket over with quicklime? Maybe he sensed there was one more question I needed to put to him, which I'd been too polite to ask last time. If his answer was to be a yes, or, rather, if it was a *no* clearly indicating its opposite, and if he knew I knew his version of events was not without its deficiencies, then we'd no longer be able to speak eye to eye. The news was that Roberto had misbehaved of late, broken street rules, stepped onto other buskers' patches or else invaded their aural space, drowning them out with his music. A week before the mighty conflagration, some musicians from Calabria came to Naples. Roberto joined them on stage and they began to scold him because he was outplaying them. 'It is not the right moment,' one of them said, 'wait a bit.' Roberto flew into a rage. Maybe that is it, he has fallen victim to excessive pride. Anyway it's not how things are done on the streets of Naples.

I first met Roberto in the spring of 2016. A few bars of his music were enough to persuade me that his musical roots go deep. A man possessed, he played the tarantella of his native Calabria with a rawness, a sureness that quickened the senses. As people strolled past him the rhythm of his music entered their bodies. A monk cakewalked across the street and kissed him on the forehead. I need only pause to remember those performances, which took place almost always at sundown, and I can still hear his playing and his voice. What he played was, for lack of a better phrase, 'the real thing', issuing from somewhere deep within the earth itself, that quality which Spaniards, or the more sensitive of them, call *duende*. The poet Lorca describes it better than anyone: 'Those black sounds are the mystery,' he writes, 'the roots fastened in the mire that we all know and ignore.' Marcello Squillante who knows what's what tells me Roberto hearkens back to a musical tradition that is all but gone. What happens, though, when one pours lighter fluid over those roots? When one destroys what maketh one? 'Where is the *duende*?' Lorca continues. 'Through the empty arch comes a wind, a mental wind blowing relentlessly over the heads of the dead, in search of new landscapes and unknown accents; a wind that smells of baby's spittle, crushed glass, and jellyfish veil, announcing the constant baptism of newly created things.' Plummy? You bet it is. *The constant baptism of newly created things.* I'll take Lorca's plums any day over academic prunes.

One evening I arrived and rather than playing accordion Roberto was on guitar, which was not his area of expertise, the roughly struck chords serving merely as a vehicle for his voice. One of the strings was broken, shivered with every move he made. Something was not right with him. Suddenly he leapt from his place on the doorstep, tears in his eyes, saying that two young men on a motorbike, one of them with a gun tucked in his belt, had mugged him, grabbed his accordion, and made off with it. Despairingly he cried that he'd never be able to afford another instrument and that it was his only source of income. Just then Naples became a most sorrowful place. The next day I related the news to another street performer who immediately responded, saying that he would speak to other musicians about banding together to help Roberto. There would be shows everywhere and the takings from them would go towards the purchase of another instrument for him. It was in front of the very man who effected his rescue that a year later Roberto would set fire to his accordion. The spontaneity with which people rose to his cause was enough to demonstrate there is as much light as shadow in Naples. A couple of days later, I went to a Pulcinella performance in the Villa Communale, the lovely park close to the Bay of Naples. Musicians performed as well, including the man who would accuse Roberto of almost killing a small girl with his accordion. A leaflet had been printed for distribution to passers-by:

> He is Roberto the Calabrese. He plays in the centre of Naples. When you meet him you will have the sensation that he is at one with his accordion. You will have the impression that the accordion is a continuation of his own arms and that the music comes out of his head, from his beard, from his mouth, from his feet. Last week two mean people with a gun stopped him, they stole the accordion from him, and ran away. Today we are playing for Roberto and the money you will put in our hats will be to buy another accordion for him and to give him back his smile so that he might give us back his music.

The amount required for the purchase of a new accordion was quickly reached. When I next saw Roberto he was beaming. 'God is here,' he said. We agreed he would relate his story to me. Roberto, my translator Silvia Corsi, and I sat at an outside table, spaghetti and wine. We would have been under a tarpaulin but for the fact it had been stolen the night before. A man with a peasant's laugh of two notes, and with not a little braggadocio in the mix, a bundle of pipe dreams too, Roberto contradicted himself at every turn, and his scant regard for chronology was such that later I would have to smooth out some of the creases. This is not to say he was speaking untruths but that his life was as messy as he claimed it was. As is often the case with people who are penniless and profess to have no interest in money, money was very often the subject of conversation. Roberto told me he once burned some money, real money in a real fire, what sounded to me like the application of a wayward principle.

'You are a young man with an ancient voice,' I told him. 'The earth moves through your feet, rises through your body.' Lorca's *duende*, again. At this point Roberto's guitar which had been carelessly propped against a chair slid to the ground with a hollow crash, its five strings humming into the air.

'There is something happening here,' he replied. 'I felt something fall inside me as you spoke. Your words thrilled me. And then my guitar fainted in empathy. A few years ago, after a long journey, I began to recollect the details of my life. You talk about the earth. There is also the Holy Mother, mother of us all.'

'You are religious?'

'Yes, don't I look it?'

I remembered the cassocked cakewalker.

'I am absolutely devoted to the Holy Mary. A *mariano* is someone who is devoted to her. We have these festas for her where we play the *tammurriata*, a very ancient music, which is rooted in the deepest ground. There is a mountain called Monte Falerio above the Amalfi Coast, and going up it is a path that leads to the Sanctuary of the Madonna dell'Avvocata where there are three days of festivities. Pilgrims ascend the mountain to the rhythm of the tammorra. When I make that journey I gain strength from the mountain. You spoke of the earth. My grandfather was a farmer who grew potatoes in Sila in Calabria.'

So this man who looked like he'd just stepped down from a mountain really was from the mountain. The high plateau of La Sila was home to the ancient Bruttii, a tribe of settlers and farmers who fell victim to Rome. It is also home to wild wolves and the ancient pines known as the *giganti della Sila* that live for several hundred years, and it is where one finds *soppressata*, the spicy sausages Roberto told me his grandfather made. Out of that same environment came the hydra-headed 'Ndràngheta, the most feared of Italy's criminal organisations, whose sacred vows are accompanied by a suicide pill to be taken in the event the initiate is ever put in a position where he might be forced to betray his clan. Their name derives from the Greek ἀνδραγαθία (*andragathía*) whose meaning conflates heroism, loyalty, and manly virtue. Was there ever so much irony packed into a single word? Their wives may have other views on the matters of heroism, loyalty, and virtue but they know enough not to give voice to them. God help the woman who does. And then there are those women who are every bit as ruthless as the men. The 'Ndràngheta which began on a hilltop is now a global syndicate.

A seller of roses stopped by our table. Roberto reached into his pocket and gave him a euro.

'*Bella rosa*,' he said, presenting it to Silvia, 'a rose for a rose.'

A homeless gentleman buys a pretty lady a rose, which she accepts with grace. It was all so very Chaplinesque that a bit of me wishes the story could end there.

'I was deeply tied to my grandfather,' he continued. 'When I was inside my mother's womb – I don't remember this – and my grandfather played the accordion she had to get away from him because I would be dancing the tarantella inside her. That is why I came out of her with a sort of illness, a madness about music. I was born with epilepsy. I had these terrible crises. My mother would go mad with fear, running from place to place, wherever she thought she might find a solution. I remember nothing of these episodes, probably because I was in the middle of them, but people who saw them tell me they were horrible. Normally those attacks last for five minutes, but with me they would go on for fifteen minutes or more. My grandfather was born in 1905, went through two World Wars, worked the soil until he was eighty-six, after which he couldn't do it any more, and died at ninety-eight years of age. He gave me my first accordion, saying, "Here you are. Learn to play." My father who was a bricklayer also played the accordion exceptionally well, but such was his destiny that he broke his hands and couldn't play any more. I had a perfect ear. I could produce any sound I wanted to, my voice too, I knew all the tonalities. I have the capacity dogs have. I can hear every sound. It is as if I was born inside a folkloric groove. By the time I was eight I could play the tarantella and all its musical passages, which was when the crises stopped and I didn't need medication any more. All I had to do was play and everything would go well for me. This is why I still have to play every day, at least one song, in order to maintain my health. The maximum I can go without music is two days. I need it in order to survive.'

Scientific research supports Calabrian folk cure. It confirms what ancient physicians such as Galen knew all along, that music has medicinal properties. Recent studies have demonstrated that people with epilepsy process music in a different way in that their brains very quickly synchronise with the melodies. Most epileptic seizures take place in the temporal lobe, which is where musical sound is processed. Mozart and, surprisingly perhaps, John Coltrane, have proved beneficial in reducing seizures.

Roberto with his fork began to tap the rims of the glasses on our table.

They each sounded a different note.

'This is how everything begins. The separate noises come together and develop into musical sound. That is the meaning of the word tarantella. It is the deep ground of our music. *Tammurriata* is more about rhythm.'

Roberto then spoke at some length of his childhood, which is where he got himself into a chronological tangle. It was as if the pain of those memories would not permit a straight line. He told me how his brothers hated him because their mother doted on him, and their father, although a musician himself, also hated and regularly beat him. There were broad hints that he'd been cheated out of his inheritance, although, from his description of life at home, it cannot have amounted to very much, at most a dilapidated house in a dying village.

'One day I will grow potatoes or I will tell someone to grow them for me.'

Was Roberto projecting himself into his grandfather's shoes? What would his grandfather say to his grandson destroying the musical holy of holies?

'I've had a messy life, I must say. The reason I'm able to continue is that when I die I know something of me will remain here. All those who have died – my friends, my mother, my grandfather – they're inside me. Their souls guide me. I think about them all the time. I blink and there they are, in front of me. I can't live without the dead. They each carry a piece of history in themselves and we must carry their story onwards. We should never forget them. They force me to see the consequences of the things I've done. Yes, it's been a messy life, all right.'

'Are you now settled in Naples?'

'More or less. I am getting tired of this journey, but I really love Naples. It has always been a point of reference for me. It is where the south begins. All the world's strength comes from here.'

'You would never go back to Calabria?'

'I can't, not yet, maybe not ever, but I'll always sing to and for Calabria. After many years of being on the road I did go back just the once. When my father saw me he cried over what he'd done to me, but I couldn't stay there. I'd been away for too long. It is a bitter land. The 'Ndràngheta is incredibly strong. You can't see them, but they operate all the time. My brother works for them, not directly, but if you work in Calabria whether you like it or not, whatever work you do, even if it's laying bricks, you end up working for them. They own everything. As soon as you are born they know how to settle you. I remember what they obliged me to do when I was young. They told me, "Get on top of that car over there and dance." I did as I was told. I was a strange boy anyway. I've had friends who were killed by the 'Ndràngheta.'

'Is it any better here?'

'It is very difficult to understand what is happening in Naples. Young people are lost in drugs. It's worse than it was in the 1980s.'

A man with glassy eyes was telling me this, but then I have never been of the mind that one who takes drugs and condemns them is necessarily a hypocrite.

'You see kids going crazy on coke and acid,' he continued. 'If you have a joint it doesn't matter, but this is like burned youth. Yes, I'll call it that, *burned youth*. A while back, some boy was killed for ten euros' worth of hashish. Another boy came with a knife and killed him. That's why I don't want children. These people are not even in the Camorra. If the Camorra knows you are doing this or that they will blow you away. It is in their interest to keep everything on the level. These kids run out of money and they start robbing people. They have got to come down from whatever they're on otherwise they end up doing whatever they are told to do.'

A question began to take shape in my thoughts, but there it stayed.

'My new accordion will arrive soon,' he continued. 'Already I'm starting to picture it. I will make a big party in the piazza. This tells you my worth for these people. They worked out a solution for me. Something new is coming out of this, a flower out of the emptiness.'

This was a year ago. Whatever that flower was, its scent had long gone. There were many people who felt they'd been compromised or taken for a ride. They were saying that for their sake and his own Roberto should get the hell out of Naples. Somebody told me that whoever stole his accordion may have stolen his mind as well. Others said he'd fried his brains on coke. The brain is not as easily recoverable as an instrument. Again, who would knowingly destroy the object that separates him from destitution or even a pauper's grave? After he did so, he spoke in a rambling fashion until six in the morning, vacillating between blaming other musicians and confessing he was unwell. There were rumours that he was about to be committed to an insane asylum although the woman who told me this said that while it's true that he had emotional problems he had the clarity required to deal with his demons. I, too, feel he is not yet beyond the reach of our entreaties. Suppose what they said was true, however, and the events of a year ago, as Roberto had related them to me, were in fact staged, which is to say he was the sole architect of a nebulous tangle. There is, of course, the distinct possibility that everything he told me is true. Somebody said to me, 'What you are doing is real but so, too, is what Roberto does. There is a big danger in coming here and thinking you'll ever find the *real* Naples.' My interlocutor was right, of course. It is an infinitely complex place.

What's with the vanishing act, Roberto? There's just one little question I want to ask you, a straight answer to which might clear the atmosphere. It's so muggy down here I can hardly breathe. Roberto, tell me, did you know who your attackers were?

Leopardi's Stomach

The first time I went to Naples was not in any spatial sense but when, confined for a month to my bed in London, I read, through a haze of opiates, Iris Origo's *Leopardi: A Study in Solitude* (1953). That was over three decades ago. I was quite ready to be taken anywhere. Naples claimed me. So why did it take me so long to actually get there? Damascus intervened, and would continue to do so for fifteen years, but somewhere inside me remained that earlier tug on my affections. I seemed to know the very dimensions of the city that so narrowly contained the last four years of Giacomo Leopardi's life, which is not to say Miss Origo goes into any great detail about Naples, but that the empathy she feels for the poet is such I was able to inhabit, if in imagination only, a world through which no cars drove, where there were no endless suburbs of concrete or shaved heads offering dope. Actually the greater part of the city was squeezed into a single café. A great biographer, Origo enables the reader to walk with her subject, dine, and perhaps even die with him. There is surely much that can now be added to her book, but it was a pioneering work in English and the hand responsible for it a most capable one, a book that is one's first love.

Leopardi was born in a sepulchre. Arguably he remained there. Death might be said to have been a release. Was Origo's the right book to be reading in my cloistered state? Misery loves company, they say, which I don't think is wholly true: the unchecked spillage of one's woes will just as often bring them increase. The fact I was in pain may to some degree have summoned the ghost of Leopardi's agonies and, with it, my sympathy, which, after all, is a species of enthusiasm, and yet, bleak though his artistic vision is, and I can think of no poet who puts one's capacity for pain to the test more than he does, he strengthens rather than weakens the spirit, and the reason for this is because no matter how dark the darkness is it can be its own source of light and, in Leopardi's case, sometimes blindingly so. A small cripple rumbles the universe. Although he has been described as an atheist what he attacks is not so much religion, which for him was a necessary illusion vastly superior to 'the barbarism of reason', as the smug certainties of the religiose mind. I should think that having had a mother who thought the death of an infant was for it a shortcut to heaven, and therefore a cause for celebration, would be enough to sour anyone's milk. She was a lousy cook too.

I have been dipping into the massive journal Leopardi kept throughout much of his life, the *Zibaldone*, which is as difficult to absorb as it is rich in substance, its consumption akin to eating Christmas pudding in June. It deals with literature, philology, and philosophy, and a thousand things more. If one had to choose a main theme, something to which he returns over and over again, it would be that Reason on its own is insufficient to the begetting of mankind's happiness and that, if too blindly pursued, it will in fact lead in the opposite direction. This was not as obvious in Leopardi's time as it has since become. The man's intellect was enormous such that at times one wants for a single breath of ordinary existence. This said, the appearance of the English translation, though horribly packaged, some 2,500 pages under single covers that will not survive any one reading of the book's contents – an Anglophone world more respectful of Leopardi's genius would have graced him with six clothbound volumes – is one of the most important literary events of recent times. It's a shame the writing of it did not continue into his final years in Naples, but then it's doubtful he would have admitted into its pages the din of the streets outside. The *Zibaldone* is, rather, a massive brain, arguably the century's most acute. Very rarely does it ever strike a personal note.

Leopardi and his friend Antonio Ranieri arrived in Naples on 2 October 1833. Three days later, he wrote to his father:

> I arrived here happily, that is to say without injury and without misadventure. My health otherwise is not up to much and my eyes are still in the same state. Yet I find the mildness of the climate, the beauty of the city, and the amiable and good-natured temperament of the inhabitants very agreeable.

Six months later, he was rather less enamoured of the place. 'The Naples climate is of some benefit to me; but in other respects living here doesn't suit me very well.' One year later, he was in full revolt, speaking of the need to get away 'from these scoundrels and buffoons, high class and low, all thieves and rogues, b.f. [*baron fottuti*, which is highly impolite] who fully deserve the Spaniards and the gallows'. Strangely, though, as the city becomes imperilled with cholera he seems to become more reconciled to the place. I suspect it was because he knew he had produced his best work there. If he was bound to be miserable then it hardly matters where, but he may have been marginally less so in Naples, which, in the Leopardian universe is a mighty bundle. A jovial Leopardi is almost too horrible to contemplate. The poet died, aged thirty-eight, on 14 June 1837, the Feast of Saint Antonio. That morning he consumed close to three pounds of the *confetti cannellini di Sulmona*, the sugared almonds with a sliver of cinnamon on the inside, for which the town of Sulmona remains famous, its other claim to fame being that Ovid was born there. At five in the afternoon, he had a hot broth followed by sorbet, the combination of hot and cold being one stated cause for his death from pulmonary oedema, or dropsy as it was then called. At least that's what was written on the death certificate by Doctor Stefano Mollica who never actually attended to him.

Here we enter a shadowy world of half-truths and morbidities. Antonio Ranieri's account of his seven-year friendship with the poet, *Sette anni di sodalizio con Giacomo Leopardi* ('Seven Years of Friendship with Giacomo Leopardi', 1880), is famously unreliable. When looking at Ranieri's photograph I can't tell whether I am looking into the face of a buffoon or a sage. Maybe, though, it's a bit of both. It has been suggested that when he wrote his memoir he was going a bit senile, but I should think there was rather more than poor memory at stake and that it is the sadly familiar story of the lesser man proclaiming himself the hero in the life of the greater man, which ought to sweeten our view of him a little, were it not that over a century later all we feel is annoyance. All things considered, he did take care of Leopardi and, a common enough scenario, probably did so to the point of being both jealous and possessive of him. Were it not that Ranieri arranged for his invalid friend to go and breathe the fresh air between Torre del Greco and Vesuvius we would have been deprived of Leopardi's greatest poem 'La ginestra o, il fiore del deserto' ('Broom, or The Flower of the Desert'). The old codger was merely seeking his dues.

Still there's no getting away from the fact that Ranieri's account is full of holes. Why did the kindly Dr Niccolò Mannella who *did* attend to the poet in his final hours decline to write the cause of death on the death certificate? Was it dropsy or cholera that took the poet's life? The bit of Ranieri's story that presents the most difficulties is where he claims to have prevented his friend's corpse from joining the many thousands of victims of cholera in the mass grave at Fontanelle. It had been decreed that all who died from the epidemic, rich and poor alike, should be taken to either Poggioreale or the tuff caves of Fontanelle and there their naked bodies covered with quicklime. These were, for the time, sensible emergency measures. Maybe Ranieri's failure to prevent such a fate for his friend prompted him to create a fiction he found increasingly awkward to escape. There is written evidence that the poet was indeed taken to Fontanelle, a document from the Ufficio di Stato Civile ('*documento* n° 568') which states: 'Giacomo Leopardi mort il 14 giugno 1837, sepolto nel cimitero dei colerisi. Ha ricevuto i sacramenti.' Ranieri claims that with a bribe of coin and fresh fish he managed to get the priest at the church of San Vitale in Fuorigrotta to conduct a funeral. Some priests can be had at a price. A funeral did take place. But *whose*? The coffin must have sat lightly on the shoulders of its bearers. When the tomb was examined in 1900 there were some bones, the most substantial of which were two femurs a bit too long for Leopardi's height, but no skull or thoracic cage bones, either of which would have been enough to point to the identity of the person whose paltry remains these supposedly were. Stranger still, there was also a shoe that in later years was purchased by the opera singer Beniamino Gigli and donated by him to the city of Recanati, which is where both he and Leopardi were born. Where was the other shoe? After the church of San Vitale was demolished in 1939 in order to make way for one of Mussolini's architectural schemes these motley remains were moved to the Parco Vergiliano a Piedigrotta, very close to where the magus and author of the *Aeneid* is said to have been buried. It is a lovely spot, tucked away from the nearby traffic tunnel, with its congestion and noise. There one may peer into the entrance of the *Crypta neapolitana* that goes all the way to Pozzuoli, which was constructed by Lucius Cocceius Auctus who also built the *Grotta di Cocceio* going from Lake Avernus to Cumae. I was late getting there, the gates were locked, but the kindly attendant allowed me in and walked me to the grave. The tomb is anything but humble. Leopardi would surely have poked fun at it and if indeed the bones it covers are not his then he would have cackled at me, my head bowed in reverence. This raises the question of what it is that one reveres, memory or substance. If, as many scholars insist, the poet died of cholera then it stands to reason that one of the tens of thousands of skulls on display at the *cimitero delle Fontanelle* is his. Might I not for just an instant have peered into the sockets that once housed Leopardi's eyes?

I was so taken with Origo's account of Leopardi's final days that as soon as I was back on my feet I wrote a poem, a monologue of five pages in length, in which I dared to appropriate, for my own purposes, the poet's voice. I will have to seek pardon from his Shade. 'Giacomo Leopardi in Naples' takes for its setting the Due Sicilie café on the Largo della Carità, which is long gone, but is roughly where Via Toledo bulges into the Piazza Carità and where, on one side of the street, abominable architecture now blights the scene. The café was Leopardi's favourite. The poem is set in 1837, not long before he dies. There is a cholera epidemic but rather than heed advice to escape an unhealthy atmosphere he stuffs his face with Vito Pinto's 'matchless ices'. Sometimes he'd order two or three at a time. Pinto gets a mention in his satire, 'I nuovi credenti' ('The New Believers'), a minor work that has been rightly excluded from his *Canti* but which, nevertheless, provides a window into Leopardi's Naples. In it, he attacks the 'gastronomic hedonism' of Neapolitans, which is an interesting case of the pot calling the kettle black. Leopardi tended to eat alone, and although he was keenly aware that to do so was considered a disgrace by the ancient Greeks and Romans and in his *Zibaldone* readily admits that he would have deserved their contempt, he defends his stance. 'I can be compared with the bird the Greeks call a porphyrion,' he writes, 'if the account of Athenaeus and Aleian is true that it doesn't like witnesses when it is eating.' Although I did my best to picture Naples as it was then, there comes into the poem the odd London scene, a particular wine bar in Kensington, for example, which, the only time I was there, was full of young male yuppies with spread legs, blaring at the tops of their voices. The glorification of the brute made the 1980s a lousy decade. I should think the voices that filled the Due Sicilie were not nearly as brash as theirs but I made them so nevertheless.

All Naples is one huge, sleepless pantomime
As was that other place the gods covered with ashes.
The mountain broods beneath its canopy of smoke
While these revellers with their booming voices and
    pointed shoes,
These plumed creatures whom progress loves,
Make corridors in air.
The pursuit of happiness brings them none.
They drape the skeleton of all things with their festering
    pride,
And fearing the tumble through endless space wage war
    upon silence.
Should they win, where then my verses?

That Naples should have to bear responsibility for certain of my confederates is a matter that will have to be decided in the courts of poetic justice. And then it was in a London café, the Troubadour on Old Brompton Road, a place just arty and pretentious enough for me to be able to hide in full view, scribbling verses, where I discovered, or was rather given, the keystone I'd so badly required for the poem's completion. At a small round table with a candle at its centre, I was playing about with a coffee spoon. The line came so quickly I feared there wouldn't be time to write it before it dissolved in a rush of caffeine: 'Yet still I see my silver spoon rise / And then dip towards the round horizon of my table where God is a flickering candle.' I knew then I had only a short distance to go before Leopardi, *my* Leopardi, would take his final leave.

Vito places the chairs on the tables;
Moonlight sweeps the floor bare.
This is a strange forest which I must now leave.
Say Giacomo Leopardi found peace at Naples.

It is a questionable business quoting oneself and it borders on downright crass, but doing so is vital to what I am about to relate. A maker is always to some degree oblivious to what he makes. Although I think I got Leopardi right, it was not until I got to Naples, many years later, that I would grasp the full import of the poem's closing line.

First, however, there is another connection I wish to make. One day I walked into the Enitharmon Bookshop in Bury Street in central London and there, to my astonishment, a rather glamorous woman with sparkling eyes, a huge flower in her hair, was reading my Leopardi poem. We were introduced by the lady working there. I was somewhat tongue-tied as I'd never before caught anyone in the act of reading a poem of mine. We spoke for barely more than a minute, during which time we exchanged cards. A filmmaker and artist, Chiara Ambrosio sent me a video link to a film she made, the superbly titled *La Frequenza Fantasma* ('The Ghost Frequency') which is her haunting exploration of a dying village in the mountains of Calabria. I have never actually discussed the title with her, and she may think I've got hold of the wrong end of the stick, but the phrase applies to a specific tone, inaudible to most people, whose frequency makes the eyes vibrate, sometimes producing optical illusions in the periphery of one's field of vision. We allow ourselves to believe we are seeing ghosts and maybe those sound waves are where ghosts feel most comfortable. Chiara and I met later and she told me about the year she spent in Naples, the city she calls her true home – her father lives in a village close to the summit of Vesuvius – and she also spoke of the so-called cult of skulls, *il culto delle anime pezzentelle*. A spark such as I remember from school experiments made with an electrostatic machine flew from one side of my skull to the other. Chiara set in motion an old promise made to myself. Originally, though, it was through the dark prism of Leopardi's life and poetry that I knew I'd one day have to go to Naples.

It might even be said I was swept there upon a single line, which, to these ears, strikes me as one of the most perfect in Italian poetry, 'Scende la luna e si scolora il mondo', from 'Il tramonto della luna' ('The Setting of the Moon'), the last six lines of which, so legend has it, Leopardi, as he lay dying in his room on Vico Pero, dictated to Ranieri. A good story, it is apparently untrue. The line I have just quoted was the product of a mind in extremis and of itself a small miracle of concision. It has been said of certain poets that one can take any single line of theirs, write it on a slip of paper, and then drop it on the street for someone else to pick up, and that it would be immediately identifiable as having come from the hand of that poet, an exaggeration maybe but a nice one all the same. Origo who is of sounder mind writes, 'In the work of every great poet there are a few lines so happy, so characteristic, that – even if quoted out of their texture – they bear an unmistakable signature.' The line is virtually untranslatable, which is not to say one cannot get at its meaning but there is, so I believe, no possibility of putting it into decent English verse. It has become for me a kind of litmus test I apply to the various translators of Leopardi. If, in English, the line gets a quarter of a way to where the poet meant us to be, the translator has probably done reasonably well elsewhere. The translations of that single line range from one so hopeless I will not offend the translator's sensibilities by reproducing it here to Jonathan Galassi's adequate but, as I'm sure he'd agree, insufficiently poetic 'the moon descends, the world goes colour-less'. The translations are, all of them, inadequate. I have no solution to offer, no improvement to make, other than to suggest that the line be left in the original Italian as untranslatable. As for its meaning, Origo captures it perfectly: 'The poet compares the vanishing of joy and colour from a man's life, as his end draws near, to the slow fading of a landscape, at the setting of the moon.' I would add only a suggestion of bone whitening beneath moonlight.

Leopardi is probably the most moonstruck of poets.

The moon makes solitude bearable.

I visited the Palazzo Cammarota on Santa Maria Ogni Bene in the Quartieri Spagnoli where, from December 1833 to May 1835, Leopardi lived with Antonio Ranieri. The place was, in his day, already converted into apartments. I entered the courtyard and wondering which of the apartments might have been his, I wandered up the stairs, sometimes studying the nameplates on the doors, tempted to knock at one of them for an answer but not quite foolhardy enough to do so. When I was back at ground level I saw a man at an open window of one of the apartments facing into the courtyard. I asked him if he could tell me where Leopardi lived, and he scratched his head, saying, 'Leopardi, Leopardi' as though it rang a distant bell and then he went to ask someone and when he returned he told me he didn't know of any Leopardi living here. It would have been too impolite to tell him that there can't have been a day when he did not pass through the entrance to the old palazzo, where above it is written that the poet had lived here.

I pictured Leopardi walking through narrow streets, mostly unchanged, perhaps making a detour into my favourite market in Naples, La Pignasecca, wearing his old turquoise overcoat over grubby clothes, a colourful kerchief around his neck, stud-ying the wonderful snacks on offer. And then maybe he stops to make the purchase of a lottery ticket or offer advice on the same. A male hunchback is a figure of good luck in Mediterranean countries. This is not, alas, extended to the female of the species. I also went to visit the slightly sad affair that is the Villa delle Ginestre where, when it was the Villa Ferrigni owned by Ranieri's relatives, Leopardi wrote the great poem that would one day give the place its new name. I had been expecting rather more of the place, but maybe here I should address my own ingratitude. What do we look for when we visit the homes of mighty eminences? Sometimes, though, it works as long as we are sufficiently receptive. It's the wanting more that drives away host spirits. The square villa backs onto a landscape that culminates in Mount Vesuvius in the distance. At the front is a lovely solar clock with the motto *Sine sole sileo* ('Without the sun, I am silent'). A single room is devoted to what one is told is the original furniture. The rest of the building is empty although I did sneak down to the kitchen and there took a photograph of the old oven with its decorative tiles, which I was glad to have done for the joy it brought out in the man I later showed it to.

Paola Villani, a professor in Italian literature, an expert in Leopardi, is a scholar not of the cold water species one finds in so many university faculties but a passionate woman whose heart is where her mind is, a combination that seems to be all but forgotten by students and teachers of literature. She spoke of her frustrations at not being able to persuade the city authorities to create a Leopardi centre. As for Leopardi's relationship with Naples, it struck me that there were few outward signs of reverence for him, no public statues or cafés bearing his name, not even a brand of chocolate.

A cigarette alight, crackling with nervous energy, she told me why this was so.

'You must remember that until 1947 the late Leopardi was not really known in Italy because literary criticism ran in the direction of the idyllic Leopardi, the Leopardi of "L'infinito" ("The Infinite") and "A Silvia" ("To Silvia") and not the philosophical author of *Operette morali* ("Moral Tales") and "La ginestra" which were considered not as good as the earlier work. We were given this picture of Leopardi, the same as you had in England, but which was never really him. The canon was determined by Carducci, D'Annunzio, and Francesco de Sanctis. We didn't read the poet but the literary studies of him, which gave us only a single aspect of his character. In 1947, two major critics, quite independently of each other, published two important studies of this second Leopardi, the Leopardi of Naples. That was the *real* Leopardi, the Leopardi of "La ginestra" and "Il tramonto della luna". The recent film about him is not good.* In the first part of the movie his life is presented historically and, as far as it goes, is true enough, but when it comes to Naples suddenly there is this

---

* Mario Martone's *Il giovane favoloso* (2014). It has its moments, but the scene in which a self-pitying Leopardi curls up in the grass to the strains of a mushy pop song deserves the most severe penalty in the courts of poetic justice.

"artistic" take. This is a film, of course, and not an essay, but I can't understand why the first part is historical and in the second part the city is depicted as this hell, a Naples without poetry or order, its people living like animals. This simply wasn't the case. We had many great thinkers here. The film was based on Antonio Ranieri's memoir of Leopardi, in which the author says that without him Leopardi would have been alone in Naples. Ranieri makes himself the hero of the Leopardi story. But Naples was quite happy to have this poet, so he was absolutely *not* alone. He stood against the *other* Naples, a different thing altogether, the Neapolitan intellectuals who were Catholic and those others who believed in political engagement. Leopardi asked where we were going with this. We can have progress, scientific and technological, he said, but we will not be any the happier for it. This is why in "La ginestra" it may be said of Leopardi that he took a stand against Naples, when he writes "Qui mira e qui ti specchia, / Secol superbo e sciocco" ("Look here and see yourself reflected, / proud and foolish century"). This is why he didn't live with or participate in this Neapolitan elite and so, in this sense, yes, he was alone.'

'I think all great poets are alone,' I said. I knew the intellectuals, for their part, did not take to this smelly misanthrope, sour head sunk between his shoulders, reddened eyes, stuffing his face.

'Yes, yes, of course,' Villani replied, a sardonic edge in her voice. 'This is one literary *topos*. Poets *must* paint themselves as alone. If you are not alone, you are not a poet. They want to present themselves not as they are but as they *must* be.'

She is not a woman to put up with moonshine.

At the Biblioteca Nazionale di Napoli, in the company of Doctor Maria Racaglia who administers both the Leopardi and Ranieri archives, I pored over the original manuscripts of Leopardi's poems 'L'infinito' and 'A Silvia' and his major prose works, the *Operette morali* and *Zibaldone*. Say I was moved.

Say I was not so much moved as entranced. Say entrancement is of a higher order than tears because Leopardi was not looking for our pity nor was he looking for the mop that would soak them up. Suffer he most certainly did, and he may have been at times, in his suffering, insufferable, but surely he knew pain is of itself never a resolution. The classical mind knows better than to whinge. It knows ice cream beats the blues for at least the length of time it takes to melt in Neapolitan sunshine. It's why he kept ordering more of Vito's incomparable ices, sometimes several at a time. Polyphagic, yes, but shambolic? What those manuscripts showed me was that his was one of the most orderly minds in all literature. On every page of the *Operette morali* there is a faint vertical crease creating an inner margin inside of which Leopardi jotted occasional notes or alternative readings for words in the main text which began immediately on the crease. Maybe this is what moved me most, the mental image I had of him folding with absolute precision each page before he began to write. It struck me as the very essence of a man in solitude, the quirky solutions he devises. When I asked Doctor Racaglia whether she thought Leopardi might have found, if only in snatches, happiness in Naples, she replied, 'His problems were still with him, but we can say that in comparison to what he'd experienced elsewhere he was quite happy here or at least not quite as unhappy.' Somehow that qualifying *quite* seemed more than enough for a man struggling with the infinite.

The business of looking for poetical traces is a peculiar one. I shun it as a rule. If one were to go in search of Keats in London one might go to the house where he lived, although it is furnished not with his but other people's furniture, and then one might visit the operating theatre of the hospital where he studied medicine, but it is not as though one can go along the streets picking up spirit traces. Why did I think this might be possible with Leopardi in Naples? Quite simply, when one explores another city one is more impressionable whereas at home overfamiliarity dims the picture. Naples is just a bit careless with its luminaries or would prefer to deal with no more than a few at a time. Leopardi has been scrubbed out of that picture, or else those parts of the picture which contained him have gone. What I really needed was someone in whom the poet resides, which is not to diminish the passion of Paola Villani, Maria Racaglia, and their worthy colleagues, but the ultimate value of any artist is the degree to which he survives in the minds of ordinary people although, really, there are no ordinary people. What I was looking for, and maybe this is a private quirk of mine, is an element of surprise, and this I would find in the burly figure of a man who has been elected 'l'ultimo monzù napoletano'.

All I knew of Antonio Tubelli was that he owned a small eatery, Timpani e Tempura, in the old centre, which was much beloved of local gastronomes and that his passion for cooking was in some way connected to his love of Leopardi's poetry. Now in his seventies, for many years he worked for an aeronautical firm and there became a union leader. At some point he studied cuisine with a chef called Tommaso Di Benedetto who thrust into his hands the book that would change his life, Vincenzo Corrado's *Il Cuoco Galante*. Published in Naples in 1773, *The Gallant Cook* may be said to be the mother of all modern cookbooks, its author having created not only a culinary vocabulary but also, in the presentation of his dishes, a blend of fantasy and choreography, edible architecture. This probably owes much to his earlier studies in mathematics, astronomy, and philosophy, not that these can be said to have had a direct influence but that they shaped his mind for adventure. It is also considered the first Italian cookbook to take into account the whole of Mediterranean as well as local cuisine. Spurred on, Tubelli visited the archives of the Banco di Napoli where he discovered shopping lists for the royal kitchens. This was followed by a reading of Antonio Latini's *Lo scalco alla moderna* ('The Kitchen Steward', 1694) which contains, among many things, the earliest recipes for tomato sauce although strangely the author fails to make the quantum leap that would see it combined with pasta. Then Tubelli fell upon Ippolito Cavalcanti's *Trattato di cucina teorico-pratica* (1837), a compendium of Neapolitan cuisine in which, for the first time in print if not in practice, tomato is wed to vermicelli, a discovery beside which, in terms of what shapes our existence, puts those of Galileo, Newton, and Einstein in the shade. What is of historical importance here is that all three books were published in Naples, the third of them in the Neapolitan language. In 1988, carrying lightly the burden of history and with the poetry of Leopardi simmering in his thoughts, Tubelli, together with his brother Lucio, struck out for new pastures.

I went to the Vico della Quercia not far from the Piazza Dante where Timpani e Tempura was supposed to be and found it gone, nothing in its place. I asked various people whether they knew of Tubelli's whereabouts but nobody could answer me. The only place I didn't try was the workshop of an elderly cobbler, the walls of which were adorned with pin-ups of naked women. He had dimmed the lights and was having his lunch. I returned a few days later. Tubelli was his friend and so I learned from him that he had moved a couple of years earlier to a shopping centre close to the harbour. These days Tubelli is enjoying an extended moment of fame, which has now brought him from the not wholly loveable harbour area into the pleasanter environs of the Chaia area on the Bay of Naples.

'Which came first,' I asked him, 'the egg or Leopardi?'

I had in mind Aldo Buzzi's delightful book, *The Perfect Egg: And Other Secrets* (2005). The delicacy with which Buzzi approaches the making of a simple omelette makes my own efforts look like an exercise in culinary abuse.

'*Allora!*' Tubelli chuckled. '"*Why* did I meet with Leopardi?" is the question. First I must tell you a few things because they'll help you understand better my relationship to him. I chose a life in gastronomy out of passion. I was passionate about it not because I was heir to anyone but because everything starts from a very big feeling from my side and it never slows down. I always knew that Neapolitan cooking ... and this is confirmed by the historical texts I'll refer to ... is a huge and important cuisine. At the end of the 1980s, however, it had become poorer and cheaper such that even I needed to be convinced of its importance. The fact that Neapolitan cooking was on a downward slide pushed my curiosity towards it, which was why I began to look at the historical sources. What was the source of its greatness? And why did it go downhill? The answer to the second question is that it sank because of a worldwide plague of *nouvelle cuisine*.'

Tubelli paused as if allowing for the immensity of the tragedy to sink in. I, too, had been reduced to the indignity of pushing a single spear of asparagus over the polar expanse of an over-sized plate, as if form alone could redeem poverty of substance. We had been fooled into paying for the space surrounding each morsel of food, and yet to my shame whenever a waiter asked me if everything was all right my response would be positive albeit sometimes a very quiet *yes*, which meant I'd entered into collusion with enemy forces. Such lies engender in oneself a species of impotence combined with latent violence. This was yet another feature of a frightful decade of yuppiedom. We'd been sold a pig in a poke – all poke, little pig – and at double the price. I would have preferred stodge.

'And the ingredients were getting cheap too,' Tubelli continued. 'We had dropped our culinary traditions in order to go down this wrong path. When I realised this I decided to go more deeply into the situation. I had the opportunity to visit the Biblioteca Nazionale here in Naples where there are these extraordinary documents, which tell us with great clarity the rules of Neapolitan cuisine and which show it in all its greatness. Why am I saying *greatness*? When I talk about Neapolitan cuisine I am thinking of Naples as the historical capital of a huge territory – the southern part of Lazio, Campania, Abruzzo, towards Calabria and Sicily – and so an immense volume of cooking. I am speaking not only about the products from those different territories but also about the local cultures and then the different cultures brought here by rulers and governors from elsewhere. The Arabs, the Spanish, the French, the Austrians in the person of Queen Maria Carolina, wife of Ferdinando, brought their own cultures into ours – it was an entwining of them and the roots of this place, which resulted in something gastronomically different from the rest of Italy. Its richness was incredible. When did that culture begin to decline? It was after the unity of Italy and when Savoy grabbed southern Italy and stole from it its most positive aspects.'

My translator Silvia Corsi who is from Torino in the north nudged me.

'I think he may have it in for me,' she whispered. 'I'm of the House of Savoy.'

It was too late. Tubelli was now in full swing although it has to be said there was some mischief in his eyes.

'We will go back to Leopardi in a minute, but first I have to say this. When I go to Torino, I always say this to them, "The Kingdom of Savoy compared to that of the Bourbons was like a little hole of a chicken egg." So now, going back to our Giacomo, Neapolitan cooking had been the best in the world after the French. All this helped me to understand the deep roots of our cuisine. At the beginning of the twentieth century Neapolitan cooking was fish-based, but that was just one side of it. The real roots are in the earth. I got to know all the products of this territory, from both the maritime and agricultural points of view. I tried to understand why some products were dropped and substituted by others because I could see that the products replaced had been great in themselves. I knew they had to be brought back because they expressed wonderful flavours not found elsewhere. I really wanted the main characteristics of our cooking to re-emerge. First of all, there is the healthiness of the food and tied to this, pleasure. So then, it was not only about being fed but also getting pleasure in the erotic, the *sinful* sense of the word. This is about my meeting with Giacomo Leopardi. Don't worry! I need to go through all this in order to arrive at him. A good friend of mine, Domenico Pasquariello, who is the co-author of our book *Leopardi a tavola* ('Leopardi at the Table') – a great painter, a multitasker, and a philosopher interested in actualities – started reading the poet at a certain point in his life. At the National Library there is the manuscript of the *Zibaldone*. I wanted to peek at it in its authentic form, and there, tucked in among this and Leopardi's correspondence, there was a single page, a list of forty-nine dishes, the food he felt most impassioned about when he lived here. They were numbered one to forty-nine. This was Leopardi's habit when he was writing his thoughts, he'd number them and from the number he could later go back to his original thought. It was like a filing system. A genius, the greatest we have in Italy.'

1. Tortellini di magro.
2. Maccheroni, o tagliolini.
3. Capellini al burro.
4. Bodin di capellini.
5. Bodin di latte.
6. Bodin di polenta.
7. Bodin di riso.
8. Riso al burro.
9. Frittelle di riso.
10. Frittelle di mela o pere.
11. Frittelle di borragine.
12. Frittelle di semolino.
13. Gnocchi di semolino.
14. Gnocchi di polenta.
15. Bignè.
16. Bignè di patate.
17. Patate al burro.
18. Carciofi fritti, al burro, con salsa d'uova.
19. Zucche fritta, ec.
20. Fiori di zucca fritti.
21. Cavoli fiori ec.
22. Selleri ec.
23. Ricotta fritta.
24. Gavazzoli.
25. Bodin di ricotta.
26. Pan dorato.
27. Latte fritto, crema ec.
28. Purèe di faginoli, ec.
29. Cervelli fritti, al burro, in citron.
30. Pesce.
31. Paste frolle al burro o strutto, pasticcetti ec.
32. Paste sfogliate.
33. Spinaci.
34. Uova ec.
35. Latte a bagno-maria.
36. Gnocchi di latte.
37. Erbe strasinate.
38. Papa.
39. Cacio cotto.
40. Polpette ec.
41. Anipol fritti.
42. Prosciutto ec.
43. Tonno ec.
44. Frappe.
45. Pasticcini di maccheroni o maccheroncini, di grasso o di magro.
46. Fegatini.
47. Zucche o insalate ec. con ripieno d'carne.
48. Lingua ec.
49. Polmate di riso.

Sing, O goddess, of macaroni, ravioli, semolina and polenta gnocchi, puff pastries, fried pumpkin, pancakes with apples and pears. A kind of wish list, compiled by Leopardi in the final months of his life, it is a cholesterol nightmare though a most heavenly one. Number twenty-five on the list, *bodin di ricotta*, is the pudding that Leopardi liked best. This is how it's made. You take a large bowl and sift 600 grams of *ricotta di bufala* and work into it 150 grams of icing sugar, adding four egg yolks, one at a time. Add a small glass of rum and a tot of maraschino liqueur, 100 grams of chocolate bits, 150 grams of candied lemon and orange peel, and ten crushed walnuts. Place in small bowls and cool for at least three hours, and when the time is ripe take a small silver spoon to it and suffer the consequences.

Oddly enough, Leopardi did not like tomatoes, which explains their absence from the list he made.

'Leopardi died young,' Tubelli continued. 'This enormous mind was too big for little Recanati where he was born and where he suffered from the family atmosphere, especially from the mother who looked upon Leopardi's health problems as a form of divine grace. On the other side, we had the father, a "ball-breaker", as we say in Italy, and a bitter person. Well, if you had to live with such a wife you would find your freedom elsewhere, which I'm sure he did, but he was also an intellectual. I don't know if you have ever been to the Palazzo Leopardi in Recanati. There is a huge library, one of the greatest in Italy. So that, roughly, is the aristocratic ambience in which he grew up and which explains in part the exuberance of his intellectual mind, but even this was too little and he looked for spaces in which to develop his ideas – he was a revolutionary really, a man who could see the alternatives, how things should have gone, and why they didn't because of the system at that time. During the night he needed fresh air and transformed what had been a health problem into an interest in astronomy and astrology. This was the greatness of his mind, that it was capable of going everywhere. He toured around Italy at this time and when he arrived in Florence he met the two people who would be most fundamental to his life, Antonio Ranieri and his friend, Pasquale Ignarra. And here we go!'

Tubelli laughed as if he was about to lead a battle charge.

'We know their story. Ranieri and Ignarra became exiles in Florence after the suppressed Neapolitan Revolution of 1799 which was quickly cut off in blood. Lord Nelson and the English people helped to spill some of this blood.'

'My apologies!'

'It's your turn now,' Silvia interjected.

'No, no, no no no!' Tubelli cried. 'Nelson is a big pain in my memory. To show the power of England he hanged Caracciolo, a big man, and threw his body into the sea in a most despicable way, although later his body was recovered and given a proper burial.'

Tubelli was certainly right to point to a disgraceful episode, which is not only the blackest mark in Lord Nelson's career but also an affront to justice. Francesco Caracciolo, a Neapolitan admiral who sided with the revolutionaries of 1799, was charged with high treason, and having been denied the request that he be judged by British officers, was tried on Nelson's flagship *H.M.S. Foudroyant* by a court martial of five Neapolitan officers, all of whom were politically on the other side. No witnesses were allowed for the defence, the verdict was hasty, a sentence of life imprisonment, which Nelson, after consultation with Count Thun who presided over the military court, changed to the death penalty. Caracciolo was denied the dignity of dying like a gentleman before a firing squad. On the same day, 30 June 1799, at five in the afternoon, on Nelson's orders, he was hanged from the fore yard arm of his own ship *La Minerva* and at sunset his body was cut down and ignominiously thrown into the sea. One of the spectators was Lady Emma Hamilton who apparently enjoyed the spectacle. A few days later, when King Ferdinand was on board the *Foudroyant*, the corpse bobbed up from the depths beside the ship. When Ferdinand asked what the dead man was after, a priest at his side said he had come to demand a Christian burial for himself.

'And now, going back to our Giacomo,' said Tubelli, fresh from Pyrrhic victory. 'Ranieri's friend, Pasquale Ignarra, was a *monzù*.'

As an honorific title, the Neapolitan *monzù*, derived from the French *monsieur* (as in 'gentleman' or even 'lord'), is applied to only the very highest level of chef. It goes beyond being a *maestro*. There are restaurants and bakeries that carry the word in their name, but this is to pinch candles from a culinary saint-hood of sorts. One might say the tradition of the *monzù* began with one woman's dislike of the local cuisine. In the late eight-eenth century Maria Carolina of Austria married the eccentric Ferdinand IV, King of Naples, who would stand on the docks selling his own freshly caught fish. She disliked him as much as he disliked her, but despite his description of her sleeping like a corpse and smelling like a pig they managed from this most unhappy of marriages to produce eighteen children. Maria Caro-lina considered the local food unworthy of the court and in any event contaminated with Spanish influence. Her ill-fated sister, Marie Antoinette, came to the rescue and sent French chefs to Naples, but rather than this being disastrous to the local cuisine the combination of Gallic and ultramontane influences gave rise to a new branch of the culinary arts. The very best of the artisan chefs, Neapolitans all of them, were given the title *monzù*, the first of whom was Giuseppe Lazzaro or 'Peppino'. (It became the custom for a *monzù* to adopt a nickname.) Another *monzù* was Gennaro Spadaccino who introduced *maccheroni* to the court but because eating it with one's bare hands, as the lower classes did, was condemned as indecorous he invented the four-pronged fork which enabled one to consume the food of the poor with regal grace. And then there was Giovanni Starace who created for Queen Maria Sofia the *timpano di maccheroni* with goose liver and pheasant hearts that still bears her name. The art of the *monzù* did not necessarily require rare and expensive ingredi-ents and in fact simplicity was, and remains, very much the rule. When in 1889 Queen Margherita with her husband Umberto I toured Italy she was intrigued by the big round flatbreads the peasants ate. Much to the horror of the court circles she loved it and never missed an opportunity to join in with her subjects over a pizza. She summoned Rafaelle Esposito from his pizzeria to the palace kitchens where he made for her a special pizza topped with tomatoes, mozzarella, and fresh basil, these combining to reproduce the colours of the Italian flag. This was the *pizza margherita* that has since conquered the globe. After the end of Bourbon rule, the *monzù* moved from the court into the houses of aristocratic families who kept the culinary traditions alive. A catalogue of names before which we ordinary mortals must tremble includes other famous *monzù* – Nicola Micera, Vincenzo Ruggiano, Vicenzo Martino, Aquilino Beneduce, and, more recently, Gerardo Modugno, and, finally, the man whom I celebrate here.

'Antonio Ranieri brought Leopardi from Florence to Naples,' Tubelli continued. 'Leopardi had an intellectual life, which was quite apart from the mainstream intellectual life of the town. He didn't want to stick with the establishment, and in fact he always pointed to its dark side, and on their part they didn't look kindly on him. The meeting place for intellectuals at that time was the Gambrinus though Leopardi never went there. He would stop at Vito's café in the Piazza Carità and would eat sorbet all the time. I should have mentioned that with his list of dishes there are no recipes for them. All we have are the names. What can you derive from this list?'

'Pass.'

'Well, you can see he was interested in food. I am just answering a very simple question. What does one take notes about? Whatever one is interested in, yes? We don't have to follow strange thoughts. It's simple. You wouldn't take notes if you weren't interested. *Molto semplice!* This means food interested him. You know, of course, he also had lung trouble. Torre del Greco, near Vesuvius, was, until the 1950s, considered a very healthy place for people with respiratory problems. You can breathe the air there, the melding of the seaside with the countryside. Ranieri settled Leopardi inside the Villa delle Ginestre, which belonged to Ranieri's wife's family. From the architectural point of view it was not all that special, a simple classical country house beside a bigger villa. *Allora*, Ranieri summoned Pasquale Ignarra to come and live with them and cook for Leopardi – they had come to Naples together. Obviously Pasquale Ignarra, who was a big chef, which is to say in a spectacular place in the gastronomical hierarchy, started to play on Leopardi's strings at the table. You can see this from the letters Leopardi sent to his sister. These were the best years of his life. So we can see the value of food, the value of pleasure, when the food is prepared with attention and from it emerge all the good things one can find in every dish. Pleasure and happiness, this is the message Leopardi gives us. If you eat well, if you taste the food, it gives you happiness and health. Leopardi's mother had always given him food for a sick person, which is why I am pointing to her morbidly Catholic side. This boy really wanted to eat something else, but his mother was preparing food in the tragic style.'

Tubelli pulled another woeful face.

'Until the moment when he got together with Pasquale and Ranieri,' he continued, 'he had not had the opportunity to perceive the quality of food. Although he wasn't a boy any more, he could understand this. That is why I started to go deeply into his thinking about food. This was the starting point for me. I was able to read all the writings of Leopardi not from the point of view of a cosmic, pessimistic view of life but from another perspective more correct and less negative. When Domenico Pasquariello and I wrote our book we had to consider two different interpretations of Leopardi's thinking, a negative line and a positive one. After looking at his list of foods, we took on this less negative – well, let's say *positive* – interpretation of Leopardi's writings. From this point of view you can read Leopardi's work in a completely different way. We are talking some years ago. It was not an easy book to write. It took us three or four years. Until then, I had a typical high school knowledge of Leopardi. We were taught he was ill, negative, and desperate, so much so he would have preferred death to life. But it was not at all like that! He *wanted* to live and he was doing so at the top of his powers. My realisation of this came from seeing his list of favourite dishes. I didn't want to put the recipes in the book, I wasn't interested in that side of things, but we had to do it for the publisher who wanted the recipes included in order to sell it. Actually the book is not about those recipes but about what I've just told you, the true colours of Leopardi's time in Naples. This gives us another, very rich image of Leopardi as a man full of interest and, in his own way, positive. The letters tell us this … it's not me who says so. He says he spent the best years of his life here. How can you disagree with that? It's quite clear. This forces one to read "La ginestra" from a different point of view, from the opposite direction if you like. The *ginestra* ("broom") is seeded in volcanic soil which is rich with life. And what grows from soil rich with life? Something *full* of life! This is where Leopardi's true greatness lies. It is not about this poor soil, this poor soul, or what high school teaches us about this poor little man's life. No, it's the other way round! The volcanic soil makes this life explode. This is his testament in the spiritual sense. He says that's the way things are. Yes, his life was full of problems, but he was expressing a vitality unique in the universe. There are not many men like him in history. Thousands of years have to go by from one genius like him to another and this all came within a short span of life. If he could have lived longer what would have happened? That is what I'm saying to you.'

'Obviously studying the food he ate must have brought you close to the poet.'

'There was a TV show at the time called *Visionary People* which invited me on. The man who interviewed me asked, "When you saw this list, what did you think?" I answered, "First of all, I thought about Leopardi being interested in food. Secondly, I understood that a man of such immense character has to eat and that we very rarely see such people at the table. So I got to know him in his intimate life. This was a big fortune in my life." Do you ever pause to think about what Queen Elizabeth eats? You never think about it! One day you are going to meet up with Queen Elizabeth's dishes and you'll say, "She ate!" It was a slight exaggeration to say "intimate" but I felt closer to the real Leopardi. This was very important for me. Critics tend to stick to the philosophical or biographical side of things, but this list had always been in among these documents. It was there for everyone to see, but nobody had properly considered it.'

'Did you become obsessed with this idea? If so, can you describe it.'

'I have to say the main point for me when I worked on recovering our cuisine is that one has to be respectful towards the cultural traditions, and not only that but also towards the products themselves. If I have something in my hands coming from the sea or from the ground I must not be aggressive towards it. I want to start a process that finally exults in its qualities. When people eat what I cook they have to be able to feel and taste the original products. This is why I am very delicate in my intervention with food. These good things that come your way are from the work of the fisherman, the farmer, and the pastry man. Being respectful of nature means also being respectful of the man who works with nature. This is my philosophy. Some colleagues of mine choose differently. When you work on a product and you take from that product just one part of it … for example, a colleague of mine makes a risotto using water that is extracted from mozzarella.'

Tubelli paused here as if about to impart some terrible news.

'How can this be allowed to happen! What he does is to take the mozzarella and heat it so that all the *latte* comes out … this is an aggressive attitude because mozzarella is beautiful, but he pushes it to a temperature where the liquid part gets separated from the concrete part that he then throws away. I am not talking about whether it is good or bad to the taste. When you do this kind of thing to food it is not a natural process. That mozzarella was made by a person called a *casaro*, a man who makes cheeses, and once upon a time someone thought about how to get the ingredients to a point when it becomes mozzarella. I caught my colleague red-handed. I stopped him just in time. I told him, "Look, you've just been saved because if the person who made this mozzarella saw what you are doing to it he would kill you." "Why?" he asked me. I replied, "This man wakes up between three and four in the morning, prepares the *pasta filata*, puts his hands in hot water in order to be able to make the mozzarella as it has to be done. It is suffering … it is work … it is *sacrifice*. If only you would pause to think about this you would leave the mozzarella as it is." This aggressive way of transforming food is like Frankenstein. You change the deepest structure of the food. Cooking is not about changing structure. Cooking is a process that modifies the food, but if you make this strong intervention even before you start then…'

Tubelli, a deeply pained look in his face, lifted a glass from the table.

'Then this glass will not be a glass any more.'

We sat in uneasy silence, pondering the collapse of our world's certainties.

'Luckily in Italy we are changing this. The idea of violent intervention is beginning to go away. We are going back to the old ways. Sometimes I have this idea – well, when we speak about Leopardi it becomes quite clear – that the critical literature commits the same violent operation. They put into the author something that is not in his writing. There is something like a violent operation before you even start reading him. You read not the work itself, but rather you see it through the lens that has been created for it. When we published our book we did a presentation and put together a menu from those dishes that Leopardi listed and then we had an open discussion about the book. We did this in Naples and then in the region of Marche but *not* in Recanati. Consider this. The book is in the Leopardi library in Recanati. The lady director of the Istituto Leopardi came to one of our dinners and I asked her, "Why can't we present the book in Recanati?" She explained that the heirs of Leopardi who are in charge of the institution absolutely disagreed with our way of interpreting his thinking and writing and so they were closed to the idea. They didn't want us to go to Recanati. They wanted to preserve this image of Leopardi as this saint, just as his mother would have wished.'

'So the end for Leopardi is like his beginning?'

'Some critics follow this interpretation. Others don't. Martone, the director who made the film about Leopardi, went absolutely *their* way. Leopardi had some health problems, but the director made a monster of him in the physical sense. Sorry I'm being rough on this issue, but it was because he had to have the approval of the Recanati regime and go with the approval of the family. So he followed their line. That is the answer to your question. I did not like the film. Consider, too, that members of Martone's entourage came to obtain a copy of the book from me. They acted as if they were interested in the gastronomical theme and wanted to develop the Ignarra character. They were going to include this *monzù* chef ... but they stopped, they didn't do it. If you picture this life that Leopardi, Ignarra, and Ranieri were having together it was a happy one. They were eating together, talking all night long. They couldn't put that in the film so they by and large cancelled out this character. It is a horrible movie!'

'Your face says it all.'

'It wasn't the right way to go about it. Martone started as an alternative filmmaker – that was at the beginning of his career – but then he goes and sticks to the mainstream regime. It is always like this.'

'When you were talking earlier about cooking the mozzarella, this to me was like the making of a poem.'

'Yes, when you make a poem or prepare a dish the ingredients in both must be pure. There must be balance. There must be form. You are arrogant if you take upon yourself the right to do as you like with the product of someone's creation. Mozzarella is one such product and so there are certain things that mustn't be done to it. You can say whatever you like, but when you do something like this you are being aggressive towards nature. It is a kind of pollution. I want to protect nature. This arrogant way is like those people who cut down the trees in the Brazilian forest. It's the same thing, there is no difference. It is about the cyclical relationship between man and nature. Again, in school, they teach us that Leopardi has this idea of nature as being aggressive towards man, as being like an evil stepmother. It's the kind of interpretation that is given in Italy. You learn three things about Leopardi – he was depressed, a sad man, a monster in the physical sense, secondly, he had these pessimistic ideas, and thirdly, that nature for him is horrible. It's the other way round. During the last three years of his life he could feel another way of being with nature. You can read this in "La ginestra", a smoother and sweeter aspect of nature. It is not an evil stepmother any more. Sadly he didn't have time to develop this. Who knows what he would have done.'

'What you are telling me is more valuable than any book of literary criticism.'

'It is the difference between passion and reason.'

'I can see you at the table with Leopardi.'

'When we wrote the book I became Pasquale Ignarra. That was me! The first time we presented the book was at the Villa delle Ginestre and before we started talking about the book I asked if I could see the kitchen. It was in the northern part of the house, the freshest side, on the ground floor, but it was not open to the public because of the low ceiling so for security reasons people couldn't go there and when I got through into that place and saw this kitchen, this wonderful old stone oven, at that point I imagined myself as Pasquale Ignarra! *Bellissimo!*'

I showed Tubelli the photograph of the kitchen, at which point he gave a huge cry.'

'*Eh! Eh! Eh!*'

Tubelli summoned his brother and colleague, Lucio, to look at the image.

'On the right side there is a horrible bit, a basin from modern times – *orrible! orrible!* – but it is not in the picture, which is good.'

It was feeding time for the human race and Tubelli had to go and be high priest to this most sacred of duties but before doing so he invited us to dine.

'What do you recommend?' I asked him.

'I never make suggestions. I have my sons. I cannot say I love this son better than the others. They are my sons, I love them all. Choose what you like.'

What I can report is that the tempura on the vegetables was so light, so crisp, and so sparing of oil that it did not stain the fingers. The solo flight of each pale blond missile from the plate to the mouth was a small miracle. We think tempura is Japanese, but actually it begins with the arrival in Japan, in 1543, of three Portuguese sailors who'd lost their bearings. A trading post was begun there, which lasted until 1639, and when the Portuguese departed they left behind them a deep-fried green bean recipe, *peixinhos da horta*, which the Japanese adapted to any number of seafood and vegetable dishes. There is, however, an alternative history. According to Tubelli, who has been to Japan to study the cuisine, the word 'tempura' derives from the Latin *tempora* which refers to the periods of abstinence in the religious calendar. The monks invented the dish in order to relieve themselves from the tedium of plain boiled vegetables. Tubelli discovered the identical recipe in the records of the church at Rocca San Felice in Campania although he admits it was Portuguese Jesuit monks who exported the dish to the Far East. 'La friggitoria è arte di ricordi,' Tubelli has said elsewhere. Frying is the art of memory? One looks in vain for a redeeming quality in the English words but in Italian it is, of course, poetry pure and simple.

I believe that on the most profound level Antonio Tubelli is right when he says Leopardi had found happiness of a kind in Naples. Such happiness is only rarely recognised for what it is. The proof of it does not require anything quite so trivial as a smile although for once I trust Ranieri when he speaks of Leopardi's 'indescribable, heavenly smile'. There is a glimmer of it in some of the surviving images of him, a delicacy in his features that must have taken even his enemies by surprise. All depends on what one means by happiness, of course, and whether it needs to be fleeting for it to have value. A million glossy magazines are dedicated to the pursuit of happiness although we know well enough it cannot be pursued unless it is at the cost of bloodshed and it is something quite apart from contentment that is more enduring although all the more subject to upheaval and carnage. The poems Leopardi wrote were his consecration of love, not in the physical sense because he almost certainly died a virgin, and yet whatever that love was it meant his poems cannot be understood in the wholly negative sense. Heaven knows what the love of a woman might have done for him and there were a few who caught his fancy – his cousin Geltrude Cassi Lazzari whom he knew at a distance over just three days, or was it just two days and three nights but long enough to inspire his poem 'Il primo amore'?; the coachman's daughter, Teresa Fattorini, who sang as she sat at the loom in the window of her parents' home and died young, and although Leopardi scorned the suggestion that he was in love with her she was the inspiration for one of his

loveliest poems, 'A Silvia'; the coquettish Fanny Targioni Toz-
zetti (his 'Aspasia') who referred to him as 'il mio gobbetto' ('my
little hunchback') and who inspired 'On the Likeness of a Beautiful Woman Carved on her Sepulchral Monument', although
one senses a bit of the knife in it; the Contessa Teresa Carni-
ani Malvezzi who wrote poetry herself and was one of the few
people with whom he could communicate; Teresa Lucignani, a
mere fifteen years of age, who found him repulsive; and finally,
perhaps most vitally, 'la donna che non si trova' ('the woman
who cannot be found'). Leopardi, as is so often the case with
men who live in solitude, dwelled upon love's image rather than
love itself although the poems themselves demonstrate true
depth of feeling. Against all my better instincts, which is to say
against everything I already knew, I had allowed myself to be
caught up in the commonplace view that a melancholy vision
proceeds from a depressed mind whereas even the darkest vision,
in order to escape the confines of the brain, requires the agency
of enthusiasm. Whether we are talking of Samuel Beckett, Franz
Kafka, or the ever-melancholic W. G. Sebald, none of them could
have achieved anything of value were it not for the exhilaration
that comes of giving voice to even their darkest thoughts and if
one looks deeper there is even, if one listens carefully enough, a
sound of laughter close to inaudible. Such 'art' as does emerge
from a depressed state, so-called 'confessional poetry', for
example, is rarely more than the rather unwholesome business
of people expressing themselves. They continue to do so all over
the place and there's no mop porous enough to absorb the mess
they make. This is why when reading Leopardi I am able to tolerate a pessimism so deep that it exceeds even mine. I already had
the answer years ago, when, in the poem in which I appropriated
his voice, I wrote 'the darkness which goes so deep can only be
pure sunlight in reverse'. And yet it took a *monzù* to remind me
of what I've always known. *Say Giacomo Leopardi found peace
in Naples*. And yes, he really did enjoy his food, and yes, I will

have the pear and ricotta ice cream that has been one of the great discoveries of my time in Naples, but not before I have feasted upon Antonio Tubelli's *timballo allo scammaro* which is of monastic origin, an oven-baked pasta dish made with anchovies, olives, and pecorino cheese, simplicity itself, as simple as 'scende la luna·e si scolora il mondo' but untranslatable all the same.

Raimondo di Sangro & the Veil of Knowledge

Raimondo di Sangro, Prince of Sansevero, finding himself under increasing scrutiny from no fewer than seven cardinals, had them killed and from their skin and bones ingeniously fashioned seven chairs. It is not recorded over what period of time this was done, but presumably the skins had to be sufficiently tanned before they could bear a sitter's posterior weight. As for the bones they may have been removed from the corpses after the extensive draining process known as *scolatura* by the *schiattamuorti* who were specially trained for that purpose.* A grisly business, rather unhealthy too, it's understandable why Raimondo chose to remain on the designer side of things. We know enough of his character to be able to say that he was nothing if not inventive, able to make the most of the materials closest to hand, and that he appears not to have been particularly vindictive. There are two contemporary accounts of the prince, both by Neapolitans, the jurist and historian Giangiuseppe Origlia

---

* The rather unfriendly Neapolitan curse *puozza sculà* ('may you drain away') is still in use although the practice that gave rise to it is not.

Paolino, and the other by his friend, the writer and philosopher Antonio Genovesi who describes him as 'short, with a big head, of pleasing and youthful appearance, a witty philosopher, greatly devoted to the mechanical sciences, very amiable and sweet in manner, scholarly and retiring, a lover of conversation with literary people'. Sweetness of manner is not necessarily a barrier to unpredictable behaviour, but it can be said diminutive stature often brings out the worst as well as the best in people. Genovesi also writes, 'If it weren't for his flaw of an excess of imagination, which leads him to see things that are not very likely to exist, he could pass as one of the perfect philosophers.' This is somewhat at odds with what we hear of a man who seemed able to achieve the greater part of whatever he put his mind to, although sometimes we have had to take his word for it as very little of what he achieved survives. Maybe Genovesi is right, though, and the business of the philosopher is to philosophise and not to make furniture. Still it takes imagination to see things as they are or as they might be. What Raimondo left behind, although the overall vision was his, is the best of what other people made for him and such ideas as he had, which were many in number, at the time of his death literally went up in smoke. We are, however, able to detect enough patterns in the ashes to be able to say that the history of the eighteenth-century Enlightenment in Naples is to a great extent his story. Many of his followers went on to become significant figures, among them the nobleman Fortunato Bartolomeo de Félice whose massive *Encyclopédie d'Yverdon* would be a compendium of the new thinking. There is no evidence of any of the seven chairs having survived, no catalogues, no auction records for their sale, and such researches as I have conducted into the simultaneous disappearance of the seven cardinals who Raimondo then put to fresh use have turned up not a single bone.

✳

It's terrible to begin a chapter on a lie or what may be construed as a cheap ploy in order to grab the reader's attention, but then I do so in order to show the furthermost reaches of the 'black legend' surrounding Raimondo di Sangro of which the above is just one instance. There is material sufficient for any number of *gialli*, the 'yellow' horror movies with which not all but a good number of Italians entertain themselves. Although I've yet to meet an aficionado, somebody, somewhere, must be watching them, and whatever it is about them that brings the viewer such pleasure is perhaps related to the take on truth that passes for much of the country's journalism and which feeds an insatiable appetite for the scandalous and the macabre. One can easily imagine the newspapers today full of *cronaca nera* (black news) about Raimondo, each new revelation just a bit murkier than the last. Certainly some of the more outlandish gossip about him endures. All this obscures the fact that he is one of the most fascinating figures of his day, which is not to suggest Raimondo was without praise during his own lifetime. We have the admiring accounts of physicists, geographers, historians, philosophers, and yes, even a cardinal, Gian Vincenzo Antonio Ganganelli, who wrote a letter to Raimondo saying of him that he was perfectly capable of 'creating a second world from the first' – arrestingly perceptive words from one who would later become pope.* It could serve as Raimondo's epitaph although typically he devised his own: 'Vir mirus ... in perscrutandis reconditis naturæ arcanis celeberrimus ...' ('an extraordinary

---

* Pope Clement XIV would award the fourteen-year-old Mozart with the Order of the Golden Spur after the latter, hearing it only the once, committed to memory the whole of Allegri's 'Miserere mei, Deus', the distribution of which outside the papal chapel was forbidden on pain of excommunication. One pope at a time, though, because we have yet to meet Benedict XIV who was pope during the period of Raimondo's greatest difficulties.

man ... renowned for his ability to investigate the most concealed of nature's secrets').

So why is Raimondo di Sangro important now? Quackery has been one charge levelled against him with respect to his alchemical activities, but alchemy, as any investigation of its etymology demonstrates, was the midwife to chemistry. Some of the greatest minds partook of it – Sir Isaac Newton, Roger Bacon, Jacob Boehme, Robert Boyle, to name but four. Raimondo may have taken alchemy a little past its sell-by date, but with him it was never less than a serious enquiry into the nature of things. One may choose to locate in him the meeting point between the old superstitious Naples and the Naples of the Enlightenment, and any discussion of the dualistic nature of the city can be said to have its beginnings in him. It may be argued that only now has his time come. This we owe to recent research, critical re-evaluation, and the absence of the suffocating muzzle of religion, although in truth I don't think Raimondo was quite as much at odds with the Church as admirers and detractors alike suggest. Where he collided with it was usually in those areas of debate with which the Vatican is now perfectly at home. One might say he was ahead of his time. It's a dusty phrase, though, because to be ahead of one's time usually means that one is, more than most people, *absolutely of one's time.*

It goes without saying that he attracted rumours to himself or, more to the point, he may have been quite happy for them to issue from his own office. This probably was done more in the spirit of good humour than menace. So it may well be that Raimondo 'kept it up', so to speak, until he attracted the attention of the Church authorities. We know his biggest headache was Cardinal Spinelli who somehow escaped the fate of his seven confederates. Spinelli belonged to that ultra conservative faction in the College of Cardinals known as the *zelanti*, and his religious zeal was such that Charles III of Spain, King of Naples, had him quietly removed. Another powerful figure with whom

Raimondo had to contend was the prime minister of the time, Bernardo Tanucci, who, although an enlightened man and a foe of the Church to the extent that he shut down convents and monasteries, had little time for Raimondo and his ideas and at one point had him arrested on a flimsy pretext. The fact that Raimondo was, and continued to be, shown in a dark light is to some degree responsible for having kept his story alive.

Clearly Raimondo was happy to test the credulity of his superstitious neighbours while they, from their side, were incredulous as to the things they saw, particularly late at night when they passed his studio, in the basement of the Palazzo Sansevero, which he called La Fenice ('The Phoenix') after the mythical bird that rises from its own ashes. What they saw through the barred window of the Palazzo Sansevero were 'wandering flames, hellish lights' accompanied by strange smells and booming noises. It ought to be remembered that the streets at that time were very dark and so it took little to bring an added sense of menace to the atmosphere. We know now that Raimondo was experimenting with fireworks and that he was the first person to have introduced several shades of the colour green although, according to Giangiuseppe Origlia's account he had already broadened their chromatic range with the addition of 'turquoise, citrus yellow, the yellow of the orange, white tending towards the colour of milk, the red colour of rubies' and many other hues. Over time the black legend grew ever larger and, more often than not, quite untrue.

What *is* true, although here we must reflect a little on the times in which he lived, was that Raimondo, a lover of bel canto, procured young boys for the purpose of their becoming singers with angelic voices. This required they be castrated, after which the unfortunates were sent to the Conservatory of the Poor of Jesus Christ in Naples. *Castrati* were, and continued to be, a fact of existence. (The very last *castrato*, Alessandro Moreschi, died in 1922.) Raimondo may also have been responding to the idea of the absolute perfection born of 'primordial androgyny' that had been doing the rounds in masonic circles.

Word on the street was that he was in league with the Devil. Where there is fear, truth is of little consequence and there is nothing quite so threatening to the backward mind as another's intelligence. It is said, although I have yet to witness this, that the older people of Naples still cross themselves at the mention of his name or when passing the Cappella Sansevero. And yet they are the same poor and uneducated people who, with their amalgam of fear, respect, and superstition, managed to create through their legends a kind of lingering subterranean existence for the man and his place, when both were all but ignored for a couple of centuries. There was not nearly as much hostility for Raimondo from them as from those in high places.

It is quite inexplicable that the English with their love of the arcane and the eccentric should have ignored Raimondo although he does merit a couple of pages in Harold Acton's history of the Bourbons. There is little about his life that does not fascinate. The first thing to notice is that there is a jump in the noble line, which is to say that the sixth prince of Sansevero was not Raimondo's father Antonio, Duke of Torremaggiore, but his grandfather Paolo. Raimondo's mother, Cecilia Gaetani dell'Aquila d'Aragona, died shortly after he was born on 30 January 1710, after which the father became for the greater part of his son's life an absentee. Antonio di Sangro was a dark figure. It may be that his wife's sudden death caused him to lose his moral compass because his actions seem to anticipate Act I, sc. i of Mozart's *Don Giovanni*. Antonio raped a young woman, slew her father, and then, very much unlike the Don who would flee not even Death, fled to Austria where he sought the protection of the emperor. There is a dark twist in a man who feels resentment towards those whom he has wronged, and in some kind of mental storm he returned to his hometown of Torremaggiore and there killed his chief accuser, the mayor, Nicola Rossi, which, by any measure, was an unwise thing to do. Wealth protects, however, as do indulgent mothers sometimes. Antonio's mother paid for him to enter a monastery where he renounced his titles, took priestly vows, and stayed for the rest of his life. There is a tendency in the modern mind to look upon the Church as an institution prepared to wash out any old stain for a price whereas the reality is, and has always been, that ultimately each man must wash his own clothes. So it may well be that Antonio di Sangro really did spend the rest of his days in penance. Raimondo's parents would later be memorialised with two statues in the Cappella Sansevero, which, as we shall see, are of themselves extraordinary puzzles.

Young Raimondo fell under the care of his grandfather Paolo and lived with him at the Palazzo Sansevero on Piazza San Domenico Maggiore. It must have made for a haunted childhood because it was at this very address that one of the most notorious murders in Italian history took place. On the evening of 16 October 1590 the composer Carlo Gesualdo, finding his wife, Donna Maria d'Avalos, in the arms of her lover, Fabrizio Carafa, slew them both, paying particular attention to the wounds he inflicted upon Donna Maria's body, stabbing her repeatedly 'in those parts which she ought to have kept honest', and then dumped both naked bodies in the courtyard where they were left on display for a week. It is said that the place is still haunted and that the distressed, scantily clad ghost of Maria d'Avalos goes looking for her lover, walking back and forth between the palazzo and the obelisk in Piazza San Domenico Maggiore.

Paolo sent his grandson, aged ten, to the Jesuit College in Rome where he excelled at his studies and was nicknamed 'Precipitoso', suggestive of one who is always in a hurry. The school, one of the most enlightened in Italy, incubated in Raimondo the notion that although truth may be veiled it will be revealed to those most deserving of it, and in this respect we have a foretaste of the masonic activities to come. Certainly he would have imbibed the spirit of Athanasius Kircher, the German Jesuit scholar who taught at the college for over forty years, who had created a marvellous *wunderkammer* there, some of which was still in existence, and whose hermetic works, particularly those relating to Egyptian hieroglyphics, must have produced an incalculable effect on the boy's mind. A brilliant student, he mastered eight languages, Arabic and Hebrew among them, philosophy, pyrotechnics, and the natural sciences. In 1726, when he was sixteen, his grandfather died and the title of prince flew over the father's head and straight onto Raimondo's. When he was nineteen Raimondo came up with the first of many inventions: a folding stage that greatly impressed Nicola Michetti, Royal Engineer to Tsar Peter the Great. Raimondo claimed that the idea for the stage came to him in a dream, in which he was presented with the design by Archimedes. In 1730, aged twenty, he returned to Naples and the palazzo that was now his.

He married by proxy his first cousin, Carlotta Gaetani dell'Aquila d'Aragona – she was fourteen at the time and lived in Flanders – and the official ceremony took place six years later. A poem was written for the event by the great philosopher Giambattista Vico and a musical prelude composed by Giambattista Pergolesi, which serves to remind us that Naples was, and had always been, fertile ground for men of intellect. The marriage was a happy one and produced five children. It was during this period that he would forge the most important friendship of his life, with Charles of Bourbon, whom he charmed with the gift of another of his inventions, a waterproof cape. Charles or Carlos, who looked so much like the proboscis monkey (*Nasalis larvatus*) native to Borneo, was to be his protector and later made him Knight of the Order of San Gennaro which, as we shall see, could not have been a more ironic title. Raimondo also invented for the monarch an ingenious hydraulic machine and a double-barrelled harquebus capable of firing both gunpowder and compressed air. After distinguishing himself in the military and producing a treatise on how best to employ the infantry, which Frederick of Prussia praised, he was made member of the Accademia della Crusca, the Italian equivalent of the Académie Française, where he adopted the name 'Esercitato' ('the exercised') which would later slip, maybe as a deliberate clue to his identity, into the title of his most significant, anonymously published, book. After the battle of Velletri, where he distinguished himself, Raimondo was given access by Pope Benedict XIV to the Index Librorum Prohibitorum in the Vatican, which, on the latter's part, was a miscalculation.

Soon enough Raimondo took what was to be the next logical step for someone devoted to the values of the Enlightenment, which included having a keen interest in science, and became involved with Freemasonry. Such were his leadership qualities that in 1750 he founded and was made Grand Master of the Orient Lodge. He translated masonic texts and clandestinely printed them on his press. About this time he also invented a printing machine that could produce several colours at a single pressing. In 1751 (although the title page says 1750) Raimondo published his *Apologetic Letter by a cultivated member of the Crusca Academy containing the Defence of the book entitled* Letters of a Peruvian Woman *with respect to her assumption about the Quipu, written to the Duchess S*****.

The book to which he refers, *Lettres d'une Péruvienne*, was first published in 1747. It was an immensely popular epistolary novel by Françoise de Graffigny, which purports to be the account of an Incan woman abducted by Spaniards and then rescued by the French, who then take her to France where she records her observations. It is in fact a sly dissection of French society and manners. It was a strange work for Raimondo to utilise, but maybe its very popularity was reason enough for him to use it as a vehicle for his own revolutionary ideas, the knife smuggled in with the cake, so to speak. What fascinated him above all was the ancient Peruvian *quipu*, a system of notations based on the use of coloured knots, which served not only as an aide-mémoire but also as a means for calculating future events. Modern research points to this having been, in the main, a numeric system and not analogous to the letters of any alphabet, although it has been suggested that it might have served as a system of representative symbols. This is where a Neapolitan woman, Clara Miccinelli, enters the picture. A school teacher and writer, she claimed to own a *quipu* by means of which she was able to put a fresh interpretation on the Jesuit presence in Peru. It was later deemed to be a forgery. The complex story can be read in Jeremy Mumford's *Clara Miccinelli's Cabinet of Wonders* (2000). What concerns us here is that she had decidedly eccentric notions, not least of which was the link she made between her *quipu* and Raimondo di Sangro whose 'spirit' sent her written messages asking her to re-evaluate his scientific discoveries and philosophical beliefs. In his article, Mumford writes at length about her 'cabinet of wonders', noting that she 'has a history of finding strange documents in surprising places'. It had been my intention to seek her out, not because I wished to expose her but because I am interested in how the dead impact on the living, some of whom claim to be Raimondo's reincarnation. There is a certain sweetness in those who pursue, and always find, the impossible. Sadly, with Signorina Miccinelli, this is no longer possible. She died while I was last in Naples.

As such Raimondo's book touched upon cabalistic and esoteric matters that were at odds with the teachings of the Church especially when it came to explaining the book of Genesis, the necessity for free thought, and the relationship between sacred and profane history. This, in addition to his masonic activities, was to herald a period of difficulties. The following year, on 28 May 1751, the Holy Office issued a Bull, the Providas Romanorum Pontificum, which called for the excommunication of Freemasons, Raimondo among their number. On 29 February 1752, his *Apologetic Letter* was placed in the Index of Banned

Books, which had been Raimondo's pleasure once to peruse. A couple of years later, Pope Benedict would write a letter in which he expresses his disquiet, describing Raimondo's book as 'full of sentiments and expressions at the very least seriously suspicious of error in Catholic dogma, and too favourable to the perverse and detestable systems of strong spirits, deists, Materialists, Cabbalists, etc.'.

Anticipating trouble, and clearly something of an artful dodger, Raimondo had recanted his masonic activities in advance of the Papal Bull, and on 26 December 1750 presented Carlo with a list of all the Freemasons in the city, which exceeded a thousand in number. Depending on how one reads this, Raimondo's action can be taken as a betrayal of his colleagues, which is how they saw it, or a cunning scheme to save them from the attentions of Cardinal Spinelli and the Holy Office. Carlo, discovering that the list contained at least half the people in his court, on 2 July 1751 issued what amounted to a 'solemn admonition', nothing more, and in the process took the wind out of Spinelli's sails. Raimondo was not forgiven by his fellows, however, and was subsequently denounced in Masonic lodges throughout Europe. Raimondo wrote to Pope Benedict XIV assuring him that he had dropped his Masonic beliefs and the Pope in turn revoked Raimondo's excommunication. I can't help but wonder if between them there is not to be found one of the great unexamined relationships of the time, which, if voiced, could become material for a dramatic dialogue between two men of great intelligence representing, respectively, the Catholic Church and Neapolitan Radical Enlightenment, each one pushing at the other's boundaries. One need only stare into the face of Pope Benedict as rendered in oils by Pierre Subleyras or in marble by Pietro Bracci to be able to observe in it an uncommon intelligence. Benedict, one of the greatest scholars of his time, promoted scientific learning, which included anatomical studies, took a great interest in the arts and ancient literature, and, much to his credit, condemned the enslavement of indigenous peoples. I have a suspicion that Raimondo may have had this last point in mind when he adopted the *quipu* as a form of argument. One man's enlightenment is often another man's endarkenment, however, and despite his many liberal qualities (and the fact that he asked the Holy Office to reconsider the removal of the *Lettera Apologetica* from the Index) Benedict was forced into a conservative position.

Although Raimondo's Masonic phase was a relatively short one, covering only two years, it is difficult to resist the notion that the spirit of it accompanied him over the years to come. The accusations by his fellow masons stung Raimondo deeply and he withdrew from public life, spending more and more time in La Fenice where he involved himself in pursuits of a more private scientific nature. If suppression of his activities had been the intention, what this exclusion from public life did was to initiate a period of experimentation and invention unrivalled since the days of Leonardo da Vinci and conducted in as many directions. A stop at his studio became a feature of the Grand Tour and what Raimondo sought to do was nothing less than to amaze his visitors. The range of his activities was breathtaking and includes the production of artificial gems and coloured glass, a technique for desalinating sea water, an amphibious carriage that worked on land and water alike (which was made to look as if it was drawn by horses but actually was moved by an ingenious system of wheeled blades), a cannon so light a single soldier could carry two of them, and a number of medicines that saved lives. One of the more extraordinary inventions, and probably the most fully documented, was a 'perpetual light' which could burn uninterrupted for three months at a time, the material for which was obtained from human skulls, a highly concentrated mixture of magnesium and phosphate. There survive seven letters, written in Italian, in April 1753, from Raimondo di Sangro to an unnamed friend, and a similar correspondence, in French, to Jean-Antoine Nollet, abbot and physicist, who once arranged for two hundred monks to stand in a circle about a mile in circumference, with wires connected to them, and then ran an electric shock which passed through them at the same time in order to demonstrate the speed at which electricity moves. The monks fell and Nollet's reputation rose. So excited was Raimondo by his discovery of the 'perpetual flame' that he related it to Nollet in words bordering on the erotic: 'I stay for a few hours sitting down to love myself alone, so to speak, with my new phenomenon.' The letters Raimondo wrote dwell at length on this light that owes its existence to the *Mercurius philosophorum*, the study of which takes us deeply into alchemy, *Mercurius* taking the shape of a serpent, which encircles the earth and is ready to strike at any time. The skull is also the alchemical symbol of the *caput mortuum* (literally 'dead head'), the raw material from which one looks for the Philosopher's Stone. Typically Raimondo conceals as much as he reveals and never fully spells out the recipe for his magical compound.

We now begin to move into a Faustian zone. Raimondo indulged not only in the study of alchemy but also palingenesis, the reconstruction of bodies from their ashes, which, together with metempsychosis (the transmigration of the soul), is at the centre of much alchemical thinking. Usually it involved the regeneration of plant forms but Giangiuseppe Origlia describes how Raimondo would burn river crabs, from which insects were born, which he would then irrigate with oxblood after which he employed a secret technique to generate more crabs. Could it be Raimondo was playing an elaborate visual joke on his friend? There were also rumours that he was able to make blood out of water or even air, and that he came up with an explanation for ghosts, describing them as latent forms of energy that became visible in particular physical and chemical conditions. It is quite likely that during this period Raimondo made the acquaintance of the occultist and magician, Count Cagliostro, who, when he was tried in 1790 by the Roman tribunal of the Holy Inquisition, claimed that his knowledge of alchemy was acquired in Naples from 'a prince who had a great passion for chemistry'. This could have been none other than Raimondo although, incredibly, the documents relating to the trial are still under lock and key at the Vatican. In any event, Raimondo was no longer about to suffer the consequences.

As to Raimondo's most controversial experiment, it is a wonder he was not torn limb from limb by his already suspicious neighbours. The French astronomer and Freemason, Joseph Jérôme de Lalande – who said of Raimondo that he was not an academic but an entire academy – and the French mathematician and geographer, Charles Marie de la Condamine, were witnesses, the latter several times in 1754, to Raimondo's duplication of the miracle of San Gennaro. Three times a year the dry blood of the patron saint of Naples liquefies. Sometimes it fails to do so, which augurs a period of trouble. This was the case in 1939 and again in 1980, the year of the Irpinia earthquake. It also failed in 1751, the year when the activities of the Masonic Lodge drew forth Benedict's Providas Romanorum Pontificum. Raimondo was playing with fire. La Condamine's *Journal of a Tour to Italy,* translated from French into English in 1763, is the most concise eyewitness account we have, although he knows better than to reveal the names of Raimondo and his assistant.

This is what I have been an eyewitness to on several occasions, not only the evening I mentioned, in presence of their highnesses, but since more particularly, and in broad day, at the keepers of the machine, where I had all the necessary time to examine it. I observed beneath the phial two small cones, I know not of what material, with their points opposed to each other, which he informed me were perforated with a small opening. He further added, that they were hollow, and that the lower cone was moveable, in such a manner that its orifice sometimes met with that of the upper cone, and at other times did not; all this was purely accidental, and just as the motion impressed on the phial caused, or not, the axes of the two cones to concur. As for the dust which I saw in the phial, they told me it was an amalgama of mercury, lead, tin, and bismuth; that the bismuth, which mingles but very imperfectly with the other ingredients, prevented the mixture from becoming an absolute fixed paste, and gave it the form of a powder too thick to pass through the little opening which communicated with the two cones. Lastly, they added, that in a circular channel, concealed in the mounting, was contained some running quicksilver; that by shaking the phial irregularly, when the orifices of the two cones met, this mercury insinuated itself in a greater or less quantity, and liquefied the amalgama; that it came to pass sometimes, that by the variety of motions impressed on the machine, the mercury, so introduced, returned again by the same opening, and that then the amalgama ceased to be fluid. I relate with all possible exactness what the possessor of this ingenious machine told me, and which I also set down in writing the same day: All that I can certify for fact is, that it performed its operations extremely well. He promised me at that time an exact description of it, together with a draught of all its parts, to be communicated to the Academy. He has since renewed the same promise to me in writing, but has not yet fulfilled it.

As might a chef with his recipes, Raimondo held back on divulging certain ingredients.

There is almost always a lengthy queue of people waiting to get inside the Cappella Sansevero and although I'd much rather have the place to myself I have to accept that its draw is perfectly understandable. The statue of the *Cristo velato* ('Veiled

Christ') is worth the journey from anywhere. This Christ is ours. One feels his bodily weight as if the depression he makes upon the mattress where he lies is somehow translated into our own innate sense of measure. The empathy is absolute. The *cappella*, which at times feels more like a temple, is a jewel of Neapolitan baroque. Actually, I'd say it is *the* jewel, the closest rival being the Church of Pio Monte della Misericordia, where one may gaze in wonder at Caravaggio's *Seven Works of Mercy* – but while the splendour of this church is concentrated into a single image, in the Cappella Sansevero it is the complex iconography of the whole that floods the mind and eye. It is not overblown, however. Harold Acton, perhaps too much the aesthete at times, winces at the art inside and seems not to want to like it quite as much he does. 'But none can deny their hallucinating technical skill,' he writes, 'and they will ever appeal to those who cherish realism, though in this case it is oddly mingled with eighteenth-century rococo.' The years of excessive Italian rococo may have jaundiced his view a little. It's the first time I have found it palatable because for me even late renaissance is too late. A splash of vulgarity makes Naples what it is, but there is something almost austere about the Cappella Sansevero, such that even the frills are imbued with purpose. As soon as one enters it one is startled, but the floridity of so much baroque art and architecture has been somehow made to behave. Classical Greece shows its face, keeps things trim, keeps them smart. Acton again, noting that the architects and sculptors were mostly of northern Italian stock, writes, 'In blending the grandiose with the startling, it was as if they were influenced by the volcanic atmosphere, and wished to compete with the mineral, marine and vegetable forces of nature, so that one comes to regard them as Neapolitan.' It is, after all, quite possible to become Neapolitan. Whether it is to be recommended is another matter.

Fabrizio Masucci, director of Museo Cappella Sansevero, is a direct descendent of Raimondo di Sangro. The fact he does not bear his ancestor's name is due to a tectonic shift somewhere in the marital scheme. A classicist by training – Plato his area of expertise – with aristocratic features a sculptor ought to render in stone. A painter would put him in an oval frame. When conditions are just right, not too much static in the atmosphere, one can hear a coach and horses in his voice. A powdered wig will complete the picture. Masucci has absorbed every known detail of Raimondo's life and works such that one has only to begin a question and he will have already begun to formulate an answer – the minutiae of his ancestor's life having entered his bloodstream to the degree that not only can he call upon all that is known about him, but also, without slipping the cables of common sense, speculate on what is *not* known about him. As to how he *feels* about it all, he is not a man to be drawn into an open space. At least I was not able to lure him there. When I asked him whether he ever felt imprisoned by his role of keeper of Raimondo's memory he was quick to deflect my question, saying only that he and his family feel a responsibility to let people know there is a treasure 'the most perfect possible' in Naples. As much as he loves the *cappella*, the main focus for him is the figure of Raimondo who he feels has been unjustly ignored. That he has succeeded in the first instance is beyond doubt: in 2017 the Museo Cappella Sansevero entered the FT 1000, the Financial Times index of the fastest growing companies in Europe. It's probably not quite what Raimondo would have had in mind, but surely he'd be amused. As for the second instance, which is where my interest lies, Masucci feels the figure of his ancestor has been polluted with too much bad literature.

'*Tempio o cappella?*' It was the first question I put to him.

'The first thing to understand is that Sansevero is a *cappella gentilizia* built for an aristocratic family. As was commonly the case, it was linked to the palace by means of an enclosed footbridge, the main difference between this and other such structures being that inside it there was a small temple, eight

columns creating a circular space, and a carillon that would play different kinds of music. Maybe it is easier to answer your question by referring to what Raimondo's opponents had to say about it. Cardinal Spinelli and his allies sent an official communication to the king requesting he put a stop to the works. Spinelli originally wanted the name of the place to be called Santa Maria della Pietà, but instead of being a proper *cappella* it was becoming a temple with pagan idols. One element within the *cappella* responsible for their hostile reaction was the statue of "Pudicizia" ("Modesty") which they described as pagan, saying it would embarrass or discomfort anyone. Also the word "temple" was very much within the Masonic vocabulary and the *cappella* was sometimes called "The Temple of Virtues". The statues depicting those virtues represent a braided path towards enlightenment. I don't say this to be diplomatic, but these two things, the pagan and the Christian, live together.'

'It has been said that the statue of Modesty also represents Isis.'

'There is definitely this aspect,' Masucci replied. 'Isis was veiled and as such she represented the esoteric side of life. Ancient Egypt was highly visible in masonic symbolism. The frontispiece of Diderot's *Encylopédie* represents knowledge as a veiled figure. The artist who drew it came to Naples and it is quite possible he was inspired by the statue.'

'It would seem that Raimondo was deliberately pushing at the boundaries of what was acceptable,' I suggested. 'Was this not part and parcel with his fuelling the legends around him, or was it in order to keep people at a distance so that he might go about his work without interference? May one go even further and say he liked to play a little with the people?'

'This is very much within the context of the baroque, matching the taste for wonder in that period with making people doubt their own senses. The producing of optical illusions was certainly part of this. The amphibious carriage which he created three months before his death was his swansong. Deception was a very baroque concept, saying things without actually saying them, implying other things, but nonetheless in his writings he was aiming for an audience who could understand him. So he was playing with irony, deceiving with irony, but definitely there was a public for whom he was writing these things. We have on one side the fuelling of the legend, the sense of wonder, all very much within the taste of the baroque, and on the other side there is Raimondo's need to be recognised by European society. When *Lettera Apologetica* was placed on the Index he was starting to translate it into French. So there was this ambivalent attitude.'

Irony and playfulness being the hallmarks of his character, in his *Lettera Apologetica* Raimondo proposed a new form of punctuation, the *punto ironico* (the ironic point) which, visually, is the same as the fermata or corona ⌒ , the musical notation that indicates a pause or stop, and which, by the way, the Russian composer Alfred Schnittke wittily adopted for his tombstone. When Raimondo suggested its adoption it was probable that he intended it to serve as a form of protection or alibi. When he wrote his *Supplica*, in which he begs for forgiveness (and possibly with an eye to having the *Lettera* removed from the Index), he argued that he wanted readers to understand that he was joking and that he had come up with a new way of indicating it. Any sentences that might appear disrespectful would have a ⌒ at their end. Needless to say, the argument did not wash with the church authorities.

'This surely illustrates,' I said, 'Raimondo's ability to invent whatever he needed at any given time.'

'Very little has been said about this. It was not only about inventing things that were functional, it was also a challenging environment. Raimondo was challenging himself first of all, but you must remember he was an amateur. The force driving him was this agonistic or competitive approach. If, in Dresden, someone was about to introduce the colour green for fireworks or, in England, someone was about to make a small cannon he would anticipate them and then seek to improve on both. It was the same with medicine. This is a very modern attitude. When you think about the scientific world and the rivalry among academies it is a matter of who gets there first. Around 1750 everything happens for him. It is the strongest part of his history and then he begins to isolate himself. So not only does he have lots of trouble inside a complicated environment but he also suffers a financial fall.'

'Surely his seeking to reproduce the miracle of San Gennaro didn't help matters.'

'It definitely comes across as an expression of doubt in the reality of the phenomenon. This is what people would have said about it at the time, but the experiments he made employed substances quite different to those in the San Gennaro phenomenon. Science had made such a spectacular advance – there were public shows of scientific experiments – it was the new era and very involving for everyone. Raimondo took pride in saying he could do all these things, but it was not in order to attack the tradition or to express doubt in the truth of San Gennaro. It was simply to say that there are substances which in certain conditions behave just like the liquefaction of San Gennaro's blood. It was merely to produce something similar in appearance. In the *Lettera Apologetica* he speaks of *wonder*, the *wonderful*, any other superlative, but he never mentions the word "miracle" and so the implication is that he might not have believed in it.'

'What is most profound for me,' I said, 'not only with respect to Raimondo but also to the *cappella*, is this idea of the veil of knowledge, which could be extended as a metaphor for Naples itself.'

'This is to connect to the word "esoteric" which means belonging to an inner circle. And so knowledge is reserved for the few who could lift or see through the veil. It was a recurring theme in other pieces of art, now lost, which were in his palace. It is very present in all that we see and it reaches its peak in this aristocratic capability of a few people to access knowledge. We are talking of an intellectual and not a social aristocracy. The veil you see in the various pieces of art in the *cappella* is a little bit like those elements of irony and dissimulation you find in Raimondo's own writing. It is not only knowledge but also, as we have already said, deception, irony, and the implying rather than the actual saying of things, but it also includes the *other*, which is to say that Raimondo allows the observer to see things only partially so that the journey of discovery and interpretation is left for him to complete. This is Raimondo's way of communicating in that it requires effort on the part of whoever seeks to understand the message he receives from him. If you extend the concept of the veil to the city itself what you find is similar in character to the prince. On the one side he gives spectacularly of himself while on the other he is mysterious and hides just in the way Naples does. The difference between this and other towns is that here beauty is diffused rather than concentrated in single areas. It is a city you need to discover and so it is up to you to find the veil you wish to remove.'

'And to take the idea of veil a step further it is that very fine division between life and death in Naples, so that one passes through it, back and forth.'

'I would rather stick to what I know because Naples is immense, but with the *Cristo velato* that is certainly true. This is also something that belongs to the rituals within Freemasonry because when a person seeks to enter the order he knocks at the door of the Lodge, saying "I am a blind person looking for light" or "I am a corpse seeking resurrection".'

As if summoned by a knocking at some other door within a rococo universe Fabrizio Masucci announced it was time for him to resume his duties.

The origins of the *cappella* date to the end of the sixteenth century. According to the *Napoli sacra* of Cesare d'Engenio Caracciolo, published in 1613, an innocent man was condemned to imprisonment and, while being walked to his fate, witnessed a section of garden wall collapse and reveal an image of the Virgin Mary – one that still hangs above the altar of the *cappella*, inside an oval gilt frame supported by angels. The prisoner swore that if he were proven innocent he would give a silver lamp to the Virgin. This happened, and the place became a site of blessing, one of its visitors being the mortally ill first Prince of Sansevero, Francesco Paolo di Sangro, who was granted a cure. Another version of the chapel's origins has it that Adriana Carafa della Spina, the mother of Fabrizio whom Gesualdo killed along with his adulterous wife, turned the votive shrine into a chapel in the hope that the soul of her wayward son might be redeemed. A chapel was built in 1590, Santa Maria della Pietà dei Sangro or 'Pietatella' ('The Little Piety'), which in 1613 was converted into a family burial chapel. The place was modified over the years, but it was Raimondo who, beginning work in 1744, gave the place the form we recognise now. Although the *cappella* was never completed to his specifications in his will, Raimondo instructs his son not to move anything inside it. He wanted everything kept in a precise position although he was not happy with the placing of four of the monuments. The *cappella* is a unity and was conceived as such. It is also believed that it was built over the remains of an ancient temple dedicated to the goddess Isis, with running water falling into a sacred basin. If true, this would be in perfect alignment with Raimondo's alchemical and philosophical enquires.

There are a number of statues in the *cappella*, but we shall focus on the obvious three, beginning first with *Pudicizia* ('Modesty' or 'Veiled Truth') by Antonio Corradini, a beautifully shaped young woman, naked beneath her transparent veil, which is meant to represent Raimondo's mother, her eyes closed either in ecstasy or to the passage of time. She is represented as a Roman vestal virgin, which is why I asked Masucci whether we were inside a *cappella* or a temple. Again, she may be the veiled Isis of Masonic belief, the veil being that which, as in Babylonian depictions of her, must be lifted in order to acquire knowledge. A beauty she most certainly is, but I may be looking at her with the wrong eyes. Will I ever be able to look upon her as God or the gods wish me to? As one blogger writing about this statue argues, 'The body is a temple of the Holy Ghost, not a cocktail lounge.' One senses Raimondo's hand upon Corradini's shoulder, demanding of him that he create an image of beauty that reflects the immeasurable sense of loss with which the adult invests the child he once was. An orphan cries into the beyond. Whether the statue physically resembles his mother is beside the point because it is a metaphor that is pursued. She holds in her left hand the inscription which has a deliberate crack in it to symbolise a life cut short, and between her two hands there runs a chain of roses that represents youth. The oak at her feet represents ancient knowledge.

To the right of her is the sculpture, *Disinganno* ('Disillusionment') by the Genovese Francesco Queirolo, which depicts a man struggling out of a fisherman's net, an angel representing Reason assisting him. The angel rests on a globe against which leans the Holy Bible open at the page where Christ restores light to the blind, illumination being another of the chief Masonic doctrines. The netted figure is Raimondo's father and what a complex work it is, not just physically but also metaphorically. The net may be said to represent sin or ignorance. There is an extraordinary story attached to it. When Nazi soldiers occupied Naples a group of them sought shelter inside the chapel. One of the officers could not believe the net surrounding the body could have been sculpted because then how would it have been possible for the artist to carve the human figure trapped inside. In order to prove the net was added afterwards he took his gun and with its grip smashed a bit of the rope. Only then was it finally proved that the net was integral to the sculpture. Do we thank the man with the gun or do we accuse him of a war crime?

Cristo velato ('Veiled Christ') by Giuseppe Sanmartino was commissioned to be positioned in the downstairs crypt and there lit at either end by two of Raimondo's perpetual flames. What was put there instead was one of the strangest things to have ever been put inside a chapel, but this we shall treat later. If it took an atheist to produce one of the most Christian films ever made, Pasolini's *The Gospel According to St Matthew*, then it took a man vastly at odds with Church doctrine to commission one of the most holy of sculptures. The *Cristo velato* is one of those works of art which annul doubt even though belief may not rush into the vacuum. As the Argentine novelist Héctor Bianciotti writes, 'No artist will ever give me, in the face of Sanmartino's technique in his Christ of Naples, the impression of having gone beyond what is possible.' In his description there is a powerful tension between the religious and the erotic: 'One would say that the artist enveloped him in that veil of pearly water to be able, whole, without scruples, to caress him with his breath.' If, after the example of the ancient Greeks, it has been the aim of sculptors to mimic translucence, it's here that it reaches its apotheosis. When the Marquis de Sade visited the Cappella Sansevero in 1775, just four years after Raimondo died, he remarked that there was a visitor's brochure available. Almost certainly it was penned by Raimondo himself in anticipation of people one day coming to see his gift to posterity. De Sade, not exactly a man of marked religious sensibilities, after seeing the statue of *Cristo velato* remarked on 'the drape, the fineness of the veil ... the beauty, the regularity of the proportions of the whole'. I should think there is not a single atheist who would not be moved by it. Something deeper than religion goes into one's bones. The mattress and the two pillows on which the Christ lies are compressed beneath his weight and because one *feels* that weight it makes the work all the more 'real', and then there is the fine sculpted embroidery at the edge of the shroud. It is not mere craftsmanship that induces such feeling but rather a sense of epiphany, a moment of great revelation, which demands of the object that it exist completely within the moment. As with just about everything connected to the man who commissioned it there is mystery and debate. We must dispel as quickly as possible yet another facet of the 'black legend' which states that when Giuseppe Sanmartino completed the work in 1753 Raimondo had him blinded so that he might never produce anything as fine again, which is a common enough trope, if not actually an urban legend, in the history of master-pieces. The sculptor Antonio Canova when he first saw it (and in fact tried to purchase it) said he would willingly sacrifice ten years of his own life to be able to produce such a masterpiece. I hesitate to reproduce it here because I have yet to find a single photograph that does it sufficient justice. It is sculpted anew with every gradation of the light surrounding it, such that one never sees the same work twice.

There is a single astonishing feature, which demonstrates that the sculpture is set within a single moment of time: it is where the supernaturally thin veil enters one of the Christ's nostrils. What this demonstrates is that this Christ is alive. There is also the single throb of a vein on the forehead that can be seen *through* the veil. This is a Christ who has suffered, but it is also a Christ at the very instant of returning to life. The instruments of his torture are at his feet, the crown of thorns and the shackles. It is one of the paradoxical aspects of a great work of art to make one believe in what is depicted and yet to not quite believe it is humanly possible to achieve. We find a parallel in literature in the theory that it was beyond Shakespeare's capabilities to have produced the works of Shakespeare. There are Doubting Thomases everywhere, a good number of them with no aim other than to preserve their livelihoods on the flimsiest of evidence. And so we discover arguments to the effect that Sanmartino could not have possibly sculpted a veil that is finer than any veil in existence. By comparison the veil covering *Modesty* seems the work of a novice. The suggestion is that some alchemical process must have been involved and that Raimondo had, along with all his other inventions, discovered a means of transforming material into marble with a combination of calcium hydrate or slaked lime. It is an understandable error because one's first reaction upon seeing the sculpture is to think it was impossible to make. The historical archives at the Bank of Naples have revealed a receipt of payment made to Sanmartino, dated 16 December 1752: 'And you will pay the aforementioned fifty ducats to the Magnificent Giuseppe Sanmartino on my behalf, for the statue of Our Lord in death covered by a veil also of marble.' The most puzzling aspect is that Raimondo should have included the phrase *in death* when clearly the statue suggests otherwise. First, though, it must be stated that the statue is of a single piece of marble. The rest is genius, but then we are faced with another problem: Sanmartino, as we know, went on to produce other work. The mystery is that there is nothing else that comes even close to rivalling the *Cristo velato* which as far as can be determined is Sanmartino's first recorded work. The question is: how did he get to there from nowhere? The original commission went to Antonio Corradini who died when the statue was still in the planning stages. Sanmartino worked from his sketches, but what came out at the end was very much his. Might he not have been creatively 'blinded' after having completed it?

The most bizarre addition to the *cappella* was that of two 'anatomical machines', the standing skeletons of a man and a pregnant woman in the downstairs space where the *Cristo velato* was meant to go. Arguably they ought not to be there because it was in La Fenice that they were kept. What is shocking about them is how brilliantly preserved the veins and internal organs of the two people are. It was actually Raimondo's assistant, Giuseppe Salerno, who between 1763 and 1764 made them, albeit under Raimondo's supervision. In the brochure of 1766 there is a sentence that still horrifies: 'In the Chapel one can see two Anatomic Machines, that is, skeletons, a man and a female, made by injection, which because of their being complete and of their having undergone such diligent treatment, can be said to be unique in all of Europe.' We come now to the blackest part of the black legend. It has been claimed that the bodies are of two of Raimondo's servants who he used as live guinea pigs, a mysterious substance injected into both of them while they were still alive, which moved through, and preserved, the capillary system and caused their agonising deaths. There is one problem in Raimondo's description: the syringe was not invented until a century later by Charles-Gabriel Pravaz, and yet there we have it, in his own words: *made by injection*. It is a story that even the great early twentieth-century philosopher Benedetto Croce promulgates: 'He killed two of his servants, a man and a woman, and strangely embalmed their bodies in such a way that would show all the viscera, arteries and the veins inside them, and put them in a closet.' The woman in particular seems to have been arrested in a state of shock, one arm stretched as if in final agonies, her eyes bulging with horror. She is also pregnant. Their bodies were allowed to decompose and what emerged from the decay were the perfectly 'metallised' veins and arteries, the anatomic machines. What is there to stop us from crying murder? Quite simply, scientific evidence. Very recently with the use of scanning electron microscopy (SEM) and infrared spectroscopy (FT-IR) the bodies have been closely analysed, and what is revealed is that although the skeletons are real they are merely the scaffolding for a realistic, though artificial, network of arteries, veins, and capillaries made of iron wire twisted with silk fibre and overlaid with pigmented beeswax. There were no mysterious embalming substances. Once again, Raimondo was having us on. Still, if artificial, this begs the question of how it was that he and Giuseppe Salerno had been able to produce the most accurate model to date. One researcher, Sergio Attanasio, has pointed to one flaw in the structure that would have made human life impossible. Raimondo di Sangro is free to leave the courtroom and may even be applauded for being a century ahead of his time in accurately depicting the coronary system.

The date 29 September 1889 brought partial disaster when the footbridge joining the *cappella* and the Palazzo Sansevero collapsed at the same time as the subsidence – probably due to water damage. Benedetto Croce described its destruction as being like 'a chastisement of the sky'. What was tragically damaged is the inlaid marble floor in the lower space that Raimondo commissioned the artist Francesco Celebrano to make in 1760. A fragment survives, which points to what would have been a complex labyrinth-pattern of swirled crosses and concentric squares, representing the difficult journey an initiate must make before he is considered a member of the Masonic order. It was the final touch that Raimondo would not live to see complete, and which was so intricate that restoration was considered impossible, and the chapel subsequently re-floored.

In addition to the carillon the bridge contained a remarkable clock made in the shape of a dragon which showed the day of the week, the hour, and the minutes as well as the phases of the moon. All during the construction of the *cappella* Raimondo kept inventing new methods such as the wax-based paint specially made for and used in Giuseppe Pesce's *Madonna con Bambino*. He invented a system to colour white marble. He also invented colour-fast pigments for the ceiling fresco, Francesco Maria Russo's *Glory of Paradise*.

Raimondo's death is inconclusive. Maybe he didn't die at all. It has been *said* that he died on 22 March 1771, most likely sped along by the chemicals he daily exposed himself to, which, like any chef worthy of the role, he'd taste from time to time. Once again, Cardinal Ganganelli had been perspicacious, for in one of his letters, composed in 1757, he writes to the prince, 'I always fear that your chemical experiments will be harmful to your health.' Suppose Raimondo really did die. Then we can say the serpent was coiled up inside one of his own beakers. Surely, with his scientific mind, he must have known the risks he was taking, but he continued because such men, when driven by a quest for knowledge, the more arcane the better, do not recognise obstacles. And suppose he knew he was about to die. Raimondo was acutely aware that he had never been wholly free of the suspicions of the Church, especially after replicating San Gennaro's miracle, and so, worried that any blame would fall directly upon the heads of his immediate family, he destroyed almost all of his massive archive. Whatever survived of that self-made deluge was then destroyed by his children because they, too, had been fearful of the consequences of having a father who dabbled in heretical activities. Raimondo's son, Vincenzo, went so far as to abandon taking care of the chapel.

So why are there expressions of doubt as to his demise? A story, which may or may not be true, is that Raimondo had discovered the elixir for eternal life, hence the question of whether he still lives. In his final hours, feeling death close at hand, he imbibed the magical potion that would ensure his survival one way or another. One of his servants, following his instructions, dismembered his body, and placed the parts in a trunk until such time as the potion would take full effect, at which point Raimondo would reassemble himself. Most annoyingly, the process was interrupted by the arrival of his relatives. Raimondo, as is sometimes the case when faced with unwelcome family members, upped and screamed, then collapsed in a heap at the bottom of the trunk ◠

What *is* true is that the whereabouts of his body remains a mystery to this day. It is not beneath the funerary stone whose inscription bears his name and describes the internee as 'an admirable man, born to dare everything'. Trust Raimondo, it was not inscribed in the usual method but with some formula of his own invention.

Fabrizio Masucci has a rather more rational approach to this.

'While I do not have any proof of where his remains are,' he says, 'there is no reason why they shouldn't be here. It is all part of the legend surrounding him. Probably it is in the subterranean area where the other bones are kept.'

The great irony is that the single image in the *cappella* to have deteriorated is the oil-on-copper painting of the man whose experiments were devoted to creating permanence. Masucci reminds me that it was for some time exposed to the elements, while the portrait of his son Vincenzo, also done on copper and with the same pigments, survives because it was in a sheltered place. Still it is hard to resist the notion that the painting is symbolic of a man very quietly taking his leave from the *cappella* or temple that is his greatest memorial. The plaque he placed there says that he who commissioned these works was moved by a desire to *astonish, discover and teach*. As for the stories, and God knows the Neapolitans love stories, they continue. Old people living nearby speak of strange appearances, a strange light that glows on Christmas and Easter nights, a smell of incense in the surrounding alleys, peculiar music emanating from inside the empty building, and the sound of footsteps, spurs scraping over the stone.

Old Bones

'We believe that the dead are as far away as the sun, infinitely far away,' writes Giuseppe Marotta in his novel *Gli alunni del tempo* ('The Slaves of Time', 1960). 'But suppose that in fact they are here, behind the door, inside the plaster on the wall or in the spider's web?' A child with fever will see shapes in the damp plaster, maybe a mangled face, a scorpion, a tarantula … *something* about to spring from the wall and onto the bed where he lies. While I can revisit the boy I once was, a bit loopy with measles, *seeing things*, I could never have imagined the resonance Marotta's words would soon have for me. Sometimes, beneath the swirls of plaster, the amorphous really does take shape. I was sitting at an elderly woman's kitchen table, staring at a bare patch of wall to the right of me. Caterina had dyed black hair, crimson fingernails. She owned a collection of dolls, maybe not all that many but enough to send a shudder through me. Sinister the child's plaything in an adult's hands, more sinister still, whether by design or chance, that she should have styled her hair in imitation of her plastic curly-haired entourage. She was speaking to me of something that happened at this very table. At first I thought I misheard her or maybe there was something not quite right with the translation.

❋

Although a certain amount of sentiment clouds his prose, at his best, Giuseppe Marotta remains eminently quotable. Later in the book he writes:

> Easter is in the air. 'Donna Brigida Cacace is mixing flour, water and lard to make the *casatiello*, the Easter Cake. She uses a rectangular piece of marble that I should guess was once part of a tomb at Poggioreale. If not, why should it have the word 'inconsolable' on it? But, in fact, this unusual pastry board lends itself to an occupation destined for Easter. The death of Christ became a bread of nourishment, and surely the forgotten one who slept under the stone that she uses today to shape the ritual cake would be content. Greetings, Don, whoever you were; pray for us who eat for you.

What I'd like to know is whether *inconsolabile* shows up in bas-relief on the cake's surface. I add this passage not only because its author deserves to be better remembered in the Anglophone world, where he has been out of print for many decades, but also because Death gives yet another encore, because Death never stops taking his bows in Naples. Marotta, who grew up in poverty in the Materdei district lived in a *basso* at the bottom of the bell tower of the church of Sant'Agostino degli Scalzi. I visited the place. There is no plaque on the wall to commemorate the years he spent there. Marotta has failed to make the grade. While a handful of luminaries are elevated to sainthood in Naples, the majority go unobserved. Marotta left Naples in 1925 to work as a journalist in Milan. Creatively he remained attached to the place of his birth although it might be said that he could treat of it only at a distance. Naples got him in the end when he went back to live there and, soon after, died, aged sixty-one, on 12 October 1963 of a cerebral haemorrhage.

And while we're on the subject of literature there's a play by Eduardo De Filippo, considered by many to be one of his best, *Non ti pago* ('I Won't Pay You') which nicely illustrates the degree to which life and death in Naples intermingle. It is a tragicomedy, although with Eduardo there is a problem sometimes in distinguishing between the two, and in fact he himself said of *Non ti pago* it was a very funny comedy that in his opinion was the most tragic he had ever written. The plot begins roughly as follows: Don Ferdinando Quagliuolo manages a betting shop in Naples where continually he plays the lottery without success, which is tantamount to a cook not being able to cook for himself a decent meal in his own restaurant. Ferdinando lives in the house of his late father, but for a short period he lets it to his daughter Stella's boyfriend, Mario Bertolini, who is also his employee. Mario seems to be favoured by fortune because, unlike his boss (and future father-in-law), he wins regularly on the lottery. One night he dreams that Ferdinando's late father gives him four numbers. The next day he plays them and wins the *quaterna* amounting to four million lire, only – and this is where sweet goes to bitter – Ferdinando refuses to pay up and keeps the money for himself. Mario remonstrates, but is told by Ferdinando that the win is not his because the soul of his father was expecting to find him, Ferdinando, in the bed where he normally sleeps and had given Mario the winning numbers by mistake.

Old bones, skulls in particular, are today's fare.

I visited the massive ossuary of the Cimitero delle Fontanelle where Rione Materdei borders on Rione Sanità, an area that has been associated with the dead since ancient times – there are traces of an extensive Greco-Roman necropolis dating back to between the third and fourth centuries BC and, from a later period, remains of paleo-Christian burial sites. Fontanelle, formerly a tuff quarry, got its name from the water springs in the area and the stuff of which it is made comes from the so-called *lava dei vergini*, the mudslides caused by millennia of rainfall eroding the pyroclastic blanket covering the surrounding hills. There one may see, spread over about three thousand square metres, the forty thousand skulls (*capuzzelle*) that once housed twice as many eyes. Some of the skulls are adorned with coins, jewellery, rosaries, sweets, flowers (mostly plastic), bus tickets, and even the odd cigarette shoved between their teeth. Most poignantly, the remains of children are provided with sweets and toys, many of them placed there by mothers who have lost children of their own. There are many more bones beneath the surface, perhaps up to four metres of human remains. Some say their number stretches into the millions, but we will never know for sure. The massive cave contains three major naves, trapezoidal in shape: the section on the left known as *navata dei preti* ('the priest's nave') because the remains there come from the city's churches, *navata degli appestati* ('the nave of the victims of plague') and *navata dei pezzentelli* ('the nave of the poor little ones'), these being the anonymous poor who have never had a proper burial.

Death is a leveller, they say, the big equaliser. It's a cliché that has never quite rung true for me. I'd better watch my words because now I find myself up against the great actor, poet, and comedian Totò, and whosoever argues with Totò argues with life itself. When did you last look into Totò's face? You'd have to go back as far as Buster Keaton for the like. Genius seeps from every pore. Totò's comic poem ''A livella' ('The Leveller'), written in hendecasyllables, the Italian metre of choice, is set in a graveyard, on 2 November, which in Italy is Il Giorno dei morti ('All Souls' Day'). It is close to midnight and the speaker in the poem finds himself locked inside the cemetery. This is what he witnesses: the Marquis of Rovigo and Belluno 'with top hat, monocle and mantle' is annoyed to find himself buried beside Esposito Gennaro, a garbage collector, 'stinking to hell and with a broom in his hand'. Gennaro speaks Neapolitan as opposed to his neighbour's posh Italian, which makes any translation of the poem a challenge. I recommend Totò's own deadpan delivery of the poem.* An argument ensues and Gennaro, who to begin with is both condescending and obsequious to the marquis, finally reminds him that death is a leveller and only the living are so foolish as to suppose wealth and social standing are of importance. The poem concludes, 'Sti pagliacciate 'e fanno sulo 'e vive! / Nuje simmo serie, appartenimmo â morte', which in Vincent Lombardo's brave translation reads: 'Only the living indulge in these buffooneries: / we are serious here ... we belong to Death!'). I doff my hat to Totò, *il Principe della risata*, 'the prince of laughter', but I'll not be swayed in my view that equality, desirable though it is, is a modern chimera that many think can be legislated into existence.

At Fontanelle there really is a hierarchy of sorts, a privileged minority of skulls to which the most attention gets paid, while this one in the back row, a little over to the right, yes, the one with the missing jaw, languishes in death just as he did in life, unnoticed. Say he is the sole representative of the majority of skulls on display here. Say this is his big moment. A moment is all it will ever be, but it'll be enough: a wink in eternity, it will light up the universe just long enough for us to be able to make our solemn observance. Signor Marotta calls this stock figure of Neapolitan existence 'Uncle Nobody' in one of his stories, but he does not do so in the pejorative. 'The term is objective,' he writes, 'impartial and as exact as a weight on the scales; it describes a man's pitiful condition without the least implication of scorn.' So 'Uncle Nobody' is not what callous tongues would brand a 'loser', which is one way of burying a man alive. 'He is

---

* It can be heard on the internet. Would Totò have been the great artist he is without his face? One of my wilder sources informs me he spent many years forcing it into a jellybean shape.

Nobody, to be sure,' Marotta continues, 'but at the same time he is an Uncle.' What does one do, however, about the anonymous dead, there being so many more of them than one can handle?

We know the identities of only two people at Fontanelle, both of whom are inside glass plate coffins – Count Filippo Carafa, who died in 1793, and the mummified Donna Margherita Petrucci, who died in 1795 and whose mouth is open wide as if caught in the middle of a scream.* She is said to have died from choking on a *gnocco*.† The other 39,398 skulls are anonymous. Uncle Nobodies, all of them save for the few who have been given special status. One hopes that in their former state the majority of them loved and were in turn loved, laughed and wept, and that only a very few were absolute swine. Didn't that one over there, the dust heavy on him, fix his weights when selling vegetables? All's forgiven, however, because the good news is that there are no swine here. It is widely held that people's sins, as does the flesh, fall away from them after death. If that's where their souls are now, somewhere on the road to Paradise, it's the living who with their prayers have got them there. A little something in return wouldn't go amiss, of course, a serving of the old quid pro quo, such as an answer to one's prayers for a baby, or, if a baby is already on the way, then one's prayers for a marriage to go along with it, or, best of all, because then one can have all the babies one likes, a nice little win of the lottery. Actually, the majority of

---

*Lovers of classical music might care to learn that Filippo Carafa's brother, Marzio Domenico IV Carafa, Duke of Maddaloni, mediated in securing a commission for the composer Giovanni Battista Pergolesi's final work, his 'Stabat Mater', through the auspices of the Confraternità dei Cavalieri di San Luigi di Palazzo.

†that is, the singular of *gnocchi*. This sad event has been echoed in recent times. A news item in one of the trashier papers relates the sad fate of a man who choked to death on a panettone. The article includes a photograph of the offending cake.

graces sought are quite modest in scale, although there are some people, of course, who'll go to any lengths to feed their greedy desires. Souls can see into the future and sometimes they give of their own accord just as the soul of Ferdinando's father gives Mario his winnings, although Ferdinando, that weasel, claims otherwise.

Ophelia says to Laertes, 'There's rosemary, that's for remembrance – pray you love, remember.'* I have only recently noted the two pots of rosemary in the picture. Who sneaked them in there? The cult is supposed to be dead, but nothing will persuade me those pots have been there since 1950 or even 1969 when such behaviour was outlawed. Whoever did this must have carried within herself (surely it was a she) some residual memory of the plant's significance. During Shakespeare's day rosemary came to symbolise fidelity, and a man indifferent to its fragrance would be denied any possibility of finding an enduring love. Centuries before, particularly for the Greek scholars who prior to their examinations would put a sprig of it on their heads, rosemary was a memory booster. It was also an amulet against

---

* Shakespeare, *Hamlet*, Act IV, sc. v.

evil spirits and nightmares, and then, going back even further, it was sacred to the goddess Aphrodite; centuries later it would be associated with the Virgin Mary. And then the supposed lifespan of the plant was thought to be equal to Christ's. It was used in ritual baths and for purification ceremonies. The ancient Egyptians used it in the embalming process, and during the Middle Ages it was hung about the neck as a ward against plague. The knot of meaning gets thicker by the minute. If love is today's object then maybe these two skulls were of an amorous couple taken by plague. This is a bit fanciful as it's the living who have designs upon these particular dead and provide them with their identities. Ophelia and Laertes disagree. They say it is the original possessors of the skulls who reveal themselves, who in their adopters' dreams give out their names and stories. This belief is central to the Neapolitan 'cult of skulls' or 'cult of death', phrases bordering on the sensational but true nevertheless, and as such nothing could speak more clearly of the thin veil between life and death in Naples. The skull with the cigarette, should I reach out to it with a lighter now that death from cancer is no longer an issue?

It is difficult to resist the notion that the cult of *anime pezzentelle** has its origins in a distant forgotten past. An easier to define, somewhat less ancient one, would be the Roman ancestor worship that was centred on the domestic cult of the Lares. Prayers were offered to these spirits, although they weren't called upon for favours. There is probably a sprinkle of Hellenic influence as well and indeed, given this was Greek Italy, it may throw

---

* *Anime pezzentelle*: 'poor little souls' from the Latin *petere* – 'to ask' – although its meaning can be extended to mean 'begging souls' because they beg us to help them escape Purgatory.

a longer shadow than the Roman, but there has yet to be found the small white envelope that, when opened, will reveal the connection between all things ancient and modern. At some point there must have been a subtle shift that made clear the difference between praying *for* the dead and praying *to* them. There are plenty who support the view that the cult of the *anime pezzentelle* may go back to ancient practice, others who absolutely won't, who see in this a smear on Christian belief, and so, as with most things Neapolitan, the subject is fraught with contradiction and occasional bad feeling, *occasional* because I think the majority of Neapolitans are quite happy to countenance pagan aspects in their religion. At the same time, they would be surprised to be thought of as anything but Catholic. Christian and pagan are not mutually exclusive.

At least we can find evidence for the modern beginnings of the cult. We have already dealt with the invention of Purgatory, and although I can't quite believe in Purgatory I believe in it more than I do in Heaven or Hell, which is not to say I disbelieve in either but that I applaud the imaginative possibilities afforded by the third to 'honest doubters' such as myself. I find it more suggestive, more open, than the idea of agnosticism which to me is the most awkward of positions to take because it is tantamount to walking from one empty room into the next and into the next, *forever*. Atheism allows for no such possibilities. It is as tightly wrapped in assuredness as is absolute faith. At the same time, I do not believe the opposite of disbelief is sanctimonious mush. If God exists, He is the god of tough love.

As early as 1476 Pope Sixtus IV declared that indulgences might be earned by the living for souls in purgatory, thereby shortening the time they would have to spend there. Whether unwittingly or not, he was the author of what was to become a rather thorny issue. 'The moment the money tinkles in the collecting box,' goes a jingle from the time, 'a soul flies out of purgatory.' This would be anathema to Martin Luther who in

1517 threw his ninety-five punches. The sale of indulgences was stopped in 1567, but there is a lingering suspicion they can still be obtained on the spiritual black market. There was a growing concern in the early part of the sixteenth century as to the disposal of human remains. There were too many of them in too small a space. The church crypts favoured by the local people were filled to bursting and so in 1605, in order to make space for new arrivals, a group of Neapolitan noblemen called the Congrega di Purgatorio ad Arco formed a lay congregation called the Opera Pia and arranged for the older bones to be removed to a tuff cave outside the city gates. They were also dedicated to the idea of praying for the souls of these forgotten figures. About this time, St Robert Bellarmine (who is best remembered for being on the jury that sent Giordano Bruno to the stake, and for quashing the absurd notion set forth by Copernicus that the earth moves around the sun) said that although they could not hear specific requests, the souls in purgatory could help the living because they are that much closer to God than we are. That was a bit like announcing the winning result in advance of the race. In 1638, the church of Santa Maria delle Anime del Purgatorio ad Arco on Via Tribunali was completed with a sizable hypogeum for burying the city's poor. This would become in more recent times a major centre for the cult of *anime pezzentelle*.

Maybe it is here, on Via Tribunali in central Naples, that one should begin one's enquiries into the cult of the skulls. Outside the church (locally known as *d'e cape 'e morte* or *d'e capuzzelle*) there are three bronze skulls. There used to be four, but one of them was stolen in the early 1900s. I was told at the church that the thief, who lived locally, was punished for his sins: death cut a swathe through his family, and this was followed by substantial financial losses. Why didn't death take just him rather than his blameless relatives? Something about the story doesn't ring true. If the thief was found, why wasn't the skull recovered? Or did somebody grease somebody else's palm? This was, is, will always be, after all, Naples. Or was the story concocted in order to avoid future occurrences? The tops of the three remaining skulls are shiny from the centuries of people rubbing their hands over them for good luck. As a ward against evil, passers-by also 'make the horns' with their fingers, inserting the index and little ones into the eye sockets. The church, designed by Giovanni Cola di Franco, was from the outset dedicated to the *anime pezzentelle*, hence the many skull motifs one can spend an hour or so looking at prior to seeing the real thing in abundance. Hidden behind the altar is Dionisio Lazzari's marble sculpture of a winged skull, gorgeously done, but so oddly placed one can barely get an angle on it. The church is so designed that architecturally it mirrors the Dantesque journey from Purgatory to Paradise, so that one goes from the hypogeum below, often referred to as the 'holy land', a rather dark and bleak place, to the heavenly opulence above. It's a bit like going from the Old Kent Road to Bond Street.

This church is where the cult of the dead found its deepest expression. That it should have escaped censure is not surprising because in the seventeenth century the close relationship between the living and the dead, especially in a time of plague, would not have raised a single eyebrow. The trouble would begin in the twentieth century when, with an improvement in hygiene, the sanitised world was cleansed of its deeper imaginative properties. There was resistance to the Vatican-inspired closure of the church in 1969, with people forcing the entrance, but later, as if Nature decided to adopt the Vatican line, the earthquake of 1980 caused structural damage making the church unstable for the next few decades. It reopened in 1992, the administration in charge saying it was a place of historical importance. The question now is whether tourism will somehow diminish its significance. Although the old faithful, or such that survive of them, are discouraged they still manage to get inside and surreptitiously deposit their messages, the greater number of which are addressed to Lucia D'Amore whose skull is covered with a tiara and a bridal veil. It is to her that young women come to seek or repair love. There is one message that asks for a boyfriend's release from prison. There must be plenty more of those on file, but then there are as many different kinds of requests as there are personal difficulties.

The Lucia story comes in many versions, the most common of which is that at some point between 1780 and 1790 she was given in marriage, against her will, by her father Domenico D'Amore, Prince of Ruffano and Marquis of Ugento, to the Marquis Giacomo Santomago. Whether by design or accident she died, aged seventeen, before the marriage could be consummated. Some say she perished in a shipwreck, others from tuberculosis, and still others by her own hand. A rather more involved version speaks of a childhood love between Lucia and an unnamed boyfriend. As they got older the boyfriend, fearing that demons would inhabit and destroy their love, wanted to marry her as soon as possible. It is probably quite true that a vacillating spirit falls victim to destructive forces more easily than does a decisive one. Lucia did not want to rush things, however, and after some years of indecisiveness on her part the boyfriend, exasperated, went to another city where he found employment in a gunpowder factory. The old cliché about love and distance made Lucia realise that she had wanted him all along and so finally, by letter, they made plans for their marriage. A date was set but just days before the wedding was to take place an explosion at the factory claimed the young man's life. Lucia, in her torment, died soon after. A still darker version of the story speaks of a delay brought on by the man not being able to get leave from the factory, which would prove fatal because the demons, seeing a window of opportunity, took possession of Lucia who then told her mother her disappointment before throwing herself down a well. There are many variants on the story, which is hardly surprising given that stories such as these are constructed according to people's own predicaments, but the idea of 'suspended marriage' is a sure winner in the soap opera stakes.

During the devastating plague of 1656 some 300,000 people died. A year later, when the bodies were still being buried, Francesco Gizzio, an Oratorian priest, playwright, mathematician, and astrologer, wrote and performed a play, *La spada della misericordia* ('The Sword of Mercy') in which two corpse-gatherers, Porchione and Sardella, the Vladimir and Estragon of their time,* go about with their cart gathering bodies, pocketing any valuables, and singing, 'The cart goes wherever there is money. / For us corpse-bearers, the plague is honey.' Where they went with those carts heaped with corpses was almost certainly Fontanelle. End of story. There were further such scenes in 1764 when over 200,000 people perished in the famine. Such was the urgency in disposing of the bodies that very few of them were given a proper Catholic burial, and so the souls of the anonymous were considered to be languishing in Purgatory.

One way a soul's journey might be facilitated to Heaven was through the prayers of the living. In the 1780s the Neapolitan bishop, St Alphonsus Maria de Liguori, made a small, but significant, change to St Robert Bellarmine's teaching on Purgatory, saying that while God made the prayers of the living known to souls in Purgatory, it was also possible for the dead to help the living with specific matters. This would open the floodgates and, with it, the idea of reciprocity that is so peculiar, and central, to the Neapolitan cult of death.

At some point, we don't know when exactly, but towards the end of the seventeenth century, there was a major flood that dislodged the corpses at Fontanelle and sent them spewing into the streets for miles around. The inhabitants stayed indoors for fear of encountering their own dead relatives. We owe this

---

* Vladimir and Estragon being the two comical characters in Samuel Beckett's *Waiting for Godot*.

information to the antiquarian Andrea De Jorio, who is best remembered as a pioneer in the study of body language and who wrote a book on Neapolitan hand gestures, *La mimica degli antichi investigata nel gestire napoletano* (1832), recently translated as 'Gesture in Naples and Gesture in Classical Antiquity'. The remains were gathered and returned to what was already considered an unofficial paupers' cemetery. According to De Jorio unscrupulous gravediggers smuggled into Fontanelle, in sacks, the bodies of the rich who had been destined for church burial after which the spaces in the churches would be resold to the next in line. In June 1804, under the Napoleonic edict of Saint Cloud that forbade any burials within the city walls, even more bodies were added to the pile. The cholera epidemic of 1837 resulted in another major influx of bodies, among them, almost certainly, a poet born in a sepulchre.

A few decades later, in 1872, entered the extraordinary figure of Father Gaetano Barbati who, driven by forces invisible, and with a force of volunteers highly visible (mostly women collectively known as *'e maste* who were widowed or who had very few relatives), had the chaotically buried skeletons at Fontanelle disinterred, sorted by their anatomy – tibiae, femora, skulls, et cetera – cleaned and placed on racks or in troughs. Would it be pushing things a little if I were to suggest that one consequence of this sorting process was that the dead were separated from themselves? Was that femur here not aching for its fellow tibia there? What a panicky clattering of bones there'll be when the Last Judgment comes. Anyway, prayers were said for the dead and it is at this point that we may see, depending on one's view, either the spontaneous beginnings of the cult of the *anime pezzentelle* or the resumption of something very ancient indeed that was already in the bloodstream. Their devotees, again mostly women, adopted skulls, cleaned them, and in dreams were given the names of the hitherto anonymous dead. Sometimes they dreamt of the dead one before adopting the skull they believed was his or hers. The requests made of the *anime pezzentelle* by their devotees could be through dreams, conversation, or even written on bits of paper which were then rolled up and put into the skull's eye sockets. The dream, as was the case in ancient pagan rituals, was the main conduit between the living and the dead, an oneiric world where meetings between the living and the dead take place, and in which the dead's identity would be revealed to their adopters. It is for this reason the bones are never given tombstones because the channels of communication might be blocked. It was important that the rituals should be neither too slow nor too hasty: in the first instance they might not respond at all and, in the second, they could become too attached to the material world. It was therefore important to find a balance. Purity was a boon, and so adopting a child's skull meant joining the queue. If the dreams did not materialise there would also be women who, skilled in conversing with skulls, would for a small fee act as midwives, so to speak. The women would place their skulls on embroidered handkerchiefs and bring them candles, flowers, and prayers that would include the phrase 'a refrische 'e l'anime d'o priatorio' ('Give relief to the souls of Purgatory').

The *rinfresco* ('cooling') that brings relief from the purgatorial fire has its origins in the ancient world, the Latin *refrigerium* (literally 'refreshment'),* and the funeral banquets held on the tombs of the dead, although often they were little more than a simple votive offering of bread and wine. Aeneas, remember, pours milk and wine on his father's grave. The ritual was taken over by the early Christians who took food to the gravesites of martyrs and relatives. 'And he cried and said, Father Abraham, have mercy on me, and send Lazarus, that he may dip the tip of his finger in water, and cool my tongue; for I am tormented in this flame' (Luke 16:24). The early Christian author Tertullian

---

* For those who consider such things important it is also the word from which our 'refrigerator' comes.

speaks of the *refrigerium interim* as the refreshment given to the recently departed ones who await resurrection at the end of time. Perhaps the most eloquent description of it comes from the pen of the church historian Eliezer Gonzalez who in his *Fate of the Dead in Early Third Century North African Christianity* (2014) writes:

> *Refrigerium* is neither solely a single, defined activity such as a banquet for the dead, nor solely a single, defined place in heaven, earth, or elsewhere. *Refrigerium* is not even a discrete time, whether it be now or the hereafter. At its core, *refrigerium* consists of community in its broadest sense, the fundamental nature of which is transcendence, be it of time or space. Central to the notion of *refrigerium* seems to be the *act* of being in this transcendent community, encapsulated both metaphorically and in actuality by the sharing of meals. In this sense, it fits integrally into Roman culture, understanding of community, and of the rituals for the dead.

And this is where Gonzalez gets to the nub with respect to the reciprocity between the living and the dead. 'The practice of *refrigerium* was not merely about the earthly community sharing heavenly food with the righteous dead; it was also about the righteous dead sharing the earthly food with the living.'

After a skull was adopted, and if it did what was asked of it, it would be surrounded with a rosary, where the neck would be, and promoted from a handkerchief to a pillow adorned with lace. The Fontanelle was opened to the public and on 13 May 1877, under Cardinal Sisto Riario Sforza, the first Mass took place there. It is hardly surprising that the cult should have found its home in southern Italy where there has always been a powerful relationship between religious life and the people's engagement with the dead. The dead and the living need each other. The historian Tommasso Astarita writes in his Introduction to the photographer Margaret Stratton's book *The Living and the Dead: The Neapolitan Cult of the Skull*:

> The dead, in a sense, were even better suited to the Neapolitan conception of the relationship between humans and the supernatural than saints. The relationship between humans and the supernatural was essentially a material one based on the practical exchange of worship for protection. Saints had, after all, limited need for the worship humans offered to them; the dead, on the other hand, and especially the souls of purgatory, were themselves very much in need of help. The cult of the dead was also built on the Neapolitan focus on the physical body, which finds its expression so clearly in the cult of relics. Thus, the fundamental Neapolitan concepts of worship as a form of practical exchange and the strong link between the supernatural and the physical found a perfect connection and focus in the behaviour towards the dead – both their corpses and their souls.

Normally Mondays were set aside for observances made to the skulls, which invites comparison with the day in the pagan calendar devoted to the lunar goddess Hecate, also mistress of the Underworld, who wanders about with the souls of the dead and who I fancy struts the stage like the Queen of the Night in Mozart's *Die Zauberflöte*.

The story of 'The Captain' has never been told the same way twice. The version collected by that cultural dynamo, Roberto De Simone, has a young *camorrista*, a womaniser and liar who makes love to a girl in Fontanelle. The spirit of the Captain scolds the young man for desecrating a sacred site. The *camorrista* laughs at him, saying he is not afraid of a dead man and then, although wedlock is far from his thoughts, he boasts that he will invite him to his wedding. The day comes when he finally does get married. One of the people at the wedding banquet is

unknown to anyone there. He is dressed in black. At the end of the meal, when he is invited to reveal his identity, he replies that he has a gift for the newlyweds, which he would prefer to give them in private. They go into an adjoining room where suddenly the young man recognises him, but it is too late: the Captain, who reveals the skeleton beneath his black clothes, offers his hands to the couple and they drop dead from shock. It is said that the couple's skeletons were placed close to, or even beneath, the statue of Gaetano Barbati in the ossuary. In another version when the young man first meets the Captain he mockingly sticks his fingers into the dead man's eye sockets (there is no mention of him being a *camorrista*). The story is an old one, and probably goes back to the Spanish period, which I would like to think fed the young Mozart's imagination or that of his librettist Lorenzo Da Ponte. The Captain fits snugly into the character of the Commendatore in *Don Giovanni* which also owes much to Molière's *Dom Juan ou le Festin de pierre*. In Roberto De Simone's more recent manifestation of the Captain story there is a reference to a section of the Fontanelle called *I Tribunali*, which is where the young *camorristi* had their initiation rites and, in order to demonstrate courage, spent a night alone in the place. It was from there, too, the bosses would issue death warrants.

The Captain is a star. I wonder who left him the bottle of Pelinkovac, which is a bitter wormwood-based liqueur that comes from the Balkans. Its close relative is absinthe. I think it is fair to assume the Captain was well-travelled and had a gut lined with steel.

Another favourite is Donna Concetta – 'a capa che suda' ('the skull that sweats') – which of all the skulls at Fontanelle is the most highly polished from the hands of thousands of women. If, when touching it, one's hand gets moist, whatever you ask of it will be granted, the sweat being a form of purification. If the skull is *very* wet then it means the prayer is already taking effect. The soul in Purgatory suffers in its struggle to reach Heaven.

Sweat is a form of release. A dry skull is a bad omen because the abandoned soul is suffering. Donna Concetta acts as a talisman of fertility, helping women to conceive. And behind one legend lies another: the original Donna Concetta, a figure well-known in the neighbourhood, would go to Fontanelle in order to be similarly graced with a child. After she became pregnant she went back to Fontanelle to give thanks to the dead soul and saw the skull emitting a dazzling light while the surrounding ones were either covered in dust or opaque. She then adopted, and became devoted to, the skull that rescued her. Other popular skulls include Capa Rossa, the postman with red hair who communicates important or auspicious news in one's dreams, and Don Francesco who sends forth Shades with the winning lottery numbers. These and Lucia's skull at the church of Purgatorio ad Arco are considered public property and cannot be adopted by an individual.

Up to a few decades ago, Friday was a favoured day for going to Fontanelle, which may signify somewhat less than pure motives for doing so – to obtain the winning numbers for the lottery which would be drawn on the following day. The novelist and social commentator Matilde Serao in her *Il ventre di Napoli* ('The Belly of Naples', 1884) writes:

There is deep disappointment and boundless grief at four o'clock on Saturday afternoon. On Sunday morning, however, their imaginations take heart and go back to work: the weekly dream starts over. The lottery is the great dream that consoles the Neapolitan imagination. It is the obsession of those over-heated minds; it is the great happy vision that appeases the oppressed; it is the immense hallucination that overcomes all souls.

According to the anthropologist Domenico Scafoglio, groups of women would go arm in arm through Fontanelle chanting,

''Mparaviso ce aspettate / e priate l'Aterno Pate / pe li noste necessità / accusì ve truvate / aneme sante refriscate. / E siccomme nce vedite / accussì ce screvite / Requie, repuoso, refrisco, cunzuolo.' ('In heaven you wait for us / so you will find souls purified of sin / and because you don't see us, / you write to us. / Pray, rest, give help, and comfort yourself.')

Often the women – almost always women – would sleep close to the skulls the night before the lottery, in an additional bid to have the numbers presented to them in a dream or to be allowed visions whose interpretation could be consulted in the book of numbers, *La smorfia napolitana*. The proximity between sleepers and the dead brings with it memories of the ancients who would sleep in the temple where they might communicate in their dreams with the gods. A distinction has to be made between grace and miracle. One is granted graces by the dead but not miracles, which are the province of saints.

What, though, of the skull that failed to render grace? Some were punished, set aside like misbehaving children, or 'turned'. If nothing came of people's entreaties to them, they were reintegrated into the grey mass of skulls and replaced with more promising specimens. The more generous of them would be secured in their small *scarabattole* with padlocks. Salvatore Mazza who works as a craftsman on Via Tribunali and makes, among other things, the terracotta figures one sees in street shrines, provided me with a striking example of how people would deal with failed skulls.

'All these gifts were given with the idea that the skull would help their daughter become married, have a happy marriage, and have children. It was a way to take back from the dead after taking care of them. If these gifts were given and nothing came back from them and the daughters did not get happily married or did not have children then those who gave them would be entitled to take them back. They'd take the glass case, if there was one, and even the cushion. And because in these underground places it was very dusty they would draw a circle around the skull to show how uncared for it was. They leave this clean circle and say to it in dialect "O' vire comme staje sporca famm'a grazia e je te pulezzo." ("You see how dirty you are, so bestow your grace and I will clean you.") It is almost a threat because they want to be taken care of in death.'

The Second World War gave a fresh thrust to the cult. So many missing people there were, not only from the repeated bombings but also the sons who went off to fight on various fronts of whom nothing had been heard for ages. The adoption of a skull became for many people if not a replacement for a loved one then a form of consolation. A message left with one of the skulls on 3 April 1944, in the midst of what were very dark days indeed, reads: '*La famiglia dell'Aviere Lista Ciro trovandosi senza notizie di suo figlio da pochi giorni dopo l'Armistizio e quindi sono otto mesi ed essendo devote di voi aspetta con tanta fede da voi la bella grazia.*' The Armistice of Cassibile had been signed the previous year, on 3 September, and it had been eight months since the Ciro family had set eyes on their son; in their message they beseech the skull to be allowed to see him again. Another skull is kept in a *scarabattola* inscribed with the owner's thanks and dated 6 September 1943, which, as we now know, was the single heaviest day of bombing in Naples. By the Allies, alas. (The exquisite monastery of Santa Chiara was pulverised two days before.) The dedication was doubtless made by one who attributed her survival to the skull's bestowing of grace. During the air raids Fontanelle was used as a shelter, and there were even some whose homes were destroyed who took up semi-permanent residence. Naturally enough, this did not end with the war but extended well into the following years. Nothing quite captures the mood of those difficult post-war years as Riccardo Carbone's 1947 photograph of Fontanelle. Carbone (1897–1973), who began as an amateur photographer in the 1920s, later became a photojournalist for *Il Mattino*, and his archive of 500,000 images of which only 10,000 have been thus far digitised is one of the city's most important visual chronicles.

From the same period there is a vivid description of Fontanelle by the French writer Roger Peyrefitte who scandalised France with his novels on homosexual themes. When he finished shocking France, he then took on the Vatican with his claims that Pope Paul VI was a closet homosexual. It was quite remarkable that he briefly served as a diplomat given that he managed to offend everyone, even the ghost of Frederick the Great who he accused of having seduced the young Voltaire. Sulphur was Peyrefitte's natural element. A pederast he most certainly was, but in his 1952 travelogue *Du Vésuve à l'Etna*, the English translation of which appeared in 1954 (entitled 'South from Naples'), he puts aside his seedier nature in order to observe the scene through which he moved.

One woman in great distress approached the Father. She had lost her skull and wanted him to help her to find it. 'It's a yellow one; very shiny,' she said. They both went off to look for it, and presently with a cry of triumph he found it, handed it with a flourish to its possessor and hurried back to his own flock. It was extraordinary to see with what delight that good woman received back her precious relic. She dusted it clean with her handkerchief, kissed it fondly, and then set it carefully on a cushion behind some lighted lamps. Nor was any skull lightly chosen. You would see the would-be possessor walking slowly along the sad mound of human debris searching attentively. Suddenly he or she would stop and pick up a skull on which no name was written. There would be much turning about of the object and careful examination of all its qualities as if it had been a melon.

The cult continued through the 1950s and 1960s with such vigour that it came to be seen by the Church as neo-pagan in spirit and attitude, the fear being that it might degenerate into magical practice or even Black Masses.* The Second Vatican Council 1962–5 called for the Church to be more open to modernity, although it was not the modernity so many people craved. What happened instead is that much of its aesthetic and spiritual value went down the chute. As for the cult, there had already been misgivings among the clergy, one of whom, Don Vincenzo Scancamarra, was parish priest at the church outside Fontanelle. Father Vincenzo had witnessed rather too many instances of odd behaviour and reported his concerns to Cardinal Corrado Ursi who, on 26 June 1969, applied the brakes, describing the addressing of human remains as 'arbitrary, superstitious, and therefore inadmissible'. Fetishism, in short. Only saints could intercede with God on the behalf of the living. Fontanelle was closed and the cult of the dead suppressed. Priests were to

---

* And in fact in later years Mario Alamaro, director of the Department for Geological and Subterranean Safety and who was in charge of the restoration of Fontanelle, recalls instances when Satanists and their Black Masses had to be removed from the site.

refrain from any action that might encourage undue manifestations of worship and, likewise, the faithful were to refrain from
any act contrary to true devotion and therefore unwelcome to
God.* Memory itself had been cancelled. The ancient connection between a people and their ancestors now severed, Ursi's
response was a deathblow to the autonomy of popular culture.
After a peaceful occupation in 2010 by the inhabitants of the
area Fontanelle was reopened as a site of historic importance,
by which point most of the devotees were dead, although, on
the day of the reopening, an old woman showed up at the gates,
shouting, 'Pasquale! Pasquale! Where is my Pasquale?' When
questioned by the organisers she said she could hear her skull
calling out to her. She went straight to a pile of skulls and disinterred her Pasquale.

So often I had been told the cult was a thing of the past, its
devotees either dead or gone to ground, which is not to say they
were beneath it but somewhere invisibly on its surface. Were *all
of them* gone? This was the question I kept posing in Naples, to
which I would say the response was roughly fifty per cent 'yes'
and fifty per cent 'no', the vast majority of the *no's*, however,
informing me that although the skull devotees continue with
their practice, I would not be able to meet with any of them.
One man I spoke to, whose late mother was highly active in the
cult, after agreeing to speak to me suddenly made his excuses.
As I'd believed in his first and second excuses, my third attempt
was met with a crushing response: the matter was closed. I am

---

* As the blogger and editor of *Morbid Anatomy*, Joanna Ebenstein,
wryly puts it: 'The Fontanelle languished after its closure, and by now
most of the devotees of the site have passed on and become what they
once adored.'

not pushy by nature, and so I sped past his favourite haunt, eyes to the ground, mildly embarrassed. I spoke to Bruno Leone, Pulcinella maestro, about *anime pezzentelle*. As Pulcinella makes regular forays into the world of the dead and always manages the return journey, my seeking of Bruno's opinion was not an idle choice.

'*Anime pezzentelle* know the future,' Bruno said. 'What this means is that there exists a world where time has another meaning. And so it becomes another way of thinking about existence. People need to believe in worlds other than this one. We are not talking about Heaven or Hell here. *Anime pezzentelle*, Pulcinella, the holy fool, the very poor, children – these are five ways through which we may communicate with a fantastic world we can't see.'

'Do you think the cult is finished?' I asked him.

'If it still exists, it's not like it was. The relationship with that world has become a much more secretive one. If you talk about it you may lose your ability to communicate with it. It would be like destroying the magic, the power lost. A friend of my mother gave lottery ticket numbers to the poor and very often they won. She communicated the secret to people with whom she did not have a personal connection, which was fine, but when someone in her family asked why she couldn't do the same for them she replied that she wasn't allowed to. One day she relented and gave her son the lottery ticket number. He played it and won. The next day she was hit by a car and died.'

I must have put on a sceptical face because Bruno was quick to say that these things are impossible to validate. There are no scientific proofs, nothing with which one can say this was or was not mere coincidence. What I do believe is that the divulging of certain kinds of knowledge can rob one of the ability to utilise it. Consider the poet who speaks of the poem he is going to write because almost certainly he won't do it, or else it will be depleted of the vital energies that informed it in the first place. Consider reading a manual before making love. Consider the imaginative possibilities afforded by Purgatory, the playground of our inner lives. Dante, in putting Purgatory at the centre, brought Inferno and Paradiso into line. The creative impulse that comes with the greatest force is the easiest to lose.

'If, on the other hand,' Bruno added, 'it really is finished, this does not exclude the possibility that it might be reborn at any time.'

It ought to be said, too, that the majority of the *yes's* I encountered look upon the cult of the *anime pezzentelle* as a purely Catholic practice that might have transgressed a little, whereas the *no's* see paganism everywhere. There is no need to set one side against the other, and while there is some bad feeling between them I suspect the truth is to be found somewhere in the middle. I spoke to two people who are on opposing sides of the issue, one of them Rocco Civitelli, an independent historian, and the other, Marino Niola, anthropologist and journalist.

I met Rocco Civitelli where he instructed me to be, in front of the church of Maria Santissima del Carmine, some yards away from the entrance to Fontanelle. We basked in the sunshine. The choice to converse there rather than inside the ossuary was, I soon discovered, deliberate. Civitelli, a devout Catholic, is impatient with what he perceives as too much willingness on the part of people, among whose number he surely put me, to see the pagan bursting through every seam and fissure of the Christian edifice. A long-time researcher of the place, he is also President of IRiS Fontanelle, the organisation whose aim is to spread cultural and religious awareness in the area of Rione Sanità. Enthusiasm drives his engine, even if at times it puts him on the same track as an oncoming one. 'With the work of research and documentation,' writes journalist Eleonora

Iasevoli, 'the association has succeeded in demonstrating that the ossuary is not a representative monument of the superstition and paganism of the Neapolitan people, but a testimony of the relocation and the role of the Neapolitan Church in the face of transformations and tragedies experienced by the city in the nineteenth and twentieth centuries.' That is the official view. What I find most laudable is Civitelli's attempt to prevent Fontanelle from becoming a theme park, so that it retains its character as a sacred place. It had been my own first thought upon visiting it. What if it was to become merely another item on the tourist itinerary? I had a brief vision of busloads of people and a booth outside selling 'Skull & Bones' or 'I ♥ Fontanelle' T-shirts. Civitelli began by inviting me to dig the hole into which I was bound to tumble.

'So what is *your* opinion?' he asked me.

Struggling a little, I told him I'd like to understand better the cult of the skulls and that although I knew of its recent history it felt very ancient to me, almost Greek in character.

The sound my question made as it hit the bottom of a very deep hole was just about audible.

Civitelli shrugged.

'There are plenty of Greek graves in Sanità and Materdei and in the hills surrounding here. There are plenty of ossuaries all over the world. What's so different about this one? Something I should tell you is that although the cult would *seem* to be linked to a Greek or pagan one, actually it is much more strongly connected to the Church. This was a Christian practice. As soon as you go inside Fontanelle you will notice the Via Crucis that evokes the birth and death of Christ. The popular view of Naples is that it's a folkloric city and so in the minds of many people the cult of skulls can be seen as something that can be separated from the Church. This is a dangerous, though fashionable, view. It is dangerous for Fontanelle in particular because it fails to acknowledge the fact that it was the Church that established this place. We meet here, just outside this place, in order to stress this. This church was built later, but if you go inside Fontanelle, on the left you'll see a small area that was the first church. The cemetery was built along the lines of the Church itself. One begins with the birth of Christ and then there is Calvary, the mount where Christ was crucified. You can see the Tribunal in the central nave, a crucifix on a mound of skulls and bones, which represents the judgement of God on man. When this place was established, Italy was still a young state. Naples was passing through a period of depression. There was the cholera, then earthquakes, Vesuvius, and in that period, after 1861, the Church established this place as the punishment that God visits upon man for having abandoned the faith.'

'This is a form of punishment?'

I'd heard nothing to support this, and in any case why punish those who happened to be in the vicinity when the bacterium *Yersinia pestis* manifested itself first in fever, then weakness and headache, and finally death? Even Francesco Gizzio, author of *La spada della Misericordia* ('The Sword of Mercy'), writes that the plague was occasioned by God's wrath over our sins, and then argues that it was also a sign of His divine mercy: God punishes us in life so as not to punish us after death. If ever there was an article of faith that stumps me, it is this one. Would God punish the baby who dies in its sinful mother's arms?

'Yes,' Civitelli replied, 'this was a cult of penitence. It could just as easily have been Paris, where there is a huge catacomb and, at the basilica of Sacré-Cœur, there is a chapel dedicated to the souls of purgatory, where we are reminded that people abandoned God. It's the same thing here, but there is nothing written because Naples is such a difficult city to rule. You have to figure out for yourself the meaning of this place.'

'If, as you say, this was a Christian practice,' I asked, 'why did the Bishop of Naples stop the cult in 1969?'

'Why do you think?'

I said something to the effect that people may have lost the necessary distance between the dead and the living and that perhaps the cult had become more important for them than religion.

'The Church lives in an everlasting conflict because it stands for eternal principles,' he replied, 'but it also has to live inside history and history is always changing. The closure of the cemetery was linked to a historical process that the church was going through in the 1960s, the end of a huge period commencing with the Council of Trent and ending with Vatican II [the Second Vatican Council]. There were new principles that had to be put into practice, one of which was to focus attention on Christ and not on devotions. As you say, when the link becomes too thin religion loses its way. There are many places like this, in Palermo and Rome, where you can see exposed corpses. The problem arose when the cult became that of the unknown dead. This is another subject, but at the end of the nineteenth century the Church approved of the cult. And then, later, it didn't. Outside this church it is written that Gaetano Barbati, an extraordinary man of the Church, edified this place. The Church uses things to its own purposes, and in this case the cult of *anime pezzentelle* was one of devotion and expiation. At one point Italy was seen as the conqueror of the Vatican State and as something bad, but then the Pope said the unity of Italy was a form of divine providence. The Church, even if it didn't want to, changed with the times. This is the contradiction, the fact that the Church stands for eternal values but lives within history. Cardinal Ursi who closed Fontanelle may be seen from one side as an authority far removed from the people, as someone who forbade what they loved, but, when seen from the other side, what he did was to close a discussion inside the Church. The priests were told they had to shut this place and of course some of them argued back, saying the cult brought the Church lots of money from the masses. Cardinal Ursi said, "Okay, but you still have to close it – I don't care how – this thing must be brought to an end."'

'What about the perception of ordinary people?' I asked. 'When you deal with superstition there is always something a bit outside religion – you mention Palermo and Paris – but here there is something unique and I want to know why it is different and whether it is attached to some bigger attitude towards death such as living in the shadow of a volcano.'

'In the whole Catholic world, even in England before the Reformation, there were kinds of behaviour similar to this. Another problem, maybe one you might wish to discuss in your book, is why people choose to see Naples as championing superstition. The problem concerns not only the representation of Naples in general but also the representation that Neapolitans make of themselves. The London of the ninth century, the Paris of the twelfth century, and the Naples of the nineteenth were not so different from each other. So why has Naples continued to be presented in this way? With respect to Fontanelle one thing different from other places is its munificence. It is particular to Naples that it likes to represent things in a spectacular way and this is equally true of Fontanelle. This is an ossuary, but it is not macabre. What the Capuchins did, for example, is gloomier, creepier, but there is nothing of that here. Why do you come to Naples and not, for example, to Milan? It is because Naples set itself up as a city of superstition and popular culture. One way to see into this phenomenon is that tradition is always invented. It is not something negative but at the same time it must be explored because it can't be determined just by spotting something here or there. Naples may excel as a folkloric city, but this is a construction.'

'Is it so wrong to see it this way, when the folkloric, as long as it is not contaminated by commercialism, is the deepest expression of a people?'

'I don't know if it is incorrect. It is a way. You have to choose. If I go to England where there were once similar kinds of phenomena, I may want to learn more about the traditional culture.

You come to Naples and see people living in narrow streets and now you are looking into the cult of skulls, so it is a matter of choice. I must confess that from a touristic point of view this is really convenient and it's why many people come here. We must be clear. Naples has nothing other cities don't have except, perhaps, for the bay.'

'So why does Naples feel completely different?' I countered. 'I want to reach a deeper understanding of it, which is to say I don't wish to make touristic mistakes.'

'So what is so unique about Naples?' Rocco asked.

'I am not talking about buildings or art or even what we find here, but what I perceive to be a special Neapolitan soul. They say melody was born here. Something happened to Leopardi when he came here. There is something that distinguishes this from other places, but when it comes to matters of the soul it becomes difficult to put into words.'

'So you are interested in the reasons why Leopardi came here. He came here because this is the place most closely linked to Virgil. He went to Florence, then to Rome, and finally Naples. It was not that Naples was a special city. English people prefer the coast, Capri, Sorrento, so one of the principal reasons that brings them here is the beauty and then maybe they see other things here. It would be interesting to discuss with you why in general tourists see only the opposite of their homeland. You are Protestant and I am Catholic therefore Catholics are superstitious. You are liberal and we are not, therefore we are conservative. This is "Herodotus Syndrome". When Herodotus first went to Egypt he thought it was the complete opposite to Greece. If I go to a place I am likely to see in that place all the things that are different from my homeland, so maybe this is one reason why tourists love Naples. This reflects the different ways in which Protestantism and Catholicism faced various kinds of problems. In the sixteenth century the Protestant church closed the argument. They still think that there is nothing in the irrational aspects of Catholicism to interest them. They see this, also the Eucharistic miracle, as superstition. At the end of Mass people here receive the *ostia*, the body of Christ, and for Protestants even this is a form of superstition. So there is a strong division and this influences the way in which the first watches the second. It is why people coming from northern countries see Naples as a society totally opposite to theirs. This perception is not wrong, it is proper, but the problem is that it has been used by Neapolitans to represent themselves. They cannot face their history without thinking of that representation of themselves, as a folkloric society based on superstition.'

Why assume I was Protestant, when indeed I'm not? Why assume I was assuming anything at all when all I wanted to do is get into the minds of people here? Why this business with 'Herodotus Syndrome', which, as far as I could tell, is Civitelli's phrase? We go with what we have, and, with luck and intelligence, we return with considerably more. I think Rocco caught these thoughts flying through me and shifted gears a little.

'There were two periods when the cult rose sharply,' he continued, 'in 1861, when the Kingdom of Naples was defeated by Garibaldi's forces, and towards the end of the Second World War when the city was occupied by the Nazis and then the Allies. It was a terrible situation. My grandmother would come here to avoid the bombing. This was the cult of devotion and penitence and in these periods of danger and desperation it rose to its height. You saw those small boxes where the skulls are kept, *scarabattole,* which is also the name for the boxes in which relics of saints are kept, another proof of the link between the souls of purgatory and the cult of saints. If you read the dates on them, they are mostly from the 1940s and 1950s. People often adopted skulls because they represented a lost parent or someone who was yet to be found, many of them in Russia or Africa. Women came here to pray for a son who had not yet come back home or who had died. When a son did come back the women said thank you to the skulls. It was not uncommon. The prisoners taken by the English came back, but it was not always like that for others. It depended on which front they were on. The grandfather of my best friend was never found. At the end of the Second World War the situation at Fontanelle was impossible to control. There were people who sold bones to medics and students, others who took skulls home. Fontanelle is a testimony to the tragedies of the Neapolitan people. I came here with two friends of mine, two girls, who were not in the least bit religious. They entered and seeing all these coins and things placed on the skulls they took a couple of coins from their pockets and placed them on a skull. I asked them, "Why did you do this?" She replied, "I was moved by the atmosphere." So the things you see do not always represent what we believe. If I enter and see skulls with coins on them, I might think there is still an active cult of skulls, and I might think Naples is a pagan place. But there is no link, no document, there is nothing that links the practice of people to their motivation or intentions. Superstition sells.'

'So these were Neapolitans, not tourists, who put coins there?'

'We made a survey. We asked a couple of guards to discover how many people who come here are still linked to the cult. There was something like ten people, in their eighties and nineties. This does not mean it is not important to them but that the cult is no longer sizable. There may still be traces of it, but today the meaning has deeply changed and is more connected to what you feel because it is a huge representation of the mystery of death. It is no longer linked to the Church, but the historical passages that have brought the cemetery to what it is now are complex. They are not pagan, however. They are Christian. The majority of people who come here are young. They are not interested in superstition but in what for them is a new way of representing death, and from this a huge range of feelings can arise. Once upon a time, death was everywhere. You were likely to see the bodies of your parents when they were buried in church but now, after the eighteenth century, when the cemetery was moved outside the city, people were taken far from death. If you are Neapolitan and feel religion strongly in your heart you don't come here. You go elsewhere. There is a new spiritual tourism. There is a joke. One skull says to another, "Why aren't we being buried?" The other skull replies, "We must represent popular culture." "What is popular culture?" "It is a touristic invention." "So Neapolitans should be superstitious and pagan?" "Yes. If not, he is not Neapolitan." "Who says so?" "The Dutch anthropologist down at the city hall." That is say, the intellectuals.'

I think I got the message. My own position is not quite what I think Rocco Civitelli thinks it is, but any standoffishness on his part is perfectly understandable given that I think the presence of pagan survivals ought not to be considered a threat but perhaps even an aid to belief because, *signore e signori*, if we are about to slip off the world's edge, or indeed have already done so (slim likelihood of our cognisance), what better reassurance than the idea of a continuum, one in which we may look back to whatever was there in the beginning, which we fondly imagine awaits our backward glance? The ouroboros, the serpent devouring its own tail, the infinite cycle of life and death, creation and destruction – they are all contained within this continuum. Also, there is in most of us the desire to be remembered, and remembrance is at the very heart of *anime pezzentelle*.

As we walked back through Rione Sanità, Civitelli stopped at a *pasticceria*, the Poppella, and got us each a *fiocco di neve* ('snowflake', a ball of dough filled with cream) which was new to Naples and causing a bit of a stir in culinary circles. It was here that they were first made, and the efforts of other *pasticcerias* in other parts of Naples to duplicate the recipe had failed. Civitelli saw in this further evidence of Neapolitan inventiveness, which, although I can't quite join the dots, he managed to equate with the composition of Pergolesi's 'Stabat Mater'. He asked me what I considered the greatest Neapolitan work of music and when, admittedly a little facetiously, I replied Totò's 'Malafemmena', which I do love, we entered upon musical warfare. We argued over the merits and demerits of Wagner, all the way down the hill to the *centro storico*. He found himself reluctantly praising the sound of the invader. The weight taken from his shoulders, 'Herodotus Syndrome' sent back into the cave whence it came, a warm handshake goodbye, Rocco Civitelli had become a most clubbable man.

God alone, God in the singular, which is to say, 'there is but one God, the Father, of whom are all things, and we in him' (I Corinthians 8:6), is at the very heart of Christendom. According to the anthropologist Marino Niola this is evidence for the disappearance of the gods, our God being at the end of a long line of Greek and Roman deities. Clearly Niola is about to follow Giordano Bruno to the stake. What would happen, though, if we were to bring the old gods out of retirement? Would they relocate from Mount Olympus to Brussels? Would they be issuing endless directives, the small print of which would make us nostalgic for city states? The old gods worked best as extensions of the best and worst in ourselves. They could be called upon with immediate results when we needed to get a job done. As bureaucrats, though, they would be as reliable as plumbers on a midnight call. These were matters I would like to have raised with Niola, the Professor of Anthropology of Symbols, Cultural Anthropology and Nutritional Anthropology at the Università degli Studi Suor Orsola Benincasa di Napoli, but beneath the tarpaulin of the elegant Gran Caffè La Caffettiera, on the Piazza dei Martiri, I had to force myself to keep to the subject of *anime pezzentelle*.

Marino Niola is the author of numerous books, among them, and central to my own enquiries, *Il purgatorio a Napoli* (2003). He has worked with the artist Rebecca Horn who created an installation of 333 cast iron skulls coming up through the paving stones of the Piazza del Plebiscito, above them seventy-seven suspended mother-of-pearl-like fluorescent halos. The work, entitled *Spiriti di madreperla*, while liked by many did not win universal approval, although the disappearance of two skulls on the opening night may have been down to thieves who were aficionados rather than scrap metal dealers. Niola is in the perilous zone of having his opinion sought on any number of issues, the great danger here being that he may, or has already become, a popular cultural figure. He studied under the great anthropologists Claude Lévi-Strauss and Alfonso Maria Di Nola. Gastronomy, together with its anthropological aspects, has been his focus of late; his recent book *Homo Dieteticus: A Journey Through the Food Tribes* arrives at some dark conclusions with respect to our attitudes towards food, suggesting it has become a new religion with its own 'demonization of desire' and with God acting as 'a sort of improper dietician', His modern-day prophets being the instigators of food fads and food phobias. Such is the consequence of being in a world that has lost a classical sense of the divine. We go where our stomachs are. On a cheerier note, Niola says of the gods that their favourite desserts were based on honey, almonds, and sesame.

'Many people tell me the cult is finished. What do you say to this?'

'It is like a river that flows underground. The deeper it is, the stronger. It is there, but you can't see it … a flowing, hidden river … but because rationality has won the day this belief stems mainly from people of the lower classes.'

'Some people say this is a Catholic ritual,' I said, 'others pagan in origin.'

'The relationship with death is so vital that for many people here it has become a religion.'

'One of the themes of my book is how life and death intersect here – in art, in music, in Pulcinella…'

'This is the baroque aspect of Naples, the relationship with death and the fact that death becomes a form of theatre. Death is useful to life. That is why I am saying that here death is like a religion because it comes *before* God, *before* Christ. God is a powerful state whereas death is more like a family member.'

'Would you say this is animism in the ancient sense?'

'Yes, it is polytheism. Goethe, when he travelled here, noted this.'

'If we say to the people who practise *anime pezzentelle* that this is animism, what would their response be?'

'Many of them wouldn't understand the word, but they are more ancient than they realise.'

'So knowledge precedes understanding?'

'This is knowledge that goes beyond the mind, which comes through the body before going to the head.'

'Are there stories from your own experiences?'

'I've been in this field since 1979. Actually I was still a student when I started. The first time I went to Fontanelle I met a man there who told me a story about the Captain. You know the story. He goes to the wedding of the man who did not believe in him. "You invited me," he said, "and I'm here." Mozart's opera *Don Giovanni* is set in Spain but it owes much to his time in Naples.'

'Yes, the Captain as Commendatore. Do you think the young Mozart might have breathed the atmosphere of *anime pezzentelle*?'

'I think he must have felt this exchange with death.'

'This idea of life and death, does it come from living in the shadow of a volcano?'

'Yes, much of it, Vesuvius from one side and Campi Flegrei from the other. There is something under our feet that is stronger than ourselves. If you look at the ancient literature, Virgil, for example, when they wrote about Hades they put it here.'

'I would like to know more about the *capuzzelle*. The people in the cult, did they argue with the skull if they did not get what they wanted?'

'They had a sort of dialogue. It is like when you talk with saints and holy figures. People prayed for the dead and in return would ask for grace and miracles.'

'What happens if the miracles don't come?'

'The one who is a believer usually thinks that he has received something or at least he will convince himself something has happened and that he did not waste his time. What this means is that a miracle happens no matter what. It is, however, a psychological miracle.'

'Theoretically the skull could belong to a murderer or evil person.'

'They know this, but it doesn't matter. There is a widespread belief that one who was a murderer in life after death becomes pure. Most of the *capuzzelle* are from people who died through various forms of violence … cholera, war, famine, drowning at sea, "death by water" as in T. S. Eliot's phrase … and had no ceremony. They become powerful spirits because they need living people. They can't accept what happened to themselves.'

'So they need completion. How would you describe the actual practice? Was it just women who did this?'

'Mostly women, but also a few men. Women in Mediterranean culture are always dealing with death and with bodies. They weep over the dead just as they did in ancient depictions you find in museums.'

'Is it true that the Camorra took their vows in Fontanelle?'

'This is a legend that was propagated in the movies. It used to be said the first Camorra in the eighteenth century did, but this might be a black legend.'

'So in terms of actual practice did people touch the skulls or move them? Or did they leave them in one place?'

'They would go there, choose a skull, and the skull would later appear to them in dreams and say to them, "You will recognise me."'

'What happens if two people adopt the same skull?'

'One skull can be adopted by two people, even more. The more miracles a skull produces the more people will tend to favour it. There is a kind of hit parade. When a skull is adopted by someone it is important to keep it clean because the cleaner the skull the purer the soul is.'

I related what Salvatore Mazzo told me about drawing a circle in the dust surrounding a skull that failed to deliver.

'Yes, this is quite true. It is about cleaning for a miracle.'

'But the circle was an expression of anger that the skull was not doing its work.'

'It was a magic circle.'

'Which keeps the spirit trapped inside?'

'Yes, the spirit stays inside the circle and finds peace when someone takes care of it.'

'Do people feel this is a secret that if revealed would result in the skull losing its power?'

'Yes, otherwise that person betrays the contract made with the skull.'

'Does this mean the people who do speak are no longer members of the cult?'

'Not quite. I found that they did not tell me everything. They tended to hold something back. Or they talked about what they did with another skull before they adopted a new one in the same way people might talk about past loves but not the present one.'

'Quite often I see a Pulcinella with a skull. Is there a connection between the two?'

'Pulcinella represents the souls of dead people. Generally masks are dead people. Pulcinella wears the white sheet of death and a black face. The name itself means "little chicken". In the past chickens were sacred to the goddess Hecate, the Queen of the Night. So there is a connection.'

'But Pulcinella never dies.'

'He keeps on being reborn and assumes a figure of present times. He is always returning.'

'Pulcinella seems to be an ambassador, moving between the two worlds.'

'Pulcinella is the representation of Hermes, the god of messages, also called Chthonius by the Greeks, which means "underground", where he connects between life and death. The French writer, Michel Leiris, used to say that here in Naples you need to move through shadows.'

'Do you think the cult is based in something ancient – Greek, Roman, or Etruscan?'

'Definitely Greek.'

'Is there anything in Greece similar to this cult?'

'No longer. They have eliminated, forgotten everything. The real Greeks are here in Naples and then Puglia is neo-Greek.'

'There is no archaeological evidence for the skull cult in this area?'

'No, nothing at all. But there is imaginary truth such as you will find in the ancient Roman mosaic of a skull with a bottle of water. It represents the thirst of dead people. They need to be refreshed. The relationship with the *capuzzelle* is called *rinfresco*.'

'Would you say this is where it begins?'

'Yes. The idea that dead people are always thirsty is very ancient. Almost every pagan culture believes the dead need water. The living people keep the dead alive. When Ulysses goes down into Hades he sheds the blood of a ram and a ewe so that the dead might drink it.'

'There are people in Naples who don't like it when I suggest this has pagan origins. They say this is Catholic in origin.'

'The fact they are Catholic does not mean they are not pagan. Catholicism embodies paganism, which is why saints often have the names of ancient gods, Saint Venera, for example.'

'This for me is a city where Christianity and paganism meet.'

'Yes, thanks to Catholicism this is possible. Protestantism never allowed for this. They believe He is just one God. This is a first step in the direction of not believing in anything at all.'

'Are there other stories about the cult?'

'A woman told me she dreamed of her daughter who died young. In the dream the girl said to her mother, "You did not bury me in the correct way. You did not put a nice dress on me so I cannot pass through." Her mother went to Fontanelle and left a new dress there. She went home and when after a few days she returned to the cemetery she found the dress wet and dirty at the hem. The spirit of the daughter wore it and passed through finally and found peace. Another person, a man this time, had a dream. He was worried because he was told he had to have surgery, so he went to Fontanelle to pray to a skull of a man who was a doctor. The doctor answered him in the dream and told him he did not need surgery because in the hospital they were wrong with his diagnosis. The man went back to the hospital and was told this was indeed the case.'

'Did these messages come through dreams or conversation?'

'In dreams, although sometimes when believers speak of this you can't tell whether they are describing a real dream or a vision. When they used to go to the cemetery of Fontanelle they got into a mystical state somewhere between dream and reality. What this means is that there are places or crossroads where there is an exchange between reality and vision. The Greeks used to say the place itself produces the dream'

'Such as one had in Cumae with the Sibyl?'

'Yes, she was in this visionary state.'

What induces in Rocco Civitelli something approaching missionary zeal is, so I believe, for Marino Niola an old story told many times. Whereas the former is expansive in his responses, the latter abbreviates. As for Niola, I know from my own experience that what was once uppermost in my thoughts becomes a little patchier with each retelling, such that I begin to leave out the connecting threads altogether and leave my interlocutor with, yes, old bones. It's what we do, we who make more journeys than one. It's what they do, who stick to a single path of choice. I'm not saying one is better than the other, only that it makes getting at the core of things all that much harder, what with brevity on one side and, on the other, a surfeit of enthusiasm that creates its own obstacles. Sometimes one wants for a single sentence, a staccato burst that will light up the whole stadium at once. Civitelli is right when he says one has to figure out for oneself the meaning of this place. Niola is right when he speaks of a flowing, hidden river. It's not that I think I'll ever 'crack' Naples, but from time to time I need to tell myself and a few unfortunates that I am doing just that. It's why I write. It's why I tip my hat to the ghost of Giuseppe Marotta. Truth in Naples is always somewhere in the middle, only the middle is invisible. The middle is only what we suppose it to be, there being very little evidence for its existence. It's like trying to plug a black hole in outer space. You get sucked into all sorts of imponderables. What is true everywhere, in Naples is twice as true.

Anna Maria Ortese, in her book *Corpo celeste* ('Celestial Body') writes, 'I believe in all that I do not see, and I believe little in that which I do see.' What she says, my friend Mariagrazia Barsanti amplified:

'In order to understand the Neapolitan mentality, their attitudes, and behaviour, you have to consider always the two things together, life and death.' The reasons for this, she explained, go back to the seventeenth century, which was a tough time for the Neapolitan people. They'd already had many different foreign sovereigns and rulers. Social conditions were horrible, and they continue to be so, but she emphasised *this* is the real Naples, not that of the bourgeoisie. If one is to know the city it is necessary to observe its people living in poor conditions. And so, to go back to the roots of the *anime pezzentelle* and the threats imposed by foreign rule, the religious curia, themselves under pressure and maybe just a little too solicitous of their own welfare, had to calm people. They did so by instilling in them a sense of guilt. The people could survive only by hoping that one day they would be accepted in heaven otherwise it was impossible to live under such pressure.'

This was still very much the case when in the 1890s Matilde Serao wrote about conditions in Naples. Anyone writing about Naples now has to add to the mix plenty of drugs and violence because these days Heaven is what you get through the wrong end of the telescope. It's minuscule. Some say it's not there at all, but that Hell most certainly is.

'This made it all that much easier for people to take refuge in an intangible dimension, the world of the dead,' Mariagrazia continued, 'and so they began to establish a deep relationship with the dead, taking care of their skulls and bones. This is a very long tradition in Naples, and the two dimensions, the subterranean and what we find here at ground level, have always lived together because it is impossible to survive by living a normal life. It is a peculiar feature of our people, this giving to the intangible a sort of life.'

I think it is there, in the second half of her final sentence, that I found the words that had hitherto eluded me, *this giving to the intangible a sort of life*. Call it, if you like, a Pulcinella kind of existence.

There is something not a little disturbing in the Cimitero delle Fontanelle having become a 'destination' and maybe tourism has done what the Church failed to do and taken the oomph out of a solemn, albeit heterodox, practice. One may go just a bit further and say that there is a certain beauty to be found in it, a form of remembrance deeper than one can put words to, which no amount of intellectuality can touch, and which, where there is very little thought at all, puts to chase the mindless adjectives that sometimes have been applied to the place. Creepy is not what it is. And yet what it is, I am still not quite sure. What I do think is that those who would erase the anomalies of folk culture, which is the soil from which all such things come, erase a vital part of themselves. Feeling modern, they wish to be spared embarrassment. The savageries we eliminate are replaced by sleeker and deadlier savageries. And so while we may smile at the stories relating to specific skulls or to those who sought to trifle with them, and although we may laugh when we hear they were objects of veneration because the souls to which they are attached could see into the future and so provide people with the winning lottery ticket numbers, there's a danger that we will cease to respect the fact every last one of those old bones was wrapped with life and invested with all the thought – good and evil, profound and trite – of which man is capable because then, perhaps, it really will be time to roll a stone across the entrance of Fontanelle.

Crimson fingernails, dyed black hair, a scattering of dolls with eyes that unblinkingly stare. Maybe they comfort an elderly woman in her solitude. She pointed to the wooden model of a ship on top of the cupboard full of dolls and antiques, saying, 'There's the ship that will carry me away.' Caterina seems to live with death. She lost her husband some years ago and there were other family losses, so many I could not count them. All the people her age, both on the street and in the building where she lives, have gone. There's little joy in being the last one standing.

Where she lives completes the scene. It used to be a convent adjoining the church of Sant'Agrippino. Soon after the end of the Second World War, the nuns were relocated and the convent was

converted into minuscule apartments for the poor, the greater number of whom had been made homeless by the bombing, some of the most intense in all of Italy, with whole areas of the old city turned to rubble. The basic structure of the building remains as it was, the corridors with their simple groin vaults, the stone steps worn down over time. Somehow one thinks of nuns as weightless, but apparently the world is as much subject to erosion from centuries of nuns' feet as from anyone else's. The apartment in which she has lived for the greater part of her life comprises two sections of the old corridor and a small room to the left, her bedroom, which was the sacristy once. There was a squint, now blocked, through which the priest could look down into the interior of the church next door. One terrible day towards the end of the war he would have seen the bodies of young children who'd been killed in the bombing. Caterina has a childhood memory of them laid out in neat rows on the church floor, those boys and girls, side by side, as if inside some infernal classroom.

Caterina's father worked at the nearby Trianon Theatre as a ticket collector. A photograph shows him and his wife standing proudly, in their best clothes, on either side of the wooden ticket box. I saw Caterina in both of them, or rather both of them in her. As her family had nowhere to live they were given leave to stay in the theatre while the convent was made habitable. She remembers skipping school in order to watch the afternoon performances. The family was desperately poor and she would be sent to a man on Vico Scassacocchi who had a huge vat in which he cooked meat – one dreads to think which cuts or from what species – but for a few lira she could buy a ladle of broth that would then be poured over scraps of stale bread or, if they were lucky, the precooked pasta or potatoes that were sometimes available for sale. Quite often one develops an aversion to food associated with hard times. Sometimes it is the opposite, and one is grateful to what got one through them. My mother was devoted to eggs, which, during a difficult period in my parents' lives, were the only food available. To Caterina, however, chicken is anathema. As it was almost the only meat available during the war, it was not so much the chicken that repelled her as the conditions in which the chicken made its home, the filth of the streets, that same filth being the chicken's main source of nutrition. It meant that to some degree one ate what the chicken ate. This said, the bad times she remembers are also associated with the best of times when, as she says, the people of the neighbourhood were still pure. She will not slight the dead by speaking of those who were not. She wants to die with a clear conscience, she told me, and so the stories she tells me are hers alone.

Caterina spoke of Forcella in days past with something like nostalgia, but that probably is because there is no one else alive from those times. She speaks of how outside the door of her apartment, in the arched corridors, the neighbours would have their Christmas and Easter meals, each of them contributing something, all of them now ghosts at ghostly tables. These days she will not allow anyone in. She is afraid of what is out there. Suddenly came words that at first were almost impossible to believe, which made the shapes in the plaster come furiously alive. This she saw with her own eyes. The story as she told it was verified by other women present. During the earthquake of 1980, the wall to the right of where we were sitting burst open and from it issued a baby's skeleton, a small clatter of bones landing on the kitchen table. It is believed there are further bodies similarly immured. I had somehow imagined these events took place in another century, but, no, they were in the final years of the Second World War. The priest of the time would pay visits to the nuns at odd hours. Those dead babies were the consequence. Presumably the babies, or at least this one, had been smothered at birth and buried inside the convent wall. Caterina called the superintendent of the building who carefully replaced the skeleton in the cavity of the wall and plastered it over.

'You mean the bones are still inside!'

'Yes,' she replied, 'they're still there.'

'And the priest was never accused?'

This was met with a shrug of the shoulders. It is not known whether what he did was ever brought to the attention of the church authorities, but then there is nothing as secretive as common knowledge. Walter Benjamin begins his essay on Naples with an anecdote of a priest drawn on a cart through the streets of Naples for indecent offences. Whereas in his piece the story takes a comical turn, in this one the dolls become something other than what they were at first. They seem to take on another meaning as if theirs were the eyes of children denied their own lives. Outside, in the vaulted corridor, Caterina's young daughter saw the ghosts of the priest and one of the nuns whom he violated. I was flummoxed when Caterina explained that the reason her daughter could see ghosts is because when she was baptised, the priest, whether through laziness or by mistake, did not say all the words he was supposed to say, thereby rendering the baptism flawed or incomplete. All this happened beside the church on whose portal, remember, one may see the Latin words which comprise Forcella's motto: AD BENE AGENDVM NATI SVMVS ('We were born to do good').

The subject of priests got Caterina on another track and she described how as a young woman she went to confession with her sister.

'When I finished it was my sister's turn and the priest asked her, "Where do you put your hands when you sleep?" I ask you. Who is clean and who is dirty? It was such a terrible question to ask a woman. I still go to church on Sundays, but I have never had anything to do with priests after that.'

And then came yet more words for which I was absolutely unprepared, which I'd been told several times I would never hear from anyone's lips.

'There is a church a few streets over called Sant'Agostino alla Zecca, where there used to be a lot of skulls just like at Fontanelle. There was a secret crypt which they opened and there they found the desiccated bodies of monks sitting upright in the wall's niches. They had been positioned that way so as to drain the liquid from their bodies. With other people I went down to "light a fire" and pray for them. I went to the crypt every Monday because I fell in love with one of the skulls. I would go down there to pray and light a candle for it. I remember writing my name on a piece of paper which I then slipped under the skull.'

Only the day before, I had been told I would never meet anyone in the cult.

'When you went to pray to the skull did you ask for favours?'

'I made prayers for myself, for my husband, his mother, his sister and brother. I sought grace for them.'

'Did you feel your prayers were answered?'

'Sometimes yes, sometimes no. It depends. Maybe people more religious than me deserve more grace.'

'Did you feel a presence behind the skull? Did you think you were communicating with the ghost of this person?'

'I did not feel a presence. It was more like a statue.'

'How did you feel when the bishop of Naples put a stop to this practice?'

'It will start again. Then I will go to Sanità.'

'So you are still a member of the cult?'

'The cult exists, but after the earthquake in 1980 they closed the church.'

'This is a beautiful thing to remember the dead,' I said, 'but it feels like something ancient in this culture.'

'Yes, I agree. It is beautiful and it's probably older than Christianity. You feel the dead very close. We did not fight over the skulls. That is why we put our names beneath them. Everyone has his own skull. If you want a certain skull it might be someone else's property, that person's name will be there, so you can't take it. They put candles, flowers, and the name. I did not clean the skull because I was a little bit scared. Other people did but for me it was too much.'

'And other people who had skulls?'

'Sometimes they would write numbers for the lotto and place them under the skulls to be sure they'd work. I never won!'

'Is it true sometimes people would argue with the skulls, saying, "You did not help me"?'

'Never. There was a lot of respect between people and the skulls. It's because they are dead people. Also we were scared because if we argued with them they might come into our dreams and scare us to death. So we were very quiet with them.'

'Do you have any stories about the *anime pezzentelle*?'

'One time three young men from Sanità went to the Cimitero Fontanelle to steal things because they knew people would often leave valuable objects close to the skulls, money sometimes. They went inside during the night. The first one, after taking something, ran away and clambered up the wall to escape, the second one did the same, but third one said, "Wait a minute, I'd like to see the numbers under this skull because I'll play them tomorrow in the lotto. Wait for me." But the others had already fled. Suddenly he felt something catch the back of his coat. Actually it was just a bit of metal on the wall, but he was so terrified he didn't dare look behind him, and cried, "Please, please leave me alone. I won't do it any more. It will be the last time." Obviously he thought a dead person had grabbed his coat from behind. So he talked for ten minutes, pleading with whoever it was and then died from fear.'

'How do we know this if he was alone?'

'The next day the other two came back and found him dead, standing up against the wall, his coat caught on a hook. Some years ago, people used to put valuable objects on the skulls but not any more because of all the theft.'

The church where Caterina found her skull, Sant'Agostino alla Zecca, dates back to 1259 when it was founded by Charles I of Anjou. One of its permanent residents is the composer Niccolò Jommelli (1714–74) of whom Charles Burney wrote, 'He is extremely corpulent, and his face reminds me of Handel, although he is much softer and more pleasant in his manners.' I listened to his 'Requiem' which is a thing of beauty. When he died he was ranked one of the greatest composers of his time whereas now, O Fortuna, only a few people have heard of him. The church was closed after the Irpinia earthquake in 1980 and its restoration has been subject to endless bureaucratic tangles. Part of the bell tower collapsed in April 2011, only a matter of luck that there weren't people below, and then thieves broke in and stole ten of the slender marble columns without anyone appearing to notice. There are rumours it is about to reopen, but I have gone there several times and have yet to see any signs of activity.

The bodies of the monks, among whose company was Caterina's beloved skull, have been removed from the *scolatoi*, which can be translated as 'dish rack' or 'draining board' but in this

instance refers to the area where the bodies of the dead were placed on *cantarelle*, special chairs made of stone, resembling toilet seats set inside wall cavities. They were placed in a foetal position in order to drain them of their fluids before burial or removal to an ossuary took place. This was considered a necessary rite of passage. The image above appeared in the *Corriere del Mezzogiorno* in October 2011. The article on Sant'Agostino alla Zecca draws attention to 'the graffiti that "embellish" the ancient burials with names of girls and references to romantic as well as sacrilegious loves' that were added over the years following the church's closure. It was not quite Eros and Thanatos, I suppose, but with what vigour the young, while Death smiles at them, perform their rapturous dance.

'And you really think the *anime pezzentelle* will come back?'

Caterina had no doubts on that score.

'Yes, even the priests say so.'

There was one more visit I had to make. A five-minute walk away from Sant'Agostino alla Zecca, on the busy Corso Umberto, one may find the side entrance to another church called San Pietro ad Aram. One can pass it any number of times without noticing it's there. As one enters the first thing one notices is how vast it is, as if it were some kind of optical illusion, a big place tucked inside a small one. The sad reality is that decades of poor urban planning have resulted in the church being hemmed in on all sides, so that now even its main entrance is inaccessible. It seems to be there hardly at all. This said, it's well worth a visit. Among several fine sculptures is Giovanni da Nola's bas-relief of the *Madonna delle Grazie*, at her feet, their arms in supplication, a group of figures rising out of the flames. Made between 1530 and 1545, it suggests an early instance of the cult of *anime pezzentelle*. It also predates the current structure that was built between 1650 and 1690 and which replaced an earlier church built in AD 870 or thereabouts. This in turn was erected over an earlier paleo-Christian church and, beneath that, an ancient Greek temple. If what one is told is true, San Pietro ad Aram can lay claim to being the first Christian church in Europe. According to legend it was here, in AD 44, that the Apostle Peter, on his journey from Antioch to Rome, stopped and celebrated Mass, which surely would have made it the first such liturgical event outside the Levant. Maybe the Vatican ought to be in Naples. The stone that served as the altar was called the Ara Petri and in the years that followed Mass was celebrated by saints Silvestro I, Pelagio, Gregorio Magno, and Nestoriano, not that any of these names will strike an immediate chord. Obscure saints fare badly on the hit parade. It was also here that an elderly woman called Candida who suffered from migraine asked to be healed by the Apostle. She was subsequently baptised by him and in gratitude – strange the forms it takes – she spent the rest of her days in a small cell. She is a credible candidate for the first nun ever. The remains of her cell survive in the crypt (although in her day it would have been on street level) and on its back wall is a faded fresco thought to have been painted by her. Saint Candida the Elder, as she later became, died there in AD 78. Almost within arm's reach of her cell was a well that also survives, whose waters were said to have miraculous properties that include the relieving of women's labour pains and headaches. Another Neapolitan convert, a friend of Candida's called Aspren, was also healed and baptised by Peter and later became the first bishop of Naples. There is a connecting theme here. In 1899, the Bayer pharmaceutical company saw fit to adopt his name for a new wonder drug called aspirin whose healing agent, salicylic acid, was first isolated by another Neapolitan called Raffaele Piria.

Antonio Paciello is the caretaker at San Pietro ad Aram, a remarkable figure who sports tattoos and walks as if on a rolling ship, which is apt given that he describes the church as a boat ferrying the *anime pezzentelle*. There is an actual boat at the rear of the church which symbolises the plight of migrants who have drowned at sea and for whom, just recently, Easter prayers were said. And to take further the analogy of ships and voyages, Antonio said the first historical mention of the soul is in Homer's *Odyssey* where the wandering hero meets the shade of his mother Anticleia. 'What we took from the Greek cult of the dead,' Antonio told me, 'we brought into Christian culture.' I didn't tell him the Egyptians got there first, the soul being very much at the centre of their belief system, but in terms of the old Hellenic culture in southern Italy his words were highly suggestive. So much of what one sees *feels* Greek. Antonio who has trained in martial arts comes from a background of poverty and violence. Without Evil, he said, you can't see Good. The business card he gave me bears the words HANAWA SAKURAJI HITO WA BUSHI, a mediaeval Japanese proverb which translates as 'the best blossom is the cherry blossom, the best man the warrior'. I wouldn't want to tackle him, there being more than a bit of the samurai about him, but there's something about his eyes that radiates tenderness, deep spirituality, and intelligence – an awful lot to absorb at a single take, I know, but what I saw in them stays with me still. Antonio's eyes see further than most eyes, although an optician might declare otherwise. The dead, he sees them. Sometimes, he tells me, people come in off the street and simply disappear into the walls. The dead, for him, are alive. I see no reason to doubt him, which is to say I'm inclined to believe what other people believe. It's the pact one makes, unless, of course, one makes a career of unmasking people. Antonio struck me as steady as they come. It's a judgement I'm prepared to stand by. The poor who early in the morning come to the church for sustenance are deeply fond of him and he is fond of them. I say judge a man not by what he says but by what he does. Again, it's something one can read in the eyes.

Antonio took me around the church, pointing out its many esoteric features. Some of what he told me seemed to be cobbled together from rather obscure sources, sometimes he was wrong with his dates, but what mattered was that in a sense the church's story was his story, and were it not for San Pietro ad Aram and the Franciscan brotherhood, which is responsible for its running, he would be in a bad place. The greater number of the church's mysteries reside in the crypt, beginning with the marble pillars, ancient Egyptian in origin, seven of them reddish in hue, and an eighth, Greek, that is a greyish-white. The seven red columns, represent the constellation of the Great Bear or Ursa Major which, Antonio told me, had been a symbol of the Knights Templar, and the eighth one I'm not quite sure what he said it represents other than when one looks into the skies one sees, positioned close to the last star in the constellation, another solitary and pale. It was not Polaris, this much I know. Whether those pillars were really pharaonic in origin or the Great Bear a symbol for the Knights Templar I have not been able to establish, but what Antonio brought to bear is an extraordinary blending of different cultures. The Egyptians had a strong presence in Naples.

As we went deeper into the crypt I saw glass cases full of human bones, a mere fraction of the many thousands that are now concealed behind the walls and inside tunnels. Candles flickered in front of them. In one of the alcoves were words written inside a snake-like bubble: IN NOVISSIMO DIE DE TERRA SURRECTURUS SUM. Job 19: 'In the last day I shall rise.' The most peculiar thing I saw were enlarged early photographic images of ghostly figures – men, women, and children, and separate individual portraits labelled 'the captain', 'the doctor', 'the duchess', 'the judge' – all of which had been taken from the internet and made to stand in for the *anime pezzentelle*. Their interchangeability, the fact that what they stand for had little bearing on who they actually were, was perhaps the most bizarre aspect of the place. As long as the figure labelled 'Dottore Alfonso' looked like a doctor (although at first I thought it was Gustave Flaubert), the captain a captain and the judge a judge, they would serve their purpose. After all, what are our bodies but mere disguises for something else? Antonio told me that when he first started coming to the church he didn't tell his wife. Maybe, shy in the eyes of God, he didn't want to reveal his hand too soon. One night she had a dream in which she and Antonio were surrounded by children and when finally she visited the place they turned out to be the children in one of the photographic images. It was in this spot, he told me, that the souls of children had first manifested themselves. Those candles, though, who put them there?

'People come here on Monday mornings,' Antonio continued, 'lighting their candles, praying for the *anime pezzentelle*.'

'You mean it still happens?'

'Yes, thanks to the brotherhood that keeps the cult alive.'

This was later verified by the priest who told me this is the only church in Naples where people continue to pray for the *anime pezzentelle*.

'Have you seen them?' I asked Antonio.

'I have seen and felt their loneliness and pain. Even if we think we are alone in this room, we're not. We are surrounded by the souls of purgatory. They are thirsty for our prayers. I didn't believe in these things before. Then I understood that there are souls that got separated from God, anonymous, taken by war and plague, and so they need our prayers to get them back to Him. I was close to death for three years. This allowed me to see what normally one can't see. Also the tufa which is everywhere in Naples activates an organ in the middle of the brain and shows you things you can't actually see. Do you want to play a game? When you go back to London there will be a place where you often go, a park or somewhere. You'll look at the trees. You will notice a tree, or maybe just a plant, maybe a rose – if you stay close to a rose you will be regenerated – whichever it is, it contains more light than the others. And you will stand close to it and stay there awhile. It will enable you to see more deeply into things than before. My grandmother was like me. She had my eyes. There are movements in your eyes that allow you to understand who it is you are talking to or that enable you to see exactly how things stand. This is something I got from her. This is important for me, especially when I'm speaking to new people or I'm in a new situation because the first sensation is felt here.'

Antonio pointed to the top of the bridge of his nose.

'You know if you have to run or whether someone is good or not. The closer you are to nature the more your mind opens up, the more it sees. The earth is alive and we interact with all things here. At the end we will physically cease to exist, but we are never separated from God. We were born to bring paradise here on earth. We are God's dream.'

We are God's dream. One of most persistent things about Naples is the way even the most uneducated people are able to give voice to things beyond their reach. They are not locked inside some prison of the inarticulate from which the only escape is a stream of expletives. They are in their poverty rich in expression. I had found what I'd come looking for, solid evidence for the continuation of a practice that was all but gone. It may not be quite as it used to be. Apparently people no longer come in expectation of graces or miracles, although who's to say for sure. What are the secret bargains a man in prayer seeks to strike with God? Are our prayers always unstained by self-interest? Dreams remain an important element and there is little control over what we ask for in them. Sometimes, Antonio said, in those dreams people are told to come here.

'It is not by chance that you are here,' he added. 'You were probably called.'

I might have said I came in pursuit of a subject, but then he might have asked me why the pursuit in the first place? Caterina may be right, of course, and everything does come back. Antonio may be right when he speaks of the inherent energy within all things that sooner or later forces everything back to where it belongs. What was that about Vesuvius containing magnetic powers that absorb what one takes to it and returns it in kind? Maybe it takes a volcano to make one recognise just how fickle, how vain, are our notions of permanence. Maybe it takes old bones.

The Devil at Play in the Quartieri Spagnoli

The Spanish Quarter is the most densely populated area of Naples, the grid of streets so tightly packed the sun falls in some places for only minutes at a time – one must rush out with a demitasse to catch it before it goes – and in other places never at all. The Quartieri Spagnoli,* to revert to the mellifluous original, occupies 800,000 square metres. Arithmetic is obdurate. What does it actually mean, 800,000 square metres? Giuseppe Marotta, *scrittore*, comes up with something the mind may grasp, a spiritually precise measurement of the place: 'God Almighty must have created the Quartieri for the sole purpose of hearing Himself praised and blasphemed the greatest possible number of times in the smallest possible area.' Zena Rotundi, street harpist, lives here. 'Sometimes, in the house where I live,' she tells me, 'I hear people screaming.' I've heard, and continue to hear, the very same from my bed in Forcella, a man in the small hours, no telling from which direction his voice comes. 'It is one of the clichés about Naples,' she continues, 'that people

---

* I realise it ought to be translated in the plural but as such it sits uneasily on the tongue.

are always screaming, but there is a reason for it. You have to see what happened to them to make them behave like this. And yet I see light in the Quartieri Spagnoli.' As there is in Forcella, dark though it is. It's in the people, not all of them, but enough to make me not seek to go elsewhere. Zena finds the old Naples still very much alive in the Quartieri Spagnoli, the Neapolitan language there the best preserved of anywhere.

The name derives from when in 1536 the Spanish viceroy of Naples, Don Pedro Alvarez de Toledo, established a safety zone for the Spanish garrisons. A city-builder he may have been, a man of vision certainly, but he was also a ruthless figure. There was no crime so petty it did not merit a death sentence, some 18,000 executions at his own count, which serves to provide a lesson rarely absorbed, that the more brutal on crime we are the more it flourishes.* Some irony that Don Pedro who almost succeeded in bringing the Inquisition to Naples should have been responsible for creating a zone whose name became synonymous with vice. It had become as much a haven for the prostitutes as for the Spanish soldiers who had only to step outside for their fleeting pleasure. One of the early residents of the Quartieri Spagnoli, a young harquebusier who had yet to make a name for himself, lived there in 1570, and again from 1572 to 1575: Miguel de Cervantes, *escritor*. The work he believed his best, superior even to *Don Quixote*, was *Journey to Parnassus*, which most people agree is close to unreadable. It serves our purposes, however, because in it the elderly author recalls the Naples of his youth. 'Esta ciudad es Nápoles la ilustre, / Que yo pies sus ruas mas de un año / De Italia gloria, y aun del mundo lustre.'† Something

---

* Peter Gunn, in his *Naples: A Palimpsest* (1961), wryly notes: 'It may be true, as Campanella said, that if there had to be foreign rulers in Italy, the Spaniards were best fitted to rule; the tragedy is that this should have been so.'

† 'Tis Naples' self, that city of great fame, / Whose streets I paced for

else brought him to his good opinion of the place. The young Cervantes fell in love with a woman who in his first novel *La Galatea* he calls 'Silena' and with whom it is believed – for he says as much in the heavy slog of a poem he wrote towards the end of his life – he had an illegitimate son called Promontorio. After he left Naples he saw neither of them again except through the magnifying lens of his prose and verse without which we would never have known of their existence. We must think of him not as a scoundrel or a bounder but as a man separated from them by circumstance for there is something haunting in the way he writes about them, as if they inhabit some misty, lost archipelago of love. I keep watching out for a young Cervantes on a motorbike.

It is at once the most inviting and forbidding of places, at once atmospheric and associated with massive unemployment and street crime. Many Neapolitans avoid the Quartieri Spagnoli or else stick to the two streets closest and parallel to the busy Via Toledo. Atmospheric it most certainly is, but at whose expense? I try to read faces. Some undecipherable code appears to be in operation, towards what end is not readily discernible, but it's what one finds in a people that has seen tough times. It's why one must go with care because the deeper one goes into the Quartieri Spagnoli the more sensitive one must be with respect to those who live there. One should not go flashing one's wealth at them nor should one go inside a tourist bubble. There are approaches as to how to behave. Sometimes it feels as if one is walking through someone's living room, which, in a sense, is what the street becomes when in the hot summer months the inhabitants move their furniture outside where they eat, drink, sing, laugh, and argue. I'll repeat what Sartre, *écrivain*, says when he describes Neapolitans as 'the only people you can actually

better than a year. / Italia's pride, that sets the world aflame.' – from *Viaje del Parnaso*, translated by James Y. Gibson (1883).

watch living their lives, from top to bottom, head to toe'. So much else about the place he simply didn't get, but then I wonder how much real life ever passed through the filter of his intellect. Was he not some froggy-eyed abstraction puffing on a pipe?

Despite its reputation for violence, I never felt deeply uncomfortable there, which is not to say I did not keep my eyes open. It is what a writer needs at times, a sense of *edge*. One is fired up into something resembling the calm out of which it is possible to write although sometimes, just sometimes, one needs the battle zone too. The bedrock hereabouts is perilously thin. There is danger from above, Vesuvius, and from below, the extensive subterranean caves, and the surface is an almighty scramble. It can give at any time.

One writer who captures this sense of foreboding is Nicola Pugliese whose claustrophobic novel *Malacqua* is nothing less than a metaphysical fix on the city. The secondary title says it all: *Four Days of Rain in the City of Naples, waiting for the Occurrence of an Extraordinary Event.* I reject the claim that it is an analogy for the so-called *Anni di piombo* ('The Years of Lead') that signalled Italy's social unrest of the 1960s through to the 1980s. Would one say of Kafka's *The Trial* that it is a comment on the Czech judicial system of the early 1900s? Nor am I comfortable with the comparisons that have been made with the 'magic realism' of Gabriel Garcìa Márquez. *Malacqua* is very much its own creature, many of its fantastical elements real enough – the sinkholes that appear from time to time are actual sinkholes – but then strange things do happen, some of it mildly bonkers, the likes of which I have not previously encountered in literature. There are dolls that scream and coins that produce strange music. At the end of the book there is a release of sorts, as ordinary in its physicality as it is passing strange in its essence. The thing most inexplicable about its author is that when his book was published to great applause (and correspondingly good sales) he refused to allow any further printings of it. A strange contract made with some unknown principle, only death would break it. *Malacqua* is back on the shelves and on everyone's tongues.

At one point in the book the rain flows in torrents downwards from the Quartieri Spagnoli into Via Toledo. On that main thoroughfare, which defines the outer edge of the Quartieri Spagnoli, one night I encountered the corpse of a druggie who'd been shot through his right eye, his dog pacing back and forth in front of him, as if to say *what now? What next?* I had seen the poor wretch several times before. Several times I steered a wide berth of the sudden hand he'd thrust under my nose. Should I be ashamed that I took to bed the image of that nervously pacing dog rather than its owner? *What next?* The dog's fate haunted me. *What now?* As for the poor druggie – no, *man*, a man surely, a babe once, 'a brother to jackals, and a companion to owls' – one can only speculate because it is not as if his miserable existence will be the subject of any further inquiries. An inch of space in the daily rag will be, unless these words of mine count, his only death notice. The most likely explanation for his erasure, for erasure is what it was, is that a precisely aimed bullet bore the simple message – hereabouts one does not try to operate outside the System.

I have walked to the back of the Quartieri Spagnoli several times, the most threatening thing that happened to me being when a girl of about ten asked to see my watch. She wasn't interested in the time. She wasn't interested in my watch either, a most regular timepiece. I'd gone there to see more of what I'd spotted a few days earlier, street art of a kind very different to any I've seen before, which had stayed with me, in the way certain dreams do. The paintings clearly issued from the same hand (or hands) and with a comical, bordering-on-diabolical spirit behind them that at times reminded me of Miró, other times of Picasso, but which also stand alone. There is nothing quite like them, over two hundred in all that together form some

kind of human bestiary. The majority of them are painted over
the steel doors of *bassi* and in no more than four solid colours at
a time, usually some combination of cobalt blue, burnt sienna,
yellow ochre, a red of some temperature I can't find a word for,
and, just occasionally, an army tank green which actually is the
original green of the door not painted over, and finally, though
sparingly used, black and white. Despite the limitations of the
palette the way colour and shape combine never wearies the eye.
There is artifice, not necessarily what one finds on the walls of
galleries, but artifice all the same, which, like much street music,
looks to its surroundings for it to be able to deliver a message.

The paintings are integral to the place, not some alien colonisation of it. Shall I say they are organic? Yes, why not. They
do not intrude or defile. What the paintings depict are scenes
from another world, though not wholly remote from this one,
strange figures, close to surreal but then again not quite, some
of them resembling futuristic knights in armour, their weapons
ranging from bow and arrow, to spears and swords, to guns and
semi-automatics, and, most deadly of all, a peashooter. Some
of the figures have limbs that abruptly stop and then continue
in another part of the picture, often beyond the door's natural
frame. Here one sees a couple of figures joined together by a
single arm and there a man with a Cuban flag blowing out of the
back of his head, and elsewhere a snorkeler with a small bouquet
of flowers held above the water's surface, a rider wearing something like a dog's mask atop a two-legged horse, a dancing man
holding an umbrella over two legs that exist independently of a
body, an almost human figure whose head is on the end of his
arm, another with his head morphed into a key, a strange creature whose arms form a single hoop over a blue mountain with
three crosses on top of it. (So Calvary is here, in the Quartieri
Spagnoli.)

I struggle to find words to describe their strange combination
of playfulness and dark forces although, as with so much else

in Naples, they seem to occupy some kind of purgatory. They are what occurs in the spiritual hinterland between uncertain life and absolute death because the first death is not really death at all but a stage on the way to absolute death, so that death hereabouts comes twice. Sadly many of the paintings are covered with graffiti or else the rust is beginning to work its way through the paint, and the sense one has is that sooner or later they will deteriorate or else be stolen, perhaps sold to a savvy collector. I would be quite happy to possess one. I'd be happier still to resist the temptation to remove it from the surroundings that give these images such force. I wish there was someone to keep them in good order, some kind of curator outside the holy temples of Art and Commerce, such as one who feeds stray cats, who does so simply out of love.

I wanted to know who was responsible for this extraordinary work and so for the next two days I walked all over the area, asking questions, most of which were met with shrugs, before someone took me inside a small art gallery, switched on the computer, and led me to a website for cyop&kaf, lower case and without spaces, the name adopted by a couple of street artists who, when finally I got to meet them, asked me not to reveal their true identities. As I would discover later, many people in Naples know exactly who they are. There are many who have cyop&kaf's number stored on their mobile phones. The kids on the block salute them. They walk like local heroes through the Spanish Quarter, stopping every few minutes to talk to people. Were they to go into politics, they'd surely win a seat, only one, mind you, because they work as a single voice. They of all Neapolitans are perhaps the most openly invisible.

So what does their name mean? Any answers veer dangerously in the direction of academe. Mine are born of mischief. CYOP is the English acronym for 'Create Your Own Path' or 'Choose Your Own Palette' the second of which is the happier of two choices. KAF stands for either the Kenyan or the Kuwaiti Air

Force, neither of which makes sense so away with those, but in the lower case *kaf* is the Icelandic noun for 'the state of being submerged' which is another happy choice because several of cyop&kaf's works depict such a figure.

Kaf is also the twenty-second letter of the Arabic alphabet, which is thought to derive from the pictogram of a hand, again not such a bad choice, but then it is highly unlikely that cyop&kaf went to the extent of studying a dictionary of English acronyms, and, as far as I can gauge, neither of them speaks Arabic or Icelandic. A moniker plucked out of the air, Italo Calvino might have baptised them so in one of his stories. Actually there is no precise meaning or at least not one that they will admit to. The fact that I offer the above interpretations at all is simply an attempt to enter into the spirit of fun and seriousness that informs their work in equal measure.

Sommerso (2012)

My first impression upon meeting cyop&kaf was one of extreme wariness from their side for they knew they were already in the position of breaking one of the cardinal rules of street art, which is the preservation of anonymity. We quickly struck a deal, their words for my silence.

'We come from a graffiti past and so we don't go about displaying our names. It's not interesting for us.'

'The people who built churches in the Middle Ages didn't leave their names either,' I replied. 'I was walking through the Spanish Quarter and after seeing more and more of your amazing works I had this notion. Suppose, heaven forbid, Vesuvius explodes and buries Naples. I would wager that in a thousand years from now tourists will be paying twenty euros to look at your excavated works and they will be asking themselves, "What kind of people were these?" "What did they believe?" "What was their civilisation like?"'

cyop&kaf sat in stony-faced silence.

'Do I have to leave?'

'You know the way,' said cyop (or was it kaf?) in a deadpan voice.

'There is one thing we'd like to know,' said kaf (or was it cyop?). 'We never talk to people. This is our principle. Obviously when we are on the streets we talk with everyone. We hope that our work speaks for itself. Our question to you is this: why do you think that by talking to us you will get anything more than you already have?'

This was shrewd, admirably so, such that I had to wonder if I'd ever be able to get through all the protective layers with which they covered their artifice. I replied that while I agreed that any work should stand on its own it is never wholly possible to separate it from the maker's life. Maybe I should have said makers' lives.

'The point is that for us these two things, our work and our lives, are *absolutely* related. We operate in broad daylight, with people passing by us all the time, and so we are very much inside life.'

'So how do those passers-by respond to what you do?'

'They know we're here, but they don't look at us as artists with a capital A. We're just painters. When you say *pittore* in Italian it is not related to the word "art" but to the painter himself. Caravaggio can be a *pittore* or he may be a housepainter. We are just a couple of familiar faces doing some other type of work. Some of the people living here think we are students wasting our time. They don't care about our aims.'

'What fascinates me about your work is that there is an extraordinary forest of symbols and images. I don't think you can say it is *not* art.'

'We don't care whether it is or not.'

'But you do it, so it must be important.'

'It is more like an accident. We don't plan anything in advance. What we do here in our studio is another kind of work. We do other things and so the language we use differs from project to project. It depends what we are working on.'

'May I ask about the visual language of these particular wall paintings? I suspect there is rather more thought going into them than you care to admit to.'

'That might be the case. It is not that we don't admit it, but we don't like this sacralisation of art, especially as for us this is just a daily activity.'

'This is precisely what interests me. I am not writing about the paintings in the Museo di Capodimonte but about something that is in the public domain and reaching into people's daily lives. I suspect that behind what you do there is a philosophy of some kind. You may not want to call it so but we all have, to some degree or another, our separate philosophies.'

'We are simply adding another layer to the many other layers of this city. This is our story. Capodimonte flows in our blood. We carry Masaccio's *Crucifixion* inside ourselves.'

'So what you are doing is ancient as well as new?'

'As you said earlier, if Vesuvius explodes … but we have stopped painting on the streets. We are starting to make sculptures, not sculpture in the direct sense, but more like those made from the empty spaces in Pompeii when archaeologists poured plaster into bodily forms. It is the same mechanism in that we obtain a positive from a negative. We try to imagine what would happen if people now were caught in a similar position, trapped by lava. They'd probably be in front of TV sets or computers. Our civilisation would not be nearly as interesting as Pompeii's was. People will be asking how in the hell we got to be like this.'

'Did you begin as a team?'

'Step by step. We started painting trains, each his own car, and then we began to work together more and more. One time the police fired warning shots into the air, chased us away. You have to be really quick. It was compulsory to work fast with the trains and this is how we work still, as quickly as possible.'

'Why did you stop with the street art?'

'It was a moment of crisis for us. There was too much bullshit about "street art" and so now we keep silent, well away from the noise.'

'You mean too much vanity was fed into it?'

'Our first step in pushing ego aside was to work as a couple, and then we started with our monthly newspaper *Napoli Monitor*. We are now a group of journalists and illustrators.'

'I don't want to turn what you do into a tourist site.'

'That is one of the reasons we stopped. There was a real risk that this area would be turned into a tourist spot. Our intention was for Neapolitan people to come here. They don't come because the very words "Quartieri Spagnoli" signify danger. We even produced a map to show them where our works are. People tend to go into the first two streets parallel to Via Toledo, take their photos, and stop there. We are inviting them to probe a

Omertà (2012)

little deeper. At this moment of art criticism it is dangerous to do something like this.'

'Politically?'

'No. The problem is that a lot of people began to exploit this street art wave in order to make touristic business for themselves. This was never our aim. We wanted people from other neighbourhoods to come here and see for themselves.'

'You have a definite style. I see plenty of squiggles on the walls about Naples, with interesting exceptions here and there, and then I see your work which is all of a piece. Quite often, for example, there is this devilish figure.'

'A lot of people tell us this. There are some even who erase our work because they say it is satanic.'

'It's like the Devil at play,' I suggest, 'in the Quartieri Spagnoli.'

'The people living here are not angry with us as such, but they say that we fail to notice the Devil is working through us and that he uses us as his instrument.'

'I am wondering if you are able to talk about some of the images I like best, where they came from.'

'If we remember.'

They are difficult people, cyop&kaf, but difficult in the right way.

'They make me think of African art,' I ventured, 'in that they are full of this primitive power. You have to be careful because people will start stealing them or they'll end up in galleries.'

'This is happening already. One year we worked in Taranto, which was a very different situation, an industrial city where they make steel, and where, accordingly, the colours and the shapes change. The reds are deeper there, for example. Our paintings were done on solid iron doors. People are so poor they have to sell the iron.'

'I really like this one. The dogs, they too, seem to like it.'

'This is quite a different picture when the dogs are not there. This painting changes according to the life surrounding it. Its title *L'arco di trionfo* ("The Arch of Triumph") has a double meaning. We always try to point out the connection between this microcosmos, which is the Quartieri Spagnoli, and the outside world, because usually people look at the area and say it is like a private club, but actually it is very connected with the rest of the world. It is a mirror. We like to show those connections, also with our titles, and often with reference to what is behind the doors.'

'It looks to me like the dogs have had an argument about its meaning and now they are silent. There is a great deal of mediaeval imagery in your work. Here, for instance, we have a bowman and jester rolled into one.'

'We don't call it mediaeval. We call it "media evil" which

L'arco di trionfo (2012)

historically is where we are now. There is a bow in the painting, not a weapon one uses any more. The weapons in our paintings do not come from any specific time. We are trying to describe what happens to people in relation to the media, what happens to people who use it and what happens to those used by it. There is an element of witchcraft. Nobody really knows how the media works – it is a sort of magic – we don't know what it does, but we still use it. Our works all have titles, which is very important, and which we choose sometimes a year after we've done a painting. When we are in the act of painting everything we do is based on instinct. We also listen because when we start our work people look at us, begin to talk, and gradually their stories emerge. And then those stories enter our paintings. Two of our paintings,

Congiura ("Conspiracy") and *Omertà*,* refer to the fact there are a lot of criminals around here and so the atmosphere of the Quartieri Spagnoli enters into the painting. *Congiura* actually depicts a fight between two brothers because sometimes families here fight among themselves in order to control the place. *Omertà* is a form of mutual protection. "I know something, but I won't tell you what it is because I am helping him." We keep silent in order to help each other. This is an invitation to *omertà*. There is a subject, a character, who is inviting another character not to speak.'

'Which is an interesting paradox, no?'

'Yes, I tell you not to speak, which implies something bad is going to happen to you if you do. There is a person you don't see in the picture who is saying to me, "Shhh, don't talk." Except I can see him.'

'So it is an act of complicity with the street itself.'

'If you like. It is a double negative. A person tells you not to lie, but because he is wearing a mask actually it is him who lies.'

cyop&kaf have produced a book that is a summary of their three-year project in the Quartieri Spagnoli. It is called *Quore Spinato* ('Barbed Heart'), a heart with thorns around it, the 'Q' replacing the 'C' of the Italian for heart (*cuore*). And, of course, the 'Q' and 'S' are the initials of the area. The book is 'a fragmented tale' whose pages have already been written on the walls of the Quartieri Spagnoli, whose totality cyop&kaf describe as 'a book in the open air'. The Introduction to their book, written in the first person singular, is a forthright statement of their intentions.

Now my challenge is this: I have put into this work the actions, the environment and the characters, but, unknown reader, *you*

---

* *Omertà* refers to the code of silence imposed by the Mafia and the Camorra, which includes not speaking to the police.

construct the plot. It may be a complex novel or a series of short stories. It doesn't matter. All I ask of my paintings is that they contain a small dose of ambiguity that will allow the reader who is on his journey to ask himself at least the hint of a question – it's like when you find only a scrap of a letter, a postcard, or maybe just a shop receipt and you start imagining the mystery of the lives they point to.

As for what happened between themselves and the people of the area, this is a private story cyop&kaf are not prepared to divulge.

Everything in between, between myself and every single page written between the lines and wrinkles of this wonderful neighbourhood is private history and does not deserve to be sold. It would be like prostitution. Have you ever seen love put on display? Those people who just show off, who make a show of participation, gentrification or social intervention, all they're doing is just building up their own careers. They put themselves in the window, selling themselves like old prostitutes. There is nothing to show. Moreover, there is much still to do.

cyop&kaf admit that some of the inhabitants of the area find their work disturbing and ask them whether they might not paint prettier things, what they call 'the dictatorship of prettiness'. The Introduction continues:

I am not out to please anyone. I absorb. While their emotional participation is very precious to me, so too is my autonomy. If I started to console them I'd risk putting myself in a field where a lot of other people are. I would be among those who continually try to hide what is wrong in this world, who try to sweep disaster under the carpet.

These are not just fighting words. They are a declaration of independence.

The book is handsomely made, about the size of a brick, a bit wider, and of a similar weight, just perfect for hurling through a window or for use as a weapon against the pretensions of artspeak. cyop&kaf don't waffle. Its final pages are devoted to the oral histories of some of the inhabitants based on interviews with them by Luca Rossomando and Riccardo Rosa. They include a woman who worked in the brothels in the 1950s, another story called 'A Love' about a person who made contraband and, as a consequence, risked losing his woman who was sick, and a chapter called 'Il piatto a tavola' ('The Dish is on the Table') about a barber who goes on his motorcycle from house to house to cut hair. He doesn't have a barbershop – he *is* the barbershop. There are a lot of people in the neighbourhood who are on remand and have to stay at home. So he goes and cuts their hair. Other chapters are about work, unstable people, dealers, Bruno who sells the water in the street, the unemployed, small bits of different stories about people.

'We have collected a lot of stories. We work on the streets for four or five hours a day and so we meet a lot of people. It is a good method of getting into relationships with the people. There is a chapter about some of the local children. The children participate most when we paint, helping mix the colours and often they paint the background colour.'

Interestingly, cyop&kaf cite the American oral historian Studs Terkel as one of their influences.

'We did this picture and the person whose house it was gave us the gift of a religious emblem, an embroidery of thorns with a heart at its centre.* We had the sense our path was almost fin-

---

* The Sacred Heart of Jesus, which has its origins in a vision given to the seventeenth-century mystic, Saint Margaret Mary Alacoque. The thorns represent Christ's suffering as well as the crown he wore

ished. We had done almost two hundred paintings and we were looking for a name to give to the book we were going to produce. When he made this gift to us, we realised that "Quore Spinato" would be the right name because metaphorically speaking the Quartieri Spagnoli is like a heart enclosed with spikes. If you want to get to the heart of this place you have to pass through these thorns. You have to deserve to arrive at this destination although you might be a little wounded on the way.'

Allegory was in the mix then. I began to feel the obstacles lift one by one.

'Do I detect a sense of a religious radicalism?'

'We are not religious, but the religious feeling here is so powerful you cannot ignore it. We are Christian even if we don't wish to be. You can't act as if this enormous apparatus of the Church does not exist.'

'But there is also an element of the pagan in Naples.'

'There are all these layers, one above the other, and you cannot separate them. Beneath us are the catacombs. You can start from hell and arrive at paradise. It is a multiple city and so it is impossible to speak of any one definable soul. There are so many layers, so many things to live for. You see the very rich, the extremely poor, beautiful places, and horrible ones. In the Quartieri Spagnoli you may see a *basso* where poor people live, and on the upper floor, in the same building, there'll be a lawyer with seventeenth-century paintings on his walls. All this in one building and these people are continually meeting and colliding with each other. It is the strength of this place. One reason why we do not talk much about our art to people here is that there is a tendency in the Neapolitan mind to become foggy. Our book about Naples is *without* the fog. One can see things as they really are.'

---

during the Passion. QS = *Quis separabit?* as in *Quis nos separabit a caritate Christi?* ('Who shall separate us from the love of Christ?').

'It is as I suspected,' I said. 'There is a sense of ancient and modern.'

'We all build cages for ourselves. Dante, when he wrote the *Commedia*, created for himself a cage of metrical rhyme, *terza rima*, which enabled him to write as freely as if it were prose or free verse. The form holds one back a little, but it's so one might fly all the more freely after that. If you stick to metre you have a very different approach to creativity. It is very powerful. It's like when you tell a horse to go faster you say *pronante*. It gives you a push, gives you strength. Form and limit expand your creativity. We decided to use only four colours in our paintings. It is our cage that helps us towards creating a vision of the world. It is not even completely a choice. It's not that we go to shops to buy paint. We find paint or else it is given to us. Sometimes it is what is left over from building sites or what has been used to paint the metal doors. If we were to go to a shop and see all the different colours we would be put in an awkward position. It would be too much.'

'Lotta Continua was an extra-parliamentary group of the far left in the early 1970s to which my father belonged. We are simply using the name of that movement in order to say the struggle continues, and "anche di notte" comes from the No Parking sign on the door: "even at night". The man who lived inside there was impassioned about Cuba and shouted it from the window. So this is what we gave him. There was nothing planned. It came out of a few seconds of conversation.'

'I can appreciate that you don't plan anything and I can well understand your reluctance to explain any of your images, and yet there remains in people a desire to reach for some kind of interpretation.'

'You pointed earlier to the frogman. We will never tell you it is *not* a frogman. If you want to see it like that it's up to you. What we do gives people the freedom to see the painting as they like.'

'It has struck me that many of your images are about being submerged.'

Lotta continua (anche di notte) (2012)

'They are about being caught between elements. It is a mirror of a very common state of mind in which one can't really breathe. We try to breathe – we are a bit inside, a bit outside – but you shouldn't think too much about this. The meaning comes on its own. We don't think about this when we are making these images but if we look back we can put them into context.'

'Do you see this as an image of suffocation in this society or even within this neighbourhood?'

'It is not necessarily about this place ... a specific moment or condition maybe, floating existences. Again, the Quartieri is a microcosm of society and in the end it is the whole cosmos.'

I mention Pugliese's *Malacqua* which they both admire, saying it describes a condition of soul rather than state.

'Yes, four days of continuous rain in a city that can't stand rain, and which can't even manage it. The streets are falling apart, the ground collapses. It seems as though things happen but really they don't. Everything is suspended. It is a bit like these floating existences we paint that are suspended, half submerged. It is the condition we inhabit in Naples, which you recognise only when you get out of here. Only then do you realise how much danger we are in. It is not a feeling of danger as such but rather of having to be aware and paying attention all the time. You always need to be focused.'

At the corner of Piazzetta Concordia there is a painting so badly disfigured now I had to ask them to provide me with an image of it as it used to be.

Indice di borsa (2013)

'We painted a door where they make high-quality women's bags, which is why you see a bag in the picture. The title *Indice di borsa* is a play on words. *Borsa* is a bag but it means also the stock exchange, the *borsa valori*. These bags they make are of really high quality and sell at incredible prices. Gucci, Prada, they go for a fortune, but the men who work ten hours a day making them don't know anything about the enormous amount of money they are generating for other people. Well, probably they do but they have to work, and so for us it was important to point out the relationship between this door, what goes on behind it, and what happens on Wall Street.'

I had, just then, a memory of some images in the Archaeological Museum.

'This is what the ancient inhabitants of Pompeii did when they painted their signs as indicators to what they did. We look at them as art now while the ghosts of these people say no, no, they are simply our trade signs.'

'We do not plan anything. A painting will take shape from the moment we start and quite often from some feature that is already there. We began to paint a figure around a hole made from a bullet in one of the metal doors. We painted a drop of blood coming from this hole, which in the picture is at the man's throat. The figure to the left is aiming at him with a peashooter that is perfectly in line with the bullet hole.

'There is an interesting story behind this painting which we titled *Buchi neri* ("Black Holes") although when we started we knew nothing about it. This man who always hangs about in the square came up to us after we finished the painting. "This is incredible," he cried. "This is *my* story!" He told us about his life in crime. One time he made a big mistake and burgled the wrong house. It was the Boss's house in another neighbourhood. The Boss sent his people to kill him. They shot him in the head and in the throat, but incredibly he didn't die. He showed us the scars.'

I pointed to another of their paintings over which someone had drawn a phallus. A ghost from Pompeii had been on the loose.

'How do you feel when you see your work being vandalised?'

'But we are vandalising the streets already! So it is impossible

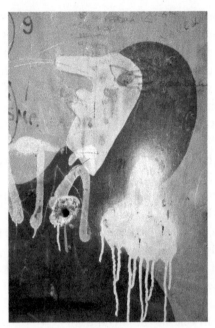

Buchi neri (2013)

for our work to be vandalised. If someone wants to add another layer to what we've done, that's fine.'

'Surely, though, there is good vandalism and bad vandalism.'

'We do not control that. When you do something on the street it is out of your control.'

'So you don't feel sad when you see your work deteriorate?'

'No, it takes on another kind of life.'

'In a way the worst thing that can happen to you is to get official recognition.'

'Yes, too many people know about us already. The point is that they are a step behind us. The book covers our work from 2011 to 2013. It's over. We are somewhere else now. Originally the idea was to write a book, not this one, but another that is actually written *on* the city if it were paper. We didn't really intend to do a book as such but rather a book about a book that is already written on the walls. We wanted something without a beginning or an end. The pages ought to be loose so you can arrange them as you like, which would be like an exploded novel. You can walk by these pictures and build up your own story based on what you see. It is not evident in the printed book whereas this *other* book can be read on different layers. You can go deeper and deeper or you can remain on the surface, which-ever you prefer. There is a place nearby, an abandoned palazzo where we made these pictures on the walls that later collapsed. This was in 2008 before we started this project. When, in 2011, the whole building fell down concrete walls were put up in its place. We redid the earlier paintings over the concrete. There is an empty space at the centre, which served as a cinema for five days. We showed movies and people brought chairs from their homes. A screen was hung from the old water pipes. When we launched the book we threw a party there. We hung some paint-ings on the walls, not ours but some by a friend of ours. We had taken some photographs of the walls of the Quartieri Spagnoli, one of which had a slogan written on it: "God put us on earth to create Hell."'

'There is such a strong relationship between the city and what you do with it.'

'We are not of that breed of Neapolitan who can live anywhere or who is here merely by chance. We are deeply rooted although sometimes it is healthy to get away for a while. Sometimes we work elsewhere and we're able to breathe for a while, but that also enables us to stay in Naples. There was a recent diaspora, a whole genera-tion of people who went away because there is very little work here. We stay where we are. We act as filters. Someone said of us that we are filters for the Devil, but we also act as filters between the writers for the magazine and the populace, and when we paint we become filters. Whatever happens around us is filtered into the painting. Here, for example, is an old one. *Apriti!* ("Open up!"). The idea comes from Aladdin's "Open Sesame". There was a keysmith working behind that door. We enjoy making puns. We are telling you these things, but we don't want the stories to be explicit.'

'There is another square where there is an entrance to what used to be a bomb shelter during the war. Some young people set it up as an exhibition space. We put on an exhibition called *Buio* ("Darkness"). *Io* is I, I in darkness. No more than ten people could go down at a time. There was a corridor, a path for them to follow. We made transparent paintings. They couldn't see anything, just these empty white walls. Then they heard the sound of air raid sirens. The lights were switched off and the pictures which we made with ultraviolet paint would appear. This is when we feel street art becomes more important than what you see in the galleries with all their intellectual expressions, such that much conceptual art has become a sort of decadence. The important thing for us is to understand *where* we are doing these things. We act differently depending on where we are.'

'You say you were in Taranto for a year so how can you afford to keep your studio here? Do you have subsidies?'

'No, but Naples is a cheap town to live in. We sell paintings, work on graphics and illustrations. We don't make much money, but it's enough to put the dish on the table. At the moment we are involved in a TV series being shot in Naples. In 2013, we made a film called *Il segreto* ("The Secret"). We are not film directors as such, but for ten years we had been doing the magazine in which we wrote up the stories we heard from people. Those people were not idiots. They all had a story to tell. The story in the movie is about kids. They have nothing to say about the past because some of them are as young as five – they are *pure action* – in their case you need only a movie. There is nothing to listen to. So we changed media and took up the camera because that was the only instrument with which we could tell their story. It was not that we wanted to make a movie and chose a subject for it. It was the other way round. The subject needed a movie for it

Apriti! (2011)

to be told. We wanted to tell their story because it is important that one can say something about kids nowadays. The *segreto* is the place where the boys hide discarded Christmas trees. They collect and store them there for what will be a bonfire. All the gangs in the city are after getting those trees.'

'Is this a traditional game?'

'No, it has been only in the last twenty years or so. Before, the bonfires were made not with Christmas trees but with pieces of wood. The ritual came from the countryside. After the Second World War, we started to have Christmas trees, which is a relatively new tradition here. There used to be lots of trees whereas nowadays people use plastic trees, making the real ones much harder to find, which is why there is this war between the different quarters.'

'So the war is based on nothing other than this specific game?'
'Yes, so that your fire will be bigger than the other gangs'.'

Although nowhere in the film does it explicitly say so, *Il segreto* draws upon an old ritual that children have no or very little knowledge of. And yet it is for them to re-enact, albeit with a modern twist, what their ancestors have been doing for centuries. It falls on the Feast of St Anthony (*La festa di Sant'Antonio Abate* or, in local dialect, *'O cippo 'e Sant'Antuono*), on the evening of 17 January. Massive bonfires are lit to mark the end of winter and the beginning of a new season, a ritual that has its origins in pagan times and which is common to almost all world cultures. The ancient Romans celebrated something very similar, the *Feriae Sementivae*, a moveable festival dedicated to Tellus (Mother Earth) and Ceres, the goddess of agriculture, who we ought to bow our heads to every time we pour ourselves a bowl of cereal. Sowing-time invited prayers for a good outcome. The timing was critical because cold weather could disrupt agricultural activities. One of the features of that festival was the making of large bonfires, fire being the element that simultaneously destroys and purifies. This ancient tradition survives through into the dialect verse of present times, 'sant'Andùon', sant'Andùon', pigli't 'o viecch' e damm 'o nuovo' ('St Anthony, St Anthony, take the old and give me the new'), and in the village of Calatri one hears words reminiscent of our own Hallowe'en when children go from door to door, saying, 'Trikk' trakk' e trùon, e ddamm' 'na lèuna p' sand'Andùon; si nn' m' la vò rà chi t' pozza fà app'ccià' ('Bang, boom and thunder! Give me some wood for St Anthony. If you refuse, may you burn!') The bonfires are called *cippi* – *cippo* in the singular – and in the smaller towns and villages the tradition survives, with the inhabitants paying their respects to this third-century Egyptian hermit saint who is not to be confused with Saint Anthony of Padua. A founder of the true monastic life, Saint Anthony the Abbot spent much of his time resisting the Devil's temptations. Clearly abstinence did him good as he lived to be 106. One legend is that he went to hell and, while the Devil was otherwise engaged, had his piglet steal a firebrand to take back to the people above. Was it with this very fire that the pig was cooked? Pigs are known for their intelligence. This would have been a bad move for a pig to make. Saint Anthony the Abbot became particularly important in southern Italy, gaining a cult status among the peasants, and is the patron saint of farming, pork butchers, bacon, domestic animals (including pigs*), bakers, basket makers, and gravediggers. He also protects against skin disease and shingles, the Italian for which, appropriately enough, is 'il fuoco di Sant'Antonio' ('St Anthony's fire'). This was a saint who saw to local needs.

What we get in *Il Segreto* is not the reclaiming of time, which is to say the historical continuum within which the above festivals take place, but rather the reclaiming of space. All gang wars are about physical space. And when the gangsters put on nifty suits, physical becomes political space. The camera follows the activities of children, aged between five and fifteen, modern *scugnizzi*, 'urchins' (or even, according to one writer, 'turbo-*scugnizzi*') over ten days, going through the narrow streets of the Quartieri Spagnoli looking for Christmas trees, sometimes asking in advance for them in hotels and other business spaces. There is an incredible sense of urgency in what they do. They go about their nocturnal

---

* Jeff Matthews in his encyclopaedic website *Naples: Life, Death & Miracles* notes: 'In the 1100s, the order of the Knights Hospitallers, an organisation that cared for the sick across Europe, adopted Anthony as its patron saint. He is often depicted with a pig because pork fat was also used as a treatment for skin diseases. This led swineherds to take Anthony as their patron, and he thus became the patron saint of charcutiers (pork butchers) and also the patron saint of bacon! (I didn't know that bacon even had a saint. Theologically, I detect some conflict of interest in having the same saint protect (1) the pig, (2) the butcher, and (3) the bacon. Maybe I'm missing something.)'

patrols or on their raids, dragging their booty behind them to the secret place, the vacant shell of what was once an old palazzo, where, on 17 January, they will have the bonfire. There is no plot as such, but there is mounting tension as they compete against neighbouring gangs for trees. There is a last-minute obstacle the boys have to overcome. It is not an action movie but it is, as any child can tell you, an epic adventure. If, while watching the film, one does not re-enter one's own childhood, even through the filter of one's life experiences, then it will seem very flat indeed. It is, at base, the story of a consummation. An adult goes behind appearances and although cyop&kaf are much too savvy to say so – there is no forced message in their film – adulthood is being constructed bit by bit inside each of the children. It may not be the adulthood their families wish for them. Checco Lecco's gang is on the loose, and while they are probably sluggards in the class-room, which often enough is a sign of intelligence, they are quick on their feet and with their wit. They are, above all, unpredict-able. The predictable one is bound to lose. They knock at the doors of apartments such as they themselves will never inhabit; they have an ambivalent relationship to authority, whether it be their elders or the police; they negotiate with owners of small businesses and with building administrators, pushing their case with miniature violence in their voices; they have something resembling mob rule and ape the sense of camaraderie between thieves. These are all recognisable tropes. When will collecting the trees become something else? The children are not so rootless or rudderless as they appear, for there is already a code, even if it is discernible only to themselves. The brief glimpses of the adult world in the film are of mostly bemused, sometimes annoyed, faces. What the participants of this serious game need most of all, however, is to keep their own faces. And the more face they have, the greater their goals will be.

Il Segreto is, on the face of it, a documentary, but then perhaps it is not quite one or, rather, just a bit more than one. It is pushing at something rather bigger that is never actually verbalised because for most of the participants it will be so very little. This rustling of trees may prove to be the biggest victory of their lives. The mighty conflagration at the end is, give or take a hiccup or two, exactly what is supposed to happen. The Quartieri Spagnoli itself has the leading role. The secret heart of that area is a mirror to the whole of Naples, just as Naples is a mirror to the world. One critic, Alberto Berardi, responding to the film drew parallels with what the French film critic and director Alexandre Astruc wrote in 1948:

> I would like to call this new age of cinema the age of *camérastylo* (camera-pen). This metaphor has a very precise sense. By it I mean that the cinema will gradually break free from the tyranny of what is visual, from the image for its own sake, from the immediate and concrete demands of the narrative, to become a means of writing just as flexible and subtle as written language.

I don't think that Berardi's mention of this is out of place nor is his pointing to the paradox of 'the secret': 'It contains the idea that there is something hidden that cannot be said or revealed,' he writes, 'and that at the same time this something is said and revealed to some in order to create a bond.'

Il segreto is at one with all that cyop&kaf do. It is urban art, although perhaps they wouldn't like to say so because their strength lies in their nonchalance, their refusal to be drawn on various issues, although not for a moment can one doubt their integrity. It's there in heaps, but they are not about to be caught shovelling it. The film has won awards, one of them for 'the convinced, lucid and passionate approach to reality with multiple nuances, that of a true, intense and contradictory Naples at the same time'.

As for what they say of it, cyop&kaf are more direct than usual and might even be accused of being moralists: 'A film that looks more closely at things can make a contribution, we hope, to isolate the comfortable and simplistic reading of the clash, beneath Vesuvius, between good and evil, black and white. Working amid nuances brings to light a different truth.' As for myself, it triggered a memory of my seven-year-old self dragging a decommissioned Christmas tree over a snowy field and the swishing sound it made.

There is often in such games of war an ultimate prize. What better than the so-called 'Beast' in the florid Galleria Umberto I, the most luxurious shopping centre in Naples, which was the setting for several of the American writer John Horne Burns's wartime stories? Stealing the biggest Christmas tree in Naples from there takes raw nerve. It means dragging it through the cavernous place, well in sight of the powers that be, and then getting it from there over the main thoroughfare of Via Toledo and up into the narrow streets where the branches of the tree will brush the walls on both sides. It had been done. And then the authorities got wise. CCTV replaced the Almighty's eye. And so the kids got wiser still, resorting to all manner of subterfuge. Sometimes they get caught, it's true. More often, as soon as the police arrive, they scatter in all directions. A year ago, they got it. They must have been kings in their world. It rather reminds me of what Norman Lewis wrote in *Naples '44* when, almost in passing, he notes that one night an American ship was spirited out of the Bay of Naples.

'So this is a rehearsal for what will one day become the dark side of Naples?'

'It is one aspect, but remember this is a game among children. Maybe they fight with their hands at most, but it's nothing unique.'

'Surely, though, it is good education for the future.'

cyop&kaf were not about to betray the trust they have with young people hereabouts. I noticed on the wall of their studio an image of the ouroboros, a serpent consuming its own tail, and I could not resist showing them the Sicilian proverb I'd shown almost everyone here.

'As a comment on Naples do you feel it's accurate?'

'We are too much inside here to be able to say. We have seen so many different levels of the city, different people, so when anyone talks in a general way about Naples it is always much too general. It is imprecise. When I hear all these definitions they seem too small to contain all the city's different aspects. We are like two filters talking together. I saw you working with someone who was talking, talking, talking. You were like a filter. You would disappear inside yourself and let the person talk on. The filter is already there because of the things you are going to write, but we are like filters in ourselves.'

I will conclude with words from the beginning of their Introduction to *Quore Spinata*:

Some time ago, a friend of mine asked me: but why do you do this? I realized she had more answers than me. Maybe she imagined I did it to improve the neighbourhood or because I liked to stay with people. Maybe, and if it's true it doesn't matter; but I am more inclined to believe that I do it because I have to, I am simply allowing my obsessions to run free. The characters I paint, they actually draw me, not vice versa. Armed to the teeth, self-destructive, misfits, more modern than modern, they drag me and force me to give life to them and to put them inside that frame of meaning that is called the metropolis. You can't fight it when a passion is so strong you walk through its flames without thinking, even though you know you can be burned at any moment, just as some surfaces (only in name, because if you look closer they have really deep stories to tell you), when the billboards hiding them are destroyed and what is revealed are layers and layers of posters singed by time and that give birth to very disquieting beings.

One may grow to love such disquietude.

Signor Volcano

Percy Bysshe Shelley, a shrewd observer otherwise, was dismissive of Solfatara when he visited it in December 1818: 'There is a poetical description in the Civil War of Petronius,' he writes to Thomas Love Peacock, 'beginning Est locus, & in which the verses of the poet are infinitely finer than what he describes for it is not a very curious place.' Vesuvius, on the other hand, fascinated him. This is no great surprise given that the nineteenth-century mind preferred the alpine to the elfin, geysers to trickles, symphonies to bagatelles. Why go south of Mont Blanc if Vesuvius was not one's objective? Solfatara, by comparison, is a collapsed soufflé, a crater sans eminence, a rotten egg of a place. One smells the sulphur before one even gets there. All it ever does is to stink, bubble, and fume. There's no saying, though, what a poet will add to his grab bag of stored images and it's not altogether unreasonable to suppose that the Cave of Demogorgon, at the beginning of Act II, sc. ii of Shelley's poetic drama *Prometheus Unbound*, contains the memory of a local guide at Solfatara thumping the ground with a stick in order to produce the echoing sound that still unsettles visitors today, which gives the impression of there being very little beneath one's feet other than a rather thin crust and, under that, a dome-like cavern.

Actually the booming sound is produced by tiny veins of gases. Most pleasingly to the ear, the Italian for this is *rimbombo*. The poetical mind imagines itself stretched like a drum skin over an abyss. It's where it functions best, anticipating doom.

One of the Oceanides asks, 'What veiled form sits on that ebon throne?' Shelley at Solfatara: it was not Greece, where he'd never been, but Italy that fed the physical attributes of his poetic vision. As Mary Shelley wrote in her 'Note' to the afore-mentioned poem, 'Shelley loved to idealize the real – to gift the mechanism of the material universe with a soul and a voice.'

I see a mighty darkness
Filling the seat of power, and rays of gloom
Dart round, as light from the meridian sun.
—Ungazed upon and shapeless; neither limb,
Nor form, nor outline; yet we feel it is
A living Spirit.

Solfatara (from the Latin *sulpha terra* 'land of sulphur') or Strabo's *forum Vulcani* is for me a most curious place. Would it be a volcanologist's idea of blasphemy were I to say it fascinates me even more than Vesuvius? But then I prefer string quartets to symphonies. An elliptical space covering approximately thirty-three hectares, which for those of us who know no better is roughly eighty-two acres, the volcanic crater of Solfatara, one of forty in the area, is deemed inactive. Strange when, depending on where one is, it goes from warm to hot to the touch, and with the swell of the magma chamber below is subject to the uplift and subsidence known as bradyseism. It feels very much alive. There is a curious tendency in the mind to think history stops in the hour and the spot where one stands, whereas, of course, the story is far from over.

Solfatara's bare expanses would seem to be empty of life. Not so. There is a bubbling pool of mineral-rich muddy water in the middle of it, which is home to a rare form of archaea, the lowest form of cellular life, *Sulfolobus solfataricus*. Somewhat charmingly, because of its penchant for hot places, it has been described as an extremophile. Also unique to the area is a creature called *Seira tongiorgii* which one is tempted to call a bug, which really is not a bug at all but a species of Collembola that belong to the grand order of hexapods, at which point an inattentive mind might revert to calling them bugs because bugs are what they most resemble. The male of the species collects spermatophores from the female without having to go to the bother of making love. I saw a graffiti in Naples, GENDER IS OVER, which would suggest the human race is headed for some kind of class reunion with its collembolic origins. Surely, though, Neapolitans are too highly sexed for it to be true.

Standing with one's back to the entrance of Solfatara and, on the outer ridge, an unsightly building development for which we have other kinds of dark seismic forces to thank, what one sees rising from fissures in the ground are plumes of sulphuric smoke, the most impressive of which is the Bocca Grande ('big mouth'), with its continually burning coals covering a colour spectrum that goes from the most beautiful yellow to the most beautiful reddish-orange. This, according to the highly impressionable ancients whose minds were more alert to the poetic than ours, was the dwelling of the god of fire. It is difficult to determine whether one is better or worse for breathing in the sulphuric fumes, although from Roman times onwards they have been said to have curative properties. The Samnite goddess Mefitis reigned here long before the Roman gods – to her we owe the word 'mephitic', which denotes foul-smelling gases. The goddess of foul smells is also, curiously enough, the Samnite goddess of love, ritual prostitution being one of the features of her temples. Paradoxically, she is a protectress against those same poisonous gases, and until relatively recently she would be called upon to avert bad smells issuing from sewers. She ought to have been kept on the payroll but sadly has slipped into the minor ranks of gods and goddesses.

Pliny the Elder mentions the 'Fontes Leucogei', the whitish aluminous waters found in Solfatara and elsewhere. It has not much changed for centuries. The toga'd Romans basked there, the barbarians put a stop to such fripperies, and the Middle Ages saw considerable mining of the extra rich mineral deposits which comprise a list to warm any alchemist's heart with, in addition to the various alums, alunogen, arsenopyrite, arsenschwefel, coquimbite, dimorphite, epsomite, galuberrite, goldichite, gypsum, halotrichite, kalinite, kaolinite, krausite, leucite, mascagnite, mendozite, metavoltine, mirabilite, natrolite, opal, orpiment, pararealgar, pickeringite, pyrite, realgar, russoite, rutile, salammoniac, sanidine, sassolite, sulfuite, sulphur, thénardite, trona, tschermigite, voltaite, and, my favourite, yayapaiite. And yet at a single glance, the untrained eye sees only an expanse the colour of sun-bleached bone. 'Colours that destroy the soul,' said Petronius of the place. Solfatara is a place of wonders geological, biological, and mythological. In the late fourteenth century during Aragonese rule, it became a royal hunting reserve where wild boar were pursued. It would later become an obligatory stop on the Grand Tour when it became a regular feature in travelogues of the time. If Shelley claims to have been unimpressed I suspect he was perhaps more impressed than he let on, either that or some of Lord Byron's facetiousness had rubbed off on him.

Solfatara's visitors have been legion. One is tempted to imagine Dante among their number, though there is no evidence for this – yet there is a passage in his *Commedia* that describes it perfectly. The great comedian Totò was filmed there, in toga and laurel crown, as the mean-spirited Baron Antonio Peletti, who in order that he might see the error of his ways is tricked into what he is led to believe is the afterlife. After *47 morto che parla* (1950) who needs the small fry that is Alighieri's *Commedia*? Silius Italicus in his *Punica* would have us believe the Carthaginian Hannibal was shown Solfatara and its environs by his nobles. It is not certain whether this was based on fact or if the author was taking his readers on a tour of the places he himself loved. The line in the poem – the longest surviving epic in Latin – most fitting to my perennial theme is when Hannibal, leaving his winter headquarters in Capua, is compared to a glossy serpent coming out of hibernation, 'lifting its head and breathing out gore'.

It was at Solfatara on the emperor Diocletian's orders that San Gennaro, who would become the patron saint of Naples, was beheaded on 19 September AD 305 along with his companions Festus, Desiderius, Sossius, Eutyches, Acutius, and Proculus, the last-named being the deacon of nearby Pozzuoli, or Puteoli as it was then known. (There is an interesting etymology here in that Puteoli might derive from the Latin *puteo* 'to stink', although there is also *puteus* which means 'well' or 'dungeon'.) So incredibly strange would have been Gennaro's last glimpse of the world. There is a dramatic painting of the event done circa 1630 by Aniello Falcone, and then later a drawing by Salvator Rosa, both of which show the fumaroles in the background. Another version tells that Gennaro was martyred outside the perimeter of the volcano where today there stands a church to his memory, with a stone that turns red with the memory of the blood shed by the executioner's axe. Yet another version of events, albeit not particularly convincing, is that Gennaro was martyred inside the perimeter of Solfatara and that his head rolled *up* the hill to where the church stands.

Giulio Cesare Capaccio (1552–1634), poet, historian, and theologian, in one of his books notes a local disturbance around Solfatara, when it would appear some resident demons broke loose. At the church of San Gennaro, some Capuchin monks living nearby told Capaccio of their troubles with the devils, who terrorised them with their howls. Capaccio goes on to relate an earlier incident involving a young man from Puglia who had been robbed in Naples, and who allowed himself to be tempted by the chief devil who said he would arrange for the man's stolen property to be returned in exchange for his soul. The man from Puglia betook himself to Solfatara where, with blood from his own arm, he produced his Faustian contract.

Petrarch, weary of the pressures of Naples, visited the Phlegrean Fields in November 1343 and although he soundly dismisses the magical tale that Virgil had constructed a crypt going all the way from Naples to Pozzuoli – saying that while Virgil may have been a poet, he was no stonemason – he found the great poet's spirit everywhere. Speaking of the sulphur baths that drew people to the area, he poses the question: 'Who would believe that, close to the mansions of the dead, Nature should have placed powerful remedies for the preservation of life?' In his letter to Cardinal Colonna he continues:

Near Avernus and Acheron are situated that barren land whence rises continually a salutary vapour, which is a cure for several diseases, and those hot-springs that vomit hot and sulphureous cinders. I have seen the baths which Nature has prepared; but the avarice of physicians has rendered them of doubtful use. This does not, however, prevent them from being visited by the invalids of all the neighbouring towns.

The benefits are noted in the early thirteenth-century text *Trattato dei bagni* which is drawn from Pietro da Eboli's earlier *De balneis Puteolanis* in which it is said that in addition to curing headaches and stomach aches, improving eyesight and fighting fever, a bath at Solfatara also 'settles the nerves, alleviates scabies and strengthens enfeebled limbs'. (More recently, it has been suggested that the presence of hydrogen sulphide acts as a natural Viagra.) And then came Petrarch's follower Giovanni Boccaccio whose first literary efforts were spawned by Naples where he lived for over a decade.

Most thrillingly for English literature, it is difficult to resist the notion that John Milton, when he went to Naples at the end of November 1638, visited the place. He might have done so in the company of the elderly Marquis of Villa, Giovanni Battista Manso, who was not only a patron to poets, Torquato Tasso in particular, but also, as one of the governors, commissioned Caravaggio's *Seven Works of Mercy* which hangs in the church of Pio Monte della Misericordia in Naples. Milton had been just a shade on the preachy side, and in one of his letters admits that he had been 'unwilling to be more circumspect in relation to religion', and because of this Manso was somewhat reluctant to show him about Naples for fear of the young prig giving too much vent to his religious prejudices. It might be supposed that Manso, wanting to spare himself embarrassment, reckoned an empty space would be a better place for his guest to dump his Protestant sympathies. There was, on the other hand, considerable respect between the two men. Manso presented Milton with a clever Latin distich which extends Pope Gregory the Great's pun on 'Angle': 'Ut mens, forma, decor, mos, si pietas sic, / Non Anglus, verùm herculè Angelus ipse fores' ('If your piety were equal to your mind, beauty, fame, face, and manners, you would be, by Hercules, in truth not an Angle, but an angel'), and Milton wrote a poem in Latin to Manso, which, among other things, thanks him for his hospitality. At the beginning of *Paradise Lost* Milton speaks of a 'dreary Plain, forlorn and wilde, the seat of desolation', a 'land that burn'd with solid, as the Lake with liquid fire', 'a singed bottom all involv'd with stench and smoak', 'uneasie steps over the burning Marle', 'a fiery Deluge, fed with ever-burning Sulphur'. This, surely, is Solfatara. Vesuvius, which he also visited, cannot be described in these terms. Milton at Solfatara? This is as far as I am prepared to go into the realms of speculative thought, which is to say I don't know if he ever went there but I know enough to know that such a possibility cannot be dismissed.

One day in June 1770, after visiting Cumae, a fourteen-year-old composer went to Solfatara. The name of Wolfgang Amadeus Mozart was already on everyone's lips. The reason he was in Italy was partly business, partly Grand Tour, all of it orchestrated by his father Leopold who wanted his son to make contact with the opera houses of Milan, Rome, and Naples in order to secure future commissions and also, in order to finance the journey, to perform for the nobility whenever possible. Wisely, Leopold wanted his son to absorb Italian culture and language. In Naples Mozart gave a concert organised by William Hamilton and others, and attended the opera at the Teatro di San Carlo twice, one such visit being the first performance of Niccolò Jommelli's *Armida abbandonata* which he deemed beautiful but 'too serious and old-fashioned for the theatre'. San Carlo did try to commission a work from him, but he was already committed to an earlier offer made in Milan. An invitation to play at the royal court was not forthcoming and so the rest of his time was spent sightseeing, with trips to Vesuvius, Herculaneum, Pompeii, and the Phlegrean Fields. We have been left in one of his letters a precise record of what he wore, a brand-new suit which he had made in Naples: 'My costume is of the colour of cinnamon and is made of piquéd Florentine cloth with silver lace and is lined with apple green silk.' Mozart, fashion victim. As to his impressions of Solfatara, he says nothing, but it is not too fanciful to suppose that the memory of the place would revisit Mozart years later when Lorenzo da Ponte wrote the libretto for his opera, *Così fan tutte*, which is set in Naples and contains a mention of Vulcan's cave.

Mostly, we are afforded mere glimpses of Solfatara through the eyes of its visitors, or, as in the case of Hans Christian Andersen, an olfactory memory of it while walking by smelting furnaces somewhere in Sweden. Herman Melville visited there. In his journal for 20 February 1857 he notes, 'Went to Solfatara – smoke – landscape not so very beautiful. – Sulphurous & aridity.'

Wordsmiths both, one might have hoped for rather more from them. There is also the French painter, Élisabeth Louise Vigée Le Brun, Marie Antoinette's official portraitist, who painted Maria Carolina, Queen of Naples, and the famous painting of Lady Emma Hamilton in one of her classical 'attitudes', a dancing Bacchante with her tambourine, Vesuvius puffing in the distance. (Le Brun wrote of Lady Emma that 'she lacked style, and dressed very badly when it was a question of everyday attire'). Solfatara, for her, was hellish. She wrote in her journals:

> I went to see, with M. Amaury Duval and M. Sacaut, the Solfatara which is still burning. It was June, the sun darting on our heads as we walked on a fire. I have never in my life suffered so terribly from the heat. To make matters worse, I had my daughter with me; I covered her with my robe, but this was so flimsy a protection that I trembled every moment to see her fall unconscious. She said to me several times, 'Mother, one can die of heat, can't one?' God knows I was in despair at having taken her. At length we perceived on the hill a kind of cottage, in which, thank heaven, we were given permission to rest. The heat had suffocated us so much that neither of us could act or speak. After a quarter of an hour, Monsieur Duval remembered that he had an orange in his pocket, which made us cry out with joy, for this orange was the manna in the desert.

So brightly glows that orange.

Louise Colet, Flaubert's ex-lover, also visited the place. Goethe sketched it, quite a wonderful sketch that anticipates the Impressionists, its lines absolutely free. Of his visit to the Phlegrean Fields he writes of:

> gentle drives, happy walks through the most extraordinary country in the world. Beneath the purest sky the unsafest

ground. Ruins of unimaginable prosperity, mangled and unappealing. Boiling waters, charms exhaling sulphur, mounds of clinker hostile to plant life, bare repulsive spaces and yet in the end a vegetation always luxuriant, intruding wherever it can, rising above all the death, around lakes and streams, even firmly establishing the most magnificent oak forest on the walls of an ancient crater.

The topography once again, as in Shelley, standing in for Greece, would enter his poem 'Der Wandrer' ('The Wanderer').
Stendhal was there, but of this we have only his silence.
Scandinavian kings and queens too, Greek royalty, et cetera.
There is a tremendous scene in Roberto Rossellini's 1954 film *Viaggio in Italia*, considered by many to be his finest, when Katherine Joyce, played by Ingrid Bergman, goes with a guide to Solfatara, one in a series of outings during which she tries to come to terms with her failing marriage. She and her husband, Alex, played with tremendous understatement by George Sanders, have come to Naples to sell a villa left to them by an 'Uncle Homer', which provides some backing for the notion advanced by Jacopo Martorelli that a poet of that name had come to settle in Naples some millennia before. While being guided through Solfatara Bergman kneels down a little, takes a cigarette from her handbag, and, right on cue, a flame leaps up from a fissure in the ground and lights it. What do Virgil, Hannibal, Goethe, Hans Christian Anderson, and even the patron saint of Naples have on this? The scene was not choreographed – it was as if the whole of Nature had put itself at the service of a gorgeous woman with a slightly strange mouth. (Maybe it is worth pointing out here another great actress's mouth, one of the unusual features in the explosive amalgam that is Sophia Loren's face. She was born just outside the boundary of Solfatara.)

Bergman was at this point married to Rossellini who left the actress Anna Magnani for her. The story of that separation has entered Roman lore. Rossellini and Magnani were staying at the Hotel Savoy in Rome when he announced he was going to take the dogs for a walk and instead took a plane to New York. The choice facing him was between the Nordic cool of Bergman and a woman, maybe less beautiful but rather more striking, who in her person represented all that we of northern climes most love and fear in the Italian female. She was volcanic, Bergman glacial.

A documentary was made about Magnani and Bergman called *The War of the Volcanoes*. Rossellini began his affair with Bergman during the shoot of *Stromboli*, resulting in her pregnancy, after which his spurned wife starred in a rival film called *Volcano*. Interestingly both were set on active volcanic islands and both flopped at the box office, the latter fading into obscurity forever, the other now resurrected as one of Rossellini's masterpieces. Omens abounded. The projector broke down at the first screening of *Volcano* in Rome, but not before Magnani got her side of the story across.

So who might this be? [Next page.] One of Proust's characters on a day's outing from the pages of *À la recherche du temps perdu*? Alexander Graham Bell trying to place a call through to Hades? It is the American, Frank Alvord Perret, trying out one of his many inventions at Solfatara. The year is 1907 and he is on his geophone listening for murmurs deep under the crater's surface. A curious path brought him here. When his family moved from Philadelphia, where he was born in 1867, to New York, Perret went to study at the Brooklyn Polytechnic Institute and from there, a natural entrepreneur, he became a self-taught electrical engineer when electricity was still in its infancy. With an eye to a brightly lit future, he started up his own business (the Elektron Manufacturing Co.), produced several new breeds of motors, and was soon noticed by Thomas Edison who took him

on as his assistant. Together they developed a battery-operated car which ultimately failed because of the inadequate life of batteries in those days. A workaholic one minute, a catatonic depressive the next, in 1904 Perret had a serious mental break-down and on the advice of his doctor went to Naples for a rest cure. Of what was his doctor's conjuror's coat made? Vesuvius would be his salvation at a point when it spelled doom for others. His new life might have been prefigured in a chromolithograph of Vesuvius erupting over Pompeii, which Perret's father kept on the wall of his office.

At the *Osservatorio Vesuviano,* on the north-east slope of the volcano, Perret came under the protective wing of its director, Raffaele Vittorio Matteucci, who also was quite the character. A burly figure, with a dirty French postcard seducer's moustache, Matteucci's relationship to Vesuvius was that of a man pos-sessed by a difficult lover:

'I could not leave her,' he told an interviewer. 'I am wedded to her forever; my few friends say that her breath will scorch and wither my poor life one of these days; that she will bury my house in streams of liquid metal or raze it to its very foundations.

Already she has hurt me, has injured me sorely, yet I forgive her, I wait upon her, I am hers always.'

Sometimes the best cure for a mind in extremis is another mind in extremis. Matteucci's found its perfect match in Perret's. As assistant to Matteucci, Perret introduced the idea of keeping photographic records.

One evening, in February 1906, Perret thought he heard a buzzing sound through his pillow. A bit unorthodox in his scientific approach, he jumped up and clamped his teeth over the railing of his iron bedstead. The sound grew louder. This, in effect, was the first seismograph. At the same time Perret set down the principles of harmonic tremor, this being the continuous rhythmic earthquake that often precedes and accompanies volcanic eruptions. Soon after, he developed a machine for measuring the earth's activity, and when in April of that same year Vesuvius finally erupted he and Matteucci radioed warning signals to the folk in Naples. Countless lives were saved. King Vittorio Emanuele III presented him with a medal that he would always treasure. A volcano had the effect of steadying a man's jangled nerves. Many were the times Perret was singed by flame, bruised by stone, and choked by fumes, but an ancient goddess, maybe a bit gone in the teeth but a dazzler nonetheless, watched over him. Although he would later visit volcanoes at Kīlauea in the Hawaiian Islands, Mount Pelée in Martinique where he almost lost his life, Sakurajima in Japan, and elsewhere, Vesuvius held him in her thrall for the next fifteen years. On Mount Pelée he got so close to the eruption that his observation hut, truly a room with a view, was surrounded but miraculously untouched by the lava flow. It was there he made the spooky observation that pyroclastic flows, that is, the massive clouds of moving rock, hot gases, and ash make virtually no sound at all. (There is something poetical here, but its application continues to elude me.) Something else about Perret intrigues me. There is a photograph of him and another man in Hawaii carrying a blob of molten lava hanging from a stick like the carcass of a newly shot creature. A few moments later, their clothes caught fire. What is striking about this and other images of him, including the one at Solfatara, is that he is always so dapper – a quality not always associated with lonely men – from his winged collar and crisply knotted tie right down to white spats on his shoes.

The only thing stronger than death is style.

Small wonder volcanologists, well, some of them, are not a little touched. A rather sullen and isolated figure, with no woman in his life (unless Vesuvius is really a woman), perhaps the only members of the human race Perret loved without reserve were children, such that in later life, back in New York City, he would go after work to an orphanage in Brooklyn and there play with them until bedtime. There is no hint of impropriety here. It was with children that he felt most comfortable.

With no training in geology or chemistry but with an inventive flare, he became the poet of volcanology. Perret's writing has been noted for its lyrical qualities, which is not to say he surrendered truth to fancy. It is to be wondered whether he read Giacomo Leopardi's 'La ginestra' in which the great Italian poet contemplates Vesuvius and man's fate. Yes, surely, for he lived a while at Torre del Greco close to where Leopardi found temporary refuge from the cholera in Naples. As late as 1950 Perret's *The Vesuvius Eruption of 1906: Study of a Volcanic Cycle* (1924) was saluted as 'the most graphic and complete account ever published on any volcanic eruption and its aftermath'.

Giorgio Angarano arrived soundlessly behind me on his bicycle, *precisely* at the spot where, a year and a half later, there would be a terrible reversal of fortune, and his world would be turned upside down. Angarano is the current owner of Solfatara – perhaps the only person in the world to privately own a volcano

– and if a man could be said to be a volcano he is the best candidate, the very earth's voice. Signor Volcano. We had got off on a bad footing, which is more easily done than not done. Already I'd heard from others that he was not an easy man, more likely to shoo away people who come to him with questions he judged idle. Somehow I had got the days confused and arrived on the morning he had an appointment to see his optometrist. Scowling, he told me to go about Solfatara and if he could find time later he'd find me. I was with my interpreter, Silvia Corsi, who may have had a soothing influence on him. I had caught him unawares, and he was a man with bigger things on his mind. I think it was when I asked whether he thought Virgil had walked here that he said I could come back two weeks later. Whatever it was, I had passed some kind of examination as he stood in silence listening to the translator, even though, as it turned out, he had sufficient English to speak directly to me.

'Solfatara,' he said, 'is the mother of us all.'

I told Giorgio I was very nervous, and indeed rather humbled, to be talking to a man who owns a volcano but then he reassured me that he was nervous speaking to a poet, and so perhaps we were in the same predicament.

'You have something I don't have,' he said, 'and I have something you don't have.'

'So you say' I replied, 'but when we first spoke you were inspired enough to say that this place is the mother of us all whereas normally one would think of a volcano as a destructive force.'

'This is something very special for us. Solfatara is like a big womb. In 1982, we had an earthquake here, actually a hundred earthquakes a day, which was problematic because this mother of ours was now behaving badly towards us. A mother is supposed to be good with her children, no? But it looked as if she was about to punish us for something. All the people who work here, many of whom were actually born here, me too, are the sons and daughters, nephews and nieces, of people who worked here before. One of the three people who was born inside here died two weeks ago.'

I did a quick calculation and realised it was on the day after I first visited the place.

'Maurizio, our night watchman, died in the same place where he was born. Throughout his whole life he never left this place. It was like the film with Peter Sellers, *Being There*, in which the main character, Chauncey, never goes out of his house. When the family dies he has to leave and so discovers the world outside, but he is very naive and a bit peculiar and because of this combination he becomes president of the United States. So, coming back to Maurizio, he died here because he did not want to leave. He said, "If I leave, I will die alone." There were three brothers – Maurizio, Fabio, and Ugo – they were born, literally, inside this place. My sister Maria was at Maurizio's baptism. She saw him and his brothers being born, watched them grow up, and *their* parents were born, lived, and worked here – three or four generations, ours and theirs, growing together. Their father lived as if he were still in the Middle Ages. A true country man, he worked the soil, making wine from the grapes, and so forth. On Thursdays he would dress up and go to my grandfather's house and there they played *scopone*, a very Neapolitan card game. When I was a boy, three centuries ago, I saw this. Maurizio spent all his life here … a most peculiar man, I have to say, but a wonderful night watchman. The job was the only thing that gave meaning to his life. Solfatara was like family, a mother to him. He never went anywhere else, never married, and had no immediate family of his own. Now his nephew is working in his place. Now we discover he was a really generous person, helping a lot of people, buying food and giving it to them. It is because all of us are tied together, we are close to each other, our family and their family. It is the only way we can continue.'

I wondered aloud why a place such as Solfatara required a night watchman. What was there to protect where surely nothing ever changes? It would be here forever although, equally, it might not be here a few hours hence.

'We have the camping first of all, so we are obliged to have a night watchman. Secondly, it is a big place and not as safe as it was once upon a time. When I was young we had two guards with double-barrelled hunting rifles. They walked at night with them. They, too, were men of the soil.'

'Did they ever shoot anyone?'

'It's possible. It is a good place to get rid of someone with the boiling water and burning stones. We had a suicide here in 1938 when this place was completely abandoned, somebody who came here and shot himself. It is another aspect of our history here. I can tell you a lot of things about the real soul of Solfatara. I am the last dinosaur of this place. There is no one to continue after me. There was the son of a cousin of mine but he got cancer, did nothing to cure himself, and stayed here until the last day of his life. I brought him here. I have a peculiar relationship with this place. I try to keep myself safe by living elsewhere. I have a home in Naples. The people who came before me, they arrived and built up a sort of mediaeval court about themselves. They did nothing else. Nobody among them got married because they substituted wives with Solfatara. Solfatara is a projection of our ideas. It is not real. A woman is also a projection of our ideas, but at least with a woman you can develop a relationship and move forward whereas Solfatara is more like a stepmother. You cannot defend yourself against her. It is easier in a way. You don't have to think. You don't have to reflect. My father died when I was a kid and was not part of the Solfatara family. It is my mother who is. When someone decides to get married the person marrying into the family has to be accepted by them. It is very strong, *molto forte*. You can live here, but it doesn't allow you to develop. It blocks you really. The fathers and then their sons worked here. It's the same for me. I've got a son, a jazz musi-cian and composer, who lives in London. He refused our Vulcan mother as being too oppressive, as all mothers are. You can meet my mother, 103 years old, she lives here. She reads the two daily newspapers. We say she is "Queen Victoria of Solfatara". She is the only one higher than Solfatara itself and for me she has always been the more dangerous of the two. I have to go away and leave my mother with Solfatara. I go round and see other mothers. Mothers are everywhere.'

'You are wonderful!'

'It's the hat,' he replied.

'All wisdom passes through the hat.'

'Yes, true, but women can modify themselves, they can change their hair, jewellery, the colour of their lips whereas men have almost nothing. We put on our hats, at an angle, and only then are we able to communicate.'

'So, really, we are very simple creatures.'

'You have a strong female component in yourself and women can feel this. I, too, have it. Usually men are afraid of women so maybe because of this men are afraid of you. Men are intimidated by the complexity of women, but you are not a simple person. You have the complexity of a woman. You are part of the conversation so we have to talk about you as well, especially with a Panama hat like yours.'

I could never have imagined having this conversation in the eye of a volcano, beside a bubbling pool, the smell of sulphur fumes, with a man in a cowboy hat straddling a bicycle. I had to pinch myself a little, that I'd come here not for an analysis of the male and female components of my character but for the human stories attached to the place and in particular how it came to be privately owned. I knew, however, this could not be achieved without meeting the twinkle in Signor Volcano's eye.

'A woman is always a form of grace,' Giorgio concluded.

I asked him how a volcano could fall into private hands.

The story is this: in 1861 the De Luca family from Cardinale in Calabria bought Solfatara for 72.000 lire from Senator Domenico Assanti who, in 1860, had taken part in the Spedizione dei Mille, Garibaldi's legendary 'Expedition of the Thousand'. The De Lucas were five brothers: Sebastiano, Domenico, Giuseppe, Vincenzo, and Eugenio, and two sisters, Isabella and Maria, and of them only Eugenio produced heirs, Martino and Francesco, and the current owners descend from Martino. Some of them were expelled from the family tree. There is something about expulsion that captures the vulgar imagination. Solfatara would appear to have produced at least one demon although there was another, Sebastiano, grandson of Eugenio, who went to Brazil. Whether he should be considered a 'black sheep' or 'free spirit' is open to debate, but whatever he did, it was enough to have him exorcised from the family circle.

"'You don't know the world,' Sebastiano told me, "until you've seen a black woman's arse."'

Sebastiano had three wives and eighteen sons of varying hues. He sold his share of Solfatara because he needed the money and also because he thought it was due to explode. Had he stayed the volcano would now be owned by twenty-five people. Another son, Mariano, Sebastiano's brother, died young from a heart attack, probably, Giorgio suggested, because he was too pure and could not withstand a family so assertive. His widow, too fond of pleasure, sold her share.

'There has been this genetic selection,' Giorgio said. 'Only the most rigorous people in love with the idea of owning a volcano have remained. This is limiting, but at the same time it is a force for protecting the Big Mother. There are a lot of psychoanalytic aspects to this story. You might say the place has had two souls in that the owners of Solfatara have been divided into two types, one, the less materialistic – my sister and myself – and two, the more materialistic who think more about money and things than about people, whereas for my sister and me people are the richest part of life. Today my pockets are getting bigger because I am talking to you.'

'Tell me about your own relationship to this place. When you walk through it at night, for example.'

'It is hard to say. I have spent my life here. For me, it is like a living person, with the love/hate that you might have towards that person. For the greater part of my life I've been obliged to stay here. I have been provided with a strong structure that my family gave me, but at the same time this structure can be an obstacle to change. I have always to fight these two things. Tradition is very important for me, but change is important too. I work with this dilemma, caught between tradition and change.'

'Did you ever want to escape?'

'Yes, maybe, but I didn't dare. When I was young I had two or three chances to escape. Once a photographer asked me to go around the world with him, but I decided to remain here. I studied physics but never followed that path. So I stayed. Solfatara with its family rules has, in a way, castrated me. Change is important. You should push situations a little to allow change. On the other hand, Solfatara has been a way of keeping something safely burning inside me, something that makes me feel alive. So I have not died inside. I have been helped by women because women have seen what I could not see. They saw in me a flame and that I wasn't a conformist. This place can kill you because of its rules. It is a very obliging, yet very structured, place. That's how it was with Maurizio, who lived and died here. He couldn't think about anything else. Although he didn't realise it, he was obsessed by the place. I knew it though. I could watch him with an outsider's eyes. Solfatara is like a siren, a mermaid, with a powerful memory. You can stay, and it will help you but at the same time it holds you back. It obliges you to remain here.'

'Will I find you here next year?'

'I have decided to stay on because every three years I have to renew my contract as administrator. Then I will have to decide whether or not to do it again.'

'I thought you owned the place.'

'Yes, I do, but we have a society that organises the tourism here and so I have to decide whether to continue to be a part of the society and have official charge as administrator. My Uncle Gegè remained in charge until the day of his death. This is why I may choose to stop my role before dying.'

'You want to abdicate? I think you will renew it.'

'Everybody tells me the same thing. It is not possible to leave, you have to remain here. The church was for life, you stayed a holy man.'

'Suppose you announce your resignation and people accept it, then surely you will be very upset.'

'I am preparing the field. I don't know if someone has already shot me. I imagine trying to get out of here and people with guns preventing me from doing so. As a king is the point of reference for the people of his country, an element of continuity, I am the point of reference here. It's a place that has to develop. I am curious, I want to see the future while I'm still alive. It is difficult to decide because I feel protected by this place.'

'Maybe you are the only one crazy enough to do it.'

'Yes, but I am also crazy enough to decide to stop. All the others finished their work in Solfatara only when they died, again like kings, but I may stop before that happens.'

'But how could you when you look like some kind of god on your bicycle?'

'Well, I'll continue to do it in that case. I will demand more money from the tourists. Anyone who wants a picture of me has to pay one euro, but with a hat it will be three. French TV came here. They wanted a shot of me riding away on the bicycle, wearing my hat, just like in a cowboy movie. They didn't pay me. Not even a euro, *niente*. The BBC made a film about this place and then they said their budget was very small.'

I began to reach into my pocket for a coin.

'Do you feel a pagan atmosphere here?'

'Pagan in the sense that divinities live within things? Is that what you mean, as in *animistic*? Solfatara in itself is a divinity – the stones, the place itself – so this is animistic, not pagan. Sometimes I remember when psychologically speaking I was weaker than I am now ... over there the earth moves from time to time and then it falls. I used to be afraid of this. I thought it was a sign that the divinity here was angry for some reason and punishing us. I don't feel like that any more. Somehow it has moved inside where I can control it. The people who raised me are still inside me, like ghosts. Somehow I did change things here. I created a small revolution, but at the beginning I was afraid because I thought that all my ghosts were looking at me, saying, "What are you doing?" Last year I did something that had never been done before. I put up an electrical lighting structure. It took a lot of time. I organised this so that people might come here at night. We prepare fish on the burning stones. We do hard-boiled eggs. The fish is easier. During the tour we stop and offer wine and fish. This has been seen by some as a desecration of the place, more like entertainment. It was really hard for me personally because people were looking at what I'd done as being not serious enough when set against the sacredness of the place. I thought many times, "What have I done?".'

'Do you have bad dreams?'

'Sometimes, after a big dinner.'

'Are the dreams worse when it is cooked over volcanic stone?'

'Tonight if I have a nightmare, I will know the cause.'

Giorgio then took me to see his sister, Maria Angarano, de facto historian of the place. We entered the palazzo, which, incredibly, and wholly in keeping with everything else strange about the place, is within the walled kingdom of Solfatara only a few yards from where the volcano proper begins. I took a lift upstairs, and out of it I stepped into another world, one that could have come out of a late Visconti film, antiques, paintings on the wall, a chiming clock. It was an aristocratic atmosphere, rendered more bizarre by the surroundings. She provided me with a potted history of the place. Solfatara has had a number of owners, among them ancestors of the poet Jacopo Sannazaro whose likeness Titian so powerfully rendered. We spoke of the De Luca ancestors, in particular the most famous among them, Sebastiano De Luca, who was a director of the Sorbonne University of Paris in the nineteenth century.

Maria Angarano describes Sebastiano as 'a mysterious figure, lonely, almost a "Sorcerer's Apprentice"'. An introverted figure, his communication skills poor, he found solace in the study of nature. Sebastiano was born in 1820 in Cardinale, in the province of Catanzaro, and later pursued his studies in Naples from 1838 to 1842 in the fields of chemistry and natural sciences. He took part in the short-lived uprising in 1848 and was sentenced to twenty-five years in prison, but miraculously he escaped arrest by jumping onto a French steamer that took him to Marseilles. From there he went to Paris where he found himself in the company of exiles and also some of the foremost scientists of the day, in particular M. Berthelot with whom he would collaborate on many scientific projects. There he smoked hashish and wrote, in French, a scientific book about the experience. He returned to Italy in 1857, first teaching at the University of Pisa and finally, the air now clear of political intrigue, back in Naples in 1862 where, as chemistry professor at the University of Naples for the last two decades of his life, he did much to advance the fortunes of the scientific life of that city. A restless spirit, he moved through an astonishing number of areas of study, which included an examination of the urinary bladder of the river tortoise, silkworms, dyes, rare lichen, the extraction of mannitol from the leaves and fruit of the olive, fermentation, wheat which in turn led him to study the grains found in the ruins of Pompeii where he also looked at water found in a bronze vessel, oil in amphorae, and human bones. And then, as one might expect, he did extensive research at Solfatara on the nature of fumaroles, the properties of volcanic tuff, the mineral waters and their therapeutic properties. The result of this research was his book *Ricerche Sperimentali, con note e documenti, sulla Solfatara di Pozzuoli* (1882). Also he had a working relationship with the archaeologist Giuseppe Fiorelli, who excavated Pompeii, the first to do so in a systematic fashion. De Luca and he compared the soil in Solfatara with that in Pompeii. Sebastiano De Luca died on 17 April 1880 shortly after being made a senator in the city that so many years before he had had to flee.

'None of them had children except for Eugenio from whose line we come,' Maria continued. 'He was the simpler one, the one least involved with the Solfatara story, but he was the one who provided the heritage. Eugenio is a name that comes back in the family again. The other brothers were all in important roles – one was a political deputy after the unification of Italy, another was a cartographer who made a peculiar three-dimensional map of the world, which was considered quite a novelty for the time, another was a doctor of medicine, Domenico De Luca, an eye specialist who used Solfatara water as a cure for certain eye problems. This he did for free, and because he did not want his patients to have to pay for the treatment he was ostracised by the administrator of the Ospedale degli Incurabili. Some of his papers, including ones on the effect of Solfatara water on cancerous wounds and chest diseases, were included in his brother Sebastiano's book. A lot of illnesses could be cured by this water, also sterility and rheumatism. All of these men left something of themselves in this place. About the women we know nothing. It wasn't possible then for women to be involved. They worked in the house. Solfatara passed from hand to hand, from one generation to the next and, step by step, it was opened to the public. During our grandfather's time only royal families from all around the world came here. There is a register here of important visitors to the place.'

Giorgio's immediate predecessor was his maternal uncle, Eugenio De Luca, born 1911, a war hero who took part in the defence of Florence. He continued to be known by his *nom de guerre* 'Gegè'. After the war he decided to open Solfatara to the general public and created the camping ground which still operates. When interviewed in 2001 and asked whether he was afraid of living inside a volcano, he replied, 'I am accustomed to living with the earth's shaky moods. Fear? Not at all. The nightmare of an eruption? We never felt it, not even during the evacuation of Pozzuoli when at night we couldn't sleep for the noise of the volcano. The strangest experience? Maybe it was at the beginning of the 1970 crisis, before the ground began to lift. It seemed as if Solfatara was sleeping. All was quiet. Somebody accused us of activating special gas devices in order to make the mud boil at the centre so as to create a spectacle.'

'My brother Giorgio,' Maria continued, 'opened the door to technology. At night, thanks to him, we now have plays and concerts. He has found new ways of using the place.'

I asked Maria to describe her own relationship to the place.

'Actually Giorgio, although in the evenings he goes to Naples, lives here almost all the time. I hope I will never have to go away for any reason. First of all, there are the personal memories of my husband who is not here any more. All that took place before me is now part of me. I could never live anywhere else.'

'Do you agree with Giorgio that Solfatara is the mother of your family?'

'Yes, absolutely! All of us, not just me, had this idea when we were young to get away from here, but then everybody comes back here. My daughters are here and my nephews are here. This house will be for some nephew.'

'This is like an aristocracy of the volcano.'

'Actually the records started only in the nineteenth century. The one who was the deputy then started to collect the letters from people like Mazzini and Garibaldi who passed through here. The poet Salvatore Di Giacomo when he wrote his guide to Solfatara stayed here. So, too, did Eduardo De Filippo's family.'

'Does this place have mystical associations for you?'

'When I am in a bad mood I go down the stairs, go out at sundown, and walk around Solfatara. I feel serene. I have resorted to this ever since I was a child.'

'For most people this would be a threatening environment.'

'Yes, the biggest fear is about what can happen here, earthquakes, bradyseism. This is what frightens us most nowadays, but we are fatalistic.'

'How does living in such an area affect one's thinking?'

'It obliges you to accept everything that can happen and provides you with a true scale of priorities. You do not become stuck in matters of little importance.'

'So, then, this is an environment that heals?'

'Absolutely. At the beginning I came here only during summertime, as soon as school was finished, but then when I got married I came here and settled. I've been here forty-five years.'

'Do you feel strong pagan associations here?'

'Yes, very much so. The spiritual aspect of Solfatara has been here since long before Christianity. We were talking about Vulcan. That's the reason why a lot of authors were inspired by this place, especially when writing about the passing from one dimension to the other, from above ground to underneath it. That is lot to do with paganism. A god dwelled in the underworld and you could go there. We have many tales about going from life to death and sometimes from death to life. The mentality of Neapolitan people with respect to death makes them less afraid of it. We move from paganism to Christianity and then back again. This an aspect of Naples that is unique.'

An eighteenth-century palazzo inside the perimeters of a volcano, who would have thought it?

When I asked Maria whether she felt safe here she said that while a sudden shift in the earth's surface could result in a building collapsing in the area outside Solfatara, that inside it was comparatively safe. One might notice the chandelier swaying a little.

A few minutes later, Giorgio and I sat in the sunshine of the Solfatara café. This was prefaced by a lovely bit of burlesque: I offered to pay for the coffees. Giorgio stood aside. I placed a note on the counter and the waiter behind it looked at it quizzically, mock-examined it further, and said, 'It's no good.' There was some disgust in his voice. I wondered whether I'd accidentally slipped him a fake note. 'Surely it is,' I argued, but he was having none of it. 'It is not our money,' he said, 'you will have to get it changed. We accept only kroner here.' I turned to the expressionless face of Signor Volcano, master comedian, and I wondered how often he and the waiter had produced this little act between themselves.

'You put people in the situation so they can talk to you,' Giorgio said to me. 'This is the *maieutikos* which you find in Socrates. My mother helped women to give birth.* It is

---

* This is all rather splendid given that Socrates's mother was also

also what happens with good conversation. It gives birth to ideas.'

Giorgio had one more surprise for me. Solfatara had notoriety as a duelling ground. The duels were done in secret, behind closed gates, always at dawn. They were concluded at 'first blood' when honour was satisfied and not at death when, for at least one of the combatants, honour was but a dissipated perfume. Afterwards the custom would be for both parties to repair to a local *osteria* where they would find reconciliation over a bottle. As a child Giorgio witnessed the last duel in Solfatara, perhaps the last in Italy, between the senator Gaetano Fiorentino and the lawyer Attilio Romano. Monarchists both, albeit of different branches, they had exchanged insults in the newspapers and later in private communications on the subject of Carlo Delcroix, another monarchist who, in 1917, after losing his hands and eyes while attempting to diffuse an unexploded bomb, was awarded the Silver Cross for Military Valour.* Fiorentino, under the penname of 'Florentinus', had expressed doubt in Delcroix's courage, saying the accident took place behind lines, and so drew the ire of Romano who saw this not only as a slur upon his friend but upon all Italian war heroes. What was at stake ultimately were the values and responsibilities of the royal house although one might ask *what* royal house and *what* values and *what* responsibilities. The monarchy had been dissolved in 1946, but in certain quarters sentiment remained strong and when such feelings are heightened men

---

a midwife. *Maieutikos*, which pertains to the Socratic method of bringing forth or eliciting ideas in other people, derives from *maia*, the Greek for 'midwife'.

* Delcroix would later throw his weight behind Mussolini, and appears as the war hero 'Uncle Carlo' in Ezra Pound's *Cantos*. In defence of Delcroix he soon repented of his support for 'Il Duce' after the latter's alliance with Nazi Germany.

of feeling tend to factionalise: monarchist reaches for the throat of monarchist with the consequence that a third party forms and so it goes until, thoroughly splintered, monarchists are no more. Still, justice had to be seen to be done. There was a court case, which was irresolute in its findings. When words fail, it is time to resort to violence.

On the morning of 23 March 1955 the duel took place, by which point the original grievance had been substituted by mutual dislike or what is sometimes called 'bad chemistry' between the two men. At a distance all this seems rather byzantine, but it was probably no less so at the time. The duel lasted an hour. An Olympic champion sabreur, Arturo De Vecchi, acted as referee. Achille Lauro, the mighty shipowner, founder of the People's Monarchist Party and mayor of Naples, said he would like to have been there, but found reason not to be. Doctors were on hand, one for each side, with their supplies of bandages. There was a minor spillage of blood. The senator won. A reconciliation of sorts was said to have taken place, and indeed there is a photograph of the two shaking hands. Giorgio remembers it differently: Romano and Fiorentino continued to seethe. Duelling was, and remains, a punishable offence not only in the eyes of the law but also the Church. The police discovered they were about to fight and on the morning fixed for the duel they knocked at the gates of Solfatara. Gegè in a newspaper interview given not long before his death remembered the moment well: 'I was sweating cold but I managed to convince them that between the vaporous fumes there was nothing going on. The duel took place and, as usual, it was not fatal. The senator won but no sooner was the fight finished than the *carabinieri* arrived and made charges. The De Luca family decided, very appropriately, that this historical cycle had become too embarrassing and so, not without a hint of regret for the many emotions, "provate e procurate", tried and procured, the last duel in Solfatara, perhaps in the whole of Europe, took place.'

There are perfectly reasonable people who say that duelling is a foolish exercise, which, of course, is a perfectly reasonable thing to say, but with its demise went the even more foolish notions of honour and manhood.

The matter did not stop there, however, for the Church authorities got wind of the duel and excommunicated both parties. Scarcely able to believe this, I discovered that according to Session XXV, Chapter XIX of the Council of Trent the Church does indeed excommunicate 'those who fight duels, those who challenge or accept challenge thereunto, all accomplices, all who help or countenance such combats, all who designedly assist thereat, finally all who permit duelling or who do not prevent it in so far as lies in their power, no matter what their rank or dignity, be it royal or imperial'.

'Well,' said Giorgio, 'it was cheaper than going to court, a bit of blood, and then a nice restaurant. I remember it well. I was ten years old at the time. It was a long time ago and yet not so long ago. It was during the first years of television. On Sunday you could watch the Pope on television. My mother had us kneel in front of the screen.'

As Giorgio saw me to the entrance to Solfatara he stopped and, staring down at the invisible line that separated his world from the one outside, he said, 'I can't go any further with you.' He moved the tip of one of his shoes a centimetre more. 'My world stops here.'

A year later, I saw Giorgio again, briefly. It was the busy season at Solfatara and the fact I was able to see him at all was cause enough to celebrate. I had a question for him that had been sitting in my thoughts ever since I sat with his sister surrounded by antiques, paintings, a chiming clock, and the chandelier that swayed a little when Solfatara quavered.

'Some people – the Dutch geologist and writer, Salomon Kroonenberg, for example – say that geological features are what determine the creation of myth and not the other way round. Would you say that in the case of Solfatara geology has led to the creation of a strange aristocracy?'

'It's true, we might be looked upon as aristocrats, but we are so only behind these walls. When we go outside, we become normal people. We have been raised like this and so, too, the people who work here – the son of the farmer who is himself a farmer, the son of the one who ran the bookshop who is now the bookshop manager – they have grown up as if inside the walls of a castle. There is a hierarchy in which they feel themselves part of a feudal system and so it is difficult to introduce change. This solid structure is what they are used to.'

'Last year you were unsure as to whether you would continue. Will you renew your contract?'

'I am trying to organise a bridge between myself and the next generation. I compare myself to the agave plant we have growing here, which, although it has a long life, flowers only once and then dies. It is a monocotyledon, a special plant that produces just this one enormous flower. I am trying to produce a flower for the next generation and then I will be ready to die.'

A most appropriate choice, the agave with its spiked leaves, a flower at its centre. What could be more emblematic of one whose reputation is that of a difficult, rather spiky, character who is mellow on the inside? The name of the plant derives from the Greek *agavos*, which translates as 'noble or 'illustrious' and this, too, fits the bill: Giorgio is so in both respects of the word, an aristocrat among the fumaroles. For the Aztec goddess Mayahuel the agave was a symbol of longevity although whether the tequila that is produced from the plant is a destroyer or a preservative is debatable. Sulphur, a killer when excessive, in milder doses would appear to be a formula for a long life. 'Gegè' had worked until the day of his death, aged ninety-six, and only four months before, Giorgio's mother, the 'Queen Victoria of Solfatara', died aged 104 and a half, in the same bed in which she had been born. Her death came as a surprise. She had been in good health. She was the missing link in my story and I had very much hoped to meet her. Giorgio and I sat over our espressos in a café just outside the gates of Solfatara, which was most unusual for him because he did not like to stray outside his kingdom for any length of time. I told him I did not wish to be intrusive, but thought that his mother must have played a huge role in the history of the place. A melancholy chord was struck and it would continue to vibrate for the next few minutes.

'I still don't know the role she played on me,' he replied. 'I thought I could pass over her death without too much damage. I'm old enough and my mother was much older than me. It is a natural thing, one might think, but something terrible happened to me. I had some problems, physical as well as emotional, for which I am still paying the consequences. A mother is rooted at the very bottom of one's soul. Normally, as one's mother approaches death, one begins to see things with a clearer, deeper perspective. This was not possible for me. There was always this wall. You would think that with death the wall would collapse but no, it's still there. When she died I suffered a temporary loss of memory. I lost all sense of space and time. I was completely lost. And then someone said to me, "Do you realise you've had a personal loss?" This I sensed but I couldn't remember who it was. Then I began to worry about my son. I developed a rash and became absolutely desperate. Suddenly I remembered. "It's my mother, yes?" "Yes, it was your mother." I started to cry. That was the moment I realised I'd had this terrible weight on my shoulders.'

I told Giorgio I was in a similar place, such that my coming to Naples was tempting the Fates. My mother was unwell.

'My suggestion to you is to break the walls down before it is too late,' he said. 'You should not leave unfinished business. You have to talk to her otherwise she will follow you for the rest of your life. Don't do as I did. I didn't have time to open the door that had always been closed between us. The moment she died and there was no one behind the door I fell.'

'This may be our shared fate, Giorgio.'

'We look for our mothers in other women.'

'I try not to!'

'I'm talking of dialogue, not seduction, *empathy*.'

'Maybe,' I said, 'your mother's spirit has entered that of the Big Mother of Solfatara.'

'Yes, I depend on this.'

Giorgio's phone rang. He was being called away on business. The spell was broken and he was able, once more, to joke.

'I have been out of Solfatara for more than ten minutes and I begin to dissolve.'

'Maybe you should close the gates, throw out all the tourists, and live like a hermit.'

(I could never have imagined what import those flighty words would one day have.)

'My cousin says we should allow only one tourist a year who pays a million euros instead of a million tourists who pay one euro.'

Spiky as the agave, warm inside, Giorgio gave me a goodbye embrace.

'We had only a few minutes,' he said, 'but we've found ourselves again.'

Very soon I was on the train back to Naples, my companion and translator for this visit, Fiorella Formicola, beside me. We found ourselves engaged in a curious conversation with two young American women in the next seat over, wearing pale blue badges with their Christian names, Sorella 'X' and Sorella 'Y' – I can't remember their names – 'X' and 'Y' seems a bit reductive somehow. Although they were pleasant enough, they grated on my nerves. They were both Mormon missionaries and were at pains to explain to us how Brigham Young had brought to pass what the Gospels decree, and we debated the matter a little, me saying that all creeds believe themselves to be in possession of all the answers and Fiorella asking them how they could expect to succeed in this most Catholic of countries. While I was pondering how these two girls with their perfect teeth, scrubbed complexions, and shiny eyes, neither of them out of their early twenties, and who had seen so little of the world, would be able to tame the wild heart of southern Italy my phone rang. It was my wife with news of my mother. I would have to leave Naples as quickly as possible. *My suggestion to you is to break the walls down before it is too late.* Giorgio's words will haunt me forever, that is, if *forever* is nothing more than the brief passage of one's own existence.

My flight was scheduled for five in the morning and because I knew sleep would be impossible I went to the airport at midnight only to discover it would be closed for the next four hours. I paced back and forth outside, in a chill breeze, my only companion an elderly woman with a baggage cart loaded with plastic bags, singing Neapolitan songs to me. I suspect the airport, rather than being a place of arrivals and departures, was for her the only stationary point in her life. Why do the homeless so often attach themselves to places of transience? She began to sing 'Santa Lucia' and she could not have chosen better, it being one of the songs of my childhood, although now as thinly rendered as tissue. My mother, so damaged by life, so embittered, and yet so easily won over by the Italianate, would have had tears in her eyes. Was this singing woman more than she appeared to be? An emissary from the gods perhaps? It began to rain from pink skies, the breeze stopped, and then began one of the most ferocious electrical storms I've seen, and, watching the multiple forks of lightning, I wondered what they announced and whether I was not already too late, and then it struck me that Virgil would have seen a storm such as this, which was now being offered to me to make of it what I could, as a commentary on a troubled life nearing its end or maybe already among the Shades, and then it occurred to me what a spectacle it must have made in the skies above Solfatara. *You have to talk to her otherwise this will follow you for the rest of your life.* Two weeks later, and several thousand miles to the west of Naples, in a country she would never have willingly chosen as her home, my mother angry, terrified, *incomunicabile*, breathed her last, her final struggle inside a place deep within herself to which I had no key. A week later, she was lowered into the grave in the midst of a storm so violent the priest called time on the funeral service. Blessed is the dead one, so the proverb goes, upon whose coffin the rain falls. It means she or he has safely 'arrived'. Would that the world she quit were as safe.

The serpent would strike twice.

Four months later, on 12 September, 2017, a holidaying family from Meolo, in northern Italy, visited Solfatara at the express wish of their children, Lorenzo, aged twelve, and Alessio, seven, both of whom were due to go back to school the following day. After one of the hottest summers in recent memory there had been a deluge of rain that lasted three days and flooded a large area of Solfatara. Whether this caused a breach in the surface or whether the surface was weakened and the breach was yet to be made has not been determined, but Lorenzo, running ahead, dropped out of view, which on a level plane must have been absolutely terrifying to observe, and his parents, Massimiliano Carrer and Tiziana Zaramella, rushed forward to rescue him. They, too, fell into the breach and within minutes all three were dead, most probably asphyxiated by the fumes. Alessio fled in the opposite direction and survived. There was some talk as to whether the three members of the family perished inside or outside the safety barrier. A single glance at a photograph of the scene was enough to tell me they were inside the safe zone, on the very spot where, over a year before, Giorgio arrived on his bicycle and where jokingly we took each other's measure. The news would go from bad to worse, but because I am not a journalist I will not enter into matters of an ugly nature. The media has had its orgy of sorrow and blame. I did communicate briefly with a volcanologist who conducted tours of the place, who, when I saw him last, wrote out for me, from memory, lines from Leopardi's 'La ginestra'. They were words that spoke of how puny we and our aspirations are when set against the power of nature. Did Leopardi not take his pessimism to such a degree that it became a kind of optimism? A man of considerable depth and experience, the volcanologist responded with the answer everyone knows to be true, everyone, that is, except the judicial authorities who seem to think someone must be held accountable. The accident took place on the very day a leading politician in Naples was cleared of corruption charges that had followed him for close to a decade. I will not enter upon the curious ways of Italian justice, but Solfatara has since been sequestered by the police. Why not put a barrier around the whole of Naples and its environs? All of it, north, south, and east, is a danger zone.

A recent fire destroyed much of the flora surrounding the crater at Solfatara. Whether this included the agave, I don't know, but although a symbol of longevity, I'd be surprised if it survived. A mind subject to omens might conclude it was time to quit the scene. 'Every volcano is a holy place,' the volcanologist wrote me. 'There the good and the bad, the new and the old, prosperity and tragedy, are all mixed together. Any differences between them belong to the rational world where logic operates, whereas a volcano is irrational and around the corner there always lurks a terrible danger. After many years spent on volcanoes, I am quite convinced of this.' Solfatara is closed until further notice, perhaps for good, the denizens of this strange kingdom dispersed, and Giorgio now a melancholy king in exile.

'Sono a pezzi', he wrote to me, 'I am in pieces'.

A charge of multiple homicide was brought against him. On the eve of a judicial decision that would determine his future he sent me a text message: 'There is in the worst of fortune the best of chances for a happy change.'

Euripides, *Iphigenia in Tauris*.

What will the next chapter be? It's not as if Solfatara's history will end on this sad note. So many people have moved over its bizarre landscape, and when the tragic events of late have receded in the public memory, doubtless many more will take the gamble of walking over hollow (or is it hallowed?) ground. There is, after all, something rather tantalising about impending catastrophe. Almost certainly Virgil walked here and got the idea for the passage in Book VIII of the *Aeneid* where Vulcan and his subterranean team forge weapons, the keenest of their time, for Aeneas at the behest of his mother, the goddess Venus. (Vulcan is the Greek Hephaestus, god of fire and forging, relocated to a Latin setting.) Solfatara was one of several candidates for the entrance to Hades. Avernus gets top prize although surely the way down is always, and everywhere, inside ourselves. The volcanic crust had withstood the rumble of horses, the Bourbons in full chase, wild boar in flight, and yet it could not support a small child's weight. Those who think they know Nature, Nature will consume. Leopardi said as much. One day a family decides to take in the pleasures of a strange world that for the duration of their visit, maybe no more than an hour, would be as safe as houses, and now thought itself stops at the gates. A mother dies, and then another, and, again, another. *A mother is rooted at the very bottom of one's soul.*

There has got to be a better way to take my leave of Solfatara. It's not as if gloom is in short supply. I'll settle on that image of Frank Alvord Perret, breathing in the fumes, *l'americano*, who had a knack for making do with whatever materials were available, in this instance a metal horn shaped like a witch's hat, a receiver, and a microphone, wires running between all three, which he then composed into something resembling a giant stethoscope – 'the hero of Vesuvius', Frank Alvord Perret, arguably the greatest volcanologist of them all, eavesdropping on the guttural rumblings of a world Virgil had centuries before sung into verse.

The Life and Death (and life) of Pulcinella

Pulcinella never actually dies although, yes, from time to time he does. And then he springs back to life. Giandomenico Tiepolo (1727–1804), in the dying light of the Venetian Republic, produced a strange album of 104 drawings, *Divertimento per li regazzi*, 'an incunabulum of the comic', in which he depicts the life of Pulcinella from cradle to grave. The drawings would seem to be, as the title suggests, an amusing diversion for boys and girls, whereas for the more senior of them, children my age, they are heavily freighted with irony and satire. Actually Tiepolo's dedication is aimed not so much at children as at those who are free of the restraints of conformity. I find the images are terrifying in the way that many of Goya's drawings are: wrapped in silence, they turn me into the child who hides his head beneath the blanket because total darkness is preferable to what shadows produce. The two artists might have slipped into each other's sketchbooks, Tiepolo self-imprisoned in his Villa di Zianigo, Goya in his Quinta del Sordo. One of Tiepolo's drawings depicts Pulcinella being buried by other Pulcinellas, and another image, serving as the title page, has him standing before his own grave, a small wooden ladder propped up against it as if inviting him

to inspect what one day will be a sepulchre for his own remains.

The good news is that Pulcinella will be resurrected from the dead because, you see, Pulcinella never actually dies although, and I repeat myself because I'm not sure how else to put it, from time to time he does. It's not much good asking him what he's seen on 'the other side', and in fact it's probably not much good asking him anything at all, but as with San Gennaro, as with Totò, as with pizza Margherita, his presence is required *absolutely*. One may go a step further: no Pulcinella, no Naples. And to think I'd thought of him as little more than a knob of carved wood with a black mask, white hat and smock, and a squeaky voice. Yet he fascinated me, as if there was something that needed to be got at, the getting of which would take me to the very soul of whatever it was I think I might have been after, and that the more I'd learn about him the more unfathomable he'd become. Peter Gunn, who has produced perhaps the most eloquent book on Naples, writes:

Pulcinella represents the Neapolitan's image of himself, a marvellously earthy creature, some of whose fascination lies in the fact that his immorality is so patent that one is at a loss to know whether it does not spring from sources deeper than what is ordinarily meant by wisdom or stupidity, virtue or vice.

I wade through imponderables: Pulcinella can be as simple or as complex as one likes. It is why both adults and children are drawn to him, although probably the latter have a better take on him than do the former with their accumulated knowledge. Certainly Pulcinella wouldn't have the foggiest about what some very smart people are saying about him, among them a philosopher from Rome, but he is, in his own way, shrewder than they are. What he knows and they don't is that the stick is mightier than any philosophical argument. When words fail, resort to violence. The only thing Pulcinella needs to address is his stomach and maybe a little something else, Teresina knows what. As for the black and white of which he is made, they carry all the opposites of which his audience is comprised – gravity and grace, aspiration and failure, stupidity and cunning, cruelty and kindness, and yes, life and death. Pulcinella, in other words, gives death the slip, chases skirt, and, although not all that bright himself and a bit of a coward to boot, pokes fun at power and arrogance.

Pulcinella was born in Acerra, a town nine miles outside Naples. Originally founded by the Ausoni, and later, during Roman times, inhabited by the Oscans, Akeru, as it was then called, had become a place of some importance. Hannibal sacked it in 216 BC, the Saracens in AD 881, and in October 1943 the Nazis, in addition to conducting a massacre, burned down much of the town. One thing survives: an idea, the idea of an idea, an idea almost beyond the reach of our intelligence. When I asked Irene Vecchia, *maestra*, if she knew which house Pulcinella was born in, she replied, 'They know! We don't know where it is, but *they* do.' She seems somewhat affronted by the fact the citizens of Acerra are so tight-lipped on the matter. A farmer from there, Puccio d'Aniello, is said to have become, at some point in the sixteenth century, a buffoon in a travelling troupe. A clue to Pulcinella's origins may be located in his name. Puccio's knockabout parody of the Acerran peasant was seized upon by the Commedia dell'Arte actor and playwright Silvio Fiorillo (1560–1633) whose mask of Pulcinella (or Policinella) first appears, together with his other creation, the Spanish braggart Capitan Matamoros ('Moor-killer'), in the play *La Lucilla costante* ('The constant Lucilla'). What is immediately noticeable is that from the very outset Pulcinella flouts authority, the 'body politic' as expressed in the absurdities of Capitan Matamoros whose comeuppance at the hands of one of their own would not have been lost on the Neapolitan audience. (Sometimes Pulcinella went too far. An eighteenth-century Pulcinella from Rome, Bartolomeo Cavallucci, was beaten to death at Pesaro by Spanish officers for his taunts against Spanish rule.) 'He may be a fool,' goes the line of a song I like, 'but he's our fool.' Pulcinella is protector of the city and indeed Fiorillo's play foreshadows the revolt led by the fisherman Tommaso Aniello, more fondly remembered by his nickname 'Masaniello'. This is only one of several theories, another being that the name derives from *pulcino*, a newborn chick, which explains the squawky voice. Pulcinella was not so much born as hatched.

Pulcinella has relatives all over Europe, our Mr Punch being one of them, and incredibly we have a date for when the latter was conceived. Samuel Pepys in his diary entry for 9 May 1662 notes a visit to Covent Garden: 'Thence to see an Italian puppet play that is within the rayles there, which is very pretty, the best that ever I saw, and with a great resort of gallants.' The performance was by the Italian puppeteer Pietro Gimonde or 'Signor Bologna', and almost immediately Pulcinella entered British folklore albeit in a fresh guise. (Would it offend Anglo-Saxon sensibilities if I were to say that when compared to Pulcinella, Mr Punch lacks nuance?) Other relatives include Kasper in Germany, Jan Klaassen in Holland, Mester Jakel in Denmark, Polichinelle in France, Petrushka in Russia, and so forth, but their progenitor's adopted home is Naples. The origins of Pulcinella are much older, however. As Pierre Louis Duchartre in his magisterial study *The Italian Comedy* (1929) writes, 'Pulcinella belongs to so ancient a house that the noblest of the noble barely keep their heads above the common crowd in comparison with him.' Pulcinella is associated with the fourth century BC Maccus and Bucco, both of them stock figures of Atellan farce (the *Fabulae Atellanae*, also known as the 'Oscan Games'), the first of whom had a hooked nose, a bumpy face, a hump, prominent belly, wore a half-mask, and dressed in a white, fairly wide, shirt and acted with a hen's voice, and the second, Bucco, who had an enormous mouth and flabby cheeks. There is yet another character in Atellan comedy, Kikurrus, (or Cucurucu) whose theriomorphic mask and onomatopoeic name are perhaps even closer to the mask of Pulcinella. It is worth recalling at this juncture that Acerra was the main centre for these farces, and that the name comes from Atella, which was close by. A city once big enough to strike its own coinage, Atella is now a few stony protuberances.

Charles MacFarlane in his *Popular Customs, Sports and Recollections of the South of Italy* (1846) provides a first-hand account of a puppet theatre in Naples, along with a potted history of Pulcinella's origins, and in passing manages to unravel a fine mesh of associations. A keen observer of extinct races, MacFarlane would seem to have known the Oscans better than the Oscans knew themselves:

> The old Oscan had a natural elegance, and an unfathomable store of good nature; he had no envy or malice, he loved those he made sport of, and in his most satirical allusions his object was to excite joyous and innocent laughter, and not to rouse

feelings of hatred or contempt. Hence, in the most high and palmy state of Rome, he and his Oscan farces were admired by all classes of the community.

Were these the same people who so pushed at the boundaries of decency that even their farces were sent into exile? We all, despite our claims to objectivity, take sides. The Oscans, those fun-loving people, were roundly thwacked by the less fun-loving Samnites before the Romans took over the region in third century BC, and adopted Pulcinella for themselves. Another valuable feature of MacFarlane's book is that he took note of things that have since gone, among them a figure closely resembling the modern Pulcinella that was drawn on the stuccoed wall of a guardroom at Pompeii and which, in the writer's day, was picked apart by brainless tourists. A small bronze figure, again closely resembling Pulcinella, was discovered at Herculaneum. There is nothing to suggest a Pulcinella-like presence in the Middle Ages, but then I take the admittedly shaky view that what was once in the soil re-emerges, and nowhere is that soil more fertile or more a preservative than in Campania. After all, it is from within those few square miles that so much of the world's mythology comes.

Here is MacFarlane's description of the Pulcinella theatre in Naples:

This truly national theatre was situated not far from the great theatre of San Carlo ... it was called San Carlino, or little San Carlo; and little it was, and far from being splendid in its appointments and accessories. The boxes were on a level with the street or square, but to get to the pit you had to descend some thirty feet into the bowels of the earth, and to dive down a steep staircase not unlike that by which Roderick Random and his faithful Strap dived for their dinner. The price paid for admission was very small; I think it was about a shilling for a seat in the boxes, and about sixpence for a seat in the pit.

Everywhere there is a 'fashionable world,' and a set of super-
fine people who deprive themselves of much racy and innocent
amusement from a notion that it is not *genteel*. San Carlino
was rarely visited except by the second and third rate classes
of burgesses, for the native fashionables considered it as 'low',
and very few foreigners ever acquired a sufficient knowledge
of the patois or dialect to enjoy and fully understand these
rich Neapolitan farces, and the perennial wit and humour of
our friend Punch. But before I quitted Naples this ridiculous
prejudice seemed to be on the decline, for a few young men of
family, who had wit as well as high birth, had appreciated the
genius of that living Policinella, and had made the little cellar
almost fashionable. For myself, I very often strolled away from
the gorgeous and fine and thoroughly artificial Opera-house,
to enjoy a little homely nature and drollery in San Carlino,
where I have laughed more than I shall ever laugh again. As in
every other theatre in the city, there was always present a commissary of police, to preserve order and decorum, and check
any too free use of the tongue on the stage. This representative
of the laws and of majesty itself, wore a blue court-cut coat
embroidered with silver; he sat in what we call a stage-box,
on a high-backed chair, covered with faded crimson velvet;
and behind his back there were two large wax candles and the
royal arms of the Two Sicilies painted upon a bit of board. But
not all this official splendour could repress the hilarity or stifle
the roguish impromptus of friend Punch; and we have at times
seen the starch-visaged commissary, after some vain attempts
to maintain his dignity, hold both his sides, and join in the
universal roar of laughter: and this too even when Signor
Policinella had gone beyond bounds and handled matters
strictly tabooed. What [Joseph] Forsyth said of the Molo and
the Marionettes, and out-door Punch, might be more correctly applied to San Carlino: – 'This is a theatre where any
stranger may study for nothing the manners of the people.

At the theatre of San Carlo the mind, as well as the man, seems parted off from its fellows in an elbow-chair. There all is regulation and silence: no applause, no censure, no object worthy of attention except the court and the fiddle. There the drama – but what is a drama in Naples without Punch? or what is Punch out of Naples? Here, in his native tongue, and among his own countrymen, Punch is a person of real power: he dresses up and retails all the drolleries of the day; he is the channel and sometimes the source of the passing opinions; he can inflict ridicule, he could gain a mob, or keep the whole kingdom in good humour.'

No Pulcinella, no Naples. Shall we go the whole hog and say that in his myriad dualities may be located the soul of the Neapolitan people? I've already said as much, but then I like to drive a point home. There had been attempts to suppress him. Mac-Farlane, after he left Naples, heard that the King Ferdinand II had taken steps to remove the puppet theatres. The most powerful voice against Pulcinella during this period was that of a priest, however, and there is an extraordinary eyewitness account of him by theatre manager Michael Kelly.* Father Rocco stumbles across a Pulcinella performance. Kelly writes:

I was myself a witness of the following ridiculous scene. One evening, a groupe of Lazzaroni were very attentively playing at their favourite game of *mora*; beside them was a puppet-show, in which Punch was holding forth with all his might. Father Rocco suddenly appeared amongst them. The first step

---

* Tenor, composer, theatre manager, friend of Sheridan and Mozart, Michael Kelly also wrote one of the most important music and theatre chronicles of the day, the two-volume *Reminiscences* (1826) of which it has been said: 'any statement of Kelly's is immediately suspect'.

the holy man took, was to sweep into his pouch all the money staked by the gamblers; then, turning to the spectators of Punch, he bawled out, 'So, so, ye rapscallions! instead of going out to fish for the Convents and support your families, ye must be loitering here, attending to this iniquitous Punch! this lying varlet!' Then lifting up a large wooden cross, suspended by huge beads round his waist, he lustily belaboured all within his reach, lifting up the cross at intervals, and crying out, 'Look here, you impious rogues! *Questo è il vero Pulcinella!* This is the true Punch, you impious villains.' And, strange as this mixture of religious zeal and positive blasphemy may appear, they took their thrashing with piety, and departed peaceably like good Catholics. I got out of his way with great alertness, feeling no desire to become a disciple of such a *striking* school of religious instruction.

A Bourbon king and a holy man who had 'the most unbounded power over the lower orders in Naples' were not enough to vanquish Pulcinella. 'Pulcinella will never die because it is us who need him.' I first heard those words in a film clip made at an event in Covent Garden in May 2012 celebrating the 350th anniversary of Mr Punch. 'It's an innate part of our human culture,' continued Irene Vecchia, puppeteer, 'to have a tradition of puppetry.' I was struck by the intensity in her face and by how quickly the severity of her manner could be undone with a flashing smile. 'A bit like with religion,' she said, 'each person creates as befits his own needs.' I knew from those words alone that I would have to begin my enquiries with her. I wrote, she replied. I was not to be disappointed in my instincts. The acknowledged Pulcinella maestro in Naples is Bruno Leone, but I would have been in some kind of wilderness had I not met Irene first. I suspect Bruno no longer needs to say the things she does. She's hungrier than he is, maybe keener, and, as anyone who has seen her perform can tell you, fully primed. Steeped with experience, Bruno simply gets out there and does what he does. She battles her way. When she was eighteen, after leaving high school, Irene joined a new school of *guarattelle*, which is the name given to the puppet tradition in Naples. The lessons were spread over three years but only in the months of March, April, and May. The tradition was taught in a new way: not as it used to be, from maestro to novice, but within a *bottega* (workshop) where one began with cleaning and other chores. There were ten students and the teachers were the three most outstanding Pulcinella performers in Naples, Bruno Leone, Salvatore Gatto, and Maria Imperatrice, who between them rescued Pulcinella from near-oblivion. Should they ever read these words, puppeteers in other parts of Italy might raise their voices in protest; some of them have opined that what one gets in Naples is not the real product, and one puppeteer goes as far as to write that in Naples, Pulcinella has been 'pitifully Pierrotized' (he also has no truck with France's 'stale, stinking mish-mosh'). And then comes his killer line: 'Fiorillo, Calcese, Fracanzano, and Petito, the great Neapolitan Pulcinellas, are turning in their graves.' These are fighting words indeed and, although spoken by someone who is himself a master, where I think he errs is to have separated local tradition from local people, as if application is all and context rather less. I also do not like to see my friends rubbished. I daresay that nowhere else in Italy is the relationship between people and tradition as inextricable as it is in Naples. Purists, in all areas of endeavour, are sometimes intolerant to the degree that they allow the traditions to go stale.

Irene Vecchia, who performed close to the spot where some centuries before Pulcinella made his London debut, describes it as being love at first sight, the art of puppetry being far more direct than marionettes. It's something she can't do without any more. It's enough to make me wonder what her dreams are like. When she met Bruno Leone in 1990 the chief puppeteers in Naples had been Nunzio Zampella and Giovanni Pino, the first of whom was a streetcleaner and the second a doorman in a public office.

They did their puppetry on Sundays in the old style, which is to say on the street and with a portable stage. Sometimes they made up to three times what they earned a month at their respective jobs, which begs the question as to why they continued with their regular jobs. Irene's answer was disarmingly simple.

'It is a good idea to do the first so as to maintain a high level of desire to do the second.'

Amateurs, take note. If ever there was a statement of artistic integrity this surely is a shining instance. The thing their successors have had to face is that working in the street has become much harder because of the distractions – the traffic and mobile phones alone – making it close to impossible to survive. It is also more difficult to create a high level of tension, and what is true for performance is equally true for the passing down of a tradition.

'Nobody,' Irene said, 'ever asked these people to be artists. One may go into a remote part of the Amazon and discover an old man singing and say he is an artist, but really he is just a singer. And so the older puppeteers simply *did it* while it was for the rest of the world to recognise them as artists. They did as they liked whereas now the old ways no longer work. Younger people are being asked to create theatre companies. Contracts are made, invoices issued. This has taken everything into a new dimension. The trick is how to recognise something that belongs to the code of Pulcinella but which is not a rule.'

Violence is something we associate with Pulcinella, and it is partly why both Mr Punch and Pulcinella are looked upon by many people with something approaching repugnance. We are living in a world where the line between actual violence and designer violence has become so blurred that some people do in real life what properly belongs to their fantasy world, but for Irene the depiction of violence in Pulcinella raises the very question of what truth is.

'When we look closely at cause and effect usually what we see is binary in nature, but with respect to Pulcinella this way of thinking simply doesn't apply. Pulcinella is spherical in nature. He is one and he is no one. We say that he is eternal, but at the same time he is not fixed. He is always changing. If something is fixed it can't change. The way I learned the tradition was completely different than in past times, but it is the only way it can be done nowadays. The most important moment of the show is when Pulcinella fights against all the problems thrown at him. For someone who has never seen the show it might be said that Pulcinella is a character who takes a stick and beats another figure, the conclusion being this is a violent spectacle. It is *not* violent, however … it is *powerful*. Once I gave a show at a school and this teacher who was going in and out of the room, not really looking at the performance, afterwards told me it was too violent and therefore unsuitable for children. "They love Pulcinella," she said, "and so should they take from him the idea that violence is a solution?" Anyone who can say this is looking for one truth only. This is not a good way to approach Pulcinella or life. What Pulcinella is doing is expressing the power of fear that we all have, and for children seeing puppets fight actually frees them of the need for violence. You could say the same for an adult watching the show. The problem is not Pulcinella, but that *we* are full of violence. We see a man throwing a stone and say he is violent. Meanwhile a president is dropping bombs somewhere. It is impossible now to give expression to violence, so the problem lies in our failure to express it. This is an interesting contradiction. We have become so violent we can't bear to see even the simplest expression of violence. It is too much to handle. If I can express the violence within myself then I am free *not* to do it whereas if I can't express it and suffocate or censor it then I will go and commit it elsewhere. Maybe I'll destroy everything. Violence exists, but this is not violence. It is a power linked with life – with desire, fear, hunger, and sex – it is the power of life. You can listen to, and learn to live with, this power or else you try to kill it. If you try to kill it, it becomes like a river. A river is always changing its course, adapting to the terrain, sometimes going underground, other times re-emerging, but it doesn't stop. It is still running, and it is as true for Pulcinella as it is for tradition and for life. Pulcinella doesn't die, but he sees death all the time. If I recognise death it allows me to live all the more, whereas if I don't recognise death I am closer to it. Pulcinella is one who sees death and for this reason he steals or fights. The energy he has is a love of life. If we lose the power of loving life, then we are closer to death. Human beings invent more and more ways to be closer to it because they don't want to actually see death. So when people tell me Pulcinella is too violent it scares me. How can one say this when the level of social and individual tolerance has become so low it becomes impossible to talk about it any more? When it becomes taboo to do so. If it was taboo to talk about violence against women it was because it had become so widespread we couldn't see it any more. Today, in Italy, we have started talking about it. The act of fighting is violence, true, but the problem is not in the puppets. It is because the level of taboo is too high.'

'I think it is true of all art that good recognises evil and vice versa,' I replied. 'I wonder to what degree this is true in Naples.'

'You see all these cheap representations of Pulcinella, fridge magnets and souvenirs sold to tourists. I don't like it. This is just one example, but it is a clear one. At the same time, somebody thought of it and expended much energy on it and so at least he recognises that Pulcinella is a symbol. If I see in this something representing art and value someone else will see it as representing his own values which may or may not be mine. A kind of balance, this is especially true in theatre. We like to say that for a show to be successful it has to have catharsis, but no matter how dramatic, funny, or interesting those theatrical representations are, they are always about conflict. If there is no conflict, then it's not going to be a good story. We want to see bad people doing bad things and observe how things develop from there. Greek

tragedy was always about this conflict and it shows how even
heroes can be bad at times, but then it is the only way for them
to survive. Antigone goes against the law, but it is the only way
she can belong to life. All human history, and by extension the
theatre, is bound up with what happens between good and bad
and so is dependent on the swinging movement between those
two extremes. This is what Pulcinella with his black-and-white
existence is. Truth is not in the grey. Grey is nothing. It is just one
brief moment in the movement of this big pendulum, so on its
own it is not true. It is simply a way to be conformist. The middle
way is the most polite way to classify something. Extremes are
always impolite and it is not just through one extreme or the
other – there are two extremes, and between them life is a swinging pendulum. So it is not true to say the only truth lies in the
middle.'

'Some people stay in the middle whereas, with you, Irene, it
would appear that in a sense you have married Pulcinella.'
Something like a shadow of fear moved over her face.

'Yes. Sometimes I think … look, I'm thirty-four now … who knows if I'm doing the right thing. I have no children. What is the right thing to do? This is something you can recognise from the outside whereas I can't from the inside. I think what you say is true. It is a kind of marriage. I always say that home is where Pulcinella sleeps with me. When I go to a festival, for example, and I perform for three days in the same place, I will set up the theatre in a protected zone. I don't take it down at night, but I always carry my puppets with me. Pulcinella stays wherever I am. This is nice. It is what happens when you are married to someone. You sleep together in the same place. When I think of the times I perform Pulcinella it is always a sacrifice of selfhood. Yes, but why? Why am I doing this? I don't have enough money. *Why?* Maybe this is just a justification, but I feel someone *has* to do it. Also, if it were not fundamental to our culture there would be no response. You have to do it to survive, you have to pay the bills. These are the things that take me and people like me underground. At the same time, if tomorrow I were to die that would not be a problem. Pulcinella will carry on and everything will be okay. There is nothing so important about me. So if I'm not so important, why am I doing it? Maybe it's true, someone has to do it, and like anyone who works as an artist it is a balancing act. As we talk someone is killing someone, children are dying of thirst, and another person is making loads of money because he is doing a crooked business deal, and yet here we are, the two of us, talking about life. Maybe it is completely futile what we do, but we have to do it.'

'Maybe it's because we are fools,' I proffered, 'and if the world loses the fool it is finished.'

'Exactly! The fool is the thing that makes the pendulum swing.'

'Would you say Pulcinella is a fool such as one finds elsewhere in the European tradition?'

'One of the characteristics people ascribe to Pulcinella is that he is ignorant, even stupid, but at the same time they also say that he is astute or sharp because he always finds a solution. So in this respect he is the fool you describe. Maybe he doesn't know much, but when problems arise he finds a way to solve them. So the solution is inside the situation itself and not something that comes from outside. In this way, too, he is a fool. Also many jokes arise from misunderstanding – somebody says something and Pulcinella doesn't understand or else they say something he struggles to understand. This is another aspect of his foolishness. Does he really not understand or does he understand only what he needs to understand?'

'So in a way this would seem to describe the Neapolitan spirit, which is to find a way to solve problems.'

'Also by appearing stupid and being shrewd at the same time.'

'And so how does Pulcinella represent the soul of Naples?'

'The contradiction of this city is one of the main characteristics of our story. You can see it just walking in the street. It is a city full of rich places that have been abandoned. This aspect of decay is everywhere, but Naples is not empty. It is still crowded. The power of this city ... it is the only big city in Italy that is still inhabited in its historical centre. If you look at Florence you see only tourist shops in the old centre. It is not so here. What makes the city look decayed is also the way it still lives. This is just one aspect. And so one thing that could be the truth may not be the only truth. A thing can be that thing and at the same time its opposite. It's like this in even the smallest aspects of existence. This is life here. But it is also a place where life can jump on you just when you don't want it to. Sometimes it's good, other times bad, but the difference between them may not necessarily be within things themselves but in you. Pulcinella is this and his incongruence is one of the aspects of Naples.'

'I have been looking for the soul of Naples, and Pulcinella seems to be it. He could not have come from Rome or Venice but only from Naples with its duality and contradictions.'

'I agree, but finally you can find him everywhere. He is universal. When I asked you what you think of Pulcinella it was not so much that I was looking for your understanding of him. You begin to understand him when you start to recognise yourself in Pulcinella. You can say what you like about him. It is like seeing shapes in the clouds. If I recognise a horse riding on a cloud and people say, "No, it's a cloud", I will continue to see it as a horse. It's the same with Pulcinella. We go to a place beyond expression. It is a very abstract concept. How do we render it? I do it with puppets. A poet does it with words. I don't know all the applications. This is why when working in the street we see a man or a woman passing and in that instant we can see Pulcinella in him or her. We don't know if it is expressed in his or her life, but we can recognise it, which is why everyone can recognise himself in a Pulcinella performance and laugh.'

'So is Pulcinella accidentally wise?'

'I know that wisdom is something you reach or gain from experience, but there is also something wise in small children. They know how to get attention. We know we are smarter than when we were younger – we hope! – and so we try to learn from our mistakes. Wisdom is what saves you. Pulcinella can escape problems although maybe he is not wise on his own but only in his relationship to others. In the battle between Pasquale, the stock character who is always the baddie, and Pulcinella, the latter survives but not the former. In this situation Pulcinella is wiser, but then he will start to do something stupid, singing songs for a girl, for example.'

'All art is alchemy.'

'Yes, the transformation of material. When Pulcinella appears it is the beginning of alchemy. This is why I love it. Here is a single person, the puppeteer, and there is the audience, all of the people in it looking at the spot where Pulcinella is. I can see and push things from my side. What the audience sees and feels from the other side is a form of collaboration. The show is always something alchemical that occurs between the audience and the puppets and puppeteer. It is not like when you go into a cinema and see things in one dimension only, where there is only screen and audience. With the puppet show it is mostly up to me. It is fantastic because you can feel it like a shower soaking you with all these feelings. When you do a show you have to know what is going to happen, but at the same time the less you are there the more lively the show will be and the more people will enjoy it. This is something I can say from experience.'

'You mean you lose yourself?'

'You are there and you are *not* there. Sometimes I do a show and I'm having lots of fun and when I come out from behind the stage I feel fantastic. I think the show was good, but then I see the audience. Although people might say they liked the show I can see they are not quite as amused as I was. When I am not *there*, they have more fun. Sometimes the problem lies with me, when, for example, I perform Pulcinella in one mood only, if, say, he is too naive or too childish. There is a loss of equilibrium. We were talking about violence earlier. Sometimes it is due to not getting the right feeling or because you are too concentrated on yourself or you are thinking too much about the sequence or you want to be really good and then get all narcissistic about it. You already know how it goes and so you execute it like clockwork. You are not inside the moment, however. You are thinking *about* the moment and when this happens it can result in a greater sense of violence. It is the same when one dances. You try for a certain movement because you want to reproduce the exact shape of something you saw once or which your maestro taught you. You may achieve it, but this does not mean the show is any good. And so it is with Pulcinella. The problem may be too much naiveté or just not being smart enough. It is not the show itself that is violent but what the puppeteer does which makes it so. There is a problem when you try to impress your thoughts and meaning on a puppet. You kill the puppet. The show becomes too much of one thing in that you become too stupid or too violent or too simple or, even worse, too boring, and when that happens you destroy the energy. You no longer preserve the equilibrium because you are too present. The puppet needs to be free to express itself. The life has to be there, with it. You mustn't interfere too much. You must let the characters carry on and finish whatever they do. I try to surrender to them. If you want to make theatre you have to connect with the audience but not impose on the puppets themselves. This is not based on theory but on experience and making mistakes. An actor works in a different way. As much as he or she is inside the role the more lively the character, but for a puppeteer it is quite the opposite in that as much as you are not there the puppets *can* be there.'

'You disappear into yourself …'

' … and make them live.'

'You die for the puppets?'

'You transform yourself into something else for the duration of the performance. It happens that sometimes I talk with people, saying I am feeling bad and don't want to do the show, but afterwards I feel better. It was hard in the beginning because you are in a state of transformation, but for all the bad you feel something changed in you. You *feel* it.'

'It seems that with Pulcinella there is real danger,' I suggested. 'You are on the edge all the time. Pulcinella is fighting to survive and so are you.'

'Am I living with Pulcinella or is Pulcinella living with me? Both are true. The only solution is to love doing what I do. I couldn't do it otherwise. If I did the show the same way every day I'd come to hate it.'

'I saw an interview with you in which you spoke of Pulcinella not as a puppet but as a living being and that to be able to work with him is a great privilege. You also said it is part of our human culture to have Pulcinella. It is a bit like religion in that each person creates according to need.'

'Bruno Leone, when he started out as a puppeteer thirty years ago, during his researches discovered there are traditions similar to Pulcinella throughout Europe, which, of course, stem from our Pulcinella. Originally, though, there was something strongly related to religion. In Mali there is the religious representation of the god, and the goddess speaks with the same voice as Pulcinella. In the Asian tradition the man who manipulates the shadow puppets is called the *dalang*, who is also a kind of priest, and before the performance he offers prayers to bring the puppets to life. The puppet representation is very primitive. It is like the mask, but the mask is already something more logical because a human being takes something, puts it on his face, and acts whereas with the puppet the human plays with the medium and so it is more primitive, more archaic, more animistic. You imagine that objects can have life and power and you use this power to express.'

'Puppets and marionettes strike me as one of the most extraordinary things to have issued from the human mind,' I said. 'I can understand an actor on the stage, or a singer, but to create a human representation is close to incomprehensible. When did it begin? To see that representation of ourselves in little things is almost too big to understand.'

'It's also too big to explain. I think it is more immediate. Also it is not logical. Maybe it is related to that area of art that is not analytical or logical. You take a stone or a piece of wood, transform it into something that will be charged with value, which everyone can see. We give it significance. The problem when speaking of nowadays is that we have built for ourselves lives full of objects. We need these objects. We need a key to enter the room. At the same time these objects we feel we need are not so important for life. We know Michelangelo made a statue. Putting significance into an object has been the matter of art ever since the beginning. We need some object to project what we have but which we can't see, so we give him material, we give him space and shape, we give him a body. So we are materialistic but at the same time we have our fill of things we need but don't really recognise. If now we go into the street and start a show people will stop for five minutes and feel the same fun and the same joy they had five centuries ago. We are talking about the same thing, but now they can stand only five minutes.'

I told Irene I was writing about the idea of death in life, life in death.

'Pulcinella is hatched from an egg. So the mother of Pulcinella might well be a hen. The chicken is an animal that is very linked with the other world because although it belongs to the avian family it doesn't fly. In Napoli when someone dies the family cooks *brodo di pollo*, chicken soup. This is the tradition here. On the night of a death we eat chicken soup. The chicken is also the voice of Pulcinella. Also Pulcinella is black and white. Our death is not like death in other traditions where the skull is white and the dress is black. We have the opposite. The skull is black, the dress white. It's the same with Pulcinella. It is rather scary too. Very small children when exposed to it start crying sometimes because it is so powerful. What they see comes from the other side, which is why Pulcinella never dies. Maybe he has already died but is still living. It's for this reason that the puppet show with death as a main character is my favourite because it is very powerful. I have never adopted a skull and I've never been involved in this matter – not yet maybe, there is still time – but what I like is that there is a powerful connection between *anime pezzentelle* and puppets. We say objects have a life, a soul. I know this is a piece of wood, but I take care of it as if it were alive. Taking care of a skull is taking care of an object – now it is an object whereas before it had life – it is still giving life to something that is no longer alive. I find in this something animistic. Also it is something divine, belonging to God. A person takes care of a skull, gives it sweets, cigarettes, money. It is also a connection with the parallel universe and so it is me deciding what life is. And so it is like being God – it is not God but me who decides – and so in this respect it is religious. It is pagan too because I am God, *I* decide. I present a skull with an object that has meaning for me, which is something I need in life, and so I give this object to another object that surely will have no use for it. It is different from prayer. Prayer belongs to words and music, but offering an object is a much bigger step. Why do I do it if the skull doesn't need this object? Why give sweets or cigarettes to a soul that is no longer here but somewhere else? It is like throwing stones over a wall and not knowing where they'll land. Such is the case with every play I perform with children or adults. It is always different. There is a traditional sequence I observe. Pulcinella fights with a dog, then fights with a man or a *carabiniere* – he is always fighting problems – but when he fights with death he goes a stage deeper and works on another level altogether. It is the climax of the show.'

'I did not know the black represents burnt skin.'

'It is something that sticks to you, which becomes the face.'

'Ancient Greek theatre?'

'Pulcinella always has a big nose, rather phallic, which in this respect means fertility. It also protects him against the evil eye. The shape, the wrinkles ... it is like stratification. There are many masks in the Italian tradition. The iconography of Pulcinella's mask changes over time, but what stays the same are the big nose, the wrinkles, the colour of his face – dark brown to black – and the eyes. Our eyes are not round whereas in puppets they are. Rounded eyes are useful for a puppet because they can be seen from a distance. Also they are sincere, round and clean like in animals. Chickens have round eyes.'

'You started when you were eighteen and here you are, still at it. There must be some driving force inside you.'

'Yes, it was like you see something and it becomes a relationship. When I saw Bruno and Salvatore Gatto doing their Pulcinella show it was love at first sight. Puppets are more direct, much sharper than marionettes. I can't do without it now. It doesn't depend on me or you or anyone else. If I don't perform Pulcinella he is still there. He does not depend on me. At the beginning of my studies, when I understood this, it was the reason for my instant love.'

I asked Irene Vecchia whether being a woman made it difficult for her to operate in what had been for the most part a male tradition. She raised her hands to me, the waggle of each finger containing a reprimand.

'How many fingers do I have?'

I think I counted ten. Stupid question. What could have possessed me?

Irene took me to the workshop of one of her teachers, a puppeteer of repute, Salvatore Gatto, who is also a musician, songwriter, and the author of a book for children, *Pulcinella che passione* (2006). With his shaved head, goatee, and gold earring

I'd gladly have him play Mephistopheles in my movie. Salvatore is a man who *does*. The studio was evidence of one who knows the weights and measures his profession requires of him. I wouldn't want to wrestle with him.

'So, Salvatore, how did you get into this strange life?'

'Ever since I was young ... well, it's probably even more the case now because I don't want to grow up ... if someone ever says to me, "You can't do this" then I stick to my guns. There was a time I didn't want this to be my job. Also because I come from a left-wing culture in which work is considered a form of torture, I couldn't imagine drawing money from what I saw as a pleasure. When I was sixteen I had a son. I didn't understand what being a father would be like.'

Salvatore's beautiful young wife, several months pregnant, was in attendance. I was able to deduce that Salvatore's history has been a colourful one.

'Tullio, my son, was always watching these Japanese cartoons on TV, he and his friends just sitting there, never smiling. This was how I became a puppeteer. When I was a child my grandfather made some puppets for me and so I did the same for Tullio because I wanted to distract him from the TV. At that time they called me "Signor Scotch" as in scotch tape ... we just call it "scotch" in Italian. I drank lots of Scotch too. I made a family of puppets with paper, cloth, and ... *scotch*. I started playing this new game with my son, but a young guy's attention for games is small and after six months, well, he lost interest. The puppets I made were from the Neapolitan *guarattelle* tradition which I remembered from my childhood, when my grandfather took me to the municipal park to see Giovanni Pino who would later become my maestro. It is said Bruno Leone's maestro was Nunzio Zampella and mine Giovanni Pino, but this is not strictly true – well, it's true and it's not true – they were the two maestros living at that time. I learned things from Nunzio as well so it is hard to separate them, but we'll allow this for the sake of convenience. I identify myself in Giovanni Pino, Bruno in Nunzio Zampella. I loved Pino's poetical way of life. He was ignorant in many ways, unschooled, but he was a man full of poetry and culture. It was an intense time.'

'Will your son step into your shoes?'

'As I said,' Salvatore continued, 'I made puppets for Tullio. I said to him, "I showed you Pulcinella, so now you can present your own show, your way of doing it, and then I will give you another show." The piece I wrote for him was about the circus because Tullio was doing acrobatics at the time. It became my first street performance. Tullio lost interest, but for me this was a new beginning.'

I couldn't tell whether Salvatore was disappointed or relieved, but clearly in doing what he did for his son he had effected a revolution in his own life.

'The very idea of the street thrilled me. I wanted to prove myself there because it was completely free and I would be dependent on no one but myself. As I was alone I needed to build up a relationship with the hat, which was a major obstacle to overcome. I thought this could be easily solved. I had a hat and put on it a written note: "This show is completely free, but you may leave a contribution." As to *passing the hat* only Giovanni knew how to do it properly. Me, I was too embarrassed. Actually I was terrified. The hat was very light and soft like pumice, but in my hands it felt like a heavy rock. When I first worked with Giovanni we worked out things in this fashion. When I did the show he passed the hat and vice versa. After the show all the money we collected was divided in two. I was able to see how much the maestro made. So what I did next time was to bring my own money from home and when I saw how much Giovanni got I slipped an equal amount into the hat so that when we divided the money he would end up taking all of it. I took nothing because, you see, I couldn't bear to pass the hat.'

Salvatore laughed at the memory of this.

'The maestro cottoned onto my trick. Although it was the first and only time I did this he understood immediately, so with our next show he said, "Okay, today we change the rules. When you do the show I'll pass the hat and that money will be yours and when I do the show you pass the hat and that money will be mine." Culturally I am an Arab in my ways. I can play with you, but I can't steal from you. (I say this because one time, in Morocco, I accidentally left my guitar in the street for eleven hours and no one took it. At the same time you try to make a deal with these same people and they ask for the impossible.) With these new rules in place there was nothing I could do. At first it was really horrible for me. I can still feel my skin tingle when I remember this. I turn red. Anyway when I began to work on my own I knew I needed to grow up a little. The problem, fundamentally, was about asking. My show was eleven minutes long. All I had to say were three words, and even if I did next to nothing by the end of the show my hat was always full. Something was changing inside me. I told the maestro, "I don't know why it is, but I can't take money from you." I finally overcame this awkward matter twenty-five years later when I was in Columbia. A man asked me if he could clean my shoes. I hated the idea that someone should kneel in front of me and clean my shoes. I said I didn't want him to. He replied that he was hungry. "Well, then," I said, "sit down with us for a meal." "No, I am not asking for that," he replied. "I am asking you to let me clean your shoes so I can make some money." I lied to him, saying I was allergic to shoe polish. "Okay, I'll clean them with water. Look, I don't want your help, I want money for my work." Then I understood something really important that I'd missed before. We are always exchanging something or other. You pay me money for doing something or we can always choose what we are exchanging. I'd suffered from *vergogna*, a much stronger word in Italian than your English one for shame. At first this was a cultural matter. At the same time I didn't want to lose direction. After a few more performances

Giovanni told me, "This can't be your hobby." This was incredible. I'd asked him many questions, but he never answered them and then suddenly he would say something that would give shape to my thoughts. Giovanni could make mistakes with the words he spoke, but their concept was always incredibly clear. When he told me that this couldn't be a hobby I understood what the problem was. When you look at the history of Pulcinella the people who performed did so out of necessity. They'd carry this like a cross, but for me it was a cross that would become wings.'

Salvatore pointed to the mobile sculpture he'd fashioned from wood and fire, which was an expression, he said, of the freedom he'd found, indicating to me the opposition of heaviness and lightness, gravity and grace.

'So it became my work,' he continued. 'I was doing animation at the time. I put on a show in a village, on one of our saint days of which we have many. And once a week, with Bruno and Maria, we put on these street performances. You want to know about Pulcinella but, watch out, I'm a deep man. We can spend the rest of the week talking about him.'

'When I speak to you or Irene,' I replied, 'I get the sense Pulcinella is always somebody who is at a distance, but at the same time he is *your* words, *your* movements, *your* mind ... so where is Pulcinella, there or *here*?'

'It's part of you, just like you are a part of everything. It is like calculating or trying to understand how much of oneself is Pulcinella, the dog, or Teresina the woman. When you do a show you do so with two sides of your character. You become a maestro because you have a student and at the same time that student is your maestro. We can think about Pulcinella because we are also the other characters.'

'So is Pulcinella inside or outside oneself?'

'We are still trying to answer this question. I can only speak about other people's shows because I can't see my own performance.'

'So this Pulcinella is *over there* somewhere?'

'My Pulcinella, Irene's, or Bruno's ... we are all Pulcinella.'

'You share the spirit of Pulcinella?'

'It is not only about sharing Pulcinella,' Irene interjected. 'It is also about travelling in the same direction, like a train on the rails. This is because we have these stock characters – Pulcinella who will never die, Pasquale who is always a bad man, and so forth. We have to do this without pity, cruelty, or ruthlessness. We merely alter the way we express it. My Pasquale will never have a deep voice because I am a woman. Maybe we can have him speak in a different rhythm, but he will always be the worst man ever. We don't allow him any possibility of change.'

'Once I saw a show in which Pasquale says he doesn't want to be bad,' Salvatore said. 'No problem. Changing little things is the way we still do it. It is like a wind coming when you open the window. It is an idea and the show is always flexible.'

'I think I found the serpent,' I said. 'It's Pasquale. Whether it was the journalist who wrote an article about the Camorra and was killed for it or the boy at San Gaudioso who was caught in crossfire, it is always Pasquale who's behind it.'

'Pulcinella is both good and bad,' Salvatore replied. 'Pulcinella is human so he can express feelings and emotions, but at the same time he is an expression of popular culture.'

The night before I met Bruno Leone I had two dreams. Which was the crazier I can't say because dreams have their own peculiar logic or so I hope. The first dream was clearly inspired by my earlier conversation with Irene Vecchia. I had become Pulcinella. I could feel something moving inside me, manipulating me. I went from being an inanimate object to one that was being animated by some power beyond me. I gabbled in an unknown tongue. I made people laugh. Whatever happened was not of my volition but somebody else's and I had to presume I was not in charge of my own destiny. At the same time, although I don't know how I knew this, whoever was in charge imputed all power to me. So I had to go along with the spurious notion that everything was down to me. In the second dream, Donald Trump won the American election, which at that point – 2016 – seemed wildly implausible.

'That is incredible,' said Bruno when I related my dreams to him. 'I am a candidate in the election here.'

'I will vote for you!'

'There is a political group here that has decided to use the mask of Pulcinella as their symbol. They asked me to join them. I told them I'm no good at politics. Anyway I am still thinking about it.'

'You want power?'

'It is important for them to have me on their side. They had a meeting to which I was invited. I said I would agree, but first they would have to accept my conditions. I'll use the name "Bruno de

Pulcinella" and, second, I will go on campaign only if I get to wear the mask at all times. Without the mask I am anonymous, whereas with it I'm a public figure. I cover my face in order to be visible. And because if politicians steal poetry from me I want to steal some space from them where I can make even more art and poetry.'

Bruno showed me a document he produced.

'These are the names of the people on my committee: Giordano Bruno, Federico García Lorca, Tommaso Campanella, Goethe, and my friend Giorgio Agamben. Agamben came to Naples to see my show. We met many times. After talking to me he added another six pages to the second edition of his book *Pulcinella ovvero Divertimento per li regazzi* ('Pulcinella: or Entertainment for Children', 2015). This, in turn, formed the basis for my show *Pulchi, Shake and Speare* in which Pulcinella becomes Shakespeare.'

There is something distinctly Rabelaisian about Bruno Leone. The silver braces on his teeth would seem to confirm this in some obscure way because I can't quite believe he wears them because he needs them. I was too polite to ask, but not so polite as to not raise the question here. Maybe they're meant to complement his kerchief with the silver Pulcinella slide. I got the sense of a man made of flesh but with metal in there as well, those elements combining to produce something brand new in the universe. I wonder what happens to him when he passes through airport security.

Born in 1949, in Montemurro, in the region of Basilicata, his parents, Giuseppe Antonello Leone and Maria Padula, were both painters and writers of note. There is an exhibition catalogue in which the writer says of Bruno's father that 'even the stones he collects, examines and reworks are a sort of sweepings of God, errant stones in search of a better destiny'. I think of this when recalling Bruno's studio with its accumulation of errant materials that might one day serve his creative vision. Again it is probably impolite of me to say so, but I think his mother was the superior painter although maybe his father had the wider range. What is important to note is that Bruno was born into culture. There is probably a book to be written called *The Childhood of Bruno Leone*, which would be more mythology than biography, and which would prefigure much of his later life, for example, the local pastor in Montemurro, Antonio Lapece, who made wooden toys for him. Don Antonio would doubtless be pleased to learn that one day his charge would perform for Pope Francis. This really did happen and is not a third dream. While the pontiff appeared to be struggling with the Neapolitan language, Bruno waved in front of him a small bottle of San Gennaro's blood. Maybe I should add a facsimile of a bottle of the saint's blood.

A trained architect, Bruno was hired by the City of Naples in 1979 during which time he worked additionally for the department of social services for children. It was about this time he came across the puppeteer Nunzio Zampella who would alter the course of his life. Zampella, convinced that the puppet tradition had died, sold his puppets to the museum of the Piccolo Teatro in Milan. Consumed with bitterness, he was at first reluctant to impart his knowledge. Why share knowledge that goes nowhere? Gradually, despite Zampella's discouraging noises, Bruno persuaded him to become his teacher. The main issue between them was the secret of the *pivetta*, which is the small double-edged object a puppeteer fits between the tongue and palate in order to produce Pulcinella's strange squawking voice. (Mr Punch would call it a call, swatchel, or swazzle.) A single mistake can result in one choking to death on the *pivetta*. (Salvatore Gatto swallowed his once. His maestro told him to eat a lot of potatoes.) The making and use of it were secrets Nunzio would not divulge because he wanted to push Bruno to produce, by trial and error, his own instrument. Bruno kept experimenting with different materials and when finally he got close to producing a *pivetta* Nunzio solemnly presented Bruno with his own, a moment, as one writer put it, so momentous its equivalent would be a king passing his sceptre to a young pretender. The maestro said to Bruno, 'My pupil must not be my parrot' and would then push him into territories hitherto unknown.

I think it's fair to say Bruno is the most inventive of the three puppeteers although there have been dark murmurings about authenticity. Was Bruno going beyond the pale sometimes? In 2002, together with some other puppeteers Bruno founded a puppet theatre which in the following year would be inaugurated officially as the Teatro delle Guarattelle. What was at first a hobby would one day take him all over the world as one of the great exponents of the tradition. Neapolitan remains the language of Pulcinella even when he performs to the Indians of the Amazon, the Tuareg of the Sahara (whose puppets are made of sheep and camel bones because there are no other materials available), or the Palestinians in the village of Abu Dis. Bruno goes about town on a big tricycle. The front bars support a small theatre, and it is from behind this he gives his impromptu performances. This is close to the old puppetry tradition of the streets. He also gives performances inside bigger venues, which is a distinct break with the tradition. When I saw him do the latter it was to the accompaniment of a rock band, which put the purists on edge.

An audience of one, it was my good fortune to be able to attend a dress rehearsal of *Pulchi, Shake and Speare* at his studio on the Corso Vittorio Emanuele, which is precisely where old meets new Naples. The plays begins with Bruno *as* Pulcinella *as* Shakespeare bent over a chess table with only a few pieces. The image is apt because as with a game of chess the figures are manipulated, so to speak, by their author. It begins as a production of *Macbeth* in which characters from the slopes about Vesuvius are introduced. Macbeth, in this production, is closer to the English Mr Punch than any Italian puppet. Soon Hamlet enters the scene. At one point he discovers Desdemona's

handkerchief in his own pocket. After killing the bad guy whose identity escapes me, Hamlet declares that 'to be or not to be is not a problem'. Then it is Romeo's turn, Romeo as a puppet and Giulietta as a marionette, which, given the mixing of two theatrical genres, is a most scandalous love. Tebaldo (Tybalt) is played by a Sicilian *pupo* who hails from yet another *guarattelle* tradition. And then we have Iago, who really is another version of Pasquale, reminiscing on Totò's performance as him in Pasolini's short film *Che cosa sono le nuvole?* ('What are the Clouds?'). Richard III appears as a Polichinelle (Pulcinella's French counterpart) and cleaves Iago's skull in two. Characters from the other plays get on stage and, while Richard III sleeps, conduct a final battle against Death. The show is interrupted by Bruno *as* Pulcinella *as* Shakespeare who chases Death away and judges the performance an absolute disaster. Bruno *as* Pulcinella *as* Shakespeare delivers the final words that comprise the moral of the fable, words that form the thrust of Agamben's book. 'Where there is a catastrophe, there is an escape route.' The players take their bows while Gianluca Fusco sings the Domenico Modugno song that gave the Pasolini film its title.* This is Shakespeare as Shakespeare could never have envisioned himself.

I perused Bruno's notebooks which are themselves museum pieces.

I asked Bruno about the connection between death and Pulcinella.

'Naples is one of the most important places to meet up with the problem of death. Death is a part of Pulcinella. Traditionally it is always a character inside the show. Death is always at its core. At the beginning of my career, when I was studying the puppets of my teacher, Nunzio Zampella, I was surprised to see that Death had a black head and white dress. I'd always imagined Death would be more like the figure in Ingmar Bergman's film *The Seventh Seal* with a white head and black cowl. I asked my maestro, "Why is Death in Pulcinella like this?" He told me it was because Death has the same colour as Pulcinella and as such it represents his conscience. This is very important. When you think of the basis of the Pulcinella show it is symbolic. Pulcinella enjoys life, Terasina, his girlfriend, is life, and another character, the *guappo*, is against life. The emblem of all bullies, whether *Camorristic*, political or religious, the *guappo* is like Cain in the biblical story, representing the violence of men, whereas the dog represents the violence of nature. The dog is our first fear. Our second fear is of our brother, our father, our state, all forms of authority as well as the unknown, death. Life without death is not possible. Death is not the end but a development. You can't develop without death otherwise there would be no life. This is important not only for the character but also in one's own experiences. If we are able to die, we are able to live. If we have fear

---

* Modugno made a great impact in the international music charts with his 1958 hit 'Nel blu dipinto di blu' which I can distinctly remember singing while on a playground swing.

of life, we stop. If we have fear of death, we stop life. This is at the roots of Pulcinella. Normally Pulcinella destroys Death, but sometimes, in some special shows, he might die.'

'I thought he lives forever!'

'Yes, he lives again. In one of Zampella's shows Pulcinella struggles and dies, but from inside him comes another Pulcinella who beats Death. I have developed this idea. I have a show about Don Giovanni in which Pulcinella is the confidante. Don Juan takes Pulcinella's girlfriend. He dies. At the end of the show Death arrives and announces that the show is finished. Suddenly Pulcinella revives and says, "It is not finished!" and turns into a giant.'

'So then,' I said, '*la commedia non è finita*.'

'I have done private shows for people who are about to die. The small child of a friend of mine was dying of cancer. I performed for him the day before he died. It was very hard. I do a lot of shows in hospitals for ill children, but I don't know whether or not they will die. This time I knew it was not possible to save him. The child asked for a show. It was hard, but I did it. I went and within ten minutes he was laughing. I could not see his father and mother. When I enter such a situation I don't change the show. I say to my audience, "I know you will die." If I laugh about death I say, "I don't know whether you will die. You are as alive as anybody is." It is important not to change the way I perform. Once in Switzerland I heard a mother in the theatre say to her four-year-old son, "Don't worry." When I finished the child said to his mother, "Mama, this death is nice." Once I went to school where I *did* change the show. The art director of the school was rather strange. When Death came the children cried out, "No, no, you have to kill Death." "I can't do this," I said. They stopped the show. So I killed Death for the first time. It was a surreal struggle. Afterwards I understood the children needed this because in that school the director was very hard on them. I never know what situation I'll find myself in. The show helps people, children especially, to resolve basic fears. So it is strange when teachers do not understand and say Pulcinella is too violent and so forth.'

'Some children are afraid,' I argued.

'Yes, sometimes, but then I'm very attentive to them. Normally, though, when children are afraid there is a problem within the family. I did a show in Brazil with children whose parents were suffering from AIDS. Their eyes were closed all the time. So I made the performance slow and delicate. After ten minutes they started to sing. I was so happy. It is important to hear people. Also if children are frightened I'll change, soften things a little. You have to be careful with children and respect them. Sometimes I'll say to a parent, "If your baby is frightened don't stay by the stage but near the door with your child in your arms." Sometimes they are frightened of the mask. When I see a child crying I put the mask away. When Pulcinella fights Death I come out and ask the child to kill Death. The child comes to the stage and beats him. In European culture the comedy is aggressive, whereas in other cultures this aggression is seen as rather strange. A clown is aggressive when he jokes with the public. This I don't like so much. My first time in Brazil I frightened people and it's strange, but I, too, began to be frightened. If there is a problem I need to be able to change in the space of a second the direction of the performance. Of course I bring my own way to any performance but I always listen to people.'

'What this leads to is how Pulcinella has entered the soul of the Neapolitan people,' I said, 'in that he seems to be inside them. Yesterday I spoke to Annamaria Cirillo at the Neapolis bookshop and I asked her who the three most important figures in Naples are. She put her fingers on her chin in a thoughtful manner and then replied, saying that in first place is San Gennaro, in second Totò, and in third Padre Pio. "Where is Pulcinella?" I asked her. I was somewhat surprised to hear that Padre Pio had squeaked in ahead of him. She said Pulcinella is inside all three of them.

This feels to me very ancient. Many people here have a figure or image of Pulcinella somewhere in the house. It is a bit like the household gods of ancient times.'

'I put on a show in which Pulcinella gives voice to San Gennaro. San Gennaro is a bit like Pulcinella, the difference being that Pulcinella hits people and San Gennaro doesn't. I performed this for the Pope. Also I wrote another story about Don Pulcinella de la Mancha. Surprised, you might ask yourself, "Can Pulcinella write?" Yes, but that's *his* secret. As far as the general public is concerned he can't write. I like your dreams. You dreamed of me. The last show I did in Minneapolis starred Trump as the Devil. Pulcinella beats and kills him.'

'As you are still alive your audience must have been mostly Democrats.'

'Pulcinella performed for Hezbollah in Lebanon, also for Palestinians, but then he played in Jerusalem as well. We spoke against terrorists of all kinds. Pulcinella is not ideological. If he is a revolutionary, it's only because of his love for life. This is very hard for any power to take. A love of life is against all power, all authority, even religious.'

'I didn't know before coming here how deeply Pulcinella has entered the psyche of the Neapolitan people.'

'If you begin to go inside Pulcinella you'll find it is so deep there is no end. I have worked on him for thirty-five years. I can't stop because I can't find a way to discover who he is. Pulcinella is rather more profound than Mr Punch. Punch is part of Pulcinella, not all of him, of course, whereas Pulcinella is Mr Punch and many other things.'

'What happens when you take Pulcinella from the street into the theatre? How much is lost?'

'My Pulcinella is normally in the street, but he is strong enough to be anywhere. I have played in the opera house, a show based on Stravinsky's music to an audience of eight hundred people. I have performed Pulcinella many times in the theatre and he is stronger than any actor, stronger than the biggest orchestra. It's incredible. Pulcinella is always something more, so small yet so strong.'

'Do you feel the future of Pulcinella is secure?'

'I think so. Sometimes this is difficult to see because so much of our system is the media, TV, and so forth. Pulcinella is a big but secret development. When I started out in 1978 I was the only one. Now there are five or six Pulcinellas in Naples alone. In France there might be twenty, in Cuba there's one using my puppets, in England there's Mr Punch. It had almost disappeared in France, Spain, Russia, and elsewhere, but there has been a big development in a small situation, which is different from mass media. TV does not speak of this. People always enjoy the performance. I think it is a show for the future. We mustn't forget Pulcinella speaks to the end. In the end, we are men. We can't all become martinets. It's not possible. Pulcinella helps people make a stand against authority. We need him because the powers that be don't like him. The future needs this. There is a hunger out there for Pulcinella. It is hard to understand but I know what I am saying is true. It is not a dream. It is normal to be pessimistic, but remember that thirty years ago Pulcinella almost disappeared. I played Pulcinella and now he is everywhere in the world.'

'All art is resistance,' I said.

'Yes, but Pulcinella is special. Art is one of the things that will save humanity. Pulcinella might die, but he will be born again. He never dies. He knows how to die without dying. This has a big philosophical meaning.'

'When I hear you talk, Pulcinella is not so much a puppet as a spirit.'

'Nunzio Zampella who had little schooling felt the same as me. The teaching was philosophical above technical. Pulcinella for me represents something that all Neapolitans want to be and yet at the same time he is inside each one of us.'

'As in the spirit of trying to escape the harsh conditions of life here?'

'Yes, but it is also trying to live life by not taking our problems too seriously because, as you know, we have a lot of them.'

What would Pulcinella say about the things a philosopher had to say about him? I met Giorgio Agamben at the Italian Cultural Institute in London where he gave an introductory talk to a performance by Bruno Leone. I hadn't fully taken on board that I'd been chatting to one of the great minds of our time. I should have been more on the ball because my late friend, the poet Christopher Middleton, had referred to him in my presence a number of times, and a positive word from him was like a stamp of validation. A modest figure, Giorgio Agamben had the appearance of one who might be happy enough to talk about the weather but otherwise did not wish to be disturbed too much lest it put his finely honed thoughts into disarray. A scholar of the 'bare life', the books that comprise his mighty Homo Sacer series are of particular importance. The other thing about him which gives me pause is that as a young man he played the role of Philip the Apostle in Pier Paolo Pasolini's *The Gospel According to St Matthew*, surely the most deeply spiritual film ever made by an avowed atheist. I can't determine whether it is logical or absurd that the latest title in the Homo Sacer series should be about Pulcinella. Say it comes as a surprise. Giorgio Agamben was soft-spoken and had a sympathetic, rather beautiful, face.

'When you were in London with Agamben I missed a great opportunity to talk to you together. We know Pulcinella is Shakespeare, we know he is Don Quixote, and we know too that he is a better painter than Picasso, but what about Pulcinella the philosopher? You told me once that actually he is a bit stupid, but then maybe you were having a bad day with him. Shall we pretend Agamben is sitting here and that we are about to combine his and your ideas to get at Pulcinella's philosophical side?'

'Agamben gave me ideas about Pulcinella that had never occurred to me,' Bruno replied, 'but before we speak about Pulcinella we must first ask what he means to me. The answer has changed over time. Thirty years ago, I thought about him in one way and ten years later in another way and today yet again he has changed for me. We can only barely understand the complexity of a character so simple. At the beginning it had to do with learning a tradition. The first thing I learned was that this tradition is really very contemporary. It is difficult to think of a tradition as modern, but it was for me. I saw an English rock musician, Ted Milton, doing Mr Punch. The show was very modern, but I could see in it the whole tradition of Punch. The show used the language of Dadaism and Surrealism. I saw that the tradition had something in common with the actual world. The same is true for Pulcinella. Although it is an ancient thing it is best explained through the language of the avant-garde. My first idea about Pulcinella was as something universal but also very particular. It was experimental and traditional at the same time, ancient and modern. My ideas have developed since then. This concept of the universal and the particular, the traditional and the contemporary, are concepts that are linked to time and space. That's why they have now changed somewhat. In order to understand it we draw upon the things we have been taught, but this art is outside time and space. I understood this complicated concept from practical experience alone because it is difficult to develop in the mind. Travelling through the world, I experienced the show many times and what I saw is that in different times and different places I had direct contact with people who felt the show belonged to them.'

'So what you are saying is that you have observed this world-wide, but that in the subconscious of all people there is a Pulcinella residing there.'

'Pulcinella is a language. We may compare Pulcinella to Esperanto, a language that was invented so as to communicate in a universal way, but in order to communicate in Esperanto first you have to study it whereas Pulcinella is a language we all know without having to study. My show is a language through which I can communicate with the whole world, with all cultures, at different times. It's a universal language. I use the word "language" although really it's a different form of language, very different from that with which one normally communicates. It is different from the canonical meaning of language. Esperanto is a language that uses an alphabet and words. I may use Neapolitan, English, or Spanish but if they are associated with sound and movement they become something rather more complex, a different thing from ordinary language. This has allowed me to communicate with many people without knowing their language. And they don't know mine. There is a person with whom I've had long conversations that are not easily expressible. A nomad from the desert, he speaks only Arabic. I don't speak Arabic and he didn't speak any language I know, but we managed to communicate all the same. Also I did a show in Chiapas with Mexican Indians. The audience in front of me understood something else through their idea of what was happening on stage. There had been communication of a kind, but I had spoken their language without knowing it, without an awareness of what I was saying, and from their side they had understood something that belonged to their world. The communication was there, but it is difficult to explain in words alone. We communicate with words and language, but the possibilities to communicate are huge. There are other ways that are not just words and language. Pulcinella represents one of these ways. That's why he is outside the categories of time and space. Anything we study needs to be framed in time and space.'

'So the whole world communicates in Neapolitan!'

'Neapolitan is a means not necessarily linked to language. It's the whole. We are hitting on a philosophical question: what was language before it became language? This is not only a philosophical question but also a practical one. How did man manage to communicate before words? I am lucky enough to remember. When I was a child, not yet able to speak, I made a *presepe*, a nativity, in imitation of my father's. I showed it to my mother. "See this beautiful nativity I made." But I couldn't yet speak when I said this. My mother didn't get a word of what I said. She answered with other things because obviously she did not understand me. I remember saying to myself, how is it possible that I can understand them but they can't understand me? This means there was a level of communication that was clear to me but not to them. I concluded that adults were stupid. This demonstrates that the language we have is the very limit of communication. The theatre of Pulcinella has something of this. I'm not saying Pulcinella represents this concept fully, but that he has something of this mysterious language that comes earlier and is stronger than communication.'

'T. S. Eliot says that poetry can communicate before it is understood.'

'Pulcinella represents, although maybe in a small way, a solution to this problem. For me it meant much to have an instrument to communicate with a world very few people have access to. Sometimes I realise I'm communicating with people on a level that escapes language. If I had to rely on language only, I wouldn't be able to say what I want. When I communicate with people through Pulcinella I know that I am communicating in another way, in another language that is not the normal one because in normal language I have no words to explain these kinds of concepts. I travel the world and talk to many different people from different places. Even if we don't speak the same language we communicate, thanks to Pulcinella. That is tangible evidence of the fact that there is a different level of communication between humans. The main purpose of this theatre is to show that there is another way to communicate – not between races, not between different peoples – but between human beings because they can understand each other. If philosophically we link all this to what Giorgio Agamben writes, things intertwine even more. Agamben's book on Pulcinella takes the example of Giandomenico Tiepolo. The main thing he says in this book is: *Ubi fracassorium, ibi fuggitorium* ("Where there is a catastrophe, there is an escape route"). There are other important things to talk about, but let's focus on this phrase. Agamben describes Pulcinella's mask, his non-expressive face, and notes the importance of the fact that Pulcinella doesn't make grimaces. Agamben says that comedy is closer to philosophy than tragedy. It is said that when he died Plato had a book on mimes under his head. There's Giordano Bruno, and Erasmus whose book *The Praise of Folly* says you have to be a bit mad to be able to really understand things. Agamben uses the example of Giandomenico Tiepolo who at seventy years of age, when the Venetian Republic had been sold out by the French to Austria and a thousand years of history deleted, retreated to his room at the Villa di Zianigo and began to draw Pulcinella. Agamben who is an important philosopher, also seventy years of age, thinks we are living in a catastrophic period and, following the example of Tiepolo, he brings Pulcinella into his world. He thinks the way out of this terrible moment is through Pulcinella. When I met Agamben what he told me is that the real Pulcinella resides not in the mask but in the voice. There are Pulcinellas all over the world, but only the Neapolitan one has a mask. What they have in common is the artificial voice. It is, he says, the mask of the voice. It is universal for all the Pulcinellas in the world. I was very impressed by that phrase *the mask of the voice*. Agamben mentions Henry Mayhew's *London Labour and the London Poor* (1851) in which the author asks Mr Punch about his voice.* The voice in Pulcinella shows there is something more to say when it is impossible to talk any more, just as the *lazzi*, the comical movements of Pulcinella, show there is something more to do when every action becomes impossible. This is the conclusion Agamben reached after speaking with me. This is the first step towards a new world, an escape from catastrophe.'

'Pulcinella *is* Naples,' I said. 'Why Naples?'

'Naples is the capital city for him, one of the most important in existence, which is why he chose it because it is a city that lets you speak to the world. A real Neapolitan is one who defends his territory. The wise, the ignorant, the good, and the thieves are all people who have a role in this city and although they may not have deep ideas about it they will defend their city all the same. The *real* Neapolitan is not necessarily a Neapolitan. He

---

* Mayhew's Punchman told him: 'The great difficulty in performing Punch consists in the speaking, which is done by a call or whistle in the mouth. Porsini brought the calls into this country with him from Italy and I larnt the use of mine from Porsini himself. I was six months in perfecting the use of it and now I'm reckoned one of the best speakers in the whole purfession. When I made my first appearance as a regular performer of Punch on my own account, I did feel uncommon narvous, to be sure, though I know'd the people couldn't see me behind the baize, still I felt as if the eyes of the country were upon me. It was as much as ever I could do to get the words out, and keep the figures from shaking. The fust person who went out with me was my wife. She used to stand outside and keep the boys from peeping through the baize and she used to collect the money afterwards as well. She's been dead these five years now.'

can be from anywhere in the world, English, French, Spanish, or American. If you feel that Naples is a universal capital then you, too, can be a real Neapolitan. When a tourist goes to Venice or Florence he remains a tourist, but when someone who is not from here comes to Naples he can take on the lifestyle of Neapolitan people. A lot of people fall in love with Naples because they recognise something they don't have and which they need.'

'Well,' I replied, 'Naples is a perfect mirror to my own spiritual anarchy.'

'This is the sole condition to be Neapolitan.' Bruno laughed. 'It is not an anagraphic condition or anything that falls into a neat category. It is something you *feel*. The most representative of holy fools is Pulcinella, which is why he chose Naples.'

'So *he* chose Naples and not the other way round?'

'I think so. Naples can be a fairy tale city, but open the wrong door and it can be a mess. You have to be careful to get the right door.'

Agamben writes:

The genealogy of Pulcinella does not simply go back, as folklorists argue, to the realm of the dead. He is neither dead nor a *larva*, that is, a malign ghost that takes the form of the deceased and infests the world of the living … He properly belongs to neither the world of the dead nor that of the living: he is here – irreparably here, in an inaccessible elsewhere.

The way Pulcinella seemingly moves between life and death is something I put to Bruno, and Bruno being Bruno – Bruno as Pulcinella – sprang a surprise.

'This idea is very important for me. I may be joking, but then maybe not, because recently I discovered the secret of immortality.'

'Oh, Bruno!'

He gave a modest shrug. 'Nobody's perfect!'

'Yes, but it's a big thing.'

Bruno pondered this for a moment before continuing.

'Somebody I told this to said, "I wouldn't want this. I'd prefer to die." I said, "Be careful because mortality is like the wheel of immortality." Immortality without mortality does not exist. The one needs the other in order to be. And the link to Pulcinella is there because mortality is change. So the born and the reborn can't exist without mortality. The baby that lives in the mother's belly is like a fish because it has life, but when it is born the fish that was in the belly dies. There can't be birth without dying. It is the same for the artist. I'll put a lot of effort into making a product, but if that product doesn't die I won't be able to make another one. A late friend of mine, Otello Sarti, gave me a heart-shaped stone. "This is my heart," he said, "keep it." He was a Communist, an atheist, without faith or belief in paradise. One of the last times we met he changed his mind. "I think," he said, "life exists after death." A lot of atheists change their minds before dying. I replied, "Okay, so what is this life after death?" Otello said, "The life after death is the life of other people." When you recognise that other people are so important to you, you are not alone. A part of you lives on in other people. They are different from you, to be sure, because you on your own can't do whatever you want to do, and so you need other people in order to do something you can't do on your own.'

I found myself, just then, staring at a Gordian knot with not so much as a nail file in my possession.

'And when you realise these things,' Bruno continued, 'you realise that you are immortal and you are not scared any more about death. If you apply the same concept to other people. You have to *feel* this concept, it is not enough to talk about it. If you lose someone very close to you this person doesn't live in his own memory but can live in another person. You can transpose. You don't feel your death or other people's death. This is my personal interpretation.'

'Does Pulcinella agree with you?'

'It's impossible to know *what* he thinks. We know that in his story he dies and is reborn many times. Death for him is part of a constant cycle. It doesn't represent the end of him because he is reborn every time. That is why the relationship between birth and death runs so deep in him. Without death, he is like a stone, lifeless.'

'It is no accident surely that both Pulcinella and *anime pezzentelle* come out of Naples.'

'Pulcinella dies and is reborn, but where does this happen? It's in a world of the unknown, a world of things we can't see, which is what these three elements – *anime pezzentelle*, Pulcinella, and the Neapolitan people – have in common. We live with a world we can't see, but which we know is there. Our relationship with it is permitted by Pulcinella and the *anime pezzentelle* because they are both links to the unknown.'

'Would you describe this world as pagan?'

'It is definitely not the Christian paradise, but I can't say it's pagan either. Giordano Bruno speaks of the infinite possibilities of the world. Maybe it is close to paganism, but then there are many worlds within this city. When you walk from Via Duomo onto Via Tribunali you go into another world that does not communicate with the first one. Sanità does not communicate with Vomero and Fontanelle does not communicate with Forcella. You will find a world of rich people here, a world of thieves there. They don't communicate although sometimes they fight each other. We are used to this idea of there being many different worlds. A person will ask the *anime pezzentelle* to enter his dream and give him the numbers for the lottery. What this means is that there exists a world where time has another meaning because *anime pezzentelle* know the future. *Anime pezzentelle*, Pulcinella, the fool, the poor, children – these are five ways to communicate with a fantastic world we can't see. We may talk about Pulcinella as a human being but at the same time we can talk of him as something that doesn't really exist. You can't meet him at the local bar.'

'So Pulcinella has his secret too.'

'I have my own idea about Pulcinella's secret. It's a secret that everyone knows. It complicates matters it being a secret that stays a secret even when everyone knows what it is. Once I had to do a show for children. We arrived at the puppet theatre an hour early and found it was already full of kids. I couldn't start because I was waiting for a friend so I had to find a way to get the children to play before the beginning of the show. After telling them some stories I said, "I have no more stories, so ask me questions." "How do you do the Pulcinella voice?" one of them asked. "That is a secret I can't reveal," I said. Then came another question. "Okay, so tell us Pulcinella's secret." "It is a secret so you should try to guess it," I replied, "but I will tell you something. The secret of Pulcinella is to understand the importance of things that are not important." They sat in silence for about ten minutes. Then a girl of ten said excitedly to me, "I understand!" She came over to me and whispered in my ear, "It is love." That for me is Pulcinella's secret, *love*. Everyone knows what love is, or thinks he does, but it remains a secret because it is impossible to explain. The secret of Pulcinella is you can say it to everybody but it still remains a secret.'

'Does Agamben support your ideas or do you support his or are you leaning together in the same direction?'

'I can't afford to have these debates with Agamben because he is brilliant and I'm not, but I think philosophy is very close to madness.'

'When I think of your maestro, Nunzio Zampella, surely if he heard this conversation he'd be puzzled. What we have now is surely a new kind of Pulcinella, such as he would not recognise.'

'We had the same conversations as we are having now, maybe not quite with the same elements, but along similar lines.'

'And of course Naples was the seat of philosophy for centuries.'

'A lot of good people, such as our mayor, think poor people are practical and just work, but they think and talk philosophically about things. Sometimes, in order to be closer to the poor, the mayor will say a rude word or a phrase in Neapolitan, but that kind of approach does not make him one of us.'

We left the studio and stopped at a small café on *il Corso* where Bruno had something important to impart to me, maybe even more important than the life eternal.

'When I was a child I loved elephants. I always imagined an elephant beside me in my garden at home. When I went to the zoo I played with the elephant. It was always like this. Many years later, I fell deeply in love with a girl. One night I had a dream. I was living in Palaeolithic times and I was living with this girl near the sea, in a place which I didn't think was Sicily but a tiny island close by. In the dream she and I were playing with a small elephant. When I awoke it wasn't so much a dream as something I had remembered for the whole of my life. The dream was that powerful. After many years, I was in Sicily and from there I went to the island of Levanzo, an archaeological site, where I stayed for a while. An old man lived there, who told me that in this very spot they found the fossil of a small elephant of a species that does not exist any more. When I visited the museum I discovered that the island had been joined to the mainland during Palaeolithic times.'

Was Bruno's adoration more for the elephant or the girl, I wonder. Or was it one of those perfect triangles such as history produces every so often when it's in the mood for love? Was Pulcinella sired from a combination of elements crazier than the craziest dream can produce? That is Pulcinella's secret, of course. Maybe he doesn't know he knows. Maybe he is waiting to be fed a cue. Out there, where the last drop from the drain-pipe falls with a thunderous splash and an octopus makes a dash for freedom, it's a secret everybody knows, but as I am its most recent, most temporary custodian I dare not say what it is.

Boom

An onomatopoetic word: a tourist guide dropping a heavy stone onto the surface of Solfatara, an explosion in a factory making stuff it ought not to, a big man's voice, the sound the tammorra makes. This phase of our journey begins with a familiar thumping against sun-dried goatskin stretched over a circular wooden frame. This is not to suggest the tammorra was born here. Some variant of it can be found going all the way back through ancient Greek, Egyptian, and Sumerian cultures, and it accompanied the Dionysian rites that were alive and well in Magna Graecia. What those old revellers aimed for in their music and dance may have changed spiritual clothes but not its substance. The distance between the 'Great Mother' Cybele, the ancient world's goddess of the earth, and the Virgin Mother is not as great as some Christians would like to think, although if time were to go into reverse devotees of the former would probably remove some of the latter's monotheistic traces as not adequately reflecting the plurality of existence. Those ancient dances were ecstatic, sometimes quite beyond the pale. *BOOM*. Another purpose for the instrument was its employment in physical and spiritual healing ceremonies. The tammorra was the instrument that addressed, and in turn was addressed by, the soul of the people.

So it was then, so it is now. It is at the very heart of the *tammur-riata*, which, as with Stravinsky's *Rite of Spring*, is a celebration of fertility and sexual love. *BOOM BOOM*. The dance is as erotic as it is chaste, a dynamic that has been all but forgotten in modern culture, the man's and the woman's bodies never touching, although the lyrics to some of the songs they dance to leave no one in doubt as to their sexual import. There are even masculine and feminine approaches to the playing of the instrument, the men holding it in the right hand and the women in the left, which is how the ancients perceived the division of the sexes, the right side for men and the left, the sinister side, for women.*

Paola Gargiulo at the Officina della Tammorra on Vico San Severino is a maker of the instrument, a seller of it. She also gives musical workshops. Some nights you can hear the thumping when you pass her place. Troubling though the idea of such workshops can be, and in many eyes signalling the death-knell of popular culture, there can be no doubting her sincerity. She has a peculiarly Catholic take on the history and playing of the instrument, but her religious exclusivity is not a barrier to absorbing the points she makes. If anything, what she says is an amplification of what already resides in this rather pagan heart of mine. She brings the distant past into the present without sacrificing her religious principles. I feel no contradiction whatsoever between past and present: the tammorra was put in the service of the gods and so it continues, the only difference may be that the old gang of deities has been whittled down to one. These are my words, not hers: I'll take the brunt of whatever she wishes to throw at me. She also has a deep distrust of what she calls an intellectual approach to the instrument, which I took to be a quiet warning. We began with the instrument itself and

---

* The word for 'left' in Italian is *sinistro* (masc.) or *sinistra* (fem.) and the phrase for 'left-handedness' is *uso della mano sinistra*. Women have been long known to be the more sinister of the two sexes.

as she spoke, a wealth of experience in her passionate voice, it became incumbent on me to remember I am but a trespasser on an ancient turf she struggles to protect, which she knows is subject to contaminants from outside. One thing bothered me, the souvenir tammorras with painted scenes on them that she sells to tourists, but then she told me she needs to do so in order to survive. Anyway they are unplayable. At times, I am too much the aesthete at other people's expense.

'When one considers its circular shape,' Paola began, 'what we have is an infinite line, a world that never finishes, the very essence of life. It represents the human will to escape time itself because only then might we touch the divine. The tammorra is played in two different rhythms, which represent the mother and baby in the womb. All people recognise this music because they are reminded of their mother's heartbeat in the womb. It has an infinite number of symbols and meanings. The tammorra is part of our cultural treasure, but it represents not only the music of Naples but also the songs of the people of the countryside, and is therefore the song of the world because, ultimately, every human being is a son or daughter of farmers in the countryside, and so they are also children of the world.'

'How did you get started with the tammorra?'

'I had some big problems in my life. My parents and their parents listened to this music. Although it can't make me happy in and of itself, it distracts and calms me. It is also deeply tied to religion. Many people forget this when they dance the tammurriata. The festivals of the Seven Madonnas are pilgrimages made in the direction of the Virgin Mary, but instead they are becoming increasingly pagan in character. As a Catholic I'd like to bring the tammurriata back into the fold of the Church where it is sanctioned. It is a dance that expresses love and God is love, but it has become too passionate, too sexual, and I would prefer it to be returned to a purer love. It is almost hell for me when I see people dance in a transgressive way. Thanks to the tammorra my faith was strengthened. I became truly Catholic only after playing it.'

Could it be what Paola was complaining about was not so much the erotic as a loss of balance? There seems no reason to separate the sacred from the profane when neither can exist in isolation. Any deeper reading of religious poetry, for example, will sooner or later take one into the realm of the erotic. Consider the mystic poets, the Spaniard, San Juan de la Cruz, who academic clowns now say celebrated same-sex love, or Sor Juana Inés de la Cruz, recently dubbed 'Mexico's most dangerous nun', which is great as far as it goes – mystics always walk on the wild side. And in the Muslim world – why not go there as well? – Rumi is another case in point. Those God-inebriated poets transgressed in ways incomprehensible to the modern mind, and maybe Paola Gargiulo was simply trying to prevent me from making an awful hash of things. I could see she thought I was sinking into an academic morass although I'd have liked her to realise it was not so, that all I wanted of her was for us to be able to bypass certain obstacles. Pier Paolo Pasolini's statement that folk music is 'la storia in atto', history in the making, seems perfectly adequate. As such it belongs to all time whatever the circumstances, religious or otherwise.

'At the same time,' I asked her, 'does this instrument not have a dualistic nature, sacred and profane?'

'I would like to express more of the sacred than the profane,' she replied. 'This music should express eternal and infinite love. I can't dance well with my partner, whether it be a man or a woman, if it is too competitive. The tradition vanished for a time, but it has returned and remains strong because of our religious faith. The values this music talks about are almost not of our time. They are about harvesting the wheat, ploughing the fields. If the tradition of the tammorra were to end we would lose that period of time when those values counted for so much, but fortunately, thanks to this music, this belief in old times remains in our lives. It is there for whoever needs God. Some people need Him to help solve their problems and some people are happy and don't need Him at all. The music, however, is a consequence of religious belief.'

'But is it not also a continuation of ancient belief?' I argued. 'The other night I saw on the street the same thing one sees in the mosaic of Dioskourides. Pompeii lives on in the streets of Naples. I believe there is, as you say, the religious side, but surely it still has its origins in pagan times.'

'The books say it is a continuation,' she replied, 'but they show only pictures. This is a tradition that goes from mother to daughter, father to son. The sister of Moses played the tammorra. When I started with it, it was something I recognised in my subconscious. It mustn't be made fashionable because then it becomes competitive and it is not cathartic any more. Many people don't appreciate it because they don't concentrate on the sound and rhythm. In order to appreciate it fully one needs to be hypnotised and to immerse oneself in the music, but to truly enjoy it you have to understand that these dances and songs all lead back to the life in the fields. After a hard day of work it was one way to relax your body and it produces a throaty sound in the voices. Watching it from afar, from an intellectual point of view, is not the same as living within the music itself. The tradition coming from older people is more authentic. When I went to a recent tammorra festival there were these kids from Naples playing and it was almost disturbing to my ears. I was about to leave when a second group from one of the villages around Vesuvius came on and what they played was more authentic than what the kids from Naples played because they lived the life. They were born there.'

'It has been used as funeral music.'

'A priest will sometimes allow tammorra players into the church provided the songs are directed towards the Virgin Mary but, yes, I think it's true that the departed soul is helped along by the tammorra.'

'What makes a maestro? How does one measure this?'

'Strength, physical and mental, wisdom. You have to be strong in your mind to be able to withstand all the chaos that occurs in life. A master transmits inner strength and makes everyone experience what he does. My master says he does not believe in God, but I know he believes in Him more than many of those who claim they believe. He is virtuous and radiates positive energy. You can have a big group of tammorra players where everyone but a few feel positive energy and it will be enough to nullify the negative feeling of those few. The common people manage to communicate better with simple methods whereas intellectuals are wary and keep their distance and are close-minded. The city has a great deal of solitude whereas the country is more open-hearted. I recognise that one can better oneself and become more humble and happy, so it is not only an instrument but a way to communicate with other people all over the world. If you don't love this world, you will go crazy.'

She was absolutely right, of course. A dislike of the things of this world is not what you want to take to bed with you because when morning comes the heaviness of the night before will be awfully hard to shake. Crazy is what one becomes. And here, where death hangs close, it is quite unaffordable.

If what makes a maestro is strength, 'physical and mental', then Marcello Colasurdo has it in abundance. I first heard of him from Pina Cipriani at whose husband's funeral he played. As I got closer to the subject of the tammorra his name came to me from several directions at once, as a *portatore della tradizione* ('bearer of the tradition'), a founding member of the musical Gruppo Operaio 'E Zézi whose most striking song 'Vesuvio' contains the apocalyptic message 'Tu tien' 'mman a te' sta vita meja' ('You hold in your hands this life of mine') and to the rhythm of which one may merrily dance all the way to Hades, and a *femminiello* who, from time to time, puts on a wig, rouge, and woman's clothes. I'd heard that he even appeared in one of Federico Fellini's films. The rock musician Peter Gabriel, a fan, recorded Colasurdo when the latter was with the group Spaccanapoli. I went to see Colasurdo at his home at the edge of the nearby industrial town of Pomigliano d'Arco where from his window he has a lovely view of the 'swearing mountain'* which, as long as it remains a mountain, is a friend to those who harvest grapes on its slopes. I had little problem finding the place. A young man with a teardrop tattooed at the corner of his right eye, when he saw me approach, pointed to the top floor of the apartment building, saying Marcello was in. There could be no other reason for me to be there. A teardrop tattoo means either that its bearer had taken someone's life or that he

---

* So described in the song 'Vesuvio'.

has suffered the loss of someone close to him. I discovered later that his younger sister had died.

It was a modern apartment block – drab, soulless, not the worst by any means and at one point probably desirable. It is a wonder such places are able to harbour such deep humanity, almost as if some infernal architect had been commissioned to destroy the soul and didn't quite manage it. The problem is not Italian. The problem is everywhere. The actual flat where Marcello Colasurdo lives seems to belong to another time and place. There is a slightly odd sense of being suspended, of there being nothing outside its walls, maybe just a rope ladder descending to my writing desk back in London, although every so often one is triggered back to reality by the sound of women's voices in the hallways, audible at every level of the building, usually a big commotion over very little. Opera is Italian, theatre Greek, Campania their bastard child. The sunlight struggles to get inside Marcello's place. Who allowed him just one window? Maybe, though, with Vesuvius loitering outside, it's enough. If it decides to erupt all one need do is draw the curtain.

One man's clutter is another man's treasure. We spoke inside an area just wide enough to accommodate Marcello's wheelchair on either side of which were heaps of possessions, among them a large clock dropped inside a tammorra, old instruments, a Mexican sombrero, wicker baskets of clothes, a photograph of Totò as the uniformed *pazzariello* in the movie *L'oro di Napoli* ('The Gold of Naples'), a couple of gigantic black dolls with open mouths that gave them a slightly demonic aspect, a small *presepe*,*

---

* The *presepi*, for which Naples is justly famous, are elaborately-carved Nativity scenes in which the manger and often the surrounding villages appear together with their inhabitants. They can be small or several square metres in size. The central focus is the manger where Christ was born, with figurines of the Holy Family. The Three Wise Men are added on 6 January. Roberto De Simone

a plastic Christmas tree. It may well be that with his illness, which resulted in the partial amputation of one of his feet, things have got away on him a little. Still, despite the chaos, the medications scattered about the place, there was nothing one would describe as depressing or unwholesome about the atmosphere. Marcello, with his booming voice, is one of the most animated and enthusiastic of figures. There is something rather motherly about him. Theatrical he most certainly is, a human tornado. Pasquale Scialò relates how when he and Marcello were in a fish market being interviewed for a TV programme on the relationship between fishing and folk music, Marcello suddenly grabbed a live octopus and holding it aloft sang at the top of his voice.

The first thing I wanted to know was his recollection of Franco Nico's funeral when Pina got up to dance around her husband's coffin.

'We have this song that says "I am blessing the milk that I am giving to you, which comes from this breast and that you now take with your mouth to feed yourself."* I wanted to pay tribute to him. I played the tammorra as in the ancient tradition to salute the dead because he was crossing the bridge from this to the other side. It was similar to the milk song only this time I sang over a carnation. I addressed him as if he were this flower. "I am blessing all the water I gave to you. / I have taken with my little bucket all the water from the sea." I made up the phrases as I went along, which is what we *cantatori* do, a song a mother might sing for her dead child or a woman for her deceased lover, a song of blessing

---

has written a history of the *presepe* in which he dwells on its obscure symbolism.
* Marcello Colasurdo sang the lines, as he would with all the songs he quoted. I have struggled for the right words to define his somewhat rough voice, but now I find it has been described as 'a voice born on the border between the fields of Pomigliano and the sirens of the factories', which feels just right to me.

for all that you have given that person when he was alive because everything goes back to Mother Earth. We go through a circular or return gesture. Once upon a time people would fill the graves with bread, grain, and wine in order to give back to Mother Earth what has been taken from her. This looks very much like what the ancient Egyptians did. We call death "the nose of a dog" because the human skull has this shape of a dog's nose where the person's nose used to be. "You have gone with a dog's nose, you are a traitor / you are betraying us." Often if it was an important person in the family or the head of a community who died they would add the image of the main wooden beam in the house. "You are betraying us because you were the best, and you are gone. / The support of the house is gone. / You preferred to go with a dog's nose." The ancient Greeks sang funeral songs as a tribute to the dead.'

'When Pina did her dance around the coffin,' I asked, 'was this the completion of an ancient cycle?'

'Yes, the circle of death and life.'

'And what are in those songs?'

'People would sing stories of the lives of the deceased, about when they fell in love, and how, if the family didn't want the marriage, maybe because they were too young, they arranged for an elopement. This was called the *fuitina*. They would spend the night together, and because she was no longer a virgin, it was compulsory for them to marry. The widow would sing to her dead husband, "Do you remember when my mother and father did not want us together and we jumped on a steam train." We have a saying about love: "When two people want it, even if a hundred don't, not even the strength of the sun can separate them."'

We had got from death to marriage in the twinkling of an eye. Some people do so in reverse order.

'There is a difference between the *cantante* and the *cantatore*,' Marcello continued. 'The *cantante* is simply a singer whereas the *cantatore* improvises or, rather, creates the lyrics and music, telling stories that come from real life. I am signed up with the music union as a composer not because I write but because of my function as a *cantatore* who extemporises. I am a composer who inhabits the moment. You have to pass an examination to be signed into the SIAE [the Italian Society of Authors and Publishers], which means writing a song and so I wrote one for Umberto Bossi, the leader of Lega Nord (the Northern League), a political party in the eighties that sought the secession of the north from the south of Italy. They were very prejudiced towards us. I went to Rome with my instrument and there, on the spot, composed a song against him. There was a person on the commission from Nola, a town not far from here, who knew exactly what I was talking about. He said, "The maestro is right, let him in."'

At the risk of reducing a complex musical history to a gobbet, the musical products of the Campania include the *canto a fronna,* which is just for voice. It derives from the Italian *fronda*, ('a leafy branch') and can be sounded over a great distance. When addressed to a young girl (*figliola*) or sung directly to the Madonna it becomes the *canto a figliola*. The *canto a distesa*, which translates literarily as a 'full-throated song', has its origins in country life, when during harvesting the peasants, in order to keep each other company, would sing their messages from one field to another. It is also said to have been used by prisoners to communicate to people on the outside. It was a way to get the news, call and response, like the blues in the cotton fields. The same songs were sung with or without tammorra during different celebrations. The canto *a figliola* has nothing to do with the *canzone napoletana*. It is country music. *Tammurriata* is song, literally 'song on a drum', tammorra, and dance.

'The dancer acts out what the *cantatore* is saying,' Marcello continued. 'The *tammurriata* is a challenge, it is love, and it is recalling the harvest work, the seeding … this is the seed … they take it from here.'

Marcello's hands winged away from his crotch, not lewdly, but as an expression of the workings of nature.

'You have different kinds of dances depending on what you want to say. The dance between two men is a challenge to get hold of land or a woman. When two women dance together they are saying "We are ready because our primavera, our spring, is ready. You can come and court us. We are ready for you." It is primavera for the men as well, they are ready, but you add the element of competition among them. The dancers must look at each other. It may be a loving look or a challenging one, but looking at each other is very important. When they tangle their legs they are actually fighting. One of them tries to push the other out of the circle. The winner goes and gets the woman. When a man and a woman dance it is mating. The *votata*, which means "flipping" or "turning", is more sensuous. At some point you change direction. The dancers do what the singers tell them to and so either they change direction at the end of eight or twelve beats or when the story is finished. All this takes place inside a circle. They could form a square but no, they make a circle like the moon, the earth, the sun, the planets, or the tammorra itself. It is also the mother's belly in which conception takes place. All the people forming that circle are the chromosomes, male and female. It is the human arena, and within that circle you sing of life and death. There is a choreography that goes with it. It is not that the people gather on their own, it is the dancers who set the shape, who organise the disposition of the people watching them in a circle. The singers, the dancers, the observers, they all have a specific role, but they have to be together because nothing ever happens by itself. The ancient dances were circle dances. It is probable that the Roman arenas and stages derive from them. There is a circle of people, families and friends, supporting them. "Do this, do that," they cry. "Make it stronger!" In the tammurriata they always told their own story and they still do. They tell the story of your life, your humanity.'

'When young people dance the tammurriata,' I asked him, 'do they remember its significance?'

'They are told what it is. No one told me. I just understood. But yes, they know.'

'Would you be willing to speak of your life in more detail? About being sent to the orphanage, for instance.'

'I am surprised you know about this. I was the son of a very young, very lonely mother. I carry her maiden name and am honoured to do so. A single mother, she didn't have the means to raise me. She was not from Naples. I was born in Campobasso and then we came to Naples where we were placed in an institution. I was three years old. We lived there in the Esposito* and then my mother left me to go to Pomigliano d'Arco. Because I was

---

* *Esposito* comes from the past participle *esposto* of the verb *esporre* (to expose), referring to infants who were abandoned (that is, exposed and put out in the open in front of churches, for example, where they would be taken in and notated as *esposto*). From Marcello's usage, we can take it that the Institution and 'the Esposito' are the same thing, an orphanage that took both children and their single mothers.

still underage they put me in another institution where children lived all the time. I had very few memories of my mother and she could not come to see me as to do so required the permission of a judge. On weekends, when other mothers came, I was the only one not to see mine. I was deeply pained by this, but the experience made me strong and gave me the capacity to understand other people. When my mother got married I joined her and my stepfather who behaved as a real father towards me. When I was ten years old he took me to Madonna dell'Arco where I saw the tammurriata for the first time. Also he bought me my first instrument there. The man who made, played, and sold tammorras had little children dance while he was performing, which was his way of advertising the instrument, and in order to test the strength of the goatskin he would invite a small girl to dance on the tammorra to see whether or not it would break. This is why it is called the dance of the tammorra, because you dance on it, tammurriata on the tammorra. It was the turning point in my life. I felt this music belonged to me. When the farmers came to the *cortile* [courtyard] at home and played their tammorras I would ask them why the rhythm would change here and there. I always asked questions. The *cortile* was shared by the whole community. We would drink water from the same well and on Sundays the bread was made for everyone. It was a very loving environment. The other women, though not relatives, were my "aunties". The *cortile* was my university. One saw all of life there. And death. When I was a kid I saw a woman putting bread and wine into the coffin of her husband. "Auntie Vincenza," I asked her, "why are you putting bread and wine into Pasquale's grave?" She replied, "You take from the earth and you give back to the earth." She put coins on his eyes too. "Why are you doing this, Auntie Vincenza?" "If we don't do this," she replied, "Charon won't let him through. The coffin is like a boat and the occupant takes it to the Garden of Eden where he goes and celebrates." I almost cried when she told me this. Death was not death any more, it had become life. You go back to where you were born. The first *fronna* I ever heard was in the *cortile*, a single voice singing over a corpse.'

'And you continued to live and work here?'

'It was a struggle to find work. I have been a barber, a bartender, a fruit and vegetable seller, I worked in the fields gathering potatoes, and then as a cleaner in a factory. In the 1950s Pomigliano d'Arco was a rural society. Then came the first Alfa Romeo car factory, Alfasud, which produced not only engines and cars but also weapons. It was the first step towards industrialisation. As other factories came the town became increasingly industrialised. We were seeing all these peasants, craftsmen, and artisans, going into the factories, very often paying the Camorra to be able to do that, 70.000 lire, which back then was a lot of money. They did this just to be able to have a safe salary every month.'

'How could they amass the money in the first place?'

'You paid it off little by little. Nobody could afford to do this in one go. The politicians corrupted unions. Our songs were a direct accusation against them.'

'Were the people who looked the Camorra in the eyes punished?'

'They knew exactly what to do. They did not point their fingers. If people said anything against the Camorra they'd be fired. In 1974–5 we started our group, Gruppo Operaio 'E Zézi, which gave voice to the people. We took the name from a workers' group in the 1950s. *Operaio* means factory worker and *zézi* was what the people from the villages called the street artists, clowns, and other performers who were considered a bit mad. We could not avoid singing "on our skin" ("sulla nostra pelle") about what was happening. We sang of the discomfort of the people who went from land to factory, whose lives were really messed up by schedules no longer dictated by nature. These were the reforms the post-war government favoured. It was a hard life, the life of a peasant, and so they wanted to go to the factory in order to have an easier life and a monthly salary. It simply wasn't enough any more to sing out of the tradition. We sang of what was happening right there and then.'

Marcello sang one such song which tells of a man who goes to the factory, and on his first day there he sees monsters that disgorge finished cars and he describes how lost he feels. One of his colleagues says to him, 'Look, there is a pressing machine. / Night and day *she* gives you the rhythm. / You have to go along with the rhythm.' And then, a few lines later, against words of discouragement, he replies, 'What are you talking about? / Are you saying I shouldn't come any more? / I paid 70.000 lire to be here.' The peasants in the factory formed a union and became politicised so as to get the rights they deserve. The song is based on a peasant song written during the period of the Borbone, 'Tammurriata della luna', which is about the land but here it becomes the factory. Marcello has continued in his role of political activist, addressing audiences on the value of the land they live on, about the damage being done to it, and more recently, in 2014, he took part in a workers' strike at the Fiat factory in Pomigliano d'Arco.

An event that occurred during his youth put him on this course.

'On 11 April 1975 there was an explosion at a factory in Flobert. They called it "white death" but I call it "white homicide". It would become the symbol of all deaths incurred while working. The peasants worked in factories without any safety measures. Sixty people worked in Flobert. Officially they were making toy weapons, but underneath there was a tunnel where illegally they were manufacturing fireworks. We all heard the noise. The houses shook even though it was five kilometres from here, in Sant'Anastasia, in the Romani district. People were running, many of them screaming. "What happened?" we cried. I went there and saw the slaughter. I thought I was seeing things, a head hanging above me, a decapitated body on the floor. Thirteen people were killed. There was the desperation of the families.

One person's remains they found a year later. Again we adapted an old song about what happened. "A Flobert'. We sang of how the firemen and ambulances came and there was a mother asking after her son. "Please help me to find him. He must be down here." A fireman said, "Please don't worry, signora, maybe he is safe." She turned and saw him being removed from the ground. The song was Gruppo Operaio 'E Zézi's political response.'

Marcello sang from start to end the mournful melody that sounded more like a lullaby than a protest song.

> *Viernarì unnice aprile*
> *'a Sant'Anastasia*
> *n'u tratto 'nu rummore*
> *sentiett' 'e ch' paura.*

'On Friday 11 April, at Sant'Anastasia,' it begins, 'I suddenly heard a boom and I was gripped by fear.' There have been musical precedents. The great Neapolitan poet Raffaele Viviani wrote a song about builders ''A ferriera' ('The Ironworks'). A worker falls into a cauldron of melted iron and they have to inform the wife. The head of the group of workers goes to give her the news at four in the morning. 'Your husband had an accident,' they tell her. Later in the song, Antonio's daughter holds what is left of him, described as being like the *matassa*, which is what you have when you roll wool into a ball. 'E Zézi has done much to extend the tradition. I wish, though, the song Marcello so movingly sang had a different last line.

'*O comunismo è 'a libertà.*

When was it ever freedom?

'You have described wonderfully the hardships of your life. I was told that as one who inhabits both sacred and profane worlds you would be the best person to discuss the spiritual side of the tammorra.'

'I am honoured by this. A tammorra player must know the history of his instrument. The tammorra is male and female. When a man plays it he calls it by the female name *tammorra* and when the woman plays she calls it by the masculine *tamburo*. The shepherds of old – this is half legend, half history – drove the sheep into the mountains for six months at a time. This *transumanza* (transhumance or seasonal migration) would end at Easter time. When they went up the mountain they would sacrifice a ram. The skin with the hair still on it was stretched and kept as a rough circle. With the tree's resin acting as a glue and the intestines as ties they folded it over the frame and with the skin still wet with blood the tammorra would be hung for six months. They would take the femur, from the leg bones, wrap it with another piece of skin and use it as a stick to play the tammorra. The tammorra has always been played in the shepherd's tradition all over Europe, the Middle East, North Africa, and elsewhere. At the end of the *transumanza* the shepherd took the tammorra, now dried, and the stick. It was a mute tammorra, which, like Cybele's, did not have cymbals. The sheep had lived with the smell of the blood of their father for the whole six months. The cunning shepherd would call them at the end of the *transumanza*.'

BOOM.

Marcello struck the tammorra just once to signify a slow procession.

BOOM.

The sound transported me somewhere ancient.

'The vibration, the energy, the smell of the blood of their father, the shepherd in front, and the sheep following him. *BOOM.* A long tolling sound.'

BOOM BOOM.

'This is the same rhythm the bells make when they sound for the dead, the *campana a morto*. The bell has taken the place of the tammorra. Originally the funerals were conducted to the sound of the tammorra.'

'– as with Franco Nico?'

'Yes, as with Franco Nico.'

'And the sheep followed the shepherd. It was a slow dance of death because they were going to be slaughtered.'

Marcello bleated like a sheep and a shiver went down my spine.

BOOM BOOM BOOM.

A spell had been cast, the world alchemised into a single sound, the human heart its monitor, and then just as quickly it was broken. Marcello's voice re-entered time.

'This was the original use of the drum. Over time, all ethnic groups have taken different rhythms and paths in the way they play. It is a Dionysian instrument, which obviously the Church didn't want played along with the bells. This instrument is male and female, but so too is the *campana*. The bell is like a skirt (female) with a clapper (male) inside. You have to hold it in your hand to play it. It is a phallic symbol. The sacred is within the tammorra. At first, at Montevergine, the priest wouldn't allow me to play the tammorra. The Church did not allow this old shepherd tradition from all over Europe. I told him, "I am playing sacred music in devotion to the Great Mother. This instrument which in your view is pagan is for us sacred. The fact that we are within the church makes it sacred. We have respect for the Madonna. You cannot send me away because you would be sending away not only my body but also my soul. We are praying through this instrument." Gradually the Church understood or rather it had to make a compromise. At the festa in Nola there is a ritual that duplicates the putting of seed inside Cybele's vagina. Cybele, by way of Aphrodite, became the Madonna. These are things from the pre-Christian era that the Church took over. They would put a saint over a pagan image, the same with the obelisks in Naples, which were Egyptian originally. These are things the Church

hides, but it has made these compromises because it has to be with the people. It knows the people are strong together, and that what they believe in is stronger than the Church. Montevergine is not just a celebration to have fun ... it is sacred in itself. A ritual that looks so much like all the others, it is sacred because you have a singer who is conducting it the way a priest does.'
    BOOM BOOM.

The festa at Montevergine is a stage for one of the more enigmatic aspects of southern Italy in that it is a centuries' old tradition attended by *femminielli*, men who have chosen to take on female roles. They are not necessarily homosexual although many of them are. Some are prostitutes, others are chaste – which, I suppose, is pretty much in keeping with the rest of the human race. There is nothing in the ever-growing catalogue of sexual identities to define them although maybe one can say they are a bit of this and a bit of that plus a secret ingredient which is theirs alone. There is some debate as to who or what they are, not least among themselves, and there is even occasional bad feeling towards others whom they perceive to be hogging their scene – transgender people, for example. It is all rather complex, and for an outsider to say anything at all with respect to them is to put himself where the earth's crust is at its very thinnest. A couple of academics say they are a thing of the past, which puts the living *femminiello* in a rather tight spot. A living fossil he may be, but is he happy about the death notices other people create for him? It is not easy coming to terms with one's own non-existence. Sometimes, though, nowhere is not such a bad place to be. One may prosper there, untouched by fashion or prejudice. There is a bit of a semantic hitch in that the word *femminiello* arrives late in the language. It makes its maiden appearance in a book by the Italian anthropologist Abele De

Blasio, *Usi e costumi dei camorristi, storia di ieri e di oggi* ('Habits and Customs of the Camorra: History of Yesterday and Today', 1897), which begs the question: what were *femminielli* called before they were called *femminielli*? The records are sparse. Certainly the *femminiello* is not without his parallels elsewhere, the *berdache* of certain Native American tribes, the *hijra* of southern Asia, the *muxe* of Oaxaca, and the *fa'afafine* of Samoa, all of them men who to some degree or another have adopted female roles.

Montevergine's *juta dei femminielli* ('ascent of the *femminielli*') has its origins in an event that took place in the thirteenth century, in 1256, when two young male lovers (although some say they were caught in nothing more than an embrace) were taken by villagers onto the mountain and there bound with chains to a tree where they were left to die of exposure or ravenous wolves. The Virgin intervened, covering them with a ray of sunlight, protecting them against the cold. An act of compassion in the most unlikely of settings and in the most unlikely of times, centuries later it became the reason why hundreds of *femminielli* make a pilgrimage to Montevergine on Candlemas

Day, 2 February, seeking the blessing of 'Mamma Schiavona', the name fondly given to the Black Madonna who 'gives everything and forgives everything'.

The idea of the *femminiello* goes back even further in time to when the *coribanti*, the priests of the goddess Cybele, climbed the very same mountain to the temple. If they were not already eunuchs they would soon become so. In an orgiastic ecstasy brought on by the sound of the tammorra they offered up their sex as a gift to Cybele – apparently with a sharp stone – and in order to identify with her all the more they put on female clothes. It has been suggested that the Catholic priests' sexually neutral vestments contain a memory of this. The *femminielli* have been part of the social fabric of Campania for a long time, and as figures smacking of the divine, with magical and alchemical properties, they are more or less protected from prejudice. They might be said to have moved beyond the human condition, above the material world, for in a society where sexual identity is of utmost importance the *femminiello* is always something else. Magic is what protects him in that upper zone. Magic is why he is still called upon to officiate at the tombola. Magic is what wins him public acceptance. A couple of *femminielli* I met in Torre Annunziata, Ciro 'Ciretta' Cascina and Luigi De Cristo, were most emphatic in saying it is not the *femminiello* who made Naples but Naples that made the *femminiello* and as such he is yet another instance of the city's duality. The geography is of utmost importance.

So, too, is the demographic. Ciro said the *femminiello* thrives best among the poor, in Forcella, for example, where one of the most famous *femminielli*, 'La Pullera', sold contraband cigarettes. I felt a certain patriotic pride when I learned that 'La Pullera' lived on the Vico Scassacocchi. As for the *femminiello's* magical properties, a woman I spoke to in Naples remembers how mothers would offer their newborn to him for good fortune. There is also a Neapolitan proverb: *T'e fa bene ricer' da nu prevt* *ricchion'* which translates as 'It's good for you to be blessed by a homosexual priest'.*

And then, most incredibly, there is the couvade, an anthropological term referring to the ritual found in several cultures in which a man goes through the motions of giving birth. Strabo in his *Geographica* makes mention of it. So, too, does Apollonius of Rhodes whose third century BC account is the first written evidence. James Frazer in *The Golden Bough* refers to this as 'imitative magic', its purpose to transfer the suffering of childbirth from women to men. The couvade can be traced back to ancient Egyptian culture. The Campanian version, today found more in the towns around Vesuvius than in Naples itself, is called *la figliata dei femminielli*. When I first read Curzio Malaparte's description of it in *La pelle* ('The Skin') I thought it was the product of a fevered imagination:

> Pale, his eyes wide open, his two hands pressed to his temples, the mother-to-be was beating his head again and again on the pillow and uttering shrill cries. His lips were beslavered with blood and froth, and large tears rolled down his dark, virile cheeks, forming beads on his black moustache.

And then, after several more paragraphs of prolonged agony, amid the encouraging noises of other *femminielli*, he gives birth. 'It was an old wooden statuette, a roughly carved fetish,' Malaparte continues. 'It looked like one of those phallic images that are depicted on the walls of the houses of Pompeii.' Strange progeny.

The festa at Montevergine is a tight knot of cultural memories.

---

* *Ricchion'* has come to have a rather more negative connotation than in the past when it was rather more gently used to describe homosexuals and *femminielli* alike. What is interesting is how their priestly aspect has survived in the language.

After prayers are offered to the Virgin the tammurriata begins, which roughly corresponds to the corybantic dances of ancient times.

'I saw a short film of you singing to the Virgin at Montevergine.'

'I am honoured when I go there,' Marcello replied. 'People wait for me to salute the Great Mother. The world may fall apart, but I'll still go there. The day before Easter, when it is summer inside and winter outside, I go up the holy stairs singing to the Holy Mother. We become her priests. It is religiosity that does not have an end or a time. There is no intercession by the priests. With all due respect we go there saying not *their* prayers, *their* Ave Maria's, but our own.'

'Are you not afraid that at Montevergine the tradition of the *femminiello* is being hijacked by the gay movement? Will that not politicise what has long been accepted as an act of compassion or what some people describe as a miracle of tolerance?'

'Absolutely not. Mother Earth creates all of us hermaphrodites. The world, the moon. The earth is female. A seed in the soil sprouts. Who told the seed what it should do? The *femminiello* belongs to a virgin cult. Theirs is a pure song of Mother Earth. There are a lot of plants in nature that are hermaphroditic. We have both male and female chromosomes. Some males when they grow up adopt a female attitude. It might be a good-looking boy with no beard and who has more female chromosomes, or it might be a woman with a beard who has more male chromosomes, but they are all part of nature's game. They are all sons and daughters of Mother Earth. The *femminiello* is chaste. In ancient Egypt he was the eunuch who was first taken to Isis who later becomes Cybele who later becomes the Black Madonna. At Montevergine he wears make-up not in order to disguise himself but so as to honour the Madonna. "I am doing this for you," he says. "I am making myself more beautiful for you." Two *femminielli* on a cold night in winter were rejected by the villagers who accused them, sent them to their death, but the

Madonna put a ray of the sun to warm them because their love was stronger than the cold of winter. It melted this thing called ignorance, the ignorance of those who put a finger on anyone who is different and who feel they have a right to judge. What's important is that it's love. That's why they are devoted to the Mamma Schiavona – because she welcomes them. A move was made by the Church to stop the *femminielli* attending. Who are they to tell us who can come? We are all the same. You are like me because we are male and female at the same time. Love does not recognise boundaries. You can't stop a natural law like the one of love. When priests refused me I said to them, "You can't do this. You are not the owner of the church but its guardian. The owner is *Her*, the Madonna. She is the boss."* Montevergine didn't start as a Christian celebration. It is on a mountaintop, one in the chain called Monti del Partenio. *Parthenos* in Greek means "virgin" – chaste and pure. The church was built over the temple of Cybele. I have seen with my own eyes an old woman take children of ten or eleven, a boy and a girl, and put her hands on their heads and then over their genitals. At first I thought this was blasphemy. She was a kind of priestess initiating the virgins. "Great Mother, this is all for you," she sang, "Bless the seed of these young people." She made a gesture, the same gesture the dancers of the tammurriata make, which replicates the peasants sowing seed by hand. The seed that was put in the ground in September takes the first light in February, the darkness of winter is over ... it is the Candelora. "Candelora, Candelora," we sing,

---

* This, presumably, was in reaction to the attempt made in 2012 by the Abbott of Montevergine, Monsignor Tarcisio Nazzaro, to stop the *femminielli*. He told them their prayers were not pleasing to the Virgin Mary. One unintended consequence of this was to make the Candelora more popular than ever. Until then, the event was relatively obscure outside the region; another was that it has now become, for better or worse, a symbol of gay pride.

"summer's in, winter's out. Everything is done for you, Mamma Schiavona. So make the seed productive." It is a cycle and this is what happens in August when you have the *festa del grano* because she has blessed the forces of our lives. August is the fruit. What the peasants do is to follow a cycle. They are perfectly integrated with nature. Montevergine is a festa of fecundity. The priests conceal this. They took the virgin Jesus, initiated him at the temple on 14 February.* It is all connected. This celebration calls upon the sun to send away the dark winter.'

On the wall of the room where we spoke there is a photo of Marcello dressed as a woman at a carnival in Pomigliano d'Arco, for a theatrical piece in which men took on female roles. The film director Federico Fellini saw the photo somewhere and instructed his assistants to find this Felliniesque figure for his next film, *Intervista*. It is not, to be truthful, Fellini at his best, but for Marcello it was an unforgettable experience.

'Did you talk to Fellini?'

'Sure! I played the part of a maharajah in his movie. Fellini saw this picture of me. When the production team phoned me, saying Fellini wanted me to play the part in this movie, I hung up because I thought it was a joke. A minute later, they called me back saying they were serious. The next morning they came here and took me to Rome for an audition. We were all put in a row, there were a lot of people, and Fellini meanwhile was directing that scene. He called for a break and then came over to me and hugged me. He whispered in my ear, "I have found you once again." I answered, "Maestro, I was never lost." I wasn't supposed to have a speaking role. I was to sit on this throne. Fellini started to scream, "Stop! Stop! I can't stand a Neapolitan who is quiet. Sing! Sing!" "What should I sing?" I said. He jumped up and came closer. I got up too, but he told me to remain seated

---

* This is originally the day of Candlemas before it was moved to the 2nd of the same month.

because, after all, I was the maharajah. He began to scribble. Fellini wrote words for the song that I was to sing, which he dedicated to the women who were dancing. "I should have been in love with her," he wrote. He made it up on the spot. I have a beautiful memory of that. A week later, I was back at the factory where I worked as a cleaner.'

Marcello reached up to a shelf above his kitchen sink and took down a plate of mouldy bread and a glass of water with chalky white deposit over its surface.

'Something my mother used to say to me, "You never fully leave the house where you have lived. If you die, you leave something behind." The souls that go to purgatory never leave. They stay, they drink, they eat. This way you never let them go. You leave bread and water for these souls, *rinfresco*. You have a relationship with these souls so that they'll stay with you. When you find the glass empty, the water evaporated, the white on the glass means they have come.'

It looked like limescale to me, but then I was happy enough to be persuaded of its ghostly properties.

'They feed on the same water that gave birth to them,' Marcello continued. 'They have left behind the ashes of their bones. I'm a man of the third millennium and I'm still doing this.'

'Your mother, your father, your friends, they're *here*?'

'The souls of all who have passed away … it is part of our tradition, our store of memories. The women at Fontanelle had this connection with people on the other side. They took care of their skulls. We sing of the souls in purgatory. "After nine months," begins one of the tammurriata. There is a specific story behind this. "The window had light in it, but now there is no light behind it any more." This is from a song dedicated to the dead. "Nine months after I've died you will find and take my bones because they'll make miracles. My bones will speak to you." There is a close relationship with the four elements – air, fire, water, and earth. Water is especially important in that it is connected to the idea of giving birth. "A shooting star falls from the sky and into the sea." In this, the line from another song, the star represents fecundity. It is the moment of conception, fertility, and abundance, and from the sea a daughter is born with curls in her hair and rings on her fingers. She is the divinity. The four elements are joined together. Water delivers life. We are born in water and water is female. And so, as I was saying, when you lose someone who has been close to you it is a way to keep the door open between this world and the other. In other traditions the connection becomes totemic. These symbols are used for protection for the house, the family, and the people you care about.'

'So this goes back to the ancient Greeks and the Egyptians.'

'Yes, both.'

'So then,' I asked Marcello, '*pagano o cristiano?*'

'I am of a natural law.' He laughed. 'Religion does not have a label or a time.'

The Intimate Lives of Things Inanimate

Carmen Pellegrino and Teresa Cervo

If I were to take a parallel rule such as the fine boxwood one with brass hinges that my father used when he was a ship's navigator, and which like so many other objects from my childhood has vanished – where do the things of this world go? – and on a map of Naples align the top edge of it with Via Tribunali and then draw a line along the bottom edge I'd be able to position on the same latitude the two women whose stories I'm about to relate. Why this sudden recollection of an object that had been nowhere in the upper or even the nethermost regions of my consciousness? And why *here*? Might it be the things we believe inanimate are invested with a spirit that only certain conditions release? A holy fool once said to me that all things, even stones, are possessed of a soul. This should please him, the fact I'm about to embark on matters that involve stones that communicate and the making of objects which subsequently acquire lives of their own. A couple of women have salvaged from the seabed of my memories my father's parallel rule. They ask, in my reveries and nowhere else, that I situate them in the same creative groove. There is only a ten-minute walk between where they live, but as far as I know the one has no inkling of the other. One day I might introduce them although maybe it's best to leave things be. One cannot force friendship, any more than one can force a smile or even, for that matter, a simile.

One of the women comes from a small village in the Cilento region of Campania and the other was born in Naples. The first is no less a native of the city than the second, which supports my view that it is quite possible to become Neapolitan if only on a metaphysical plane. My landlady Melania, when we first met, informed me I was already one and I'd been in the city for only a week. As she is a denizen of Forcella and has a serpent tattooed on her ankle I will take what she says as irrefutable. So what if I don't speak the language: I am not waiting to be given the key to a city whose lock I picked at first glance. As for the two ladies I'm about to introduce one is a writer and the other an artist, and in both of them I find the embodiment of many of the city's elements that have so completely taken hold of me. Both of them do a good line in death although their common aim is life.

Carmen Pellegrino always wears black, even in high summer, and if thereabouts it is as murderously hot as it's said to be – something I'd rather not investigate myself – then enquiries ought to be made as to her physical constitution, whether she suffers inordinately from the cold or if she is of another species altogether. She does as soul dictates. Some people only think they do. Most are afraid to. It's only the rare few who disengage themselves from what the world would have them do. The black she wears is not the black of style; it is what country women wear, or at least used to, as a perpetual sign of mourning although it can also be a declaration of modesty. Seen from afar, and with fanciful eyes, they might be said to be lamenting an Italy drained by many years of emigration and, more recently, by a sense of inner betrayal, political and otherwise, that has increasingly driven people into themselves. Only charlatans chasing after votes blame outside influences. The country is perfectly capable of breaking its own heart. You wonder how this can be, given its history, its culture, and the agreeableness of its people. Surely there isn't a stiletto hidden behind every smile. 'Ahi serva Italia, di dolore ostello / nave sanza nocchiere in gran tempesta, / non donna di provincie, ma bordello!'* ('Abject Italy, an inn of sorrows, a pilotless ship on a stormy sea, a princess not of provinces but a bordello').

She is what she is. There's no pill for it. She may be Emily Dickinson in reverse. She has a surprisingly girly voice. I had been expecting it to be somewhere in the lower register as befits someone of her gothic appearance but no, she speaks as might a sparrow endowed with human speech. I think I detect a rural trill, but I can't be sure. Sometimes things are only as I will them to be. She has, to be sure, certain peculiarities. She attends the funerals of complete strangers and has a passion for abandoned places, not just solitary buildings of which there are many in the south of Italy but also entire villages. They are the stuff of her two books of fiction. Such is her dedication to places ravaged by time that a new word has been coined to describe what she does: she is an *abbandonologo* or 'abandonologist', defined by *Treccani*, the Italian encyclopaedia of arts, letters, and sciences, as someone 'who scouts the territory in search of abandoned villages, the ruins of public and private edifices, abandoned buildings and activities (amusement parks, gardens, stations etc.), in order to document existence and study history'. Actually the word was first uttered by a young boy in a bookshop to whom Carmen had expressed her enthusiasm for a certain book on the subject of ruins. 'So you are an *abbandonologo*,' he replied. She was, at that precise moment, equipped with a literary handle. *Treccani* being an Italian work of reference, she is described in it as *giovane*, *molto bella* with which it is difficult to disagree although if one

---

* Dante's *Purgatorio*, Canto VI, lines 76–8.

were to say so in English it would rankle. She has published two novels, *Cade la terra* ('The Earth Falls', 2015) and *Se mi tornassi questa sera accanto* ('If Tonight I Went Back Next Door', 2017) and is currently working on a third.

The first novel is set in the fictional ghost village of Alento, which, as it so happens, closely resembles the abandoned village of Roscigno Vecchia in the province of Salerno, abandoned because at the beginning of the twentieth century it was partially destroyed by a landslide. The inhabitants were at fault because, old story, they cut down the trees that kept the soil in place. Many of them moved away from the *paese che cammina* (a lovely phrase, such as only the Italians can produce, which rather blandly translates as 'country that walks') to what would become the village of Roscigno Nuovo. It is to be hoped they don't repeat the same mistake there. Strange how people are so slow to learn from experience and yet are so quick on the uptake when invited to take a blind plunge. One person alone stayed on in the old Roscigno, 'Sister Dorina' who was born Teodora Lorenzo. As a girl she entered the convent in the *comune* of Vallo della Lucania, and then, after a crisis of faith, abandoned her vows and went back to her village where she continued to be known by her sisterly name. After the landslide she continued to live there without electricity or running water for over half a century. As hermits are rarely allowed to enjoy their solitude, and in fact are rather sociable creatures, she became the village's main attraction. People came, filmed her, and interviewed her. When she died on 12 October 2000, the press made much of her not quite so solitary existence.

The real Dorina gave birth to the fictional Estella who in Carmen Pellegrino's story leaves the convent and lives with the wealthiest family in the village. They own a grand house with an elm tree in front of it, and there Estella works as governess to a spoiled and spiteful boy, Marcello. Disaster strikes, *the earth falls*, and the inhabitants of the village leave. Estella stays on. It is the only world she knows, or is this, as the author suggests, 'a magical imposture'? She is not absolutely alone, however. She communicates with the ghosts of people who lived and died there, and once a year she arranges a banquet for them, going so far as to produce invitations and dress up for the occasion. Among the guests are an anarchist whose dreams were shattered, a girl who was forced to marry a violent thug, a blind auction- eer, and a young person who died by suicide. The idea of the dead returning to the table is a common motif in Italian folklore. One version has it that if, after dinner, one does not remove the tablecloth the dead will come to the table. In Giovanni Pascoli's poem 'La tovaglia' ('The Tablecloth') a child is told, 'Bada, che vengono i morti!' ('Beware, lest the dead should come!'). A few lines later, that same child welcomes them: 'Lascia che vengano i morti, / i buoni, i poveri morti' ('Let the dead come, the good, the poor dead'). And then in one of Pascoli's stories 'La befana' the tablecloth is left out on purpose so that the dead will take their place at the table. *Cade la terra* invites comparison with the great Mexican novel *Pedro Páramo* by Juan Rulfo, which also is set in a ghost town populated with spectral figures. The dead, as the dead tend to be, both in fiction and in how we continue to perceive them, are very much with us and are as concerned about their problems as when they were alive. What bugged them then, bugs them still. What's the point of death, one wonders, if it is merely a release into more of the same. In *Cade la terra* we read of six families, one of which experienced a tragedy that mirrors a terrible event in the author's own family.

'That story,' Carmen Pellegrino told me, 'is about a little girl called Mariuccia who, in real life, had she lived, would have been my aunt. She died, aged seven, in the 1950s because of a medical error. The doctor gave her the wrong injection which stopped her heart. My grandfather, a simple man, a peasant, was angry that his daughter should have been killed because of a stupid mistake. The doctor who was deeply arrogant admitted his mistake but then blamed the father, saying there were no electric lights in the house and that he couldn't see what he was doing. "You are living like beasts," he said, even though at that time many homes in the countryside didn't have electricity. The girl's father went crazy. "Do you want money?" he cried. "Is that why you are complaining? I'll take you to court and the law will decide what's right and what's wrong." The doctor, knowing there was nothing more to be done, laughed at him. "Do as you like," he said, "You can take me to court. I'm all right with that. They know who I am." Mariuccia died in the street while they were preparing to take her back to hospital and, incredibly, it was at the very spot where my grandmother gave birth to her. There was a little memorial plate placed there, but they got her dates wrong. It was as if her destiny was to be put inside an eternity of indifference. I had to tell her story, a true one, as some kind of recompense.'

I was curious to know more about Pellegrino's background and, naturally enough, how it impacted on her writing and choice of subject.

'I come from the small village of Polla in the mountains on the border between Campania and Basilicata. We were, within that context, middle class. My father worked in an office. Born into a peasant family ... his father was the one whose daughter died ... he was the first to graduate from university.'

'I should ask you what your first memory is because I believe that often it's what we choose it to be, and as such it points to the direction one takes in the future.'

'My baptism. I was three years old. There was a Don Camillo-like situation in our family with my father being a socialist although he had nothing to do with the so-called "Apennine socialism" you found in intellectual circles, and my mother a Catholic. He didn't want his children to be baptised but then, in 1980, there was the Irpinia earthquake with a loss of three thousand lives. My mother told my sister and me to go under the table. After this terrible event she insisted that we be baptised.

I remember walking to the church with the priest who was all dressed in white and saying to him, "You are looking very elegant today."'

'The memory of both the baptism and the earthquake,' I suggested, 'must have stayed with you as a writer.'

'Yes, always. The sense of danger and of things hanging over you, this city waiting for Vesuvius to erupt again. I moved to Naples when I was eighteen and I was completely overwhelmed. It is the only town you can float in. You feel you can belong to this place without it keeping you here by force. This is why I stay on. I travel a lot and when I come back I don't feel the need to go out and socialise. This is the only place I know where you can be alone without feeling lonely. I am a person of disquietude, but there is nothing wrong with that in Naples. I always dress in black, I am always cold, but these things don't make me a pariah. It wouldn't matter if I wore a huge hat with a parrot on it because I can do as I like. Although I live nearby I feel I can come here, to Piazza Dante, as a complete stranger.'

'One of the curious things about Naples,' I said, maybe thinking about my own emotional attachment to the place, 'is that an outsider can become Neapolitan.'

'After being here for fifteen years, only now have I officially become a resident of the city. It has its faults. Naples is tiring sometimes because you can do anything here. At three in the morning you can party and make noise. It is a constant party and sometimes quite unbearable. Also it can be a disrespectful place. A cab driver will be rude to you or you can go into a shop and the person working there makes you feel like he is doing you a favour. There is a lack of grace. You need to take a break, get out of here and breathe, but after a month or two you need to come back. You forget everything that's bad about this city. It is like a woman who at some point after giving birth forgets the pain. After ten years, my sister moved here too. She enjoys it here, but has little perception of the downside. We come from a village that has a narrow perspective and where you feel constrained. You don't have this in Naples. I think this is the happiest town in the world simply because it allows itself to be unhappy. What I said earlier about Vesuvius being a constant threat ... well, people continue to live on its slopes. When I come back here I feel released and even, in a way, protected. I am aware there are dangerous areas where you can't go, but there is humanity there too. Those people are victims too, not the dodgy ones imposing themselves on their lives. It is a complex place. I love Milan where many things happen ... plenty of culture, people doing good things ... but spending a winter there is much more difficult than spending it here.'

'What you say about Naples being a happy place reminds me of what Herman Melville wrote in his journals when he came here in 1857, calling it the "gayest city in the world". Will you ever write about Naples?'

'I couldn't. First of all, the stories about Naples would never be wholly mine as opposed to the ones where I come from. What I am writing now is set in an imaginary village. If I write about an actual place I can't go back there.'

'I would have thought this city with its *anime pezzentelle*, the cult of skulls, and Fontanelle would inspire you to write about it.'

'Not explicitly, maybe in a layered way, but not so I am aware of it. The reason why, after fifteen years here, I am still floating is that because I have not actually gone *through* the city, which is another reason why I can't write about it.'

'And yet you commune with the Neapolitan dead to an inordinate degree. You have said elsewhere that for country people it is perfectly normal to imagine the dead sitting at the same table as the living and that in your writing you seek signs of what had been their passage through life.'

'It's true that I go to the funerals of complete strangers. In the village where I come from this was normal. I lived with my grandmother for a few years ... my parents had to leave for a while ... and she would go to everybody's funerals, even if she didn't really know them. This tends to be the case in small places. When I came to Naples, aged eighteen, the first thing I noticed were these posters announcing the deaths of people. I was curious about the nicknames on them, many of which are comical. Although my village is only two hundred miles away from Naples my dialect is very different from Neapolitan and so I needed to ask people the meaning of various words and phrases. The first time I went to a funeral it was for an Antonio Esposito, which is a very common name, and on the poster was this nickname, "'O tubbato". I asked someone what it meant. At first I thought it had to do with when you are in hospital and have to breathe through a tube but no, it wasn't that. It was a play on the word *turbato* in the sense of "madness". So this Antonio Esposito was "the crazy one". There was another death notice for a Maria Esposito "the Spinster" and yet it contained words of condolence for her husband, sons, and daughter. So why, if she was married, the nickname? I thought this might provide some hint of what her life was like, but it was simply because she married late in life. Also, with so many names the same, "Esposito" for example, it is a way to distinguish one person from another. I think, too, it is a way to exorcise death, adding a little twist of irony.'

'Do people not ask who you are when you go to a funeral?'

'At funerals everybody is suspended. There is a calmness that follows death. There is no need to explain anything to anyone, but if you want to ask them questions about the deceased they are happy to answer. So people don't mind or see anything wrong with my presence. It is a bit like the abandoned places. When you go to a funeral death has already occurred. Nothing worse can happen. There is a reversal of some kind, a sense of something starting over. Anyway I'm not looking for death but for the life within. It's the same thing with abandoned places.

They are called "dead cities", but they are not dead. The houses talk to you. Nature takes over, acting upon them like an invisible gardener. Animals are there. Anything can happen because there's still life in there. This is the core. Obviously there are other things as well but this is the core.'

The Polish writer Bruno Schulz, who is one of my literary touchstones, writes: 'There is no dead matter [...] lifelessness is only a disguise behind which hide unknown forms of life. The range of these forms is infinite and their shades and nuances limitless.' What my holy fool in Damascus told me has taken many years to sink in, but that it should have done so in a city that so often reminds me of his is surely no fluke. They are both cities where the very stone speaks to me. And again, it is no accident that so much of our western mythology is bound up in a few square miles. All of it speaks, all the time.

'Again it's like when you move somewhere,' she continued. 'You look at a place and you can feel whether or not it is good for you. You ask yourself, "Does this house speak to me?" Objects do this as well. It is as if certain energies are trapped inside them. This is nothing to do with ghosts or anything like that. It is not looking for death, it's looking for life. When someone dies that person never leaves you completely. Likewise, objects trap energy. There are funerals that are more attended than some, others less so. If you didn't have many people about in life, there won't be many when you die. For some people it is a lonely death, such that for them it is not the last goodbye, it is the *only* one. This is one of the reasons I go to funerals. And then there are those lives that have been without consequence, which leave no trace, and are completely forgotten by history. I try to recall them in what I write. I intend literature as a way of saying they are not doomed to oblivion.'

'Yes, you have spoken often about giving voice to people who didn't really have one when they were alive.'

'I'm currently working on a book about child suicides. You

don't want to know about it, *nobody* does, but it exists. In this modern society removing death and sadness from our discourse is actually condemning us to unhappiness. It allows us to die without anyone taking account of the fact. The neighbours don't want to ask themselves why this person has disappeared. I read of a man, aged forty-two, who died and was found nine months later only because his bills weren't being paid. This was in one of the wealthiest regions of northern Italy. Where everything functions or is automatised you can disappear and nobody will notice. Our society wants so-called decency. It wants you to never show your feelings. You are not supposed to reveal that you are sad or desperate. This is why Naples is, within its own sadness, a happy place to be. My writing is about looking for elements of life where normally you can't find them because you think at first they are not there. They *are* there. The co-habitation of life and death not only refers to my work but also to the approach I have to life. According to the American Constitution it is the right of each individual to be allowed the pursuit of happiness. This implies ignoring the downside. If you reject the idea of unhappiness, the unhappiness within you will increase. You trap it and that's where it'll be. The more you try to get rid of it, the more it will haunt you. Italy in the past was a rather more complex place, but now things have been lowered to a very simple level. This is due to politics, the quality of communication, and television. In the past twenty years, the levels of depression in Italians have greatly increased. One of the reasons for this is because we are not going deeply enough into things. We want to be light and happy and frivolous. If you refuse to adapt to this search for happiness you will be rejected by society. You will be made to feel wrong because you are not like all the others and so you have to isolate yourself even more. That's when depression seeps in, that's why it is a growing phenomenon.'

'Would you say there is a religious or spiritual dimension in your writing?'

'Not in a religious sense, but if we are talking about animism, and by this I mean the energy within things, then yes. There is a web of energy within which people and objects are linked. There is nothing about it that I'd call a miracle. It is all very rooted. The way I think about the dead is that they're not up in the sky some-where. They are *here*. This is the only life we are given. So there is nowhere else for them to go. Obviously this is how I imagine it, but it helps me live. I am not sure what it is like in England but here, in Italy, the cynical approach to life has become very strong and so being too rational or having a materialistic approach to things takes away from what's there inside this web. When you remove something it's because you don't want to see it. We adopt

this mechanism to avoid death and pain, the fragility of existence, and imperfection. All becomes eugenics. Imagine a society
of infallible people, hard and pure, and yet incredibly lonely.
You only do those things that are functional and then you begin
to see people according to how useful they are. That is why I
go to abandoned places because they are not useful to anyone.
They've lost their function.'

'Leopardi warns against putting too much faith in reason.'

'This is exactly where we are now. We cannot accept failure.'

Pellegrino's second book touches yet again on the theme of
abandonment although it has more to do with the ruins a man
makes of his own life and the betrayal by others of the ideals that
he held dear which have brought him to an impasse. The other
main character is his daughter Lulù who keeps her distance from
him. He puts messages into bottles in the hope they will reach
her. The title of the book, *Se mi tornassi questa sera accanto*,
is taken from the opening line of Alfonso Gatto's poem 'A mio
padre'. Gatto, who is little known in English, was described by
no less than Eugenio Montale as one of the best poets of the
century. Pellegrino opens each section of her two books with
quotations from the poems of Gatto, Montale, Giovanni Pascoli,
and Antonia Pozzi. Gatto, though, is her first love.

'He was my introduction to poetry,' Pellegrino continued. 'I
was ten years old. The reason I was exposed to his poetry was
that his daughter married someone from my village. She and her
husband always came on summer holiday. The husband became
the godfather to my sister, so there is a family connection. At
that age I was attracted not by the meaning of the words but by
the way they sounded. Gatto is a deeply hermetic poet, a poet
of subtraction rather than addition, a bit like the cuttlefish in
Montale's "Ossi di sepia", which is *sarno* or without flesh. Very
much at the core of his work and thought is the relationship
between the dead and the living. Often he was accused of writing
too much about death, and in more than one interview he said,

"When I tell stories of the dead I am actually talking about life."
They called him *il poeta del canto fioco* ("the poet of the dim
song") like when the flame is weak and small. It is like a sad
whisper or the last breath of a dying person.'

'The abandoned places, are you keeping some kind of record
of them?'

'I have been working for years on something called *The Cartog-
raphy of Solitude*, which is a poetic journey through abandoned
houses, churches, and theatres, travelling through places as one
would through people's lives. It will never be finished because
things change all the time.'

Whether or not it's true, and ten out of ten it's not, the impression I have of Carmen Pellegrino is that once she has had her say
she beats a retreat into her room, embraces the shadows, for fear
the sun will burn the words she speaks.

One evening as I walked up the *vico* that leads from the corner
of Piazza Domenico Maggiore towards Via Tribunali I passed
a door that was slightly ajar and I could glimpse what seemed
to me the workings of another world. What that world was, I
couldn't properly say because I was pressed for time but something of it stayed with me. I move too quickly at times. This probably comes of an old fear I have that the things I most want to
capture in words are just about to dissolve. All, finally, does. All
that was once so painstakingly set in place perishes, even marble,
but then there are the necessary illusions by which a writer or
artist may persevere and which prevent him from surrendering to
the despairing though chummy voice inside him that says *why
this pointless exercise, why this struggle against impermanence?*
Maybe one has to be sufficiently stupid to write. 'Great poetry
is essentially *stupid*, it *believes*,' wrote Baudelaire, 'and this is
what makes for its glory and its force.' I don't think he was being

entirely cynical, nor was he saying one should produce a mighty
slog of a poem in the manner of Herman Melville's 'Naples in
the Time of Bomba' with such stirring lines as 'Ha, happy to
meet you, Punchinello! / And, merrily there, in licence free, / The
crowd they caper, droll as he.' What could he have been thinking? Odds are he thought more of this than he did *Moby Dick*
just as Cervantes thought *Viaje del Parnaso* was superior to *Don
Quixote*. Still there can be no denying the hold the city had over
Melville's imagination. At his home on 104 East Twenty-Sixth
Street, New York City, he hung a framed print of the Bay of
Naples. What I am trying to say is that for the world's sanity, by
which I mean *ours*, it is imperative that we be able to think poeti-
cally as well as scientifically, economically, and politically. Baudelaire, who tonight seems to have got his claws into me, said one
must not confuse the phantoms of reason with the phantoms of
the imagination. You'll be stuck with a heap of equations otherwise. Such is how our world has gone, with reason its pinnacle.
Leopardi would clink glasses with Baudelaire. So would Carmen
Pellegrino. So, too, the street singer who told me that in Naples
people too often mistake shit for chocolate. (Did I forget to
mention there is a bluntness in Neapolitan discourse that makes
our own verbal boorishness shy by comparison?) There's something else I wish to communicate before my next subject takes the
stage. A germ of death resides inside every creative moment. It's
there when one is in the middle of a good conversation or when
one sees more deeply into a painting than ever before. It's what
Naples throws at one on a daily basis, if not in spades then at very
least a sprinkle, its import being that we need death in order to
live. Only I wish there wasn't quite so much of it. One evening as
I walked up the *vico* that leads from the corner of Piazza Domenico Maggiore towards Via Tribunali I yet again became conscious
of the fact that I have allowed too much to slip away from me.

Several times I went back there, but the entrance was sealed by
a heavy metal door, no sign on it as to what might be inside. My

curiosity had already begun to wane a little when one morning I saw a woman sweeping the street at the open entrance, over her shoulder a dimly lit atelier of some kind. I asked her if one could go inside and she told me to come back later. She had the slightly weary look of one who has had to field one tourist too many. Who could blame her? She was merely protecting her zone. When I returned I found her busy at her worktable, putting the finishing touches to a paper sculpture, a doe-like creature with a female face, small horns, and three humps out of which grew leafless branches constructed of wire. I could have said papier mâché, but it wouldn't be quite right for what she does. It would be like saying of a painter that he does nice pictures, but then I'd rather not talk about art because that would be to get myself into an even deeper tangle. I'm after what drives it. What Teresa Cervo does is both art *and* papier mâché, but there is something else in it that defies categorisation, which summons forth a chain of associations that want not to go easily into prose.

'May I look?'

She nodded assent.

'May I take photographs?'

'No.'

I knew immediately I'd like her.

This is some of what I saw: strange beings with their bodily features sprouting into musical instruments, others with pointed noses and horns on their heads, wire ladders with paper rungs that seemed to be symbolic of something (but what?), minuscule chairs, birds, and fish (many of them), a bird with a tiny hand-written note saying, 'Give me a breath of wind', monsters with friendly faces, a group of figures flying towards a paper moon while seemingly ignoring it, a male figure with a removable face behind which were little paper butterflies, pensive female figures that might have strayed in from a novel by Colette, other women armless and eyeless, one of which instead of a torso had a couple of doors that opened onto a smaller female figure inside,

Quattrocento female busts with enormous hair and Madonna-like figures, again eyeless, holding babies. Altogether they might have come out of one of Bruno Schulz's stories. Why is he so much on my mind as I write about these two women of Naples, a world away from Drohobycz where he spun his strange tales? All these figures seemed to say to me that any attempt to describe them would be to do violence to the world of symbols they comprise, but then Schulz I'm sure could have rendered them as crackling prose. It is difficult to imagine how any of those works would survive in isolation because here, in this most dreamlike of places, they seemed all of a piece.

Strength and fragility, black iron wire, and papier mâché – would it be too much to suggest that Teresa Cervo is likewise made? When I suggested she works in a medium many people would consider perishable she informed me that ancient Chinese armour was made of paper strong enough to withstand a sword's blow. And then, speaking of the materials she uses, she told me the Italian for iron is *ferro*, which is masculine, and for paper, *carta*, which is feminine, the male not necessarily stronger than the female. She also told me she is trying to build a bridge between herself and other people, and just when I thought her answer was a touch jejune she compared this process to a synapse. Synapse: now there's a word to beat the world at Scrabble. It's from the Greek *synapsis* (συνάψις) meaning 'conjunction'. The *Oxford English Dictionary* defines it as 'the junction, or structure at the junction, between two neurons or nerve-cells'. In the nervous system it's what permits a neuron to pass an electrical or chemical signal to another neuron and as such is believed to play a vital role in the formation of memory. Maybe, although I'm not about to toss a bone to the smug certainties of neuroscience, synapse is what makes poetry happen. Maybe, too, it is responsible for 'the cloud of unknowing', which in Christian mysticism sees one happily placed in the *pleroma*, yet another choice word signifying plenitude or, at a higher level, the spiritual universe.

Sacred space, does the mere saying of it wreck the spell it makes? Cervo spoke of her installation *Il passo dell'ordito* ('The Journey Through the Warp') and how she has sought to create a sacred space, although she takes care to avoid religious analogies. (She had already related a story from her childhood that pretty much sums up a widespread Neapolitan attitude with respect to God and the clergy and how rarely the two meet in people's affections: 'After Communion I was supposed to be christened. I refused. The priest said to me, "You have to do it because God is telling you." And I replied, "I'm *not* doing it because *you* are telling me to."') She uses the metaphor of the warp on a loom to describe the journeys we make. What follows is roughly what she said to me. Also, because my wife is a weaver and I already knew the technical lingo I was able to follow Cervo's line of thought at least to the second or third turning. When the warp is opened, she says, this creates a shed or narrow passage (*passo*) that the shuttle holding the weft goes through. The Italian word for weft (*trama*) is also a play on the idea of narrative. The installation comprises thirty-two ladders (*scale*) that are suspended in space. They may be said to represent the warp and the people who pass through this space are the *trame*. A sudden beam of light catches their bodies inside the installation and projects their shadows onto the wall so that the participants are at once the actors and the spectators of this action of crossing space. This crossing over is what tells us that the space is sacred.

'Sacred space is,' she continued, 'the construction of an action. There is no contemplation, which is vertical – only action which is horizontal. I think there is no heaven or hell, only this space, empty and sacred, in which the ladders go nowhere.'

I'm not sure I fully caught the gist of what she told me, and also I suspect she hides behind words, the more convoluted they are the more they shield the thing they are meant to disclose, but what she said put me in mind of Samuel Taylor Coleridge's Eolian harp: 'O! The one Life within us and abroad, / Which meets all motion and becomes its soul.' As is properly the case, the work is better than anything she can say about it. She struck me, for all that she says to the contrary, as a woman of deep religious sensibilities. Spiritual is no longer a word I can say with ease, not since thieves ran off with it to a shallow place.

I asked her about the piece she was working on, the doe-like creature with three branches growing out of it.

'It is called *Ho tre alberi sulla schiena sottili come frecce* ("I have three trees in my back as thin as arrows"). In this work I celebrate the vital force of pain. The three arrows in the back slowly turn into trees. They represent the ways by which we may elaborate upon pain, distilling it until it becomes pure beauty. Life and death, pain and joy, there is no clear line of separation between them. They are all part of a greater organism. It's like when you have a great pain and suddenly you feel joy. It makes more sense when you have suffered and know what pain is. I carry the pain of this creature. I may have suffered, but my art makes me feel better.'

At the risk of making it sound like too much of an academic exercise, I asked where in her work one might locate aspects of Naples.

'I know this is what you are looking for, but those elements are so powerfully embedded in who I am, so deep in my roots, that I am not conscious of them nor am I able to single them out.'

She brought out for me a folding sculpture of a woman, her body a construction of wire with patches of red here and there.

'If this is the weave of my life, the red areas represent my great joys and sorrows. The work ravels or unravels according to what this woman's needs are at various points in her life. She adapts, but with all this ravelling and unravelling she also runs the risk of breaking at some point. She is to me like Naples. This city is a woman and this figure carries the history of my land and my people who, having had to endure so many different dominations, have adapted to them, although the risk of breakage is always there. I feel close to the ancestral roots of my city, but the iconography of the city as it has now become, at least on the surface, is very far away from me. I love the city deeply, which is why I have stayed here, but as with all great loves I also hate it. My roots go deeper than the stupid stereotypes that have now emerged, which make the city look crass.'

When she spoke generally of those people who have made it so, I couldn't help but wonder *which* people? Was it the obsequious accordionist in the Piazza Domenico Maggiore who murders Neapolitan tunes for the tourists? Or was it the tour guide dressed as Pulcinella who with every gesture betrays the very soul of the figure he dares to imitate? (Cervo would later tell me she hates Pulcinella because he thinks only of himself, a Neapolitan trait she loathes.) Was it the *presepe* figures on Via San Gregorio Armeno or, rather, those that have been disembowelled of significance? Or do we have to look further still to the architects of the tourist trade, who'd sell the city's soul or else reduce it to a fridge magnet? Sappho, anyone? I saw the haunting image from the Tomb of the Diver has been reproduced as a mousepad. Crassness is everywhere. Crassness is not a Neapolitan invention, of course, but maybe in a city as naked as this one it irks all the more.

'You made it here just in time,' she continued. 'Naples has been changing. On this street there used to be many artists' studios. Once upon a time people could survive doing something different, but now the city is being flattened by tourism. It's like you are being eaten alive. It is not the travellers who are the problem, but the tourists. They always need to discover a new place and they want to show others they have been there, but they don't even look at it or if they do it is through their cameras or smartphones. I feel sorrow because people are less and less able to be enchanted. During the age of the Grand Tour this was a place poets and artists came to. They left it deeply enriched, taking with them a whole world within themselves, but now people come and they leave with nothing. It is a measure of change in the human species. If you know where the chords are, and if you know how to pluck them, the city will play for you. Naples is this massive, beautiful body over which people move, just as they do in Gulliver's travels. They can't grasp the whole.'

What had been once upon a time the beautiful town of Amalfi has been, every square inch of it, given over to tourism and as such it serves as a warning to Naples. Once stripped of its soul, how can a place ever hope to regain its identity? Cervo's anger is fully justified.

I looked at another sculpture, a mesh of wire with tiny figures inside.

'*Grovigli* ("Tangles"). This is about a woman going through a tough period in her life. The wire is as messy as life itself. These tangles are either made heavier by stones or cement or become as light as lace. Out of them emerge either ladders or single threads of wire, over which move tiny female figures clad in black, who tell you the story of their journey, the attempt to liberate oneself from the controls of family or society, the great effort that detachment requires. This figure on a ladder tells the story of a woman who builds a path that can lead her away from all this, but which at the same time allows her the possibility of return. This other figure with the *fil rouge* tells the story of a woman who leaves without hesitation, who simply jumps out, abandoning herself to the red thread of new encounters.'

I was soon aware that there wasn't a single work of hers she could not elaborate on, although she made it clear that it would be the height of carelessness if she were to explain anything too much because that would be to reduce her work to a series of formulae. I had a sense of someone who physically opens a door while at the same time mentally closing it and who, although she might welcome the exposure, makes sure the light does not compromise her. Clearly, though, much of her work is autobiographical in substance. She was born in the Posillipo quarter of Naples and then lived in Secondigliano which, in her words, was not exactly a bed of roses although she was happy enough to have lived there. She describes it as an education that daily forced her to see things in a different way. She was able to not only watch with her eyes but also to listen with them. At the age of six, when her mother fell into a deep depression, she was sent to live with an aunt in Piedmont in the north of Italy. This 'very wild Neapolitan child', as she describes her younger self, was suddenly thrust into a world of strict schedules. When she returned to Naples a year and a half later she spoke a different language. She felt separated from her kin. A sense of nonbelonging was to colour the whole of her life.

'Those three arrows are the great pains in my life that later become trees. The sense of nonbelonging, though painful, yields fruit.'

'Did you slowly drift into art or was it a conscious decision?'

'I think it was there all the while, frozen inside me. I didn't know it was there. My father was a worker and my mother a housewife. They wanted me to be someone with a position in society, a lawyer or doctor, but I sought another path. I wanted to be free and not have a boss over my head. I started in the 1970s. I was young and it was at a time when everyone wanted to do something for society. When my husband and I opened this place we wanted to do something different. So we worked with leather for a while. At the beginning we did things that were useful, but now we focus on what is useless. It has become more about art.'

'So strength is in uselessness.'

'Yes, a paradox.'

The studio struck me as a place of silence set against the noise of the world outside.

'I have had this studio for fifteen years, but I decided to open the door only two years ago, doing so only while I work. I notice that when people come in here they speak in a low voice. I watch them get lost in their own space. It is like observing a light turn on inside them. Many people walk through this door, foreigners, and this includes people from the north of this country, and natives too. They are deeply touched by this dimension that survives in a city where nothing is easy. They discover there are people who still resist everything out there and whose reality is far away from what theirs has become. They have forgotten this way of living and that there are people who try to build beauty in this world. I could make pizza and become a millionaire. It is difficult, but there is this strong need in me and in people like me to continue. This is what kept me here during the most difficult years, a deep energy that belongs to the very stones. Thomas Aquinas, Giordano Bruno, all these people walked over this stone.'

On the floor was a strange assembly of vaguely human figures morphing into instruments. 'In their world,' she said in an interview, 'music is no longer allowable and so they decide to become instruments themselves, employing parts of their own bodies. They play such beautiful music that with sound alone they magically change the colour of the eyes of those listening to them.

'You can see,' she added, 'that even their own eyes change colour like this one which has one green eye and one blue eye.'

My composer friend in London spoke to me of a vision he had in which ancient Greek musicians tune their lyres to the precise frequency that causes the edifice of reason to turn into rubble.

One of the more mysterious works was the figure of a woman with doors opening onto another figure inside.

'I call this *Anima 'nserrata* or, in Italian, *Anima chiusa* ('The Locked-Up Soul'). The woman is a tabernacle protecting a small soul she can't see because she has no eyes and which she cannot open the doors to because she has no arms. She is waiting for someone else to open them in order to let the light inside. The most ancient way of touching a woman is to touch her breasts. The handles are like breasts. It is not just that you have known a woman, but also you discover what is inside her. You must open the door just a little at a time, however, otherwise the light will burn her.'

Almost all her female figures are eyeless and, once again, she has said elsewhere: 'They are without eyes because they are in a different dimension ... they are elsewhere. It is not an escape from reality nor is it mutilation, but a *seeing beyond*, a different concept from simply looking.' Seeing beyond is at the very heart of Teresa Cervo's work, its conditions being silence and the suspension of time.

'Maybe,' I proffered, 'we require chaos as well as order to be able to create.'

'Chaos is one thing, confusion another. Chaos is force, energy. Confusion merely puts you inside the boundaries of the very system that creates this confusion and so you are led into even deeper confusion. It doesn't show you anything whereas chaos makes you conscious of the divine. You become aware of your quota of divinity, what little bit of it lives inside you, whereas with confusion you are unable to perceive yourself or the world outside.'

'Do you think the cults of the *capuzzelle* and the *anime pezzentelle* will return?'

When earlier I asked Carmen Pellegrino the same question she said yes, it would, because people in Naples are still much too attached to the irrational for these things to be lost forever. Teresa Cervo disagrees.

'Our sense of death has changed too much. Once death was a part of life. Children would be taken to honour the dead, but this doesn't happen any more. The space for death has changed. Cremation is widespread. Where do the ashes go? There isn't anywhere to go to. There is a wonderful film by Vittorio de Sica,

L'oro di Napoli, in which a young boy dies. The mother walks behind his coffin throwing confetti, sugar-covered almonds.* Children run after the coffin to gather them. I remember from my childhood visiting the dead, still in their houses, and under their beds there would be dust mixed with those sweets, the same sweets that you give out at marriage. This, I believe, was done in order to temper death with sweetness. One of my earliest memories, one of the first and most powerful images in my life, was when I was six. This was fifty-four years ago. The city was poor, and at dusk not very well lit and walking through those crepuscular streets, suddenly I saw, built into a wall, the flames of the votive shrine for the *anime pezzentelle*, the candles lighting the scene just like in a small theatre. I was not so much interested in the religious aspect as in those burning figures.'

---

* The paper confetti we throw at weddings has its origin in the ancient practice of throwing grains and sweets, in particular sugar-covered almonds.

I found myself drawn to the sculptures of two women, clearly designed to be a pair, one of which is brightly coloured and holding a couple of babies and the other colourless, cradling emptiness. The first of them, I learned, was inspired by the Matres Matutae. These extraordinary tuff sculptures, housed at the Museo Campano di Capua, date from between the fourth and first centuries BC and depict seated women holding swaddled babies. They are unique. There is nothing like them anywhere else. Capua is rightly proud of them. They may be ugly, but they are theirs. Originally they were spackled and then painted. They have since reverted to the ugly stone that was their preliminary state. When they were first discovered in 1845, they were considered much too wanting of beauty for the world's eyes and so for many decades they were consigned to storage. We are nowadays perhaps less dedicated to beauty – which is not always to side with its opposite, although we do make an awful hash of it at times – and there has been a renewed interest in them. Our fascination is not misplaced. Most likely they were votive statues dedicated to a central mother goddess figure, probably the Great Mother who by the time she entered Roman mythology had become the goddess of the morning, the harbinger of new beginnings. She may be the solitary figure in the museum who clutches, instead of babies, a pomegranate in one hand and a dove in the other. Wherever you see a pomegranate you know sex is in the offing although only rarely does sex come with the prophylactic of peace. The literary scholar, Liliana Rampello, writing of these figures, is struck with wonder:

When we ponder the enigma of the Matutae, questions are pointless as they would strike a blow at beauty. All we can do is contemplate something that is both life and death, inexplicable and inextricable. Gazing at them imparts emotions that delve into the soul, as is always the case when 'fullness and majesty' are accessible 'only to the symbol, but not to the word.' This is what [Johann Jakob] Bachofen said regarding the necropolis, and thus a place of death composed of tombstones, walls and rocks; an array of *res sanctae*. Yet what is *sancta* here is life, giving life, life that became life: fertility and infertility? Fulfilment and incompleteness? Image conceals and reveals, and is never merely one thing. This is especially true with the Matutae, with their complex and multiplied variation, their stability and immutability.

Walter Benjamin, when speaking of them, employs the phrase 'chthonian sentiment' which I find oddly comforting because the further back we go in time the more difficult it is to think of those vanished people feeling anything at all. They can barely hum a tune, and one wouldn't wish to copy their recipes.

'The first mother represents fertility,' Teresa continued. 'As you can see, she wears the popular colours of the region, green and red, and holds with pride her child. As such her role in society is appreciated because she is someone who creates. She is the first mother. Beside her is the second or last mother who is colourless, white as salt. Where there is salt, nothing grows. While the first mother walks people into and through life, this one walks them into death. I was inspired by the Sardinian figure of the *accabadora*, which derives from the Spanish *acabar* "to end" or "turn off". The *accabadora* was an older woman, a widow, appointed by the community, and her role was to kill elderly sick people when there was nothing more that could be done for them. She unplugged them.'

'I take it you are talking of a mythical figure.'

'No, a real one. She actually existed up until the 1950s. The reason they chose a woman was because if a woman brings life then it ought to be a woman who takes it away. You must consider the context. This was a rural area where they were all farmers. If a farmer got ill he became a burden to society and so at his own request he would be killed. The *accabadora* would come with a wooden cudgel, a single blow aimed at a spot between the neck and the back. I wanted to draw this comparison between the mother who gives life and the one who takes it away, which amounts to the same thing. What she does is, in both instances, in the giving and taking of life, a gesture of great generosity.'

My initial instincts were spot on when I divined the workings of another world. It is one of dualities – sacred and profane, joy and horror, light and shadow, pain and its various antidotes. Teresa Cervo is a woman wrapped in silence, such that even the noise outside is somehow swallowed up in this space she has made for herself. Classical music plays while she works and that, too, is a kind of silence. A violin is mightier than a speeding motorcycle.

The Ghost Palace of Roberto De Simone

All my dead rise before me. As if on parade, countless pale faces. *I had not thought death had undone so many.* Among them are some whom I'd all but forgotten, such as one might stumble into at a village fête. I hardly know what to say to them, small talk not being my forte. And then those others with whom I converse all the time, who, as if granted an extended lease, continue to argue with me, joke, or pontificate. What will happen to them when I've gone? When all who knew them have gone? What should we be, who allow the dead to die? There will be a select few, of course, for whom the subsidised curious will produce biographies or hold annual conferences, otherwise anonymity will swallow them whole. They'll be what we absorb on a Sunday afternoon stroll through the cemetery, just names, names and more names, the carved letters on many of the graves barely legible because, yes, even stone dies. Sweetly picturesque, the world's putrescence. As for now, while I soliloquise, they live. Their spirits know whenever they've entered my thoughts and they know, too, that between the living and the dead there exists some kind of electromagnetic force. The blackbird knows this, the honeybee too. We only *think* we do. All my dead rise before me, unsummoned, vying for attention, as needy as they were in life because they, too, must be nourished although in truth I can handle only so many at a time. They emerge from the mind's fog one by one, slow sepia flashes, the time it takes for the mist from one's breath on the mirror's surface to evaporate and then, although I don't wish to be impolite, I dismiss them: I can't be too much with them or they'll suck the life out of me. Maybe I should be keeping some kind of record of those who have come and gone. This morning brings news of yet another whose name I'll have to score through in my address book. Voices that once upon a time I could summon with a few movements of my index finger, I'll never hear again. Their telephones ring into empty rooms without a scrap of furniture in them, maybe a few dead leaves imprinted onto the floorboards. Svidrigaïlov's words come back to haunt me. I wish, sometimes, they'd leave me alone: 'We always imagine eternity as something beyond our conception, something vast, vast!' he says. 'But why must it be vast? Instead of all that, what if it's one little room, like a bath house in the country, black and grimy and spiders in every corner, and that's all eternity is?'* So pale, so many of them, I ask them, *Why me?* I may yet, if I decide not to venerate it, throw away that address book before it disgorges me.

A friend of mine, aged 100, keeps in the breast pocket of his blazer a twice-folded list of all those friends of his who have died. Once a week, in church, he reads through his list of friends from beginning to end, silently speaking their names. A citadel of silence, in Naples of all places, is where I would discover another kind of mnemonic, one of a sturdier structure though not necessarily more effective, its purpose somewhat different in that it is not so much a record of friendship as the setting down of a sphere of influence. On one of the walls in the Maestro

---

* Dostoevsky, *Crime and Punishment*, translated by Constance Garnett.

Roberto De Simone's palazzo – actually not a palazzo but a spacious apartment with big rooms, high ceilings, and a hint of aristocratic decrepitude – there is an old wooden bulletin board called a *tabula hebdomadaria*. So lovely the way it rolls on the tongue. The phrase has survived almost fully intact the journey from Latin into Italian. (*Ebdomadàrio* in Italian means 'weekly' and when combined with *tabula* takes on the feminine form.) It is usually employed in monasteries, particularly by those orders sworn to silence, such as the Carthusians, as a means to indicate, with inserted slips of paper, the tasks assigned to the monks or nuns over the course of the weekly liturgical celebrations. It is improbable that there are many of these objects in private hands and I should think that most monasteries will have already opted for modern devices. The last time I visited one I caught

sight of a glowing screen tucked away in a small back room as if it were an object of mild embarrassment. The days of the *tabula hebdomadaria* are numbered, I'm afraid, just as one day what has replaced it will also be obsolete. The Maestro has put his to another use. The slips bear in his fine calligraphic hand the names of those he knew, who have died and who were most important to him, and (another difference between him and my professor friend) they include also the names of figures from the distant past who have had a bearing on his creative life.

If I had my wits about me, I might, with such a constellation of names, have got him to digress more. I was badly in need of a focus because the Maestro would not be led in any direction not of his own choosing, and what he proffered me were the generalities I might have plucked from the pages of a book. Whether this was because he is elderly or because he is obstreperous I'm not sure, but then why should he allow himself to be corralled by an interlocutor from London who he had never seen before, who on the morrow would be gone? Word on the street was that he is famously difficult and yes, it registered in his blue eyes. I could see in them the erection of a thousand defences. Clearly he refuses to play the game. *Which* game? *Any* game. Admirable is the natural dissidence of a man who refuses to wear the definitions tailored for him by those foolish enough to think they've got his measure, but if perhaps he'd got my measure just a bit more we might have skipped preliminaries and gone straight to the main course. 'If you knew me entirely,' he shrewdly told an interviewer once, 'my life would lose its meaning.' Maybe, as on his *tabula hebdomadaria*, there is little enough room as it is for admitting more people into his life. Certainly he has had his fill of luminaries. What was I compared to them? Still I got to see him twice, which, after registering astonishment in the faces of people to whom I told this, I now realise was something of a coup. Our conversations comprised five hours in total, but when I listened to the recording I realised there was not as much there as I'd thought at the time. I had planned to take the key points of a long life as scaffolding upon which I might construct a wider, twentieth-century picture of Naples and Robert De Simone's place in it. What follows is, in part, the description of a failure. May it succeed at being so.

✳

All roads lead to Roberto De Simone, even, or perhaps *especially*, those with muddy ruts or strewn with pebbles. It would seem there is no area of study so remote he has not gone there, and if we know as much as we do about the traditions, art, and music of Campania it is largely due to his perseverance. As an ethnomusicologist his legacy is already immense. The fruits of his musical journey through Campania in the 1960s can be found in *Son sei sorelle: Rituali e canti della tradizione in Campania*, a book and seven CDs (LPs in the first edition), which contain devotional songs to the 'six sisters' of the title, these being the representations of the Black Madonna, although I failed to ask him why six when seven is the number most often cited. The recordings comprise carnival music, *tammurriate*, *fronne*, funeral lamentations, work songs, harvesting songs, prison songs, lullabies, Christmas carols, all of which have been presented in an order that evokes the ritual cycle of the farmer's year. It is the record of a world all but gone or, in his words, it is 'the celebration of absence'. It is the world of that fugitive, most rascally, quarter tone. De Simone will be remembered for this alone, but he is also much more – a composer, a theatre director, and the author of numerous books dealing with folk ritual and music, Neapolitan song, Baroque music and theatre, Pulcinella, and the history of the *presepe*. He is also one of the founder members of the important folk group, Nuova Compagnia di Canto Popolare. Maestro De Simone has been bestowed with many honours including the Grande Ufficiale Ordine al Merito della Repubblica Italiana and the Chevalier d'Ordre des Arts et des Lettres. You can barely see his head for the laurels covering it, so many of them he might make a passable tree.

It may be that he has stepped on a few toes, or so one might surmise from the plaintive cries of those upon whose extremities he has moved. Small men inflict the greatest damage. Younger scholars carp at him a little, among them some who legitimately call into question his ethnological methods, such as having recorded many of the folk musicians in the studio rather than in their homes or at the festas they went to, thereby robbing the performances of context and immediacy. Fair enough, but where otherwise would we be able to hear those ghostly voices? It's not as if De Simone retouched those performances. It's not as if he behaved like some Soviet commissar of folk culture, making it serve a political ideology. What he got he got as best he could and with the best of intentions, which is to say there might be flaws here and there but that on the whole he achieved something of immense historical and cultural value. After all, it requires a certain visionary quality to capture what very soon will be gone. At least he got within crying distance of the *real* whereas for his detractors, who weren't actually there, authenticity is merely a catchword, a mask of self-righteousness. Maybe he was a bit too hasty, too much driven by enthusiasm which, depending on which way one goes with it, can be either the most creative or the most destructive force in the universe. Anyway he would say he has no truck with intellectuals, which is often the case with natural born thinkers when put in defensive mode. You could say he is a pioneer and that what pioneers achieve is done with the boldest of strokes, with a machete rather than a penknife. Small wonder he's in a foul mood. I suspect there is an element in him of one who, having quit the room in a huff, is a little wounded not to have been immediately recalled. There may even be a touch of Lear in him. Closer to ninety than eighty and confined to a wheelchair, he has beaten a retreat from the world with the result that many of his early associations are now dissolved, the people who were his familiars once now sad, angry, or puzzled that he will no longer communicate with them.

Among them are Fausta Vetere and Corrado Sfogli, members of the Nuova Compagnia di Canto Popolare. This is not to say they do not revere him but that they feel pain at having been cut off by the man who first gave them voice. Fausta was only thirteen when she first met De Simone at the RAI TV studio where she worked on a children's programme. She was fascinated by his intellect and musical knowledge and soon they began to collaborate with him on performances ranging from traditional Italian music to Jacques Brel. She spoke to me of a heady time when they would spend their afternoons playing music, making fresh discoveries. De Simone, meanwhile, was doing his research into early music, which included the discovery of a manuscript of some villanelles in a library in Wolfenbüttel. What this demonstrates is that by 1535 Neapolitan music had already reached Germany, or Saxony as it then was called. That period culminated in the formation of the Nuova Compagnia which brought to the fore the talents of Peppe Barra, Giovanni Mauriello, Eugenio Bennato, and Carlo D'Angiò. Corrado came onto the scene a bit later. The turning point came at the Spoleto Festival where the audience included the great playwright Eduardo De Filippo who would later sing the group's praises.

'Roberto then presented us with the gift that is *La gatta Cenerentola*,' Fausta continued. 'In 1975, he decided to put it on stage. We started to quarrel in the group, Bennato not wanting to go into theatre but rather to stay on the music scene. So he left. A master psychologist, Roberto got to know us well and how we balanced each other. He knew how to get deep inside us, create a perfect role for everybody, but there began a period of existential crisis and we realised there was something not quite right with us, which was why we separated.'

'Do you feel, as apparently he does, that he has been neglected by Naples?'

'He has been waiting for a tribute from the city. He had the makings of a great school, but suddenly he began to run away from it, meaning from the people surrounding him. He should have created a school, but because he didn't Naples forgot about him. I think he should have done something bigger with respect to the whole country. He would have had the recognition he was expecting, but it didn't happen.'

I described the apartment where De Simone lived as a ghost palace.

'Yes,' said Corrado, 'we have been there and know this is true. He is perfect for this city because he himself stands midway between life and death. It is a special city, different from others in that life and death are bound together. We have always had this ability to smile at death. Roberto has this charm, which is like the charm of death. You don't fear it. You are fascinated by it. You have to learn to love the hidden Naples, but he was selfish with it. He should have thought more about the children of Naples, but he abandoned them completely. He thought only of himself.'

'Was he a happy man once?'

'*Molto! Molto!*' cried Fausta. 'Happy and poor.'

Before I left them Fausta Vetere and Corrado Sfogli performed for me a seventeenth-century song 'Ricciulina' by Donato Antonio Spano (1585–1609) and, from more recent times, Pino Daniele's 'Terra mia', so beautifully sung, the second, it brought tears to my eyes. I wished silently that, just then, a man in his ghost palace would give them audience.

I also met Carlo Faiello, who between 1984 and 1998 was a member of the Nuova Compagnia di Canto Popolare and who also played double bass in the orchestra for the productions of De Simone's *La gatta Cenerentola*, *Cantata per Masaniello*, *Carmina vivianea*, and *Le disgrazie di Pulcinella*. As so many

Neapolitan performers have done, he began his musical career on the street and with a stolen guitar for which he later paid, shall we say, a modest remuneration. As I should hate for him to be arrested on account of the forgoing sentence, the plea might be made that over the years he has repaid his musical debts in good measure, most recently with the recording of his song cycle *Tra il sole e la luna* ('Between the Sun and the Moon') which is based on a fairy tale but is ultimately a synthesis of all the mythological strands of which Naples is made, and his *Miserere, Cantare la Passione* which I saw in freezing conditions at Domus Ars Centro di Cultura with the legendary singers, Antonella Morea and Emanuela Loffreda and the actress Isa Danieli in the role of the Madonna. There is nobody in these pages who has not been at some point connected with, and owes much to, Roberto De Simone.

Carlo Faiello is likewise saddened by De Simone's withdrawal from the world, seeing in this the tragic plight of a figure who has been caught between the ancient for which there is no hope of revival, only imitation, and the new which he will not admit into his life.

'Roberto thinks everyone dislikes him and so in this last period of his life, without a school to follow in his wake, he has become fully closed in on himself. He has stopped because he feels there is no possibility of development. At the same time he does not accord the possibility of renewal to anyone else. If you want to give something to someone, then you need to be able to listen to him. If you can't give any more, and there is no prospect of a future, then perhaps it is better to be closed up inside. He is the greatest figure we have, but he stopped too early and does not want to help anyone else. What he is saying is that his art stops with him.'

One person, maybe the only one to have kept a channel open to De Simone, is the singer Antonella D'Agostino whom I met at a café in Piazza Dante. I first encountered her in Michael

Radford's documentary *The Madonna and the Volcano* (1977) about the Seven Madonnas, and which contained the beginnings of the story with which I will take leave of this book. It includes an interview with a much younger De Simone and the film ends with Antonella D'Agostino making a studio recording of 'Jesce sole', the song which opens *La gatta Cenerentola*. She sang it with an intensity that haunted me for many days to come. Any voice other than hers is quite unimaginable. I watched her searing performance three times, and from that moment on it became for me the anthem of Naples.

She was in a rage, or maybe she was not in a rage at all but simply getting things done, shouting down her mobile phone, and stamping her feet at the pigeons swivelling about her. She was wearing sunglasses. I tipped my hat at her. The first few minutes of conversation with her were a bit like entering a decompression chamber, what with doubts as to my intentions and so forth, but gradually she warmed to me. The most loyal of people, she is solicitous of De Simone's reputation. The story of how she got together with him might have come straight out of one of Giambattista Basile's tales.

'The first time De Simone heard me sing was in Posillipo. He came up to me and complimented me. After some years of singing in city squares, I had just made my first record. I insisted on getting his phone number from the man at the recording studio. I am from Calabria and so I'm a tough person. I pursued him. My mother told me to let it go, but I persisted. "You have a good voice," he told me, "but you don't have to haunt me." Then he told me to go into the woods and find someone with a great voice. I did so. Yes, I was that crazy! I went into the mountains and, sure enough, I found this woman singing. I made a recording of her and phoned Roberto to say I'd found for him a great voice. "Oh God,' he said, "*you* again!" I told him I had a recording and so he said, "You have got five minutes to get over here and then you can get the hell out of my life."

When he heard it he jumped out of his seat, saying, "You really have found a wonderful voice. Congratulations!" He is a true and beautiful man, not just a genius but also a good man. He is everything to me. He is the last one left, which is why I must protect him. That is how I got to sing "Jesce sole". The song is so important to me that when I sing it I feel it on my skin. When, on the first night, the curtain rose I was alone on the stage. I sang it and the audience went crazy. After forty years, people still talk about it. A theatrical miracle like this had never happened before. After that I travelled the world with him. After my mother, comes Roberto. I will not hear anything said against him. He has problems walking, but he has two blue eyes like the sea, which says everything about him.'

An old man's most vibrant associations are often with those who are no longer alive. Some say of Roberto De Simone that he is a man who does not love, who never cries, but then it may be that he loves too much. We should bear this in mind when he rages against the cheap facsimiles of traditional culture that pass for the real thing among the very people who should know better. The introduction he wrote to his *Son sei sorelle* ('They are six sisters') is an exercise in righteous fury and indignation, the wrath of Achilles transposed into culture. Elsewhere, like Cassandra and Petronius rolled into one, he rails against what Naples has become, 'a city soaked with vulgarity', 'dull and degraded', and 'sinking into nothingness'. If I were to say he's wrong most likely he would argue, saying I wasn't there to see things as they once were, just as one day I might say the same to someone much younger than me. Yes, even if one has to dig deeply for it, *l'oro di Napoli*, I think he loves it although maybe he ought to allow others more latitude. There is a peculiar egotism in those who think the world stops with them.

✳

The palazzo where he lives – yes, I'll call it that – is full of paintings and sculptures, musical instruments, *presepi*, crockery, books, and, most interestingly, objects of an esoteric nature. It has been his dream that his collection might one day form the basis for a museum of music and folklore, but the city of Naples has been slow on the uptake. The mayor seems otherwise engaged or else too disengaged to notice what the city might lose or maybe he has already been lashed by De Simone's tongue. There are whispers that it may all go to Montemarano, a town in the province of Avellino famous for its distinctive *tarantella montemaranese*. A man begins to live as a ghost amid the things he accumulates. When finally those things take over, there'll be nobody worthy of them. I couldn't see anywhere a room that spoke of ordinary existence, not even the kitchen where even the utensils were things of beauty, everything aesthetically in its place. Among the curios there was one object in particular that caught my eye, a circular piece of slate with numbers carved into it. Anyone with a grasp of arithmetic could have worked out the *how* of it in seconds (I failed to), and as to the *why* of it I could only puzzle. Maybe this was the code that might unlock the universe.

I asked De Simone to explain it to me.

'Add the numbers in the top row. 16 + 3 + 2 + 13 = 34. Add the numbers in the second column. 3 + 10 + 6 + 15 = 34. And then do it diagonally. 16 + 10 + 7 + 1 = 34. Whichever way you look the solution will always be 34.'

'Its significance?'

'It's magic. "34" in the Kabbalah signifies we have a mind. The square is inside a circle, this representing a single year, and the circle is your mind. This is what makes culture. What it means is that culture does not die as long as it is linked to our thought. Capitalism is killing thought because people do not think any more.'

I couldn't tell whether or not he was spinning me a line for there was some mischief in his eyes. A scholar of the Kabbalah tells me he knows of nothing to this effect. According to the Pythagorean scheme, the significance of '34' is suffering, retribution, and penalties. The number in Hebrew is written with the letters *lamed* meaning authority and *daleth* door. The number identifies the person who will walk through that door. It symbolises the power of realisation in man. This small object, signifying intelligence, could serve as a talisman against everything De Simone hates or as a token of all he loves.

When I asked whether he might relate his childhood experiences of the war he immediately stonewalled me. Was this an old man's belligerence? Yes, I think so. A refusal to be steered onto any course other than the one he chose? Yes, I think so. A memory of something too painful to relate? All he would say is that he had lived through one of the most tragic moments of Neapolitan history, its occupation first by the Germans and then by the Americans. I don't think he was being careless with his words because, for him, there seemed to be little to choose between the two: a friendly bomb destroys every bit as much as an enemy one. What I do know is that there is an open letter he wrote to a 'Dottor Savoia' (the recipient's name an exercise in irony?) in which he relates a childhood memory of wartime Naples. Nineteen forty-four was a horrendous year despite the liberation of Naples by the Allies. The books of an American, John Horne Burns, an Englishman, Norman Lewis, and an Italian, Curzio Malaparte, their titles respectively, *The Gallery*, *Naples '44*, and *La pelle* ('The Skin') focus on those precise months. Three men wrote independently of each other, at times maybe even unknowingly brushing shoulders, but often it is with the happy result that a story in one book is corroborated by a similar story in another, or even both titles. Burns, a ghastly man whom Naples made human for perhaps the first and only time in his life, survives his own purple prose. Lewis, morally upright and clear-sighted, is likewise brought to love, but with a much more clinical eye. Malaparte, a compulsive liar hungry for truth, was brought to hate. The book he wrote is a warped masterpiece. All three describe a city utterly humiliated. Food was scarce, women plentiful, which would make for one of the more tragic equations in the history of modern Naples. Women turned to prostitution in order to feed their families. At the former convent of Monteoliveto, which the American troops had requisitioned as an army base, some of the soldiers, when not trading army rations for sex, would occasionally distribute them freely to the hungry. One day, a group of people, among them De Simone, aged ten, and his grandmother, visited the convent in the hope of obtaining sustenance. A soldier appeared in the courtyard with a container of meat, which he began to open as if he were about to hand it out. Suddenly he yelled, spat on the meat, and, much to the mirth of his fellows, threw the container onto the ground. A woman knelt down, removed the contaminated layer, and began to take the good meat when a second soldier pulled down his flies and pissed on the meat, spraying the woman at the same time. One can easily imagine why an old man has no desire to revisit that scene.

'My main preoccupation at the beginning was to be a composer and pianist,' continued De Simone. 'I studied at the conservatory of San Pietro a Majella in Naples. My father and aunt came from theatre. My grandfather was a comic actor, my stepmother and an aunt of mine were singers in operetta. I remember asking myself what the point of studying music was if I were to end up wearing a smoking jacket and performing for rich people.'

A jobbing musician is what in fact he became. The death of his father left him in an impecunious state, and so he taught a little, became an organist on a TV show, and played Cole Porter songs in an American club. It was during this amorphous period of his life that he began to make forays into the countryside.

'At some point you plugged into this great folk tradition,' I said, 'the art and music of Campania. This, presumably, was the great turning point in your life. Can you describe it?'

'I couldn't do much, one cannot stop history, but at least I did something. Fifty or sixty years ago, I collected and recorded the voices of the real thing. It is not fully appreciated now, but it will be in the future when the tradition is completely dead. Also I recorded and translated the fairy tales of Campania as told me by the old people. Something of them has been kept alive, but it's shallow compared to what I collected. I also wrote on the popular celebrations, the Virgilian traditions. There was no plan for what I did. I lived day by day. It is the same way I write music. It is not for intellectuals. That popular tradition is now the missing link upon which the whole world ought to be focused. The greatest losses in any culture occur when it detaches itself from what tradition really is.'

'Was the moment of crisis when the agrarian reforms were introduced?'

'It came long before, when Italy was united by force. We were defeated then. It was something decided at a table, a political project, not a realistic one. Naples has always been friendly with Venice, and Venice with Naples, but they are very different. The act of putting everything together has taken away so much from all the different cultures. I am not a Marxist, but I blame capitalism and the culture of money, the imperialism of commerce which has imposed a mass culture that is killing humanity. I studied the popular traditions, but the oral tradition is very different from what you find elsewhere. The traditions of Naples and the south of Italy are deeply religious, but not necessarily Catholic. There is a difference between Rome and Naples in the religious aspect, between the Catholic Church there and the popular religious tradition here. The Pope is not very well accepted here. We have had great popes, of course, Pius XII being one of them, whereas Pope John XXIII destroyed the Church. Vatican II destroyed tradition and in doing so it killed religion. It was the end of the fantastic Latin language. The peasants used to pray in Latin. I have great admiration for the English because they preserve a sort of cult towards the Queen. I believe the future of humanity is more on the side of the Far East. Compared to the north of Italy, it is more ancient, more ancestral, here. The peasants, the shepherds, they are for the Madonna. Who *is* the Madonna though? She is the mother of Jesus, *probably*,' at which De Simone gave a sly wink, 'but she is also an ancient divinity. With respect to the tradition it is very difficult to say who she is exactly. Also there is nothing written about it because the tradition lives in the imaginary ... it is what we dream, it is what parents tell their children, and what they, in turn, will tell their children. It is nothing one can put inside a clear definition.'

'You would seem to be half pagan.'

'We are all pagans! I am a religious person, but it doesn't matter if one is pagan or Christian. I love Christ, the *real* man, but we also have Apollo and Dionysus. I believe that the figure of Christ is similar to the latter. Christ says, "This is my body and eat it" and Dionysus said the same, "Drink my blood" and then the Bacchantes kill Dionysus and eat his flesh. We have a tradition of divine possession. You find it at Madonna dell'Arco.

They dance for the Madonna because she wants dance. There is a procession, the bands play, and the devotees make the effigy of the Madonna dance, but not inside the church – the Pope doesn't want this, the Vatican does not approve of *tarantismo*. And I say to them, "I pay taxes so let me do what I like." It is a kind of compromise, a matter of give and take. Today is San Gennaro's day. We wait for him to perform a miracle. If it does not happen then we have to be afraid. Once they used to ring the bells when the blood liquefied but not any more. That sound was not a bad noise. It was used to regulate time. Maybe in the future we won't have calendars. The TV will tell you that today you have to eat this, you have to go to bed at such and such a time, and you have to make love, but only once. The artist is not a rebel. He is someone who has to say the truth, and truth more often than not is on the other side of power.'

'But surely a desire for truth is what makes one a rebel in this world.'

'I don't care. Artists have always said what they think because they don't subscribe to dogma. Mozart never walked the path, he went his own way. Bartók is another great artist who died in misery. I am a composer. I write because I have to say the truth.'

I first came to Roberto De Simone on the wings of the song which Antonella D'Agostino immortalised. *La gatta Cenerentola* in its entirety is a response to the riches of Neapolitan music of the past, in a sense his gift to it, or what in his own words he describes as 'a mirror to the tradition'. The plot comes from Giambattista Basile's story of Zelolla in *Lo cunto de li cunti* ('The Tale of Tales', 1634), which is the earliest written version of the folk tale whose heroine we know better as Cinderella. De Simone's work is not so much an opera as a curious hybrid of musical theatre with its roots in eighteenth-century song and ancient theatre.

The lyrics of 'Jesce sole' are few and disarmingly simple. It comprises the first stanza only of what may have been a lullaby dating from the beginning of the thirteenth century. It is briefly mentioned in Boccaccio's *Decameron* and quoted in a fifteenth-century codex now in the Bibliothèque Nationale in Paris. What it turns into is a plea for deliverance. What I first listened to one magical afternoon is, to all intents and purposes, De Simone's composition, his reimagining of an old tune.

Jesce sole
nun te fa cchiù suspira'
siente mai
ca li ffigliole
hanno tanto da pria'
Jesce sole,
jesce sole!

Rise, oh sun
Rise, oh sun
Rise, oh sun
Don't make us wait any longer!

Do young girls
Really have to
Implore you so?

When I told him that for me it was the anthem of Naples he chuckled.

'I wrote it in a dream. It was written for the voice and not for the melody. You can't use your brain only, not even your heart. You have to *dream* the music. "Jesce sole" tells the story not of the real sun but of the sun at night. You may ask how, in darkness, you can see the sun rise. I had been listening to some beautiful recordings of Buddhist monks with their long trumpets and low voices. They were looking for light in the darkest notes. I wrote the song with this in mind. I didn't write it for the sun that is born each morning but for the sun of the night. Art is like this. You have to wait in darkness for the sun to be born.'

(Corrado Sfogli, when I related this, exclaimed, 'The sun does not rise!' Roberto De Simone, he said, remains in self-imposed darkness.)

'And silence, is this, too, not a condition of art, the most profound silence being that which will preserve culture?'

'It's why I live in this place because of its silence. The walls are thick and where I sleep there is no noise, no cars. I do not watch television. Noise impedes music. Silence implies listening. Silence is a culture that has been lost. It is what allows you to think. We have barbaric noise instead. In the monasteries, you work and think in silence.'

We sat in silence for a moment.

'Do you hear any noise here?' he asked.

'Just us.'

'We don't make noise, we transmit thought.'

When I told De Simone I was investigating the close relationship between life and death in Naples, he replied, 'Which death are you referring to?'

As death would seem to defy categories, the question threw me a little.

'I am thinking of Pulcinella who goes back and forth between the worlds of the living and the dead, the cult of *anime pezzentelle*, the fact Naples is in the shadow of a volcano...'

'Death in Naples takes various shapes, but you have to note the differences between them. You have a symbol of death in Pulcinella, a black and white figure, the colours of death. There is always a scene in which Pulcinella fights death. And then you have the *anime pezzentelle* whose identities we don't know, who died during plague and war and did not receive the holy sacraments. The cult of Fontanelle is now dead. It's over. When I was younger I used to go there. Most of the people who went there received the dead in their dreams. They would each adopt a skull and maybe they would build a little wooden house and put the skull inside. They would go there and pray with flowers and candles, offering refreshment to the dead. Sometimes it happened that people were possessed by the soul of the skull and they would cry and scream, but culture does not belong to history and those who belong to history alone don't understand it. Clever people think this is all superstition. There is a conflict between reason and dream. That is why Naples is not the city it used to be. It has become too rational.'

There came back to me memories of Leopardi's words on the subject of reason: 'Reason is the enemy of all greatness: reason is the enemy of nature: nature is great, reason is small.' I had something with which I hoped to pique De Simone's interest.

'I was told I'd never meet anyone in the cult, but I met a woman just a few doors away from me on the Vico Scassacocchi.'

Sure enough, De Simone perked up as if being given news of an old acquaintance.

'How old is she?'

'In her eighties.'

'So she came before the politics, before the communists. Does she still go to the cemetery?'

'No, she is not physically able to. She found her skull in the Sant'Agostino della Zecca which is closed for repairs.'

There is nothing quite like death to cheer the man of morbid sensibilities.

'I went there many times! You find all these characters among the dead. Quite often there'll be two brothers, Mario and Renato. Sometimes they are called "the two policemen". In that particular church there was the cult of "John and Robert", the Kennedy brothers, which is an instance of how history and dream connect with each other. There is also the body of a musician, the clothes he wears dating to the sixteenth century. He was from a little place in Campania and there were calls for him to be returned, but the mayor wanted the bones to be left as they were. I was once asked whether the musician should be sent back and I said no, he has always been here. Don't touch anything.'

'This woman I met on my street said the cult is like an underground river. She said everything comes back.'

'In popular culture there is always this opposition between history and metahistory. Time produces history while in this culture time is considered like a serpent that renews itself. So every bad thing that happens – war, catastrophe – comes back.'

I'd been waiting for that serpent to arrive. *Metahistory*, not a word I'd ever had cause to use, is the consideration of what history is in a philosophical sense.

'Are you really saying everything is finished?'

'Yes. There is still something, but only in those countries where consumerism has not yet arrived. Now everything is business. The only person you can trust with respect to the tradition is that old woman you met. The rest is all a bunch of lies.'

'Is it lies or is it because everything changes?'

'Official power is capitalism and consumerism and now, through TV, they have destroyed everything. People are unhappy now because this society does not allow you to think. It only wants you to buy. I don't know where I can purchase my thoughts. There is no shop for them. You go to a peasant and he tells you a fairy tale and you have bought something without money. I do not watch television, which is dangerous. I just read books and the newspapers. Naples is selling herself. People think that this is good, but it is all about consumerism. I don't go out because when I do I see how everything has changed. Once there were people selling fruit, now there are just supermarkets. Tomatoes do not come from here any more, they come from Spain. Oil does not come from Puglia but from places where it costs less. You only see telephones and clothes ... make-up. There are no stationers because nobody writes any more. Everyone speaks with a microphone. That's why it's the end of the world.'

There is a line I heard once from some mediaeval poem and which I have never been able to retrace: 'The world will come to an end when everyone walks about with a conch pressed to his ear.' Could I have imagined it? What De Simone describes, could it be an old prophecy come to pass?

'With everything gone,' I said, 'you must have a troubled heart.'

'We are witnesses. As long as God gives life to us, truth is what matters. We have a duty to tell the truth. I am eighty-five. If you ask me how things were before I can tell you. I am not unhappy about that.'

'Surely, though, tradition never stays in one place. It has to change in order to continue.'

I was surprised by his response.

'Tradition cannot change because for it to do so the relationship between man and nature would have to change. Tomorrow, at 5:30 a.m., the sun will be born again, but in September the clocks will change because the sun rises later. You cannot alter this. Tradition is like the sun. Man changes, the sun doesn't. Man does not have a relationship with the sun any more. The visit to the dead doesn't change. Night doesn't change. Dreams don't change. In ancient cultures they used to have dream culture. I no longer know what young people dream about. Who knows what they will dream of in the future. This is the end of the world in which the death of history will be presented. Christ can be considered the end of a story, but he is also the beginning of a new one. It is not likely he will come back though.'

I profoundly disagreed with him and argued that for tradition to survive it has to change. There was no moving him on this issue.

'You have a dark vision.'

'Unfortunately, yes.'

'So you have effected a divorce with Naples?'

'Officially, yes.'

'Unofficially?'

'I am still linked to San Gennaro and the Madonna dell'Arco. I am still connected to people over fifty because they still know something. Young people don't know anything.'

'But surely we must teach them, Maestro…'

'We have to teach them not to turn on the television, not to buy clothes or make-up. We still have our words which are a powerful element in this culture. Once the old taught the young, but now they are put aside.'

God knows I'm not exactly an optimist, but when pessimism is taken too far it becomes a kind of luxury, something in which to wallow like a hippo in mud.

'Do you not realise there are young people out there who love you?'

Just then, so briefly I could easily have missed it, he glanced towards the window which was just a bit too high for him to look out of from where he was, a small, tired man, full to bursting with all the wonders he'd seen in his life, sour at how those wonders have been allowed to dissipate, a weary man confined to his wheelchair.

✳

The memory of the *tabula hebdomadaria* wouldn't let go of me. I even considered making a return journey in order to quiz Roberto De Simone on this alone, but there was no saying whether he would comply with my request once I'd got there. I had been fortunate enough to meet him twice. Why did he agree to see me? Maybe I was sufficiently from outside. I had taken a photo of the *tabula hebdomadaria* and when later I enlarged it, I was able to make out clearly the names he wrote there, who, it seems, are more alive to him than the living, the ghosts who occupy his palace although that palace might just as easily be the physical manifestation of his mind. Some of the names I recognised from before, others came to light during my researches, and still others, although I dearly love to claim a full house, remain a mystery. Slowly, step by step, I was able to construct De Simone's world through his past associations and maybe then I would understand better why it is that he feels they represent a world gone, irretrievable. I knew this, of course, and it's something I've always known, but something in me refuses to acknowledge what I already believe.

All will be gone, all we ever were will cease to be.

Among the historical figures on the *tabula hebdomadaria* one finds: 'Amedeo Volfango' more widely known as Wolfgang Amadeus Mozart (1756–91) who as a boy was brought by his father to Naples, where he made a musical splash and bought himself some brand new clothes; Antonio Petito (1822–76), also known as 'Totonno' or 'the madman', actor and playwright, a semiliterate, of whom it has been said that with each play he wrote he would use a litre of ink that covered not only several reams of paper but also his own body and clothes, and who, as an interpreter of Pulcinella, provided him with the modern costume we know and invested him with greater psychological depth than had ever been seen before; Salvatore De Muto (1876–

1970), said by some to have been the greatest Pulcinella of all time only to be forgotten and left destitute, and with whom De Simone's grandfather shared the stage; Giulia De Caro (1646–97), 'la principessa del bordello', comedienne, singer, and whore who, as one of the most revered opera singers of her time, became, as one occasionally does through the restorative processes of fame, 'a virtuous and honest bride' – she might have been tailor-made for *La gatta Cenerentola* – and she sang from the balcony of a lover's palazzo through a new-fangled object called a megaphone; Leonardo Vinci (1690–1730), composer of *opere buffe* in the Neapolitan language, one of which was titled *La Partenope*, also a teacher of Pergolesi, and who, so it is said, was poisoned by a jealous husband in the wake of an ill-advised affair; and Andrea Perrucci (1651–1704), playwright and librettist, early theoretician of the *Commedia dell'arte* and whose most famous work *La Cantata dei Pastori* ('The Cantata of the Shepherds'), an edition of which was edited by De Simone, was traditionally performed on Christmas Eve.

When I asked the Maestro why Mozart and not Verdi he replied that Verdi was not the great musician everyone says he is and besides, he represents Italy and Naples is not Italy. There can be no arguing with a 1799-er.* Wagner is definitely out of

---

*I struggle with this. Naples could be its own country, and a sense of this lies at the bottom of my thinking about the place, but when it comes to lamenting the not quite five months when, from 21 January to 13 June, Naples became the Parthenopean Republic then I'm no longer sure. I had started off as a closet Bourbon with Charles III in charge, not that I am so taken by the man but because, whatever his deficiencies were, he was responsible for much of the very best of what one sees in Naples, but the achievements of one ruler need to be consolidated by the next one otherwise they evaporate, and only the buildings survive, the spirit which produced them gone. Charles's son, Ferdinand, is one of history's nincompoops. There are key dates when the city was brought low, 1799 one of them, when the dead

the picture, no space for him on the *tabula hebdomadaria* even though the gardens of the Villa Rufolo in Ravello, south of Naples, were an inspiration for his *Parsifal*. 'Il magico giardino di Klingsor è trovato,' he wrote in the guestbook of the Albergo Palumbo on 26 May 1880 while waiting for breakfast to be served – 'Klingsor's magical garden found'. At this point in our conversation the Maestro pulled one of his surprises.

'There is nothing in the whole of Wagner,' De Simone told me, 'that matches in brilliance *Sergeant Pepper's Lonely Hearts Club Band*.'

I was rendered speechless though not a little pleased by the sheer audacity of his words. My youthful enthusiasm had been vindicated by an octogenarian, which was not something I could ever have hoped for at the time.

The names of the Maestro's familiars on the *tabula hebdomadaria* include: Tita Parisi, a legendary musician with whom, as a child, De Simone studied piano on Via dei Mille, who would later describe him as 'a magnificent student, a born musician, studious and intelligent'; Concetta Barra, who has one of those rare voices that scrape heaven and hell at the same time, a haunting voice, I would have given much to have De Simone's memories of her; Vera Lombardi, a socialist (though heterodox) politician who, during the war, was involved in the antifascist movement and who at the age of ninety-one played her first and only acting role as Maria Bakunin in Mario Martone's film, *Death of a Neapolitan Mathematician*; Lea Bartorelli, better known as 'Zietta Liù' (the name she took from the slave girl in Puccini's opera *Turandot*), a journalist, a writer of children's stories, and drama teacher, one of whose students was De Simone; Giulia Ciletti, one of the last funeral mourners in Irpinia,

---

must have wept in their graves, 1944 another – but what is to be made of this dream of a republic? Roberto De Simone is the Parthenopean Republic's most illustrious citizen.

who, when De Simone finally persuaded her to record a funeral lament for a mother, broke down in tears at the memory of her own mother with whom, in her youth, she had a tempestuous relationship; the writer and film director, Pier Paolo Pasolini; the anthropologist, Ernesto De Martino, the haunting title of whose book on southern Italian tarantism, *La terra del rimorso* ('The Land of Remorse') says just about all that needs to be said on the subject; the folklorist, Gennaro Romei; the Pulcinella street performer, Nunzio Zambello who was Bruno Leone's maestro; Giusto Monaco, Greek and Latin philologist and a director of ancient classical theatre; Annabella Rossi, anthropologist and filmmaker, one of her greatest accomplishments being her leading role in the making of the TV documentary *Sud e magia, in ricordo di Ernesto De Martino* ('South and Magic, In Memory of Ernesto De Martino', 1978), her exploration of southern magic, and who collaborated with De Simone in the writing of the book *Carnevale si chiamava Vincenzo* ('The Carnival Called Vincenzo'); Pasquale Aloisio, master craftsman, maker of the intricate Christmas scenes called *presepi* and who, in December 1943, after the Nazis fled Naples, transformed with cork and moss one of their abandoned tanks into one, turning the gun barrel into a comet, an ironic gesture if ever there was one; Emanuele Esposito, another maker of *presepe* who was also the oral guardian of the complex culture of Grottaglie in the province of Taranto; the street singer, Eugenio Pragliola, who, when questioned about his illiteracy, replied, 'I have two balls, respectfully speaking, as many as a Mongol' and who provided the title to Ars Nova's first CD; 'Fruttella', the nickname of Michela Erbaggio, who, aged seventy-nine, danced around a fire and sang a lament that marked the end of the festa in Maddaloni; the singers and musicians who De Simone encountered when he was collecting songs of Campania, among them Antonio Torre 'lord of the tammorra' and his female counterpart Rosa Nocerino 'queen of the tammorra' who taught Fausta Vetere how to play it; Vito Fresolone, who played the *zampogna*, which in local dialect means 'many sounds played together', and which is the southern Italian bagpipe whose sound tears at the soul; Alfredo Ordano, whose voice was considered exceptional in its power, musicality, and timbre; Venere Veneroso 'la Spagnola', who also sang a lament for the death of the carnival; Giovanni Del Sorbo, Antonietta Salvi, Francesco Giffoni, Giovanni 'Pellecchiella' Pirozzi, and Virginia Aiello, all of whom were shepherds, farmers, and the like. There is a mysterious slip upon which is written, *La Grande Imperatrice* ('The Great Empress') whose identity took me a while to crack, who was a farmer from Avellino called Giuseppe de Martis who, once a year, at the festa in Irpinia, took on the role of the *imperatrice*, putting on a gown woven out of straw and intertwined with shells; and Gennaro Albano who will be the subject of my last chapter.

And finally, on the heavenly ledger in the ghost palace of Roberto De Simone – whether or not it has already been written in his own neat hand and tucked away somewhere safe I didn't think it proper to ask – there is a space reserved for his own name.

An Infinitesimal Particle of the Vegetal Universe

My journey ends here, as I knew it must, where the 'hot' mountain, Vesuvius, and the 'cold' mountain, Monte Somma, meet. Originally they were one. A single image of the solitary mountain survives, in a fresco from the *lararium* or holy shrine in the Casa del Centenario in Pompeii, which now is in the archaeological museum in Naples. It depicts Dionysius covered with grapes the size of nectarines and holding a *thyrsus* in one hand and a *kantharos* in the other, standing on the slope of the mountain which was, and still is, famous for its vineyards. There is a panther at his side, his preferred mode of transport and – a whiff of decadence here – he appears to be pouring it some of his wine. The *thyrsus* is a staff made from giant fennel, adorned with a ribbon and topped with a pine cone, its phallic imagery unmistakable. As a symbol of prosperity and fertility it was commonly used in religious rites. *Thyrsus*, a word to commit to one's memory storage, if not for Scrabble then at least for as long as it takes to whip up a surprise. The *kantharos*, a wine cup with two high handles, Greek in origin, was used in rituals as a symbol of rebirth and resurrection. Abundance, fertility, rebirth, resurrection: potent words, they contain all that we might wish for ourselves.

The Roman poet Martial in a celebrated epigram speaks of the mountain's verdancy, the shading vines, the noble grape, the satyrs' dance – all in all, an idyllic setting for a god devoted to pleasure – and then he clobbers the reader with the line 'Cuncta iacent flammis et tristi mersa fauilla' ('All of this lies covered in flames and sorrowful ash.') The eruption of 24 August AD 79 was powerful enough to cleave the mountain.* The geological conjunction that was formed, which in local dialect is called *ognundo*, is where, more or less, I took my enquiries with respect to one of the stranger varieties of spiritual experience.

A coiled serpent fills the lower third of the fresco. What would the artist have thought if one were to inform him that very soon it would strike? It is a remarkable image in quite the most remarkable of places. Who was the last ancient to look at it? Maybe it was the mistress of the house, a bracelet slithering down her arm as she cupped her hand over her mouth in horror at the infernal racket outside. One could get awfully fanciful here and imagine what went through her mind, incredulity at how, on the turn of a denarius, things can go belly up because so much of life up to that point had been devoted to pleasure. She died. The fresco survives, as good as new.

It speaks volumes for the duality of Naples and its surroundings that the serpent was then looked upon as a symbol of abundance, which is why it adorns so many ancient shrines. The agathodaimon, the name given to that harbinger of good fortune, comes from the Greek for 'noble spirit' or 'good daimon' and, although a young man, the agathodaimon was often depicted

---

* Another poem by Martial mentions a man who sets fire to his house in order to collect the insurance. And I thought insurance was a modern scam. Sadly, though, there was nobody left in either Pompeii or Herculaneum to put in a claim and if there were he would probably be informed there is no coverage for the tantrums of spleenful gods.

as a serpent, the vineyards and fields of plenty its domicile. Was there, as was common practice in ancient Campania, a serpent kept in the house? A propitious figure, the serpent was a symbol of the *genius*, the divine nature which resides in all things, man and nature, what we would later call soul although it is better to think of it as the guardian spirit that accompanies one from birth to death. The *genius loci* applies to the protective spirit of a place, volcanoes in particular, although Vesuvius the destroyer was yet to be. What were the early Christians thinking when they gave the serpent such a bad name? It infects my own prose. They sought in this, as in so many things, a reversal, either that or they were out to press the restart button on our story of the human race. So how much was religion, how much politics? I wish the Virgin on top of the Obelisco dell'Immacolata in the Piazza del

Gesú Nuovo would take her foot off the serpent which surely is one of God's creatures and deserves to be treated as such. To give Christianity its due, they can be a menace. One would not want to accidentally step on the *Vipera aspis* which accounts for ninety per cent of snakebites in Italy. The asp, a symbol of royalty, has been, in both Greek and Egyptian cultures, for purposes of suicide and execution, the snake of choice.*

Abundance, fertility, *death*. This may seem a rather serpentine way of setting the scene for the remarkable *festa della montagna* that is held every year on the slopes a few miles up from Somma Vesuviana, which one reaches by taking Via Caprabianca, the small country road that translates wonderfully as the 'Street of the White Goat'. Although Christian, the event evokes much that is pagan in character and substance. It begins on the first Saturday after Easter, *il sabato dei fuochi* ('the Saturday of the fires') and concludes on 3 May, which in local dialect is called *o' 3 ra croce* ('the third of the Cross'), at the Santa Maria a Castello. This second event is where all the *paranze*† join forces for a final salute to 'Mamma Schiavona', which is one of the Black Madonna's names. According to legend it was on this date in AD 326 that Helena, mother of Constantine the Great, discovered a relic of the True Cross.

There are several simultaneous celebrations on the first date, but the one I will discuss here is organised by the *paranza d'Ognundo* whose participants consider themselves to be the most traditional and perhaps the most exclusive of the various *paranze*. This I can't properly judge as I've been forever thwarted in my desire to be in several places at the same time. I will, on

---

* 'With thy sharp teeth this knot intrinsicate / Of life at once untie' – Shakespeare, *Anthony and Cleopatra*.

† On the simplest level, the word *paranza* refers to any group of people working towards a single end. As we will see, its meaning is rather more complex.

the other hand, accept their statement as true. Certainly the instruments are the ones that have always been played, the songs the ones that have always been sung albeit with minor additions here and there to accommodate the previous year's occurrences. One of the ways by which the *paranza d'Ognundo* may be distinguished from other *paranze* is that its cultural roots come from deep inside the community rather than having been reinvented for them by some culture squad on the outside. The difference is subtle but of vital importance in that it is distinct from the revivalism that some years ago spread throughout much of the south of Italy and which, on occasion, smacked of marketable culture. There comes a point when even purity becomes merchandise. The *contaminazione* which the *paranza d'Ognundo* has been at great pains to avoid is, oddly enough, considered a virtue elsewhere, even to the point of being advertised as such, especially in the popular music sphere which welcomes 'contaminating influences'.

Roberto De Simone laments the fact that in recent times the celebrations have become commercialised to the degree of having been polluted with modern devices such as loudspeakers and microphones. The whole point of the tammorra, he argues, lies in its intimate proximity to the human heartbeat and so to artificially make it louder paradoxically puts the listener at a greater remove. Certainly the Maestro is vexed by change, and much of this is understandable, but my own experience of the *paranza d'Ognundo* was to be a deeply moving one. The problem would be whether it could be captured in words because its intensity owes almost everything to non-verbal communication. It made absolute sense while I was there, but no sooner was I back in Naples than it became difficult to describe and now, back in London, almost impossible to explain. Say that it centres on a single branch of a chestnut tree that in the words of the anthropologist Fabio Birotti becomes 'una particella infinitesimale dell'universo vegetale' ('an infinitesimal particle of the vegetal universe').* I think, but I'm not sure, that what I register in the eyes of people I've attempted to describe this matter of a branch to is the question 'So?' *So, so,* so what one does is to carefully choose, which is to say one *knows* when one sees it, cut, strip a branch of its bark and protrusions after which, for the duration of a single day, that branch will be like no other in the universe.

The earliest written evidence for the origins of the *paranza d'Ognundo* can be traced back to the end of the nineteenth century. If, however, one chooses to follow the oral tradition then the year 1640 is cited, a date arrived at by the current older members of the group having spoken to elderly people who then recounted the memories of their grandfathers whose memories of their grandfathers took things back to what is essentially a date of convenience, which is to say it might be older still but it is not more recent. It is the rule of thumb by which many traditions can be traced before they evaporate into the historical mist, which often is when myth plugs the absence, but then, as if there are hidden currents beneath the soil that never change course, there come reports of traditions much older and in certain respects remarkably similar. Times there are when it is difficult to distinguish between 'pagan revival' and 'Christian renewal', although such phrases did not enter people's minds until fairly recently, with there being an imported hint of brimstone. It is worth noting in this context that the word 'pagan' is derived from the Latin *paganus* meaning 'rustic' or 'villager' and that it was only much later, in the fourth century, that the Church made it a derogatory word referring to heathens. There

---

* The reader might wish to be guided to his book, *Fuochi del Vesuvius* (Gramma Edizioni, 2011).

is no accounting for country folk and their ways. Much has been written on the similarities between the various manifestations of the Black Madonna in southern Italy and the Egyptian goddess Isis 'the Queen of Heaven, Mother of God' who exerted a powerful influence over the Bay of Naples. She was the most potent of gods and goddesses, and her spiritual governance spread from Egypt to all over the Graeco-Roman world and endured for a period longer than, thus far, the whole of the Christian era. Visually, too, there are remarkable parallels between the Black Madonna and a black Isis seated on a throne with baby Horus on her lap, often suckling him, and sometimes accompanied by her husband, her brother, Osiris, the three of them forming a holy trinity. The recent claim that the Black Madonna *is* Isis is less than subtle. The important thing here is that the older anticipates the newer and the newer evokes the older and that without its roots in the ancient world, Christianity would be a shrivelled plant.

Angelo Calabrese whom I met at the 3 May event at Santa Maria a Castello is an author, lecturer, and scientific director of the Vesuvian Academy of Ethnohistorical Traditions, his professorial air such that when he spoke the young people in the room fell silent for about twenty of the forty-five minutes I was with him, which, in Italian terms, is roughly equivalent to eternity. He places much store by the origins of words (or what my sometime translator Adriana Vasques, citing her father, calls 'il significato intimo delle parole') although at times it seems to take him down paths strange. We stumbled onto Shakespeare via Jacques Lacan, both of whom Professor Calabrese greatly admires. A handful of Englishmen with their scatty theories on Shakespeare is no match for a handful of foreigners with their rather more extreme tendencies. They, too, want their pound of Shakespearean flesh and there's no price so high they will not pay it. 'Shake sphere,' Calabrese explained, 'shaking the globe.' He is adamant in his belief that the Bard smuggled into his writing distinctly

Neapolitan figures of speech. When Hamlet quips with Rosencrantz and Guildenstern, describing King Claudius as 'a thing', and Guildenstern, not the sharpest tool in the shed, replies, 'A thing, my lord?' Hamlet's damning response is, 'Of nothing.' This fits snugly into the Lacanian universe. The French psychoanalyst was quick to see phallic connotations everywhere, and phalluses are a big thing in Naples. Calabrese informed me that 'a thing of nothing', which signifies a loss of virility, is a typical Neapolitan phrase. Shakespeare in his doublet and breeches cutting a dashing figure on Vico Scassacocchi? Anything's possible. With the respect to the etymological origins of the *paranza*, however, a subject that had absorbed him for forty years, Calabrese is unimpeachable.

'When you see these men carrying the Madonna on their shoulders through the streets, walking and dancing at the same time, it looks like the Madonna is floating on a wave. *Barca*, the Italian for boat, contains the word *arca*, as in Noah's Ark. The *paranza* is a method of fishing, two boats moving in parallel, pulling a net between them.* What is preserved, although its meaning is lost on many people, is the memory of the boat, the movement of the wave, echoed in the carrying of the Madonna. A *paranza* is any group of people, but the one we are talking about is an association that is linked to the Black Madonna, which goes back to the cult of the Egyptian Isis. The Black Madonna was once situated in the soul of Naples. When the cult could no longer be celebrated there its devotees moved from the sea to the mountain, the mountains being safer, harder to reach. There are seven Black Madonnas: the Madonna di Montevergine in the province of Avellino, the Madonna delle Galline in Pagani, the Madonna dell'Arco in Sant'Anastasia, the Madonna dei Bagni in Scafati, the Madonna di Briano in the province of Caserta, the Madonna

---

* Once the catch makes it onto your plate it becomes *frittura di paranza*.

dell'Avvocata of Maiori, and the Santa Maria a Castello here.*
The Church did not want them to be linked to the Egyptian cult
and so they made up stories about their images being found in
the sea or else buried somewhere. The churches in the Campania

---

* Although geographically close it is surprising to discover how
the festas celebrating them differ in character and tone. While
the celebrations surrounding the Madonna dell'Arco strike me as
severe, a bit hysterical at times, those for the Madonna of the Hens
at Pagani are joyous. There the whole town dances. Almost all the
legends behind them are peculiar. I particularly like the one just
mentioned, which owes its name to a flock of sixteenth-century
hens pecking at a spot on the ground until they uncovered an image
of Our Lady of Mount Carmel. What they have in common is that
they are collectively known as the 'Madonne Pacchiane', the 'gaudy
Madonnas' that belong to the peasants.

devoted to the Black Madonna were founded on places of natural power – rivers, forks in the landscape, and the like. The church here is devoted to the one they found in the ground, a farmer's sculpture – the Madonna as a peasant woman, a *real* mother. She was black once, but someone tried to scrub her white. The *paranze* devoted to these "Seven Sisters" are brotherhoods that each come from a town or village, maybe a specific part of a city or the countryside. They are all different, each one with its own chapel and traditions, but on 3 May, which is what we are here to celebrate, they gather in one place.'

'Is there also a connection between the *paranza* and Christ as the fisher of men?'

'Yes, this was a Christian symbol from the very beginning. The Catholic Church still has this symbol of the anchor. So the people of the *paranza* express these ideas with their songs, the *canto a figliola*. The thing to remember is that the *paranza* is a brotherhood.'

'Is this why the Camorra stole the word?'

'We have a saying here, "We are all in the same boat."'

Somehow, through the agency of a rather special, difficult-to-obtain Vesuvian wine, homemade, deep yellow, fizzy, and wickedly potent, we drifted into a shaggy dog tale of how Angelo Calabrese's brother smuggled out of Communist Poland the woman who would later become his wife. The story struck me as wildly funny at the time.

Scrivi maccheronicamente, più semplice possibile.

'Write macaronically,' said Lucio Albano, 'as simply as possible.'* I had been expressing my worries about how to get

---

* The reader is here advised that Lucio is not using 'macaronic' in the OED meaning of the word but as referring to the pasta.

my thoughts on what I was about to witness onto the page in a convincing fashion. Also, I knew I was a UFO on the *paranza* radar. It is easily enough done, coming to grief with the intangible. After all, even Roberto De Simone, when he came here in the 1970s on his musical researches, discovering that the *canto a figliola* had survived here in its original form as a devotional song sung directly to the Madonna, began to collect the songs and was then accused of having stolen them for his own purposes. There is a thin line between what one does in good faith and how it is perceived by others, which inevitably leads to misconjecture. I am reminded of the great debate in 1960s America where there was a similar revival of interest in folk traditions, the surge of interest being the very thing that would pollute them. The city slickers had much to answer for in their search for authenticity although country folk were often only too keen to jump on the bandwagon. You can't trade baubles for culture, however, and not expect resentment when there's nothing left at the bottom of the burlap sack, which is why a very thin layer of plastic covers much of what was once vibrant in American popular culture. Italy has been suffering the same fate but not where I was, breathing the azure, on a mountain slope where already I had been buzzing to the sound of ancient voices. The *paranza d'Ognundo* is deeply protective of its traditions and would rather be left alone. It was the day before *il sabato dei fuochi* and the men of the *paranza* were scouring the hills for the tinder with which to build the three pyres, forty bundles (*fascine*) for each one. They would stop every so often and sing their praises to Mamma Schiavona, splashing brandy on the ground for the absentee dead before raising a toast to her.

'Macaronically?'

I was being advised by a man whose notions of writing were, so I believe, the equivalent of setting a wooden beam against a sturdily made brick wall at precisely three o'clock in the afternoon.

'Macaroni,' he said. 'You know the long hollow pasta that you have to break into pieces when you cook it?* They call a person who is simple, not too bright ... well, let's say a good guy but a bit stupid and gullible ... a "macaroni". So write simply so everyone will understand. The most difficult thing is to be simple.'

'Yes,' I said, swept away by the culinary analogy, 'otherwise the macaroni will be too hard or too soft.'

Lucio looked askance at me, but then he lived in a part of the world where for something to be not *al dente* was to border on the unimaginable.

'You will achieve more by adding a lot of simple words than by taking away a few difficult ones.'

This was going a bit too far but then a few minutes later I discovered that he worked in wood. You can heap the world on the tables such men make.

Lucio is the ruggedly handsome son of Sabatino Albano who is the capo of the *paranza d'Ognundo*, a role he inherited when his father, also called Lucio Albano but more popularly known as Zì Gennaro, died.† The position of capo is not hereditary, it is elected, but such was Zì Gennaro's reputation as a man of strength and probity that the title was passed from father to son, presumably on the principle that the magic of one cannot but infiltrate the other. It is not always the wisest of strategies, but Sabatino appears to have made the best of a deeply challenging inheritance. Apparently there was a fracas or two, and even, sad to report, a spot of vandalism. The memorial stone to Zì Gennaro was broken into pieces. The Albanos, father and son, are tight-lipped on the how and why of this. It is a matter of things *not* said although now and then there is a whisper of enemies, words to the effect that 'they', whoever *they* might be, 'will make us stronger'. A siege mentality will often cause one to see enemies

---

* The real thing comes in lengthy stalks which one breaks before adding to the pot.
† *Zì* ('Uncle') is an honorific, affectionate, addition.

everywhere. Still, there is a great deal to protect oneself against. It is easy to imagine that one day Lucio will fill his father's and his grandfather's shoes because he has a commanding presence, as strong as his father's is gentle, which is not to say one is better or worse than the other, simply that they appear to have different physical and mental constitutions. A tower of strength, Lucio would have been described in the days before the dissolution of the sexes as 'a man's man' although there are fleeting moments when he seems vulnerable. He also has a temper on him. When during the course of our conversation his mobile phone rang, which he ignored, and then rang again he dashed it against the ground to the gasps of the surrounding Italians who place as great a store by their talking pieces as they once did their swords.

We spoke of Zì Gennaro whose spirit continues to dominate the place, which is how we will continue to call him so that he not be confused with his grandson who related the story to me. He was born in 1913, the last of ten children, to a relatively prosperous family in Naples. Their mother did not have enough breast milk to feed Gennaro and his brother Mario, so she went to the egg market in Naples which provided opportunities for town people to ask country people if there were any wet nurses available. The woman they found, Maria Cerciello, was from Somma Vesuviana and had recently lost a child called Gennaro, which is how Lucio became Gennaro although he kept the surname Albano. Maria formed an attachment such as often happens with women who have lost their own children, who see in the substitute at the breast features of the departed. She did not want to surrender him to the woman she referred to as 'the signora from Naples'. She told Gennaro that if she took him away he would not be able to see his friends any more. So every time his mother visited he would climb up a chestnut tree and keep himself hidden until she was gone. The fact it was a chestnut tree and not some other is most fitting.

'It is the tree of Monte Somma,' Lucio said. 'It is everything for us. The chestnut provides flour. It keeps us cool when it is hot and you can climb it and be at peace on your own with God. Before we had a chapel we made an arch of ginestra with the Madonna inside and put it under the tree.'

Often the chestnut has been called the 'bread tree' because the chestnuts were roasted and ground down into flour that was used to make bread as well as a substance similar to polenta, both of which were often the only carbohydrate available in mountainous regions. Food was short. Gennaro's mother continued to come to Somma. She paid Maria fourteen lire a month, an oddly concise figure. One day she saw Mario eating beetroots with chili and complained. 'I'm paying you so that my son can eat well,' she said to her. 'It is not enough for him.' Maria, however, couldn't afford anything else. Mario was taken back to Naples to be farmed out to another wet nurse. With the disappearance of a brother would Gennaro lose his friends as well? After many years he would still feel the pain of having been separated from his natural family, but a child operates according to his own peculiar logic. Gradually 'the lady from Naples' understood she'd lost her son and so Gennaro who had come from an urban background became a peasant with all the toughness and wiliness requisite to such an existence. A photograph of him, taken many years later, displays strong facial features akin to a mountain eagle.

There are probably childhood stories that point to how Gennaro came to be a leader of men but in the absence of those I will jump ahead to early manhood. Military service was compulsory in Fascist Italy, but because of the peculiar circumstances surrounding his childhood, the absence of identity papers, Gennaro, who was now married with children, had not been called up. Maybe fearful of being accused of desertion, he went to the police to ask why this was so. This, presumably, led him to the recruiting office where it was decided that he should go to the African frontier for six months. Six years would pass before he returned home. The English captured him at the Battle of Al-Alamein in 1942 and, after a horrific march through the desert where they quenched their thirst with animal urine and where a merciful bullet to the head put an end to the suffering of some of his comrades, Gennaro was kept in a prison camp in South Africa. He and his fellow prisoners, about twenty of them, some of whom were from Somma, formed a *paranza* and annually observed 'the Saturday of the fires'. Gennaro was an attendant to an imprisoned Italian officer from Calabria, who dined with the British officers and so had access to the canteen. When everybody had gone Gennaro would collect everything he could find, food and wine, and bring it to his fellow prisoners who at times were close to starvation. There was an English officer with whom he was on good terms, and because the officer was a good artist Gennaro asked him to draw in charcoal an image of the Madonna, which they all signed, and which later Gennaro would present as an ex voto to the Santa Maria a Castello. While imprisoned he vowed that if he and his friends survived he would continue the tradition at Somma.

Il sabato dei fuochi was interrupted during the war. Vesuvius, displeased at being ignored, erupted in 1944. In what was already a terrible year this must have been seen by the suffering populace as one portent too many. It is an odd aspect of human nature that misfortune should be thought of as somehow deserved.

Religious faith compounds this. Angry gods let loose their darts and their worshipers bare their chests. Curzio Malaparte in *La pelle* ('The Skin', 1949) describes the scene:

> The sky to the East was scarred by a huge crimson gash, which tinged the sea blood-red ... As always, the populace ascribed to that awful scourge the character of a punishment from heaven; they saw in the wrath of Vesuvius the anger of the Virgin, of the Saints, of the Gods of the Christian Olympus, who had become incensed at the sins, the corruption and the viciousness of men.

Almost every day at sunrise old women would walk up the mountain even though it was dangerous to do so in order to seek divine intervention so as to bring the war to an end.

Sabatino picked up his son's thread when Lucio, about to relate the story of Zì Gennaro's demise, broke down in tears.

'When the Germans left they set fire to our house,' said Sabatino. 'I saw everything. Before setting the fire they smashed all my mother's dishes. They felled trees in the roads to slow down the English and American advance. It was a bleak future. My father was in prison still and his house was gone. There were massacres. My grandfather was taken out to be shot and was already blindfolded but managed to escape. My brother and I took a *quattro soldi* coin with the face of Mussolini on it and we flattened his features with a hammer because this was the man who was responsible for our father being in prison. And then, with the same hammer, we smashed a bust of Mussolini to powder. We received only two letters from my father during all that time. Malicious people, *male lingue* ("bad tongues"), said my father wasn't coming back because he had found another woman whereas in fact he was surrounded by barbed wire. When finally my father and his companions were released in the spring of 1946 they were kept for forty days in a detention centre close to Naples to check if they had any illnesses. When he came home my mother told us to go to him but we did not recognise him. "You lied to us," we said. "No, he's there." Only the land tells you the truth. If you do things properly it will give its fruit. My father was very humble. "What have I done to deserve all this friendship?" he said. "All I did was to teach my children a sense of respect for nature and to be good to others." This humility is a feature of the *paranza*. My father went to the Madonna di Castello and, crawling, he licked the steps as he went up to the statue of the Madonna, his adoptive grandmother at his side with a tissue for him to wipe his tongue.'

Soon after, with the post-war revival of the *paranza d'Ognundo*, he was made its leader. There is nobody who in his recollections of Zì Gennaro does not speak of his incredible strength of character, his ability to handle farmers, politicians and *Camorristi* alike, and whose sense of justice was such that he would be called upon to settle everything from family to land disputes. This was due, in part, to an ability to listen in silence for any length of time and then to pronounce a verdict with one or two short phrases. This said, he was not beyond using his hands to settle an argument on those rare occasions when words failed him. He was also acutely aware that society had changed since before the war, not least with respect to the agrarian reforms and industrial development favoured by the Italian government during the 1950s, which effectively brought an end to Italian peasant culture.

The new society was based on men in suits and ties deciding what farmers should do. A man who looks at the clouds and can't tell you the next day's weather ought not to be put in charge. A man such as this who reaches for a cow's udder deserves the kick he gets. Eric Hobsbawm got it right when he says that 'the most dramatic change of the second half of this century, and the one which cuts us off forever from the world of the past, is the death of peasantry'. What is less easy to determine is which side

Hobsbawm is on, the Marxist point of view being always such a lamentably positive one, but at the risk of being a romantic, if being a romantic is to engage with matters of the soul, I would side with the writer and film director Pier Paolo Pasolini's verdict that it was 'anthropological genocide' and that with the shift from field to factory came consumerism on a scale that in his words was 'a fascism worse than the classical one'. Silvio Berlusconi had yet to show his face. On the other hand, it was during this period that the ideas of Antonio Gramsci (although he died almost twenty years earlier) came into prominence, particularly with respect to his view that it was advisable for intellectuals to engage with folk culture. If there has been a spasmodic revivalism it is because there is a tendency in the human mind to seize upon whatever is about to disappear over the edge. Alongside this was the rise of a monochromatic Golden Age with Italian film and literature. And maybe it wouldn't be pushing things too far if I were to mention Giovannino Guareschi's *Don Camillo* stories in which a priest and the communist mayor of a small town set out to outwit each other. Don Camillo and Mayor Peppone were my childhood fodder. It was during this same period that the *paranza d'Ognundo* became more intense, when spirituality was diminishing everywhere else.

Although Zì Gennaro was considered a 'natural obstacle'* to the pollutant of modernity, he was conscious that in order for it to survive the *festa della montagna* would have to change. The problem was how it be allowed to do so.

Sabatino drew a picture of how things used to be.

'As there were no chairs or tables they would lay sheets on the ground. It took an hour and a quarter to walk the three kilometres to the top of the hill, which is where the event was. If a priest was there he'd celebrate Mass, and if there wasn't one, the

---

* In geographical terms *obstacla naturale* can be a river or a mountain.

capo of the *paranza* took a palm leaf and holy water and blessed everyone. The *paranza* was made up mostly of old friends and extended families. After the blessing, the children ate first as they were so hungry. This was before the war. They would play and dance and afterwards they'd light the fires and then go back down to the town. It was much simpler, more contained than now, both in manifestation and in the length of time it took. After the war, both the elderly and the young could not make it up there. They were so unhealthy and unable to carry heavy supplies. There was no way for cars to get there.* My father went to the owner of the land here, which had a big chestnut tree, and asked him if they could hold the celebration in this new place called Novesca. The *paranza* kept the old name, but moved down here. At one point they wanted to build a church and had to ask the owner of the land for permission, which he gave. It changed the way we did things although the tradition remains. Instead of the thirteen fires representing Christ and twelve apostles it now became just three, representing the Father, the Son, and the Holy Spirit. In 1975 the land was given to us.'

'It must be a struggle to keep the tradition alive,' I said, 'because the world out there is conducting a war against silence.'

'Yes,' Lucio interjected. 'It is a screaming silence. That's why we're here.'

Father and son were at great pains to assure me that absolutely nothing had changed, but to what degree did they really believe this was the case? Surely the festa has become increasingly secularised with many young people coming to share in a spiritual experience not quite in accordance with what Zì Gennaro had in mind. There must have been a point in its history when values

---

* Fabio Birotti believes the real reason was that the young didn't think it was worth the journey. Values were weakening and the idea of mortifying the flesh and the physical effort involved became abhorrent to them.

were shared absolutely and observed likewise. I would later hear one dissenting voice to the effect that if Zì Gennaro were about he would not recognise the festa any more. Things cannot help but change, but even if one of the first things I noticed was the presence of a couple of drones – there to film the event from above – the fact is that a great deal has survived intact. It was why I had come here. Surely it was for the same reasons that Roberto De Simone came, although things have changed even more since his time.

The Albanos, son and father, take a dim view of De Simone's enterprise.

'When he discovered the *canto a figliola* he fell in love with it because here we had preserved the ancient tradition of Naples. Concetta Barra and the Nuova Compagnia di Canto Popolare came to our house along with ethnomusicologists and psychologists to study it. As a kind of compensation he arranged for us to go to America in 1975, in advance of the country's bicentennial celebrations, but really it was because he couldn't perform the *canto a figliola* himself. Obviously if he had tried to do so the results would have been quite different. We had kept it as a natural thing and he was an outsider who tried to imitate our sound.'

It seems inevitable that people would not take kindly to a man who collected their songs and stashed them inside boxes or pressed them onto wax. We who seek to preserve culture deep-freeze it in academe, the consequence being a loss of natural flavour. Culture is put on a life support system. It's what happens and, more often than not, for the best of reasons. Who, upon hearing a catchy tune, does not want to repeat it, even in his silences? The equation is simple: the thing an outsider values may be the only precious thing an insider has. It is where strife begins and the world appropriates what is not the world's to appropriate. Still, when Zì Gennaro died on 28 August 1989, De Simone wrote, 'With the death of Gennaro Albano one of the last great custodians of the Campania tradition disappears ... the authentic great priest of an archaic and popular religiosity, in which singing and music represent the magical means to get in touch with the celestial world.' These do not strike me as the words of a thief or a grasping academic, but rather the words of a man who loves, and is sad to watch die, his culture. On his wooden *tabula hebdomadaria* in the first column, third from the bottom, tucked in between the names of the folk percussionist Rosa Nocerino and the great Pulcinella performer Nunzio Zambello is 'Gennaro Albano'.

The most mysterious aspect of the festa is the *pertica*, the branch of the chestnut tree that for the duration of the day does not represent but actually *becomes* the Madonna with all the graces the latter implies. It is the main protagonist, 'the infinitesimal particle of the vegetal universe' without which the celebrations cannot begin. As with most plants useful to men the chestnut is invested with symbolism. A symbol of fertility and abundance, the *castanea sativa* was sacred to Zeus and, as dancers of the tammurriata will tell you, it provides the wood to make their castanets. The twelfth-century Christian mystic Hildegard von Bingen spoke of the chestnut's ability to increase vigour, prolong life, and free up the mind to allow for the absorption of ancient wisdom. It is also symbolic of honesty and justice. The early Christians thought it a symbol of chastity which, given its aphrodisiacal properties, would suggest yet another reversal of the old beliefs. Jacob, patriarch of the Israelites, combined its sap with that of poplar and hazel to bring increase to his flocks. The Hebrew for chestnut, *armon*, means 'naked' and refers to the annual shedding of the bark. When the chestnut falls from the tree, it signifies not only abundance but also sends out a message to gather and prepare for hard times ahead.

There has been much ado about paganism, its survival, continuance or resurgence, and while I do not wish to force the issue, comparison with the ancient *thyrsus* is compelling. This is not to say the *pertica* is the *thyrsus* repackaged any more than the Virgin Mary is Isis revisited, but they all come out of the same ether. Although a priest may bless the proceedings he will not extend his blessing to the *pertica*. This would be to allow too much folk religion into the Church, but at the same time the latter realises that there has to be some kind of compromise. The Church is at its most intelligent when it is prepared to admit imponderables and at its most foolish when it calls for an auto-da-fé. There are many, of course, who would argue that at core the Church is unchanged and eternal. I hope they'll weather the course. A godless universe is terrifying to contemplate. We are awfully close to it. The illusion of faith is surely better than a throng of smug faces. Sureness would be better, of course. A great deal hangs on interpretation and so maybe it's fairer to say that spiritual currents, ancient and modern, run over the same bedrock, shimmer in the common light of faith, and produce in the human heart a similar ripple.

Whereas for the *paranza d'Ognundo* the *pertica* is a Christian symbol, for Angelo Calabrese it is clearly a pagan one.

'The *pertica*,' he told me, 'signifies the umbilical cord between mother and child, the point of masculinity. You do not cut it off. You remove the skin of the branch so that it is purified. It is a pagan symbol of fertility that has been adopted by Christianity. It is adorned with ginestra because it is not a plant you can pull out of the ground with your hands. The flower is fragile and the root is strong and together they represent man's fragility and strength.'

Strength and fragility, Leopardi would make 'La ginestra' the title of his greatest poem on the human condition.

Qui su l'arida schiena
Del formidabil monte

Sterminator Vesevo,
La qual null'altro allegra arbor nè fiore,
Tuoi cespi solitari intorno spargi,
Odorata ginestra,
Contenta dei deserti.

Here on the dry flank
of the terrifying mountain,
Vesuvius the destroyer,
which no other tree or flower brightens,
you spread your solitary thickets,
scented broom,
at home in the desert.

These are things, Calabrese insists, that people no longer know the meaning of but then this strikes me as an instance of academic versus living tradition. Who's right? The business of choosing sides seems not nearly as important as recognising that the slopes of Monte Somma resound with ancient echoes.

'Do you choose the *pertica* or does it choose you?' I asked Lucio.

'The second,' he replied, 'otherwise one would never be able to find it. Nature speaks to you. She is the only one that can tell you the truth. It has to be an elder of the *paranza* who finds it. My father found this one.* It has another purpose. You put gifts on it, simple gifts such as lemons and oranges† that you then take

---

* Fabio Birotti suggests that between the seeker and the object there is a simultaneous energy radiating from both, which is to say they find each other.

† In some instances this might include the traditional *'o père e 'o musso sale e limone*, a combination of veal mouth and pig's trotters with lemon, which recalls the 'waste not, want not' attitude of the Italian peasant.

as a gift to the woman you wish to marry, remembering always to present it with the right hand. She removes the gifts and then once you've married you put over the *pertica* the sheets from the nuptial bed, what we call the sheets of love. The *pertica* represents fertility.'

'So when used in the *paranza* the *pertica* is an echo of this courtship?'

'Yes.'

'The arboreal rite (*rito arboreo*) is an important aspect. Is this finding the divinity in the branch?'

'Yes, a good way of putting it.'

'What is the relationship to Vesuvius?'

'She is the mother. You call your mother by different names, the same thing with the mountain.'

'It is also this mother who destroys.'

'She protects us.'

'But it is also a destructive force waiting to erupt again.'

'We are aware of this. We are the sons of death. We are not immortal, we are born to die. The life you have may be long or short, but it is up to you how to live it. I chose this way and I am aware I'm going to die and I am not scared because death is part of life. Vesuvius is right in front of my bedroom window. When I awake I am made aware of it. When I am away from it, on holiday or even for a day, and I don't see the silhouette of the mountain I begin to miss it. It is a mountain. It is a volcano. It is the Madonna. It is death too. When I make the journey back and see its silhouette I at once feel at home.'

'The other beautiful aspect of this festa,' I said, 'is everything that has been broken throughout the year is healed.'

'It is like a Japanese vase. The concept of a broken vase is that they fill the cracks with gold and it becomes even more beautiful once it has been repaired. Likewise, when you make a mistake and repair it, it becomes better than before the mistake was made.'

'Which would reflect on your grandfather's broken memorial stone.'

'When it was broken a few years ago, I didn't repair it. I kept the pieces as they are. Many people say to me, "When are you going to repair the stone?" A friend suggested filling the cracks with gold to make it more precious. We are still thinking about it. The breakage was done with malice. This is good because it makes us stronger.'

'What other forms of healing take place during this time?'

'We've had miracles. Zì Gennaro had a stroke which paralysed half his face. One night he was in his bedroom and said, "Madonna, you are allowing me to die. I can't do the festa any more." People came to say goodbye. His wife was in tears. He really thought it was the end. Then he dreamed of the Madonna who told him there is no way he was going to die. "Go up to the mountain," she told him. When he was a prisoner in South Africa he had asked the Madonna to allow him and his friends to live. Other people died there, but they survived. These are graces received.'

We are the sons of death.

Lucio Albano's words would continue to reverberate with me.

The following day was the Saturday of the fires.

Fabio Birotti writes: 'The woods come alive; men and vegetation appear to form a unity. On Monte Somma, ritual sets the boundaries for a natural contract, an inescapable biological bond, and of survival between the community and the surrounding territory. It is a contract of exchange made explicit through an act of identification with the wild, the mountain, the vegetation, the dead, the demons inhabiting the woods, and every other animated presence; also it is an act of mutual giving between powerful entities celestial and terrestrial: the Santa Maria a

Castello and the community of the *paranza d'Ognundo.*'

A scholar's prose bordering on the baroque, what Birotti writes captures a sense of the primeval mystery within which the relationship of man to untamed nature becomes readable. My task was to observe how this would translate into action. I wanted to see how things would actualise because this was not going to be some academic exercise: it would be the most important moment of the year in the lives of these people. Situated somewhere beyond language, only the heart would be able to decipher its occurrences.

The sun at its zenith, Lucio's body slackened as he took the *pertica* in his hand, as if suddenly, exposed and vulnerable and realising the gravity of the task ahead of him, he had for just that instant become the child he once was, the child Sabatino once was, the child Zì Gennaro once was, the children all the elders of this particular tribe once were. Maybe this is what men who are about to be sent into battle are like in the seconds before they drum up courage. Will Lucio ever see himself as I saw him then? Were these eyes of mine faulty? At the signal of Sabatino's baton the musicians started up, instantaneously, among their number Mimmo, the village simpleton who could only blather, but who was so perfect in his timing on the *triccheballacche* it might have been his sole purpose in life to play it as if only this could make him noble. And so, to the rhythmic sound of the tammorra, the *triccheballacche*, the *putipù*, and the *scetavajasse*,* Lucio, all

---

* The tammorra we already know. The *triccheballacche* is a percussion instrument, with a wooden frame containing three wooden hammers, two of which slide and beat against the middle one which is in a fixed position. The *putipù*, which is a 'friction drum', achieves its sound – which some people describe as being akin to blowing a raspberry – by pushing a bamboo stick into a cylindrical sound box covered by a membrane. The *scetavajasse* comprises two wooden sticks, one of them smooth and the other notched with

power now restored to him, strode towards the enormous chestnut tree and climbed a wooden ladder propped against it, a narrow ladder such as peasants have always made – tapered, beautiful in its simplicity – a ladder such as Jacob might in his dream have used, and up he rose, so heroic against the noonday sun, clambering higher and higher, defying gravity, the energy from the *paranza* below pushing him onwards from branch to branch, and when he got as high as it was possible for him to go he tied the *pertica* to the uppermost branch of the tree, the process of ritual grafting known as *innesto*, which binds together all the elements of the universe and admits the Madonna into our presence.* A job done, mission accomplished: the *pertica* was now *her*. At the end of the *pertica* fluttered the Italian flag that Zì Gennaro's wife had sewn. When Lucio climbed down and walked towards the crowd waiting for him at a respectful distance he began to tremble from the release of a whole year's cares. All that had been exorcised from within him was now on the surface of his face, as if this is what happens when flesh enters another dimension, as when the first astronauts went into outer space. The older members of the *paranza* had tears rolling down their cheeks because they, too, had been waiting for a mighty release. Lucio and Sabatino, father and son, threw their arms around each other, the beating of the tammorra getting louder and louder, as if to say, *Your task is done. We must dance. We must eat. We must drink. We may do as we like because the Madonna is here.* The tammurriata began, the watchers forming a circle, just as Marcello Colasurdo described it, inside of which time and space were annulled, annulled because the Madonna loves timelessness

---

metal discs, and when the former is rubbed over the latter it produces a characteristic sound which in Neapolitan is called *nfrunfrù*. The simpler the instrument the more difficult it is to describe.

* Although the *pertica* is central to all the *paranze* it is only with the *paranza d'Ognundo* that it is placed on the chestnut tree.

and because only then will her people be able to get close to her. They danced as the ancients would have danced, the rhythm very much as it always was, and then they settled at the long tables for a banquet and what a banquet it was, a banquet worthy of Mamma Schiavona with her ruddy cheeks, a no-nonsense girl straight from the farm. Was this a miracle? Yes, of course it was. What is ritual but induced miracle? Whether Christendom alone was responsible for it I'm not entirely sure.

I had never seen fireworks in daylight. The sense they produced in me was of a world gone into reverse. The valley shook with explosions and it could not have been much fun for the cats and dogs below. That evening the three pyres were set alight. Sparkles were produced from the ginestra, the leaves of the holly oak, bay leaves, and rosemary with which they were covered. Then came, from each of the *paranze*, huge firework displays. Italians are crazy about fireworks or, rather, it is in them that their craziness is made manifest. They have another function, however, which is to act as a form of exorcism, whether it be to drive out the fear of what is there or to indicate what you have been spared.

There is a primordial power in the spectacle of human figures moving about in the glow of a big fire. We go back to where we always were, where civilisation began, with fire, which, depending on how vigilant we are, will either aid or destroy us. Prometheus lives. The first Greeks to come to these shores saw the mountain as the home of Jupiter. The ancients lit fires to mark the change of the seasons. Some of those festivities were beyond the pale, at least for the early Christians who condemned such free licence – orgiastic dances, pounding drums, clashing cymbals, shrilling flutes, people bathing themselves in the blood of slain bulls, women possessed, crying aloud their hymns – but whatever garb the festivities wore, whether pagan or Christian, and however gaudy or pure, this place has been sacred forever. The fires people make are set against the greater fire that might one day destroy them.

The previous summer, there had been other fires on the wooded slopes of Vesuvius for which the Camorra has been held to blame. There were too many simultaneous fires for them to be mere coincidence, carelessness, or spontaneous combustion. Someone taking a photograph of the billowing smoke enveloping Vesuvius captured a strange formation, the image of a skull, which, as they say, went viral. Two people died in the fires, the body of one of whom was found, so said the *cronaca nera*, in the act of masturbation. Was it though? The same was said about the cast of a human figure found at Pompeii who appears to have met his fate likewise, which produced a rush of sick jokes, some of them funny, I'm afraid. The volcanologist Pier Paolo Petrone puts this down to pyroclastic rather than erotic surge, the flexing of the body after death by fire. A Neapolitan woman living in London, Erica Esposito, wept when she related to me the violence done to the mountain she calls her home.

Would these festivities heal the fracture? As the flames from the pyres rose higher, one of the members of the *paranza*, Luca Lucia, said to me that if I listened to what the fire had to say, that if I observed it closely, it would speak to me.

'Il fuoco parla, se lo osservi lui ti dice le cose' were the words he spoke and in the reddish glow of the fire I scribbled them into my notebook. They seemed, just then, the most important thing anyone had ever said to me. If I were to lose those words, I would lose the world.

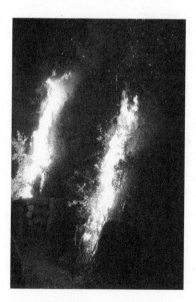

✳

It was brave of him to come. Some years ago, at the *sabato dei fuochi*, Fabio Birotti met the woman who would later become his wife. She had just recently died. Fabio came with his young sons who, as children will do, concealed the immensity of their loss, which somehow brought their sorrow even closer to home. A trained anthropologist, Birotti is the author of the most important work on the *festa della montagna*, which he also takes part in. We spoke briefly at the festa and then met again a week later, at a party where he made pizzas, shovelling them in and out of an oven in the courtyard, children rushing about high on calories, a number of musicians in attendance, among them, Dario Mogavero, one of the most highly regarded performers of the *canzoniere Vesuviano*, who, like Marcello Colasurdo, is from Pomigliano d'Arco. Several pizza slices later, after I asked Fabio why he forsook the role of pizza maker in favour of anthropology, we climbed onto the upper deck of the house where he began in rhetorical mode.

'Why do they gather and are so moved by all this? Why do they cry underneath this branch of a chestnut tree? Why do they sing beneath it? Why is there an image of the Madonna at its tip? Why do they carry it in procession to the highest tree in the area? Why, again, do they weep? Why do they cover the *pertica* with colours? And why do they dance underneath it, shout and drink? Why do they tell stories about what happened during the previous year, not only the bad but also the good things? Why are they so excited? Why are they so driven by passion, not only sexual but also full of rage? Why is this the peak of their existence? Why does this happen? Why is all of this possible only on that day? A religious person would say, "You should not be rude or swear on that day. You do not have to celebrate and party on that day. You should not think about sex on that day." Well, it's because on that day everything has to flow out of you and set you free. All this is possible because of the Madonna's presence. This happens in all rituals, in all cultures. If everything is allowed it is because it is allowed by the presence of the divinity. The ritual gives you power because in daily life it is impossible to have a face-to-face relationship with the Madonna. You are almost touching it. It becomes extra-transcendental.'

'Is it recognised by the Church?'

'Absolutely not,' Fabio replied, 'but they accept it.'

'So if this is direct religion why does the priest come for morning service?'

'The answer is simple. Some people come up only to hear the Mass and then leave. The *pertica* comes later in order to legitimise the ritual. This the Church does not approve. A hundred years ago, even fifty years ago, a priest would go to the top of the mountain but not always. Mass can be celebrated by the capo of the *paranza* if the priest is not there. The capo becomes the intermediary between the community and the divinity, a priest elected by the people.'

'We know that in one way or another this goes back to ancient times,' I suggested. 'The *pertica* and the *rito arboreo* would seem to resemble the vegetal cults.'

'The mountain ... the chestnut tree ... the *ginestra* ... all this is wild nature, which is external to the community. It is uncontrollable. It is the element that at any time can invade our anthropomorphic world. There is the wilderness outside and we are inside this humanly managed zone. We have a deep fear of an uncontrollable, wild nature that can come back at any time, occupy and destroy the harvest by which we survive. There is also the terror of the mountain exploding again. The dead as well as nature can rebel against men. The ritual empowers us so we might have control of these elements that could destroy us and everything we have made. The ritual is allowed by the Madonna. It has another function. What you have taken from nature you must give back. The *pertica*, the chestnut tree, the grafting ... the *pertica* is the joining of sky, earth, and under-world. You replicate the natural cycle so that the dead can push the seed up towards the sky, towards rebirth. This is why you have to look for and choose the most beautiful branch because it is an act of consecration, an asymmetric marriage between man and nature. The choice you make introduces three fundamental moments – the cut, the cleaning, and adornment. The *pertica* becomes the offering, the returning to nature and the Madonna. When Lucio climbed the chestnut tree with it this was a grafting to nature. Within the flowers and trees is hidden the mystery of existence, the secret intelligence that the Omnipotent One hides in them.'

'Are you saying the *pertica* does not represent the Madonna but actually *is* her?'

'It is the arboreal or vegetable outfit of the Madonna by which she shows herself to the community together with her recognis-ably human resemblance, which is represented by her image at the tip of the *pertica*.'

'Would I be wrong in seeing in this the continuation of pagan elements?'

'Do not say *pagan*. The term was introduced by the Church in order to distinguish between those who are Christian and those who are not. Everyone was pagan once. Any culture wants to put itself at the centre of the world. The *paranza d'Ognundo* is the same. It is the centre of the world just as the chestnut tree is. As the *pertica* is. It is mythical ritual logic, irrational maybe, and never meaning any one thing, but there is a thread that joins eve-rything. If we put forward our Madonna as the most important, then she is the centre of the world. Our interpretation of things has to be not only coherent but also logical and exclusive.'

I didn't tell Fabio that I saw the word 'pagan' in a rather more favourable light than he was prepared to allow. Also, the word in English doesn't carry quite as much baggage as the Italian does. I might have balked at the word 'heathen' with its suggestions of savagery and uncivilised behaviour: the ancient Romans were anything but. Virgil was a pagan. Dante, tough nut though he was, so cruel in his Christian faith at times, nevertheless did not shy away from his company. I'd gladly sup with pagans. So, I think, would he. I did say to Fabio, on the other hand, that the *paranza d'Ognundo* shared the same spiritual landscape of the ancient people and that in this respect I couldn't see any over-whelming contradiction between them and what came before, that both are forms of direct religion based on a similar compre-hension of nature.

'I am bonded to the mountain and it is bonded to me and it is what feeds me,' Fabio continued. 'The mountain is where the Madonna is and she protects me.'

'My initial understanding of the festa is that it is built on an ancient model in which the local community asked the "moun-tain" to stay quiet for another year.'

'It is that, too, managing the wild powers of nature in order to make them benevolent towards us, but the first thing is to honour the Madonna. This must be done before asking anything of her. The *pertica* is not only the centre of the world, it is also its bel-lybutton. It signifies rebirth. It is the umbilical cord that feeds your child.'

I heard in Fabio's words Angelo Calabrese's.

'The community are sons and daughters of the Madonna,' he continued. 'Mamma Schiavona, the Santa Maria a Castello, is a peasant with beautiful red cheeks. Who is the Mamma Schi-avona? What is the etymology of "schiavona"?'

The phrase translates directly as 'slave mamma'. In northern Italy *schiavona* is a type of sword but in southern dialect it means 'dark-skinned' and is therefore suggestive of one who serves. Mamma Schiavona becomes the mother of all slaves, somebody with whom an oppressed peasantry may readily identify. She is one of them. Her darkness is also that of the earth and one may go further and summon forth the earth goddess cults of old whose deities were Isis, Artemis, and Ceres, all three of whom were, at some point or other, depicted as black. It is said that early Christianity had reconfigured all three. She is, in the eyes of some, unsightly. The Madonna at Somma Vesuviana has been sometimes called 'Mamma Pacchiana' which means gaudy and uncultured, a peasant in other words (though not mine). She is, in the eyes of others, beautiful, described with a phrase from the Song of Songs (1:5–6): 'Nigra sum, sed formosa' ('I am black, but comely'). Whichever she is, she accepts all and forgives all.

'As an anthropologist are you in conflict with your own involvement in the *paranza*?'

'No. You have to immerse yourself and then suspend judgement. Immersion, suspension, detachment: you immerse yourself, but in order to analyse what you see you have to detach yourself and be able to observe it through one's own emotions. The anthropologist's role is to observe and interpret, but in the simplest way possible, through example.'

'Attached to all this is a poetic dimension,' I proffered, 'the creation of a circle within which time and space are suspended.'

'It is impossible to have all this without suspending time, without being inside another dimension. There is no way you can approach the Madonna otherwise. If you could meet her normally you'd do it every day. There is another important meaning of the celebration. It is like tearing away a veil that separates the people from the Madonna.'

The veil again, the *Cristo velato*, the veil of knowledge, the veil covering Naples.

'It creates a breach whereby people may get closer to her,' Fabio continued, 'otherwise the Madonna would have to come down to men and not the opposite. There is a mending of all that has been broken in the previous year and by extension it becomes a personal commitment for the coming year. So there is an opening, a breach formed by the supernatural invading profane time, but afterwards it needs to be closed again. We light the fires and looking into the flames recall the dead. The celebration closes, the Madonna departs, and the breach is closed for another year. The *pertica* is about stopping or suspending time. The divinity within the branch re-evokes mythical time, because another function of ritual is to replicate the original foundation myth. Ritual and myth are the two faces of the same coin. Myth is somewhere in space and time whereas ritual is myth in action. So the time of myth comes back in the here and now as it has always done. We are talking of the ubiquity of space and the reversibility of time. Through ritual one evokes Zì Gennaro and the many dead and also the stories that have come down through the oral tradition. We also obtain it through the different versions of the tammurriata which tell the story of the past, but it is also the invention of the moment. The *canto a figliola* is not just the compulsory words of myth and tradition. It also recalls events that happened during the previous year. When you study this kind of celebration as an anthropologist it is fundamental to put yourself in the position of the believer. You don't have to think with your own head, you have to allow for an exchange, otherwise you destroy what you seek to achieve. There is much emotion and commotion when the *pertica* is raised. You saw for yourself the tension, the energy, the emotion, the care with which everything was prepared. Everything one does is in honour of the Madonna and her presence. It is not just her, it is everything. It recalls the chaos of your own life, so basically your soul is compressed and what happens is a bursting out, an explosion that is spread to everyone – rage, sadness, joy, spiritual feeling, violence, and negativity – all that has been accumulated throughout the previous year. Everything must be purified. You can do it only on this one day in the presence of the Madonna. Also, it is a sexual explosion. Everything that has been suppressed inside you will come out then. It is not a contradiction. It is authorised by the presence of the Madonna. Chaos has to find order. Order through disorder. In front of the Madonna you will not be a sinner but the opposite. It is not a contradiction. You have to let it out in front of her. You laugh, you cry. Everything is allowed.'

'To what degree?'

'Until it trespasses over the line of respect.'

As surely as the current of a river takes us from its source to its mouth, we drifted into a discussion about the *canto a figliola*, an aspect of the *festa della montagna* as vital as anything else.

'I do not agree that the *canto a figliola* is a means of communication between prisoners and people on the outside. This was Roberto De Simone's theory and Sabatino accepted it, but I think its origin is much simpler. It is a peasant song. The *canto a distesa* is what you perform in order to communicate information. Peasants used it as a way of spreading news between fields. It was a way to fight loneliness and at the same time it would exorcise fatigue. It spread from peasant to prison culture and was employed by the *guappi** as a coded language so the guards wouldn't understand. The *canto a distesa* came later, though. It is usually just one voice at a time and can be heard over a great distance. *Canto a figliola* can be choral, a prayer to honour the Madonna. It contains phrases that come from the oral tradition. Some things change, but the core remains the same.'

As if on cue, rising from the courtyard, came the ancient, searing voice of Dario Mogavero, a voice such as would carry across a hundred acres. A young master (already), he learned from the elderly musicians of Pomigliano d'Arco, a town which he describes as 'the passage between peasant and urban culture'; he also studied the writings of Vittorio Imbriani who, in 1871, published his influential *Canti popolari delle provincie meridionali* ('Popular Songs of the Southern Provinces'). Dario, however, is not merely a product of what he studies: he possesses *duende*. You don't learn *duende*. You have it or you don't.

---

* The *guappi* (sing. *guappo*) were thugs, most commonly found in connection to, or employed by, the Camorra.

Speaking of which, I should have enquired after the whereabouts of that rascally quarter-tone.

✳

What were those words, again, about looking into the fire? When earlier I'd asked Lucio Albano whether the fire would tell me things that are going to happen or the things I ought to know, he replied, 'The things you need to know. It doesn't predict the future. Whatever you wish to see, you'll see. Nature will tell you things, but first you have to empty yourself. You have to allow for the creation of a space. Only then will you see them, whether they be in the form of silence or voices or actions. All manifestations of nature – flowers, trees, fire, water – you must learn how to read them and then you'll know what you need to know.' So much seems to be wrapped up in that single sentence and yet, as with fire, it is hard to pin one's thoughts to a single place.

Something, though, made me stare into the distance, a pale smudge on the horizon, the glimmer that was Naples. All my friends and acquaintances down there, what were they up to now? They, too, are heirs to an infinitesimal part of the vegetal universe. And now, while I sit at my desk in London, old words fly back at me. 'They want, and deserve, deliverance.' As she spoke those words sunlight danced over Mariagrazia's silvered eyelids. A cool breeze in the air, we had to keep shifting our chairs in order to stay in the sunshine.

Il fuoco parla, se lo osservi lui ti dice le cose.

The fire speaks; if you look at it, it tells you things.

Naples, Three Years On: An Afterword

Thomas Fuller (1654–1734), physician and churchman, compiled a collection of sayings and sage advice, *Introductio ad Sapientiam: or, The Art of Right Thinking* (1731), which includes an aphorism that has often been ascribed to him: 'Travel makes a wise Man better, and a Fool worse.' William Hazlitt (1778–1830) pilfered or, rather, improved on it: 'It is not fit that every man should travel; it makes a wise man better, and a fool worse.' The biggest fool of all, however, must be the writer who imagines he can squeeze a country or a city in between the covers of a book. Still, he tries. The best he can do is to admit to failure. As I do mine. *The Serpent Coiled in Naples* is far from complete. Where is Saint Thomas Aquinas, for it was in a small cell behind the church of San Domenico Maggiore that he completed his *Summa Theologiae*? What about the city's many philosophers, from Giordano Bruno to Benedetto Croce? And the composers of the Neapolitan School, from Alessandro and Giuseppe Scarlatti to Domenico Cimarosa? Pergolesi's 'Stabat Mater' is piped everywhere, and I wish it weren't so, not because I don't love it but because I do. The painters of the Neapolitan School, whose vision owes so much to Caravaggio, who spent his last years in Naples – where are they? And how could I not include a chapter on the historical archive of the Banco di Napoli, popularly known as *il Cartastorie* ('paper stories'), with its hanging bundles of payment slips resembling gigantic wasps' nests? There is a whole section devoted to the business transactions of Raimondo di Sangro including a receipt of payment for the block of marble from which, chip by chip, the *Cristo velato* would emerge. And, from more recent times, 'this turbulent priest' Antonio Maione, who in 1990 outraged the church authorities when he invited the Camorra boss, Nunzio Giuliano, to address the congregation from the altar of the church of Santa Maria delle Grazie in Piazza Cavour. (Seemingly, perhaps even genuinely, Nunzio had repented of his sins, but for him, as for many in whom crime is second nature, repentance had a short battery life.) When Don Antonio returned the following week to conduct mass he found the locks had been changed and a note on the church door to the effect he was 'indisposed', not only that Sunday but every Sunday to come, and so he took to preaching on the streets. Had I known about him earlier he would have had a major role in my chapter on Forcella. Since then Don Antonio has become something of a cult figure. Now in his eighties, but still with a young man's physique, he lives on a hilltop in Roccavecchia in the municipality of Pratella. When I met him he was hard at work in his garden, moving heavy stones, the blazing sun no barrier to his daily chores. I partook of fruit from his shrubs, words of wisdom from his lips. People from all over Italy come to see him, this rebel priest who years before, according to the cardinal in Naples, had conducted 'a wild liturgy'. Don Antonio presented me with a book about himself, which he inscribed: 'L'eresia è l'unica via per la verità' ('Heresy is the only way to truth'). More holy fool than apostate, there was a time once when he would have accompanied Giordano Bruno to the stake.

Napoli, c'est moi. There is a sense in which all books of travel literature are autobiographical, if only by virtue of what their authors choose to write about. Although I like to pretend I'm invisible, I can be sniffed out in my prose. I am not sure, however, if what I write meets the criteria of 'travel literature', a term I have often allowed to be applied to what I do but almost always with unease. I mean no disrespect to the genre itself, which has produced some wonderful prose, although there have been those whose artfulness has cast doubt on the genre as a whole. When I look at the writers I most admire, I can't do what they do. I don't have their gift for describing terrain nor have I mastered languages, and I haven't got saddle sores. My approach has been to journey not so much through places as through the lives of people who inhabit those places. There, on occasion, I may have a slight advantage. People talk to me. I'm not sure why this is so, but it may have to do with my curiosity about them. I never fail to be surprised by the fact that some of the most celebrated travel writers have scant regard for the people among whom they move. At worst this boils down to sheer contempt. One such author, irked by his Muslim guides, sought revenge by slipping bits of pork into their food. I will not read another book by him. And what can one say about Lawrence Durrell, whose description of place is often incomparable, but who then goes on to describe the Cairo poor as 'apes in nightgowns'? Quite often, readers blink away those motes of dust in the eye. I can't. While I'm sick to death of the language police who strip-search every utterance, there are certain things that ought not to be allowed to pass unremarked, which is different from saying they should be banned or cancelled. Whether rightly or wrongly, I believe the closer one comes to people the more vividly they reflect the world they live in. As strategies go, it's a risky one. Aside from speaking to the wrong people, especially those who tell you what they think you'd like to hear, there is also a danger of putting oneself too much at the centre of their narrative, so that one becomes the sun around whom the planets revolve. And yet if one listens to their stories, 'the which, if you with patient ears attend', one will see deeper into the world from whence they came.

There is another area in which luck has served me well – it is almost too obvious to mention – that has to do with being in the right place at the right time. It has happened too often for it to be put it down to mere coincidence. I could get almost mystical about this, but I'm not keen on the smell of incense. Actually, luck has nothing to do with it. My instincts have served me well. My very first day in Naples, I fell into a conversation with a woman who was handing out leaflets for a nearby restaurant. We got chatting and soon the talk moved from ragù to literature. Her command of English was superb and it turned out she had done her dissertation on the playwright Tom Stoppard. It is not uncommon in Italy to find people in jobs well below their education, or abilities. The country is, in so many respects, socially immobile. Would she be my enabler? That night, the question kept me awake. The following day I put it to her. She was to accompany me as my translator throughout the rest of that first sojourn and the discoveries we made together were just as much hers as they were mine. She seemed to have some inkling of my mind and was willing to roll unquestioningly with my schemes.

I try not to approach people with prepared questions. I seek, above all, good conversation. Questions provoke avoidance whereas *talk* encourages disclosure. Bigger truths emerge. I say this without wishing to get into any philosophical conundrums as to where truth lies. I record all my conversations. A journalist once advised me to switch on my recorder a couple of minutes in advance of any conversation. The idea, he said, is to put people at ease. A single clicking of a switch can set off a stampede. Apart from scribbled notes, I never write when I'm on the move. I gather or, as I was once accused, I forage. It's only when I'm back in London that I do any actual writing and, even then, only after I have dutifully transcribed everything from my recordings. This may sound ridiculous or labour-intensive, but I copy even the most trivial remarks because there's no saying what might come in useful. Quite often there are the lucky accidents, small interjections I missed at the time. There is something about background noise too – say the clattering of cutlery in a café – that will put me back inside an old scene. I'm constantly amazed by how, in certain parts of our planet, even people without any formal education are able to articulate their surroundings. Other places, one can't cut through the static or the thicket of arrested similes. When Lucio Albano said 'We are the sons of death' I felt I had just been handed a literary gem, and by someone in whose house I saw not a single book.

I'm not sure if it is useful anymore to write about going *to a place*. After all, there is nowhere we can't get to. Our explorations need to be of a different complexion. I feel it is now incumbent on one to write *out of a place*. If there have been hiccups along the way, they are best suppressed, whether it be the suspect water in an unwashed glass, the broken flush, the lumpy mattress, the fleas. When I think back to my first time in Damascus, I fell into difficulties the telling of which would not be admissible evidence in any court of law. I did write about them, the perils of happenstance, but divine intervention came in the form of a thief who stole my computer containing the only draft of my first version of the book. As a devout follower of my own cherished principle REAL MEN DON'T USE BACKUPS – these were still early days in computer technology – I had to start over, only this time it was with the realisation that one ought never to dramatise one's own experiences. The least interesting subject in any travel narrative should always be oneself.

Naples, May 2022. It was my first time back in three years. A pandemic had put the world to some inconvenience. I did follow the city's fortunes during that eclipse. Irene Vecchia set up a food stall for homeless people, which, given her public-spirited nature, didn't surprise me. It *gladdened* me. Mariagrazia Barsanti fashioned a facemask out of one of her bras. There was a marked improvement in the concentration of pollutants in the atmosphere. A man claimed he could kill any virus at any distance with the blast of a single note from his bagpipe. That inveterate chronicler of Naples, its strengths and foibles, Jeff Matthews, had himself photographed with his own prophylaxis against coronavirus, a bottle of Corona beer. Stories of good intermingled with stories of bad, oftentimes reflecting the famous ingenuity of Neapolitans when it comes to adapting to adverse circumstances. The restriction of outdoor movement in Naples was severe and drones were used to monitor people who ought to have been staying indoors, heavy fines imposed. Among the few given leave to go for walks were dog owners and very soon one heard of a model dog on wheels pulled by a rope (a proper leash was an unnecessary expenditure). It caught on. The fake dogs with their doggy shapes, wooden or wire skeletons covered with bits of pale carpet simulating poodles or dark textiles for sturdier breeds, successfully foiled the drones. It is the same mentality that resulted in the manufacture of T-shirts with single black diagonal bands across their fronts so as to fool traffic police into thinking drivers were wearing seatbelts. Why do I tolerate in Neapolitans what I find quite intolerable in other people? It's the anarchic side to their nature that, ultimately, makes them horribly likable.

The city was in a bad mood. It was unseasonably hot, added to which the pollution was once again at its most extreme. My favourite gelato, which usually is too big in any case, melted over my fingers and then the stickiness was transferred onto the handle of my walking stick and tissues made things worse. As soon as I stepped out into the daylight my shirt was soaked and it was in this state I went to see a director at one of the city's great institutions only to be asked by the secretary whether I'd made an appointment. I said I'd written from London several times and that I'd had no response. 'Sorry, but without an appointment I'm afraid the director is not available.' 'So how does one get one?' 'You must first write a letter.' Why was it I could feel the presence of *il diretorre* behind her voice? Oddly enough, after several visits to Naples, this was my first brush with Italian bureaucracy. It is impenetrable. That month, the hottest on record, I accomplished not a single thing I'd set out to do. It struck me with some force that had this been my first time here, and I'd come with the aim of writing a book, I would have absolutely no idea where to begin.

So much of what I have written about – the people I met or else the situations in which I first found them – has gone. Skimming the book, chapter by chapter, I note various absences: Domenico Garofalo has quit his perch opposite the Teatro Galleria Toledo and is now promoting modern dance, much of it in the nude, in the Low Countries; the elderly lady in Forcella, who had seen and experienced more than anyone should have, has died leaving behind her daughter who also has seen and experienced more than anyone should have; Pina Cipriani, 'the soul of Naples', still makes her absence felt and the venue where I saw her sing has become just one bar among many; Ernesto Colluta spends not nearly as much time as he would like on his farm on the edge of Lake Avernus because after his father died he took over most of the responsibilities of running the family spa; Roberto Talarico has been banned on pain of arrest from the centre of Naples after committing several acts of violence; Ars Nova Napoli have moved from success to success and are very rarely heard on the streets anymore; Antonio Tubelli, *monzù*, has now retired and those with antiquarian palates can no longer sample Leopardi's favourite dishes; Fabrizio Masucci is no longer to be found at the Museo Capella Sansevero, its directorship now having passed to his sister; the Cimitero delle Fontanelle is temporarily closed for 'structural interventions' and on a handwritten sign at the entrance is written 'Entrano solo i morti' ('Only the dead may enter'); the remarkable street art of cyop&kaf steadily deteriorates, some of it barely visible now; Solfatara is permanently closed and Giorgio Angarano's fate continues to hang in the balance; Pulcinella thrives and, a dream come true, he has his own theatre, Casa delle Guarattelle, but then, of course, Pulcinella never dies; Marcello Colasurdo, tammorra player, is in a hospital bed, almost blind, both legs amputated; Roberto De Simone sinks ever deeper into rage such that when I tried to deliver a copy of my book I was expelled, book in hand, by his manservant; when I visited Corrado Sfogli and his wife, Fausta Vetere, founding members of the Nuova Compagnia di Canto Popolare, and they sang and played for me I had no idea Corrado was fatally ill and soon to die; after a hiatus due to the pandemic the *paranza d'Ognundo* continues, although its capo, Sabatino Albano, is now infirm; my friend, Mariagrazia Barsanti, now teaches at a school closer to where she lives and therefore is no longer happily met with in the Piazza del Gesù Nuova.

And now it occurs to me – suppose some reader of mine were to go about Naples with this book in hand and seek out the things I've described. What verdict would he or she place upon a book in which so much is already obsolete? It is not the first time that I have written a book that is already out of date as soon as it hit the shelves. Wherever you look, in whichever direction, it's always the end of one thing and the beginning of another. There is a critical stage in the life of a book such as this when almost immediately it is redundant, and so it continues for an agonisingly long period of time before it enters a yet more critical stage. It comes back to life as something just a little different to what one had originally planned and either it goes straight to the basement shelves of second-hand bookshops, or it is looked upon as a valuable record of things gone.

There is another glaring absence in the book. I left it too late to visit the dilapidated building in the Rione Sanità district where the great comic actor, Totò, otherwise known as Antonio Griffo Focas Flavio Ducas Angelo Comneno Porfirogenito Gagliardi De Curtis di Bisanzio, His Imperial Highness, Palatine Count, Knight of the Holy Roman Empire, Exarch of Ravenna, Duke of Macedonia and Illyria, Prince of Constantinople, Cilicia, Thessaly, Pontus, Moldavia, Dardania, Peloponnesus, Count of Cyprus and Epirus, Count and Duke of Drivasto and Durazzo, was born. The wealth of names was nowhere reflected in coinage, for he was the illegitimate son of a Neapolitan marquis and a Sicilian woman and grew up in one of the poorest areas of Naples. It was only later in life that his father recognised him. When I was first in Naples the second-floor apartment where he was born, at Via Santa Maria Antesaecula, 109, was very briefly opened by a woman as a 'museum' to which one paid a modest entrance fee. There was a slight catch in that it was completely empty. *Scartiloffio!* It had been my intention to visit and stay for at least two or three hours, for what could be closer to the spirit of Totò than this wonderful ruse? After all, this was the man who in a short comic film sold the Trevi Fountain in Rome to an unsuspecting American tourist. Time ran out and when I returned the following year the Casa Natale di Totò was closed after complaints from gypped tourists were made to the civil authorities. There is one further twist: Totò was actually born at 107 and was a few months old when he and his mother moved into 109. When the boy was four, much to his mother's embarrassment, he would lean over from the balcony and imitate passers-by, earning him the nickname *'o spione* ('the Spy'), which doubtless explains how he became such a gifted mime. A quintessential Neapolitan story – there will always be more.

Notes

Epigraph

Anna Maria Ortese, *L'infanta sepolta* (c) 2000 Adelphi
    Edizioni S.p.A. Milano.

Chapter 1

p. 5: Giovanna Ceserani, *Italy's Lost Greece: Magna Graecia
    and the Making of the Modern World* (Oxford: Oxford
    University Press, 2011).

p. 8: The video for La Famiglia's song 'Odissea' can be viewed
    here: https://www.youtube.com/watch?v=dodAgPqUV4I

p. 9–10: Jan Kott, *Theatre Notebook 1947–1967* (London:
    Methuen, 1968).

p. 10–11: The lines from Matilde Serao's *Il ventre di Napoli*
    (1884) have been taken from a forthcoming translation of
    the book by Jon Snyder. Its publication will fill an immense
    hole in our understanding of late nineteenth-century Naples.
    I thank Professor Snyder for allowing me to use the passage
    in advance of publication.

p. 12: Giuseppe Marotta, *Neapolitan Gold*, translated by
    Frances Frenaye (London: Hogarth Press, 1950). I enter a
    plea for its re-issue.

p. 13: The 'music' on the wall of the Gesù Nuova
    can be listened to here: https://www.youtube.com/
    watch?v=CkHXVD5vEFk

p. 14: The scene in which Eduardo Di Filippo expounds on the making of coffee can be viewed here: https://www.youtube.com/watch?v=JVxoboMJzj8

p. 15: Judith Summers, *Casanova's Women: The Great Seducer and the Women He Loved* (London: Bloomsbury, 2011).

p. 15: The lines from Casanova's *Memoirs* come from the translation by Arthur Machen (London: Privately Printed for the Navarre Society, 1922).

p. 17: George L. Kelling and James Q. Wilson, 'Broken Windows: The Police and Neighbourhood Safety', *Atlantic Monthly* (March 1982).

p. 20: Harold Acton, *The Bourbons of Naples* (London: Methuen, 1956).

p. 25: Luciano De Crescenzo, *Thus Spake Bellavista: Naples, Love, and Liberty*, translated by Avril Bardone (New York: Grove Press, 1988).

p. 25–6: Peter Gunn, 'Some Thoughts on Time in Naples' in Edward Chaney and Neil Ritchie, eds, *Oxford, China and Italy: Writings in Honour of Sir Harold Acton on His Eightieth Birthday* (London: Thames & Hudson, 1985).

Chapter 2

p. 35: John Horne Burns, *The Gallery* (New York: Harper, 1947).

p. 41: Roberto Saviano, *Gomorrah: Italy's Other Mafia*, translated by Virginia Jewiss (Pan Macmillan, 2008).

p. 61: Raffaele La Capria, *The Mortal Wound*, translated by Marguerite Waldman (London: Collins, 1964).

p. 61: Curzio Malaparte, *The Skin*, translated by David Moore (New York: New York Review of Books, 2013)/*La Pelle* © 2010 Adelphi Edizioni S.p.A. Milano. This is essential reading.

Chapter 3

p. 74: The lines from Il Panormita's *Hermaphroditus* are from Eugene O'Connor's translation (Lanham, MD: Lexington Books, 2001).

p. 78–9: Giuseppe Marotta, *The Slaves of Time,* translated by Shirley Bridges (London: Dennis Dobson, 1964). Another translation of Marotta that deserves a re-issue.

p. 89: Franco Nico, *Resta ancora a Capri / Il Boom* (45 rpm, Edibi – EDB11010, 1963).

p. 99: Pina Cipriani's live performance at the Teatro Sancarluccio of 'Maronna mia' can be viewed here: https://www.youtube.com/watch?v=dvMs5DqMXe4

Chapter 4

p. 101–2: Ephorus's account of the Cimmerians has been pulled from Strabo's *Geography*, translated by Horace Leonard Jones (Loeb Classical Library, 1923).

p. 105–6: Henry Swinburne, *Travels in the Two Sicilies in the Years 1777, 1778, 1779, and 1780* (London: J. Nichols, 1790).

p. 106: Lucretius, *De Rerum Natura: The Poem on Nature*, translated by C. H. Sisson (Manchester: Carcanet, 1976).

p. 104–30: Virgil, *Aeneid*, translated by Frederick Ahl (Oxford: Oxford University Press, 2007).

p. 110: I apologise for not having taken a note of where I found the lines to the translation of *Patrologia Graeca*.

p. 111: Percy Bysshe Shelley, *The Letters of Percy Bysshe Shelley, Vol II.* (Oxford: Oxford University Press, 1964).

p. 111–12, Mary Shelley, *The Last Man* (London: Wordsworth Editions, 2004).

p. 112: Herman Melville, *Journal of a Visit to London and the Continent 1849–1850* (London: Cohen & West, 1949).

p. 114–15: Gervase of Tilbury, *Otia Imperiala: Recreation for an Emperor,* translated and edited by S. E. Banks and J. W. Binns (Oxford: Clarendon Press, 2002).

p. 122–3: Salamon Kroonenberg, *Why Hell Stinks of Sulfur: Mythology and Geology of the Underworld*, translated by Andy Brown (London: Reaktion Books, 2013).

p. 126–7: Jacques Le Goff, *The Birth of Purgatory*, translated by Arthur Goldhammer (Aldershot: Scolar Press, 1984).

Chapter 5

p. 131–2: Charles Burney, *The Present State of Music in France and Italy: or, The Journal of a Tour through those Countries, Undertaken to collect Materials for a General History of Music* (1773).

p. 143: The only surviving record of Eugenio Pragliola singing one of his 'papocchie', as he called them, was posted on the internet by Luciano Taglialatela: https://www.youtube.com/watch?v=3QL93nJYJAY

p. 144: Ars Nova's live performance of 'Canzone della vela' at the Teatro Galleria Toledo di Napoli on 5 April 2018 can be seen here: https://www.youtube.com/watch?v=QdPygRVrJVU. The behatted figure at the beginning of the film is said to be the author of this book.

p. 144: The quotation from Alan Lomax was extracted from his diary and printed in the accompanying booklet to the album *Folk Music and Song of Italy: A Sampler* (Rounder Records – Rounder 11661-1801-2).

Chapter 6

p. 163: Giacomo Leopardi, *Zibaldone* (New York: Farrar, Straus & Giroux, 2013).

p. 164: Giacomo Leopardi, *The Letters of Giacomo Leopardi*

1817–1837, translated by Prue Shaw (Leeds: Northern Universities Press, 1998).

p. 168–9: Marius Kociejowski, *Collected Poems* (Manchester: Carcanet, 2019).

p. 170–1: Giacomo Leopardi, *Canti*, translated by Jonathan Galassi (New York: Farrar, Straus & Giroux, 2010).

p. 176: Domenico Pasquariello and Antonio Tubelli, *Leopardi a tavola: 49 cibi della lista autografa di Giacomo Leopardi* (Bologna: Logo Fausto Lupetti, 2008).

Chapter 7

Astonishingly Raimondo di Sangro has no English biographer, although the historical sources are many in number. I hope this will soon be remedied by Clorinda Donato, who has kindly allowed me to use her translation of some of his writings, and from whose essays I have drawn valuable information.

p. 220: Hector Bianciotti, *Le Pas si lent de l'amour* (Paris: Gallimard, 1995).

p. 220: Marquis de Sade, *Voyage d'Italie* (Paris: Fayard, 1995).

p. 223–4: Benedetto Croce, *Storie e leggende napoletane* (Bari: Laterza & Figli, 1923).

The author is grateful to the Museo Cappella Sansevero for supplying the images for this chapter:

p. 216: *Fabrizio Masucci*
Foto di Marco Ghidelli
© Archivio Museo Cappella Sansevero
p. 219: *Pudicizia* (Antonio Corradini, 1752)
Foto di Marco Ghidelli
© Archivio Museo Cappella Sansevero
p. 219: *Disinganno* (Francesco Queirolo, 1753–4)
Foto di Marco Ghidelli
© Archivio Museo Cappella Sansevero

p. 221: *Cristo velato*, part. (Giuseppe Sanmartino, 1753)
Foto di Marco Ghidelli
© Archivio Museo Cappella Sansevero
p. 226: *Tomba di Raimondo di Sangro* (Francesco Maria Russo, 1759)
Foto di Marco Ghidelli
© Archivio Museo Cappella Sansevero

Chapter 8
p. 228: Giuseppe Marotta's *Gli alunni del tempo* (1960) I have already mentioned, although it wouldn't hurt to do so again (translated by Shirley Bridges as *The Slaves of Time* in 1964).
p. 232: Vincent Lombardo's translation of *'A livella* can be read here: http://www.freemasonryresearchforumqsa.com/a-livella.php
p. 240: The lines from Francesco Gizzio's *La spada della misericordia* are translated and discussed in David Gentilcore's lively essay 'Tempi sì calamitosi: Epidemic Disease and Public Health' in Tommaso Astarita, ed., *A Companion to Early Modern Naples* (Leiden and Boston: Brill Publishers, 2013).
p. 243: Eliezer Gonzalez, *The Fate of the Dead in Early Third Century North African Christianity* (Tübingen: Mohr Siebeck, 2014).
p. 243–4: Tommaso Astarita, 'Introduction' to Margaret Stratton's *The Living and the Dead: The Neapolitan Cult of the Skull* (Chicago: The Center for American Places at Columbia College Chicago, 2010).
p. 247: Once again, I thank Jon Snyder for allowing me to use lines from his translation of Matilde Serao's *Il ventre di Napoli*.
p. 250: Riccardo Carbone's photograph of Fontanelle has

been used with the permission of the Archivio fotografico Riccardo Carbone.

p. 250–1: Roger Peyrefitte, *South from Naples*, translated by J. H. F. McEwen (London: Thames and Hudson, 1954).

p. 254: Rocco Civitelli, *Il cimitero delle Fontanelle: Una storia napoletana* (Naples: Dante & Descartes, 2012).

p. 263: Marino Niola, *Il purgatorio a Napoli* (Rome: Meltemi, 2003).

Chapter 9

p. 289: Nicola Pugliese, *Malacqua: Four Days of Rain in the City of Naples Waiting for the Occurrence of an Extraordinary Event*, translated by Shaun Whiteside (Sheffield: And Other Stories, 2017).

Chapter 10

p. 323: Thomas Campbell, *Life of Petrarch* (London: Henry Colburn, 1841).

p. 328–31: I am indebted to Tom Gidwitz, whose website http://www.tomgidwitz.com/ includes a fuller biographical sketch of the extraordinary Frank Alvord Perret, 'The Hero of Vesuvius'.

p. 329: The photograph of Perret comes from an article 'The Day's Work of a Volcanologist' published in *The World's Work*, Vol. 25 (1907).

p. 347: The photograph of the duel is in the Riccardo Carbone archive in Naples. The author has 'adopted' the photographs relating to this event.

Chapter 11

p. 357–8: Peter Gunn, *Naples: A Palimpsest* (London: Chapman and Hall, 1961).

p. 357: The author is grateful to the Nelson-Atkins Museum of Art, Kansas City, for supplying the image of the original title-page of Tiepolo's *Divertimento per li regazzi*.

p. 360: Pierre Louis Duchartre, *The Italian Comedy: The Improvisation, Scenarios, Lives, Attributes, Portraits, and Masks of the Illustrious Characters of the Commedia dell'arte* (London: George Harrap, 1929).

p. 360–3: Charles MacFarlane, *Popular Customs, Sports and Recollections of the South of Italy* (London: Charles Knight, 1846).

p. 363–4: Michael Kelly, *Reminiscences of Michael Kelly, of the King's Theatre, and Theatre Royal Drury Lane* (London: Henry Colburn, 1826).

p. 336: Antonio Fava, *The Comic Mask in the Commedia dell'Arte: Actor Training, Improvisation, and the Poetics of Survival* (Evanston, IL: Northwestern University Press, 2007).

p. 385: Giorgio Agamben, *Pulcinella or, Entertainment for Kids in Four Scenes*, translated by Kevin Attell (London, New York & Calcutta: Seagull Books, 2018).

Chapter 13

p. 438: Carmen Pellegrino, *Cade la terra* (Florence: Giunti, 2015). Shaun Whiteside's translation will be published in 2024 (London: Prototype Publishing).

p. 447: Carmen Pellegrino, *Se mi tornassi questa sera accanto* (Florence: Giunti, 2017).

p. 426: *Le Madri di Capua – La collezione del Museo Campano* (Napoli, Quaderni del filo di perle, No. 1, 2006).

Chapter 14

p. 476–7: Roberto De Simone's letter to 'Dottor Savoia', in which he recounts his memories of the war can be seen at http://lettermagazine.it/musica/a-proposito-del-savoiardo-canterino/

p. 480: The photograph of De Simone was taken by Salvatore Laporta.

p. 481–2: The translation of 'Jesce sole' is by Ed Emery in collaboration with Jana Gough. http://www. thefreeuniversity.net/LaGattaCenerentola/english.html

Chapter 15

p. 495: The key text on the *paranza d'Ognundo* is *Fuochi del Vesuvio* by Fabio Birotti (Perugia: Gramma Edizioni, 2011).

p. 496: 'Contaminating influences': I am referring to Stephen Francis William Bennetts's thesis '"Tradizione e Contaminazione": An Ethnography of the Contemporary Southern Italian Folk Revival', submitted to The University of Western Australia in 2012. The author spent a year in Italy collecting material and is to be commended for drawing on a wide range of sources.

p. 505: The photograph of Zì Gennaro is used with the permission of Sabatino and Lucio Albano.

p. 508: Eric Hobsbawm, *The Age of Extremes: The Short Twentieth Century, 1914–1991* (London: Michael Joseph, 1994).

p. 513–14: Giacomo Leopardi, *Canti*, translated by Jonathan Galassi (New York: Farrar, Straus & Giroux, 2010).

Acknowledgements

Almost certainly there are some absentees in the following list and to them I owe my apologies, otherwise I wish to thank Lucio Albano, Sabatino Albano, Chiara Ambrosio,* Domenico Angarano, Giorgio Angarano, Maria Angarano, Ars Nova, Mariagrazia Barsanti, Tommaso Battimiello,* Fabio Birotti, John Birtwhistle, William Blissett, Angela Boriello,* Angelo Calabrese, Ciro 'Ciretta' Cascina, Federica Catalano, Teresa Cervo, Carolina Cigala, Pina Cipriani, Rocco Civitelli, Marcello Colasurdo, Ernesto Colluta, Silvia Corsi,* the gentlemen who call themselves cyop&kaf, Antonella D'Agostino, Luigi De Cristo, Letizia Del Pero, Roberto De Simone, Clorinda Donato, Erica Esposito,* Gareth Evans, Carlo Faiello, Fiorella Formicola,* Domenico Garafalo, Karen Hersch, Bruno Leone, Lucia Marinelli, Federica Martina, Bianca Mastrominico, Fabrizio Masucci, Jeff Matthews, Noonie Minogue, Mirko Mondillo, Marino Niola, Antonio Paciello, Mariella Pandolfi, Carmen Pellegrino, Maurizio Ponticello, Maria Rascaglia, Roberto Renino, Giuseppe Romano, Pasquale Rossi, Zena Rotundi, Carmela Russo, Melania Russo, Pasquale and Valeria Scialò, Corrado Sfogli, Norm Sibum, Nunzio Sisto, Ilaria Stabile, Marcella Starita, Jon Snyder, Roberto Talarico, Antonio Tubelli, Valeria Vaiano, Paolo Valerio, Adriana Vasques,* Irene Vecchia, Fausta Vetere, Paola Villani, Marina Vinto, Sofia Wood,* Svetlana 'Lana' Zhmur,* Caterina, and the two ladies on Vico Scassacocchi.

The people I have asterisked have worked as translators for me and as such I am deeply indebted to them. The epigraph from Ana Maria Ortese's *L'infanta sepolta* was especially translated for me by Jeff Matthews. His website *Naples – Life, Death & Miracles* is a virtual and indispensable encyclopaedia of the city: http://www.naplesldm.com/. He has my gratitude on any number of counts, not least for casting an editorial eye over my typescript, his commentary on it so witty and with so many asides it might make a book in its own right.

I am grateful to Harry Hall for the book's existence, and to his colleague Ella Carr who did the copy-edit and spared me much embarrassment.

A special word of thanks to my wife, Bobbie, who read the manuscript and made suggestions, most of which I have adopted. On occasion, she joined me on my travels – to Lake Avernus, for example – and I must own up that it was she who suggested we infiltrate the yellow helmets at Cuma. If she has been excluded from certain passages, it is simply in order to put myself at the centre of the universe.